THE FORCES IN AMERICAN
ECONOMIC GROWTH SERIES

Under the General Editorship of Alfred D. Chandler, Jr.

The Economic Impact
of the Cold War

D0187465

The Economic Impact of the Cold War

Sources and Readings

COMPILED AND EDITED BY

James L. Clayton

UNIVERSITY OF UTAH

Harcourt, Brace & World, Inc.

NEW YORK · CHICAGO · SAN FRANCISCO · ATLANTA

ISBN 0-15-518797-X

Library of Congress Catalog Card Number: 72–105690

PRINTED IN THE UNITED STATES OF AMERICA

For Gerrie

THE FORCES IN AMERICAN ECONOMIC GROWTH SERIES

THE *Forces in American Economic Growth series provides a documentary record of the building of the American economy. Each book in the series concentrates on the economic force or forces that generated the most compelling pressure for change at key junctures in American history. In each volume the men responsible for change speak for themselves. By presenting such a record the editors hope to enhance the reader's sense of economic reality, his awareness of underlying historic currents, and his ability to investigate and interpret business and economic change and growth.*

The series attempts to achieve this goal by presenting documents to show how new patterns of economic action occurred and how American entrepreneurs, managers, engineers, financiers, business analysts, workers, and labor-union leaders carried on their activities at different periods of history. The record provides more than mere illustration. The documents have been collected and presented in such a way as to encourage analysis and interpretation. Why did new ways come when they did and in the way they did? What stimulated and what hindered change? What was the role of personality in producing innovation and bringing economic growth?

In short, the series supplies the record, the source materials, that a reader can use to form his own judgment about the nature of economic and historical change. It allows him to be his own historian and his own interpreter of the changing American business and economic scene.

ALFRED D. CHANDLER, JR.

CONTENTS

PART I

The Cold War
and the National Economy

PART II

The Impact of the Cold War
on the Institutional Framework

PART III

The Impact of the Cold War
on Research and Development

PART IV

The Culmination of the Cold War:
Vietnam

PART V

The Legacy of the Cold War:
The Military-Industrial Complex

THE FORCES IN AMERICAN ECONOMIC GROWTH SERIES

Under the General Editorship of Alfred D. Chandler, Jr.

The Economic Impact
of the Cold War

A GENERAL INTRODUCTION
TO THE READINGS

A WISE country should keep a comfortable war under way all the time because war, and only war, solves the problem of economic progress. Although no single writer has put it quite this frankly, this proposal, or its derivatives, has been debated by informed scholars for centuries.

HOW ECONOMISTS HAVE VIEWED PAST WARS

During the seventeenth and early eighteenth centuries, most mercantilists were persuaded that war was an inevitable, legitimate, and occasionally necessary medium for economic advancement. Thus the mercantilist's primary concern was to prepare his own nation for victory. To gain victory, the mercantilists urged modification of the extensive economic regulations of the Middle Ages in order to enhance national economic power vis à vis other nations abroad. During the mid-eighteenth century, the physiocrats, who wanted a "natural" or unrestricted economy, took the opposite view, emphasizing the high costs of war to the victor as well as to the vanquished. They maintained that the mercantilists had been mistaken in regarding war as a means to prosperity and adhered to a firm belief in natural law as the best way to prosperity. This idea grew under the influence of the "classical school" of political economy, whose advocates paid little attention to war in theoretical discussions of political economy, but who generally opposed heavy military expenditures in practical politics. The classical economists, beginning with Adam Smith, assumed that the individual's desire for leisure was greater than his desire for goods and services; hence, most classical economists tended to be critical of war. Still, the classical economists saw war as one way to acquire scarce goods—although war was viewed as a wasteful and most difficult undertaking. National defense was recognized as a basic duty of the state, but these economists played down war as an instrument of progress. During the early part of this century, writers in the classical tradition were critical of the assertion that the gains of war were greater than its costs. These men therefore generally saw war as being brought about by a nationalistic, glory-seeking populace.

With the rise of Marxism, the debate shifted somewhat again. The Marxist point of view held that war, in its imperialistic stages, is actually promoted by profit-motivated capitalists. According to Marxists, exploitation diminishes the opportunity for expanding the domestic market, thus requiring new markets overseas and the eventual creation of monopolies with an exclusive control of foreign markets and resources. These two evil tendencies result in war, in which the workers are "cannon fodder" for the enrichment of entrepreneurs; consequently, Marxists have usually seen wars—except those of "national liberation"—as significantly retarding economic and human progress. Critics of the Marxists have answered that patriotic governments rather than large corporations have generally been the greater advocates of war.

Despite the teachings of most classical economists prior to World War I, in virtually every Western country there was considerable public sentiment that war was inevitable and probably even desirable. This faction of classical economists believed that, according to history, war had helped to civilize society. For example, the Persians had made the Near East safe for trade; Alexander had made the ancient world more cosmopolitan; and the Romans had built roads and established order. England was consolidated under the Wessex kings, Spain under Ferdinand, Germany under Bismarck. The United States found independence through revolution and union through civil war.

Following World War I, however, there was a marked confluence of thought between economists and the public—both entertained doubts about the beneficial results of war. By the time the *Encyclopedia of the Social Sciences* was published in 1935, Alvin Johnson could say: "Whatever may have been the case in earlier periods, scarcely anyone regards war under modern conditions as a force making for progress in civilization."[1]

With the coming of World War II, there was renewed debate concerning the significance of war in relation to economic progress. At the annual meeting of the American Economic Association in 1940, a session was devoted to the economic consequences of war since 1790.[2] At this session, Henry Oliver demonstrated that modern wars cause inflation that peaks well after hostilities are ended. Three forces raise prices during the war and cause inflation thereafter; they are, according to Oliver: (1) psychological pressures, (2) scarcity of wanted goods, and (3) governmental, business, and labor controls. Willard Thorp maintained that this inflationary period is soon followed by a "catastrophic economic crisis." He concluded that while at war, nations appear to be prosperous, but sooner or later nations must pay the penalty of having gone to war. The sudden withdrawal of the "great beneficent new employer and customer"—the government war machine—brings falling prices, stock dumping, loan calls, and unemployment, often lasting for several years. He maintained that since major wars are infrequent, we do not learn the lesson of feast and famine, and the cycle continues; but each time the economic consequences of wars become more severe because of the destructiveness and totality of modern wars. Thorp suggested that the only way to break this destructive cycle was to have the government continue as "the great peace customer" after the war.

1 Vol. 25, 340.
2 See *American Economic Review*, vol. 30 (February, 1941), 344–78.

The following year, just twenty days after Pearl Harbor, the American Economic Association met again and devoted much of its program to the economic effects of war, and especially to its impact on the postwar peacetime economy.[3] Most of the participants shared Thorp and Oliver's view of the economic consequences of war. In addition, they foresaw that World War II would bring an increase in the power of the central government and in the importance of scientists. Many were fearful of a depression. One economist, Asher Isaacs, predicted that "defense will be the keyword for decades to come."

Some other recent writers believe that these fears did not materialize after World War II because the hot war simply became a cold war, and the United States never converted to a peacetime economy. It is true that the level of federal spending from 1946 through 1950 was three times the level of the 1930's; but the Gross National Product (GNP) in constant (1958) prices fell from $355 billion in 1945 to $310 billion in 1947. Similarly, unemployment climbed to almost 6 percent in 1949 and was significantly reduced only by the Korean War boom that ended in 1953 with the cessation of hostilities. Despite heavy defense outlays, the GNP did not regain its vigorous rate of growth until the Vietnam conflict. Thus, these economists conclude that there has been no prolonged depression since World War II because there has been no end to war.

HOW ECONOMISTS HAVE VIEWED THE COLD WAR

During the past twenty-five years, thousands of articles and books have been written on the economic and political impact of the Cold War.[4] The general trend of these books and articles has been to express an ambivalent but increasingly negative attitude about the economic consequences of the Cold War.

In the early years of the Cold War but prior to the Korean conflict, economists and historians alike tended to see defense spending mainly as a prop for the economy, as the *sine qua non* for full employment, and as the basis for the prosperity of several states and certain sizeable industries.[5] Few books and articles written during that period criticized defense expenditures as wasteful or the war itself as unnecessary. At the annual meetings of the American Economic Association during 1949 and 1950, for example, the primary concern of the participants was to minimize government con-

[3] See *American Economic Review*, vol. 32 (February, 1942), 1–36, 216–17, 227–30, and 351–432.

[4] There have been over 700 articles and books written on the role of the military-industrial complex alone during the brief span of years since 1961. See *Peace Research Abstracts Journal* (Canadian Peace Research Institute, Clarkson, Ontario, Annual Indexes under category IX–37) for specific titles.

[5] See *Index of Economic Journals*, vols. 3 and 4 under section 13, for articles during that period.

trols while recognizing the dangers of war-generated inflation. It was generally agreed that the Cold War helped our economy, that military power was the best means for stopping the expansion of Communism, and that military spending was more important than building security through productive capacity.[6] Indeed some economists, afraid that the public was unduly concerned about the high cost of defense spending, spent considerable effort to show that our defense budgets would not lead the nation into bankruptcy. Shortly before the Korean conflict broke out, *Business Week,* summing up the general attitude of economists, concluded that defense spending was necessary to preserve the nation and keep the economy healthy: "Pressure for more government spending is mounting. And the prospect is that Congress will give in a little more now, then more by next year. . . . The reason is a combination of concern over tense Russian relations, and a growing fear of a rising level of unemployment here at home." [7]

The coming of the Korean conflict and the ensuing years of high military spending thereafter made the close relationship between the Cold War and unemployment even more evident. Prior to the Korean conflict the rate of unemployment had remained tenaciously high, albeit much lower than during the 1930's. In 1949 it had climbed as high as 8 percent, and immediately before the American forces were committed in Korea, it was over 5 percent. With the coming of the war, however, the rate of unemployment dropped rapidly. By October 1953 the figure was only 1.8 percent—the lowest of the decade. Conversely, the end of the war and the cutback in defense expenditures brought on a recession. But in 1957, following the spectacular Russian achievement in orbiting Sputnik I and our consequent increase in defense expenditures, the economy boomed briefly. As a result of these lessons, few economists saw the Cold War as a burden depleting our economy or undermining our long-term productive capacity.

With the coming of the Kennedy administration, economists began to intensify their studies of military spending and to shift their focus in three ways. First, because President Kennedy's administration began to stress the need to help the disadvantaged at a time when welfare programs lagged because of rising defense outlays in response to the 1961 Berlin crisis and the two Cuban crises, many economists began to emphasize the burdens created by defense expenditures. "Guns versus butter" became a fashionable subject, and argument was heated until early 1968, when it was finally conceded that costs in Vietnam required the nation to choose one or the other. Perhaps the best-known author to take this view is Seymour Melman. His book *Our Depleted Society,* published in 1965, was the first major recent work to return to the old argument that war retards human progress. Excerpts from this work are printed in Part I.

Meanwhile, Senator George McGovern (Democrat, South Dakota) became

[6] See *American Economic Review,* vol. 39 (May, 1949), 357 and vol. 40 (May, 1950), 191.
[7] *Business Week,* April 15, 1950, 15.

perhaps the most effective political figure to carry these ideas to the public. In a 1963 speech to the Senate,[8] McGovern declared that our level of military spending was distorting our economy, needlessly increasing our nuclear stockpile, wasting human resources, and restricting United States leadership throughout the world. He called for diverting $5 billion of the military budget to education, urban problems, medical assistance, control of river pollution, and so forth. Such themes were to be frequently echoed after 1963.

Second, certain economists began to view all military problems as problems of resource allocation. These economists emphasized that the important question was how to make defense spending more efficient once it was decided how much *ought* to be spent. Charles J. Hitch and Roland N. McKean in their book *The Economics of Defense in the Nuclear Age* exemplify this point of view. Since the time of the publication of their book in 1960, a whole literature—if not a distinct school—of defense economics has sprung up and is still flourishing.

Finally, a third view was taken by those economists interested in multilateral disarmament. Distrusting the balance-of-power approach, they focused on international security arrangements that would permit savings in defense expenditures and thereby allow a rise in the standard of living. A session at both the 1962 and 1968 annual meetings of the American Economic Association was devoted to this theme.[9] It estimated real costs of defense spending on a per capita basis for the first time, called for greater attention to the economic implications of defense planning, and, most important, recommended a gradual reorientation of defense programs toward goals of social and economic development.

Proponents of these three views are all inclined to see defense spending as a burden—albeit a necessary one to some degree. Those who share this outlook seem to increase in numbers as the years go by and major domestic problems remain unsolved. Perhaps in time current economic opinion will once again see war as the classical economists saw it—a detriment to human progress.

The articles that follow were selected to give the reader as broad an understanding of the economic impact of the Cold War as possible and at the same time to fit the Cold War into the perspective of history. The closer one's analysis comes to the present, the more careful he must be in his judgments; hence, the aim of this book is to help the reader to understand the major issues and to come to his own conclusions rather than blindly taking a position for or against the Cold War itself or for or against defense spending per se.

Part I emphasizes the national and regional scope of defense expenditures

8 See *Congressional Record*, August 2, 1963, 13968–95.
9 See *American Economic Review*, vol. 53 (May, 1962), 413–51 and vol. 58 (May, 1968), 398–445.

and attempts to relate these expenditures to the civilian economy. The long-range impact of the Cold War on governmental and market institutions is the subject of Part II. These selections help to show how the Cold War generated economic pressures sufficient to change the nature of the market system itself as well as the way in which our government operates. It is here that the role of personality as a factor in decision-making is most noticeable. Part III is concerned with the impact of the Cold War on research: Has the war retarded or advanced technological change? The readings also deal with the impact of the war on science and the university. Part IV examines the special problem of Vietnam. These readings focus on that war as a war within a larger war and provide an introduction to Part V, a summary chapter on the military-industrial-scientific complex. The origins, growth, and impact of this complex are discussed, and a special section has been included on "militarism" as fostered by deterrent theorists. Each chapter is self-contained, yet each adds another dimension to understanding the economic implications of contemporary warfare.

The following article by John Clark will serve as an introduction to the materials in these parts. Clark attempts to place the Cold War in historical that are pertinent in evaluating the present conflict. He argues that wars— that are pertinent in evaluating the present conflict. He argues that war— especially recent wars—have paved the way for more rapid advancement in the material conditions of life. Moreover, Clark feels there is considerable evidence that World War II and the Cold War have given rise to economic progress—especially in technology—that otherwise would not have occurred. Clark believes, however, that the preponderence of evidence supports the judgment that war tends to retard economic progress.

This essay raises a number of pertinent questions for anyone interested in the economic impact of the Cold War: Do long "cold wars" have a greater impact than shorter "hot wars"? Is our experience since World War I a good guide for what is happening now, or is it really dangerously misleading? Would we have suffered a serious depression by now if we had not spent massive sums for the Cold War? [10] Since recent American wars have tended to cost *three times* more after the fighting stops than during the period of hostilities—largely because of veterans' benefits—should not those who defend the war as necessary be required to justify the long-range costs of the Cold War as well as the immediate expenditures?

---

[10] Over seven-tenths of federal expenditures since 1946 have been for national security—an amount now totaling over a trillion dollars.

The New Economics of National Defense

· · · · · · · · · · · · · · · ·

To ANALYZE the impact of war on man's material wellbeing is a most formidable assignment. One must weigh, as we have done in Chapter 1 [which discussed the role of economic theory and military needs], the different degrees of warfare and the level of involvement in the actual fighting. It may well be, for example, that limited warfare will offer to some nations a measure of economic progress to counterbalance the destructive aspects of fighting. One is obliged to examine the consequences of war for the allocation of the factors of production among the different industries. This necessarily evokes discussion of the means of mobilizing resources and financing military expenditures. One must also attempt to evaluate the indirect influences of war on social classes and institutions for, even if war does not contribute directly to economic progress, it may still, by clearing away the debris of archaic customs and institutions, pave the way for a more rapid advance in the material conditions of life. Contrariwise, warfare may introduce social rigidities and inspire nationalistic enmities that detract from the prospects of the future. It would be manifestly absurd to pretend that we can encompass in a single chapter all the many points that arise under each heading. We can, nonetheless, survey the main influences of war, as described by economists and social historians, and tentatively set forth a few hypotheses concerning this phenomenon, which may serve to guide our approach to military-economic problems.

POPULATION

The principal ingredient in war, as well as in economics, is man. Responsibility for producing wealth and preserving national security reposes ultimately in the population. The impact of war on the quality and quantity of a nation's inhabitants is therefore of primary concern for both the economist and the military man. Apropos of this point, numerous subjective and objective factors determine size of population. At any given time, the supply of resources fixes the outside limits to population growth. The restraints imposed by man's geophysical environment, however, do not set an unalterable quota on human numbers. With the advance of technology, new natural resources are constantly being unearthed and improved methods of exploiting known reserves devised. Short of the maximum permitted by the resource element, population growth is regulated immediately by certain components of the cultural complex: the population's capacity to utilize its labor and resources; its desire and ability to form capital; the effectiveness of birth-control devices; the divergence between its objective (actual) and its subjective (desired) mode of living, in so far as these condition family size; the influence of war. The latter, surely a factor indigenous to human culture, imparts a mainly short-term bias to the rate of population growth—i.e. to birth rates, death rates, and the flow of immigration.[1]

There is ample evidence to suggest that the appeal to arms tends to retard the rate of population growth, although exceptional instances may be cited. The American Civil War apparently did foster such a result. The rate of increase in population declined from 35.5 per cent for the decade 1850–1860 to 26.6 per cent during the years 1860–1870. This decline incidentally represented the beginning of a downward secular movement in the rate of United States population growth—a movement which would persist until World War I. One authority estimates that, as a consequence of the internecine warfare, population growth was 1.3 million less than might normally have been expected for the decade.[2] History repeated itself in World War I. The population growth rate dropped from 21.4 per cent for 1900–1910 to 15.2 per cent for 1910–1920. Population grew by 3.3 million less than expected—a fall attributed mainly to the abrupt halt in immigration and, to a lesser degree, to war mortality. World War II, contrariwise, accelerated the rate of population growth in the United States. The rate rebounded from 7.3 per cent for the decade 1930–40 to 14.8 per cent in 1940–50. How much of the increment was a response to the stimulus of war prosperity, and how much merely a delayed reaction to the abnormally low rate engendered by the depressed economic conditions of the 1930's, still remains unanswered.[3]

The population of Great Britain declined absolutely during World War I from 35,358,896 in 1915 to 33,474,700 in 1918. Britain's World War II history was less stringent in this respect: population grew by some 888,000; this was a slower pace than for the period 1935 to 1940. Similarly, in Italy population expanded during World War II, but at a lower rate than that characteristic for peacetime. The long-term decline in the French population was little altered by the second world conflict; Germany, on the other hand, suffered an absolute decline of substantial proportions: approximately 6,496,000. Naturally, the figures on the war years must be accepted with some reservations. The ebb and flow of battle, the march and countermarch of refugees, and the employment of forced labor exacerbated the ills of an already uncertain collection system.

All estimates point to marked retardation of Soviet population growth as the result of the massive losses of World War II. The population of the Soviet Union in 1926 totaled 147 million; by 1939, the figure had climbed to 170.5 million, an increment of 23.5 million or 16 per cent. By 1950, the U.S.S.R. could boast of a 200-million population. However, this number

---

[1] Joseph J. Spengler, "The World Hunger—Malthus 1948," *Proceedings of the American Academy of Political Science*, 23, 2 (January, 1949), 53–71.

[2] Chester W. Wright, "The Most Enduring Economic Consequences of American Wars," *The Task of Economic History* (December, 1943, Supplement to the *Journal of Economic History*, LLI); Herman E. Krooss, *American Economic Development* (Englewood Cliffs, N.J.: Prentice-Hall, 1955), p. 471.

[3] National Industrial Conference Board, *The Economic Almanac 1960* (New York: National Industrial Conference Board, 1960), p. 1.

embraced 24.3 million people in the new territories occupied by the Soviet Union. If we adjust the data to measure population growth within the area defined by the 1939 boundaries of the Soviet Union, the Russian population grew by only 3.5 per cent for the period 1939–1950. Within the same geographical limits, the Russian population was 186.7 million in 1959, a 9.5 per cent growth over the 1939 figure. At the hands of the Nazi invaders, Russia lost a major portion of two generations—25 million persons actually killed in the fighting, and the countless number of children they would have produced. Thus, beyond the immediate human loss, the Soviet economy today suffers a severe shortage of young workers which hampers the industrial expansion of the country.[4]

Earlier wars could be equally deleterious to population growth. During the economic collapse that followed the Thirty Years War in 1618, the population of Central Europe (what was to be the German Empire of 1871–1919) fell precipitately from 21 million in 1550 to 13.5 million in 1650. In sharp contrast, the years 1815–1854 and 1871–1914, two of the least violent periods in Western history, saw nearly one half billion people added to the world population. John U. Nef observes:

> In little more than one generation the world population grew by almost as much as it had grown during the untold generations which separate Adam, the first man, from Newton, the first man of science of the seventeenth century.[5]

Because of the absence or incompleteness of population records, we know little, except for modern times, about the behavior of birth rates under the stress of wartime conditions. The consensus of opinion supports the conclusion that birth rates tend to drop during some or all of the years of an actual war period, to be partially offset by higher rates in the postwar environment, followed by the resurgence of longer-term influences on the number of births.

The data portray a mixed picture, however. All nations listed in Table I manifest secular declines in birth rates, and there are no sharp reversals of trend. The American birth rate evinces a falling secular movement until the middle years of World War II, when apparently a renewed upward swing takes hold. The German and Italian rates fit the model: decline through the war years, and then higher in the immediate postwar era. On the other hand, English and French birth rates commence to increase in 1941 and 1942 and rise steadily to 1947, after which lower rates became evident. Except for Italy, all nations had slightly higher birth rates in 1945, the concluding year of World War II, as compared with 1935, the bottom year of the Great Depression.

One might expect a more definitive picture to emerge from a consideration of death rates (Table II). After all, much of the ingenuity of war is

4 Harry Schwartz, *Russia's Soviet Economy* (Englewood Cliffs, N.J.: Prentice-Hall, 1950), pp. 26–33, 130–131.

5 John U. Nef, *Western Civilization Since the Renaissance* (New York: Harper & Row, 1963), pp. 286–287.

TABLE I   BIRTH RATES PER 1,000 INHABITANTS IN SELECTED COUNTRIES

Year	United States	England and Wales	Germany	France	Italy
1841-1845	–	32.2	36.7	28.1	–
1871-1875	37.0	35.5	39.0	25.5	36.8
1896-1900	29.8	29.3	36.0	22.0	34.0
1915	25.0	21.8	20.4	11.6	30.5
1920	23.7	25.5	25.9	21.4	31.8
1925	21.3	18.3	20.7	19.0	27.8
1930	18.9	16.8	17.5	18.0	26.7
1935	16.9	15.2	18.9	15.5	23.4
1937	17.1	14.9	18.8	14.7	22.9
1938	17.6	15.1	19.7	14.6	23.8
1939	17.3	14.8	20.4	13.6	23.6
1940	17.9	14.1	20.0	13.1	23.5
1941	18.9	13.9	18.6	14.5	20.9
1942	20.9	15.6	15.0	15.7	20.5
1943	21.5	16.2	16.0	16.1	20.0
1944	20.2	17.7	n.a.	16.2	19.4
1945	19.5	16.2	n.a.	16.6	18.3
1946	23.3	19.4	16.4	20.9	23.0
1947	25.8	20.7	16.5	21.4	22.2
1948	24.2	18.1	17.0	21.2	21.9
1949	23.9	17.0	17.2	21.1	20.3
1950	23.5	16.3	16.5	20.7	19.6
1951	24.5	15.8	16.0	19.7	18.4
1952	24.7	15.7	16.0	19.4	17.9
1953	24.6	15.9	15.8	18.9	17.7

SOURCES: National Industrial Conference Board, *The Economic Almanac 1960*, p. 15; *Demographic Yearbook of the United Nations*, 1948 and 1962.

directed toward the killing or maiming of human beings, civilian and military. Indeed, such is the case.

What may we conclude from this brief survey as to the effect of war on population growth? (1) On balance, war exercises a negative short-term effect on the rate of population growth, mainly through rising death rates and to lesser degree through falling birth rates. Since we cannot ascertain the optimum population for a given set of resources, and since so many factors —both psychological and material—determine the rate of growth, it is impossible to form conclusive judgments on the long-term effects of armed conflict on population size. The data gives some support to the opinion that other, perhaps more fundamental, causes shape the final size of a nation's population, war being but a temporary interruption in the secular performance. (2) To state the case differently, where population size is buoyed upward by other forces, war induces a short-term hiatus in the trend, but it does not appear ultimately to deter population growth. Where, however, war casualties are added to an already sloping rate of population growth, they impose

TABLE II   DEATH RATES PER 1,000 INHABITANTS IN SELECTED COUNTRIES

Year	United States	England and Wales	Germany*	France	Italy†	Japan
1933	10.7	12.5	11.2	16.0	13.7	17.7
1934	11.1	12.0	10.9	15.3	13.3	18.1
1935	10.9	12.0	11.8	15.8	14.0	16.8
1936	11.6	12.3	11.8	15.6	13.8	17.5
1937	11.3	12.6	11.7	15.4	14.3	17.0
1938	10.6	11.8	11.7	15.8	14.1	17.7
1939	10.6	12.2	12.3	15.6	13.4	17.8
1940	10.8	14.4	12.7	19.1	13.6	16.4
1941	10.5	13.7	12.1	17.4	13.9	15.7
1942	10.3	12.4	12.0	17.0	14.3	15.8
1943	10.9	13.1	12.1	16.4	15.2	16.3
1944	10.6	12.8	n.a.	19.4	15.3	17.4
1945	10.6	12.7	n.a.	16.4	13.6	29.2
1946	10.0	12.1	13.5	12.3	12.1	17.6
1947	10.1	12.4	13.2	11.6	11.5	14.6
1948	9.1	10.9	12.5	10.5	10.7	12.0
1949	9.7	11.7	13.9	10.4	10.5	11.6
1950	9.6	11.8	12.8	10.5	9.8	10.9

* Excludes deaths of military personnel in Germany for years 1935 to 1943.
† Excludes deaths in the military zone of operations 1940 to 1945.

SOURCE: National Industrial Conference Board, *The Economic Almanac, 1960*, p. 16. The data in Table II shows declining death rates for all nations cited. Although the United States once more does not conform to the pattern, for all other nations these trends are reversed during the war years by higher death rates, but reassert themselves on the termination of hostilities.

a heavy burden on a nation's demographic resources. Casualties of the eighteenth-century conflicts and of the Napoleonic Wars were comparatively easily borne by Great Britain because of a powerful rising trend in population. The demographic circumstances differed on the eve of the Great War. World War I casualties for Britain amounted to 745,000 men killed (9 per cent of all the men in the 20–45 age bracket), and 1,700,000 wounded. Ten per cent of all deaths in the decade 1911–1921 resulted from service casualties. These accentuated the effects of an already declining rate of population growth.[6] (3) The retarding influence of war on population growth varies in proportion to the degree of participation. Direct and complete participation through land warfare provokes the heaviest casualties and subverts most acutely the forces and conditions of population growth. Thus the American Civil War imposed a greater stress on population growth than the United States entanglement in both World Wars I and II. The events of the Thirty

[6] William Ashworth, *An Economic History of England 1870–1939* (New York: Barnes & Noble, 1960), pp. 285–286; W. W. Rostow, *The Process of Economic Growth* (New York: W. W. Norton, 1962), pp. 150–153.

Years War and the role of England in the numerous continental conflicts of the eighteenth, nineteenth, and twentieth centuries lend further support to the hypothesis.

INDUSTRIAL PROGRESS

Could war, which consumes so much blood and treasure, be after all the arbiter of industrial progress? If so, then history should place those societies that manifest the more egregious forms of belligerent behavior in the van-guard of those nations that enjoy a high degree of material well-being. The testimony of human experience from the earliest times speaks against the proposition. In the approximately two thousand years from the third to the first millennium B.C., the civilizations prospering and dying in Hither Asia, the Nile Valley, the regions of the Aegean Sea (Egypt, Babylonia, Assyria, the Hittites, Persia, Phoenicia, etc.) passed from the Age of Copper through the Age of Bronze to the Age of Iron. The sources of economic progress here at the threshold of organized social life are the same as those for modern societies: the extension of trade, spreading division of labor, and a deepen-ing of investment. Similarly, declining economic welfare correlates with the rise of internal troubles (civil strife) and attacks from without. Shepard B. Clough summarizes his remarks on these civilizations as follows:

> Finally, it is worth mentioning that those cultures which looked to war—
> to preying on others—as a fundamental ideology and as a way of sustain-
> ing themselves did not achieve such high levels of civilization as more
> peaceful cultures. *They devoted too large a proportion of their energies
> to destructive rather than constructive ends.* (italics added)[7]

Of course, our very limited knowledge of ancient societies makes impos-sible any conclusive demonstration of the supposition. A survey of modern European history from this vantage point will prove more to the point. The two hundred years from 1450 to 1650 saw much warlike activity on the Con-tinent: the Religious Wars of the Reformation, including the Thirty Years War; the four wars between France and Spain, with Italy as the prize, and the fateful struggle of England and Spain. The age also witnessed a plethora of technological innovations, which quickened the pace of industrial prog-ress in the late sixteenth and early seventeenth centuries, especially for England: the printing press; the blast furnace; the furnace for separating silver from argentiferous copper ore, with the help of lead; horse- and water-driven engines for draining mines; railed ways for carrying coal; furnaces using coal instead of wood; coke in drying malt; sheathing of ship bottoms with metal to fend off rotting. These fruits of their ingenuity Europeans di-rected primarily toward peaceful purposes. If they would some day trans-form the art of war, that was clearly not the source of their inspiration.

Modern war requires a vast outpouring of cheap metals, but the inven-tions that enhanced the efficiency of metals production preceded by many

---

[7] Shepard Clough, *The Rise and Fall of Civilization* (New York: McGraw Hill, 1951), pp. 47–48; see also Arnold J. Toynbee, *War and Civilization* (New York: Oxford University Press, 1950).

decades their use in warfare. A similar tale can be told of the introduction of gunpowder, firearms and cannon. The invention of gunpowder is unrelated to its subsequent use in warfare. Gunpowder was invented during relatively peaceful times for Western Europe—during the age of the Crusades —and was initially employed in mining operations. The Crusades, by the way, did stimulate the production of weapons—but traditional weapons, not novel ones. Firearms made their appearance after the Crusades. Finally, the production of cannon evolved from the method of casting church bells described by a German Benedictine monk, Theophilus, at the end of the eleventh century. The gun and the cannon never transformed the European economy; rather, they were themselves the fruit of a long period of development in which urban independence was growing and the money economy was spreading—in short, the product of peaceful industrial employments.

Nevertheless, if the new weapons did not originate in the attempt to escalate the deadliness of warfare, they may yet have contributed to economic progress during the years 1450 to 1650, by creating a mass demand for their manufacture and thereby encouraging the adoption of labor-saving techniques and a larger scale of enterprise. One must acknowledge that military imperatives have motivated some innovations (the blast furnace, for example) which, in the ensuing peace, helped to raise the output of copper, bronze, brass and iron. The stimulus provided by war from this direction was, however, more than offset by the disruptions of conflict: (1) The flight of industry from the continental war zones to England, Holland and Sweden counterbalanced the impetus to larger-scale enterprise to meet war needs. As a corollary, the rise of industrial capitalism in England and Northern Europe, joined with the regions' natural endowments, can be attributed to the relative peace and insularity of the area; (2) Contrary to Sombart's conclusions, war with firearms and cannon did not create the large industrial plant or promote the factory system. It was salt-making, alum-making, coal mining, and other nonwar industries, rather than arms manufacture, that led to the build-up of larger-scale enterprise in response to the normal expansion of the market. In fact, the warfare of the sixteenth century in some instances delayed the concentration of industry into larger units. The French monarchy, for example, subsidized the production of gunpowder in small plants scattered throughout the country; (3) Although warship design provided models for more commodious merchant vessels, the growth of commerce and water-borne trade invariably anticipated the growth of sea power. The fishing and coasting trades sustained generations of British seamen, while the construction of merchantmen offered basic job opportunities for shipwrights, carpenters and sail- and rope-makers.[8] (4) War interfered with scholarship of every description, in particular when it was concerned with pure speculation. The Thirty Years War ended for Germany a brilliant period of study in the natural sciences that ran from Copernicus (1473–1543) to Kepler (1571–1630). To recapitulate,

> . . . so far as the period from about 1494 to 1648 is concerned, such
> constructive consequences as the Europeans derived from military prepa-

[8] Alfred Thayer Mahan, *The Influence of Sea Power Upon History, 1660–1783* (New York: Sagamore Press, 1957), pp. 22–77.

rations were more than offset by the economic damage caused by these preparations and by war itself. The influence of war was to lower the material standard of living. Population and production grew mainly in those parts of Europe where there was the least fighting. War contributed less than peace to the progress of science and even of industrial technology. War enlarged the scale of economic enterprise mainly by increasing the civil services and the annual expenditures of princes and kings.[9]

War and preparations for war, on the other hand, may contribute to technological improvement in several ways. They may induce the general adoption of new types of machinery that are in current but restricted use. Mechanical improvements designed for weapons production may also have peacetime applications. In this connection, boring machines invented to produce smooth barrels for cannon were later modified to the fashioning of steam engines. Moreover, war may enlist the services of minds not normally attracted to the subject of technology, and thereby increase the attention given after the war to improvements that reduce the costs of production. Nevertheless, on balance, peaceful industry offers many more technical problems to challenge the imagination than do the exigencies of wartime necessities. War, in fact, frequently diverts attention from the solution of broadly conceived industrial problems that are prerequisite to balanced economic growth, in favor of an emphasis on those areas that appear to hold a promise of immediate gains for military operations. Such at any rate are the tentative conclusions derived from the history of Europe between 1640 and 1740.

The one hundred years from the middle of the seventeenth century to the middle of the eighteenth century brought less warfare to the continental heart of Europe, but a significant augmentation of fighting on the periphery and on the high seas. The shift in arena meant that England and the Northern countries would be proportionately more heavily engaged than during the period from 1450 to 1650. In addition to her own Civil War, England fought three naval wars with the Dutch (1652–1673), and thereafter two long coalition wars against France (the War of the Dutch Alliance, 1689–1697, and the War of the Spanish Succession, 1702–1713). Good fortune remained with England, however. Because of her insular position, England would yet not taste in full measure those bitter fruits that wars inevitably held in store for her continental neighbors.

The reader will also recollect that 1640 to 1740 was an era of limited warfare. Military engagements became less frequent, as national strategy called for wars of maneuver and attrition. Paradoxically, military service assumed a more regularized aspect: larger bodies of troops and naval personnel were kept continuously in service; the new warfare made mandatory the organization of schools for the education of officer candidates and staff service experts; heavy expenditures on naval armaments and land fortifications added to the capital costs of the military establishment. Uniforms, muskets, ammunition, and other martial appurtenances were set in standard specifications.

[9] Nef, p. 113. See also: Nef, pp. 23–41, 42–64, 65–88; Alfred Vagts, *A History of Militarism* (New York: Meridian Books, 1959), pp. 41–74; Ferdinand Schevill, *A History of Europe* (New York: Harcourt, Brace & World, 1947), pp. 65–258.

These reforms formed the genesis of the modern defense organization: a knowledge of economics and an ability for administration would henceforth supplement the purely military virtues.[10]

What did the new pattern of military affairs portend for economic progress? Previously, we have alluded to Sombart's thesis that, with the introduction of firearms, the need to supply large quantities of munitions supplied the occasion for standardization in industry, encouraged large-scale enterprise, and thereby made possible the rise of modern capitalism. Does the period from 1640 to 1740 support this contention?

At the outset, one should note that England's larger military and naval commitment apparently slowed the rate of industrial progress in that country. The expansion of coastwise shipping, particularly in coal, grew at a noticeably slower pace from 1635 to 1710, as compared with the tenfold increase for the years 1550 to 1625. Shipping generally suffered heavily in England's wars:

> The ultimate effect of the Dutch and Spanish Wars was to ruin English trade, which had begun to revive after the ravages of the Civil War. The narrow seas at this time swarmed with privateers working from Dunkirt and Ostend; and, notwithstanding the extension of the convoy system, the English merchant marine suffered severely. Under Cromwell, England had become a great military power, but at ruinous cost.[11]

The failure of Great Britain, Holland, and Sweden during this period to further their leadership in heavy industry, which they had gained from the preoccupation of others with military glory, Nef blames on the more frequent naval engagements of the states of northern Europe.[12] Not until 1785, more than two generations after the invention of the steam engine, was this new source of power used to revolutionize industrial organization in Great Britain.

Nor is it possible to attribute the movement toward standardization of product lines and capital equipment to the specifications of military procurement. Standardization was indigenous to the industrial process from its inception, at least as far back as the early Roman Empire. Large-scale enterprises in iron-making, artistic and luxury industries, and shipbuilding foreshadowed the wider adaptation of industry. Private shipbuilding yards in England were frequently as large as or larger than the government yards used to support and maintain the naval establishment. In one respect, however, the standing army and its organized supply services had undoubted influence: they served to extend the authority of the state over economic enterprise on the Continent.[13]

To review the course of European history from 1740 to 1950 would do little more than to reinforce the conclusions spelled out above. The Industrial Revolution is an oft told tale. Its development in England during the

10 Nef, pp. 202–207; Vagts, pp. 75–91.

11 G. J. Marcus, *A Naval History of England: The Formative Centuries* (Boston: Little, Brown, 1961), p. 150.

12 Nef, p. 221.

13 *Ibid.*, pp. 202–207; Schevill, pp. 261–360.

Napoleonic Wars was due less to the stimulation of the war economy than to the historic isolation of England from the main theater of land warfare. On the Continent, the Industrial Revolution did not gain momentum until the guns fell silent in 1815, inaugurating the long peace of the nineteenth century. American economic history, however, offers more precise data on the manner in which a state of war inhibits the growth of industry.

Of the three major wars in American history since the second half of the nineteenth century (Civil War, World War I and World War II), the first two definitely hampered the process of economic growth. The index of total production during the Civil War exhibited a 13.5 per cent increase for the period 1853–1865, but the increment was not sufficient to cover the demands of war production. Edwin Frickey's index of manufacturing output shows a rise of only 1 per cent for the period 1860 to 1865 (1899 = 100). Value added by manufacture, in constant dollars, was lower during the ten years 1859 to 1869 than in the previous decade. The failure of production, therefore, to rise sufficiently to cover the drain of war goods meant that civilian living standards would suffer in proportion. The Civil War, in addition, hobbled the pace of innovation. If technological progress is measured by the number of patents issued, then it must be noted that these actually declined from 1861 to 1863, while the increase for the over-all war period was at a much slower rate than that anticipated under normal conditions.

The story was not very different for World War I. Spectacular feats in the production of war goods went unmatched by a comparable growth in total output, primarily because of declining productivity and manpower shortages. Industrial production grew less than 1 per cent between 1916 and 1917, by 1918–19, it had actually fallen below the 1916 mark. The output-per-man-hour index declined from 40.8 in 1914 to 40.5 in 1919. Value added by manufacture, in constant dollars, was lower in 1919 than in 1916. Lastly, the number of patents granted dropped from 43,118 in 1918 to 37,797 in 1919.[14]

Prima facie, the vitality of the United States economy during World War II contraverts the pessimism of the preceding paragraphs. Industrial production rose 48 per cent between 1939 and 1941, and another 45 per cent by 1945. Half of total production and 80 per cent of durable-goods production were allocated to the war economy. Nevertheless, the civilian sector had approximately the same real income at the conclusion of the war in 1945 as it had had at the beginning. The war gave strong impetus to group research in science; it was the first war to mobilize scientific talent to support the war effort. Consequently, many new products that would do much to raise the level of living during the postwar period appeared on the market: antibiotic drugs, radar and other electronic devices, synthetic rubber and gasoline. Above all, atomic energy (for good or for evil) would fashion, in the fullness of time, a new society.[15]

On closer examination, the American reaction in World War II gives less substantial support to the case for war as the highroad to economic progress.

---

[14] Krooss, pp. 447–479; *Historical Statistics of the United States, Colonial Times to 1957,* supplement to *Statistical Abstract* (Washington, D.C.: Government Printing Office, 1957).

[15] Krooss, pp. 463–465.

The following year, just twenty days after Pearl Harbor, the American Economic Association met again and devoted much of its program to the economic effects of war, and especially to its impact on the postwar peacetime economy.[3] Most of the participants shared Thorp and Oliver's view of the economic consequences of war. In addition, they foresaw that World War II would bring an increase in the power of the central government and in the importance of scientists. Many were fearful of a depression. One economist, Asher Isaacs, predicted that "defense will be the keyword for decades to come."

Some other recent writers believe that these fears did not materialize after World War II because the hot war simply became a cold war, and the United States never converted to a peacetime economy. It is true that the level of federal spending from 1946 through 1950 was three times the level of the 1930's; but the Gross National Product (GNP) in constant (1958) prices fell from $355 billion in 1945 to $310 billion in 1947. Similarly, unemployment climbed to almost 6 percent in 1949 and was significantly reduced only by the Korean War boom that ended in 1953 with the cessation of hostilities. Despite heavy defense outlays, the GNP did not regain its vigorous rate of growth until the Vietnam conflict. Thus, these economists conclude that there has been no prolonged depression since World War II because there has been no end to war.

HOW ECONOMISTS HAVE VIEWED THE COLD WAR

During the past twenty-five years, thousands of articles and books have been written on the economic and political impact of the Cold War.[4] The general trend of these books and articles has been to express an ambivalent but increasingly negative attitude about the economic consequences of the Cold War.

In the early years of the Cold War but prior to the Korean conflict, economists and historians alike tended to see defense spending mainly as a prop for the economy, as the *sine qua non* for full employment, and as the basis for the prosperity of several states and certain sizeable industries.[5] Few books and articles written during that period criticized defense expenditures as wasteful or the war itself as unnecessary. At the annual meetings of the American Economic Association during 1949 and 1950, for example, the primary concern of the participants was to minimize government con-

[3] See *American Economic Review*, vol. 32 (February, 1942), 1–36, 216–17, 227–30, and 351–432.

[4] There have been over 700 articles and books written on the role of the military-industrial complex alone during the brief span of years since 1961. See *Peace Research Abstracts Journal* (Canadian Peace Research Institute, Clarkson, Ontario, Annual Indexes under category IX–37) for specific titles.

[5] See *Index of Economic Journals*, vols. 3 and 4 under section 13, for articles during that period.

trols while recognizing the dangers of war-generated inflation. It was generally agreed that the Cold War helped our economy, that military power was the best means for stopping the expansion of Communism, and that military spending was more important than building security through productive capacity.[6] Indeed some economists, afraid that the public was unduly concerned about the high cost of defense spending, spent considerable effort to show that our defense budgets would not lead the nation into bankruptcy. Shortly before the Korean conflict broke out, *Business Week,* summing up the general attitude of economists, concluded that defense spending was necessary to preserve the nation and keep the economy healthy: "Pressure for more government spending is mounting. And the prospect is that Congress will give in a little more now, then more by next year. . . . The reason is a combination of concern over tense Russian relations, and a growing fear of a rising level of unemployment here at home." [7]

The coming of the Korean conflict and the ensuing years of high military spending thereafter made the close relationship between the Cold War and unemployment even more evident. Prior to the Korean conflict the rate of unemployment had remained tenaciously high, albeit much lower than during the 1930's. In 1949 it had climbed as high as 8 percent, and immediately before the American forces were committed in Korea, it was over 5 percent. With the coming of the war, however, the rate of unemployment dropped rapidly. By October 1953 the figure was only 1.8 percent—the lowest of the decade. Conversely, the end of the war and the cutback in defense expenditures brought on a recession. But in 1957, following the spectacular Russian achievement in orbiting Sputnik I and our consequent increase in defense expenditures, the economy boomed briefly. As a result of these lessons, few economists saw the Cold War as a burden depleting our economy or undermining our long-term productive capacity.

With the coming of the Kennedy administration, economists began to intensify their studies of military spending and to shift their focus in three ways. First, because President Kennedy's administration began to stress the need to help the disadvantaged at a time when welfare programs lagged because of rising defense outlays in response to the 1961 Berlin crisis and the two Cuban crises, many economists began to emphasize the burdens created by defense expenditures. "Guns versus butter" became a fashionable subject, and argument was heated until early 1968, when it was finally conceded that costs in Vietnam required the nation to choose one or the other. Perhaps the best-known author to take this view is Seymour Melman. His book *Our Depleted Society,* published in 1965, was the first major recent work to return to the old argument that war retards human progress. Excerpts from this work are printed in Part I.

Meanwhile, Senator George McGovern (Democrat, South Dakota) became

---

[6] See *American Economic Review,* vol. 39 (May, 1949), 357 and vol. 40 (May, 1950), 191.
[7] *Business Week,* April 15, 1950, 15.

TABLE III   INDICES OF PRODUCTION

Country	1938	Industry 1953 = 100		Wheat Production 1934-1938 = 100
		1946	1948	1948
West Germany	78	n.a.	41	63
Italy	62	n.a.	62	n.a.
Austria	59	n.a.	54	n.a.
Japan	88	24	38	n.a.
France	71	60	81	40
Belgium	71	63	87	n.a.
United Kingdom	71	72	83	n.a.
U.S.S.R.	30	29	45	n.a.
Canada	41	69	70	129

SOURCE: Shepard B. Clough, *The Economic Development of Western Civilization*, p. 454.
Kaplan and Moorsteen's estimates project a very large decline in the output of civilian goods
in the Soviet Union during the years 1940-45—a decline of about 50 percent in machinery
and consumers' goods, and 40 percent in other producers' goods.

The position of the United States from 1914 to 1945 resembled that of Great
Britain during the Revolutionary and Napoleonic wars from 1792 to 1815.
A vast expanse of ocean secured by naval and air power made it certain that
the United States would be the only major power to escape both invasion
and destruction. Technical progress continued unabated, as North America
prospered from the inflation of demand induced by military preparations,
without suffering at home any of the direct destructive consequences of warfare. Moreover, the United States entered the war with substantial unemployment and idle resources. These could—at least, initially—take up the
slack of war production without concurrent adverse effects on civilian living
standards. Statistically, the low base of the 1930's also allowed the nation to
establish new industrial records as the economy worked back to full employment.

Against the wartime maintenance of American living standards has to be
placed the economic deprivations endured by much of Europe and Asia,
where the battles were fought. Table III depicts the costs of direct involvement.

Necessarily, some capital investment took place in European industry during the course of the war, even though it was spotty in character and of
small utility for balanced economic growth. Motive power increased 23 per
cent in the Netherlands from 1939 to 1945, and by 35 per cent in Denmark.
Expansion of the machine tool industry in Germany amounted to 75 per cent
from 1939 to 1943.[17] By contrast, there was little expansion in the steel industry, in the consumers' goods industries generally, in housing or in transport,

[16] N. M. Kaplan and R. H. Moorsteen, "An Index of Soviet Industrial Output," *American Economic Review*, L, 3 (June, 1960), 295-318.

[17] Shepard Clough, *The Economic Development of Western Civilization* (New York:
McGraw-Hill, 1959), p. 54.

so that bottlenecks developed in these lines during the first years of reconstruction.

SCIENCE AND WAR

War among industrial societies is as much a battle of scientific imagination as it is of bombs, bullets and resources. In both world wars, governments organized the scientific talent that had been recruited from universities and private business to serve the war effort. These endeavors bore fruit, especially after World War II, in the appearance of new sources of industrial power, novel procedures in clinical medicine, and a score of technological innovations that held the promise of better living, at least materially. Thus science contributed to the equipment and methods of war, and war made its contribution to science.

> "The intense motivation of the war effort," writes Mr. J. Carlton Ward, Jr., "stimulates men to bring to fruition many unfinished projects and to conceive, under pressure of fear for national safety, bold new ideas. The question of immediate financial returns at such times is unimportant and, in fact, irrelevant. It is possible therefore to go ahead at full speed on programs that would not be justified on the basis of profits. For these reasons many advances in technology are made during war which might have been delayed for decades or generations in times of peace. These considerations emphatically do not create a case for war. The destruction of life and property and the overthrow of institutions due to military conflict are infinitely tragic . . . ." [18]

The succeeding paragraphs will take up, as illustrative of the relation of science to war, the following aspects of the subject: atomic energy, developments in surgery, and the problem of basic research.

Atomic energy was only partially the creation of war. The theory of atoms was in fact developed by the Greek philosophers as early as the fifth century B.C. The modern father of atomic studies, John Dalton (1766–1844), a British scholar, carried the theory of atoms much further than had the Greeks, and during the nineteenth century many scientists added to the fund of knowledge about the atom. The French physicist Henri Becquerel, for example, opened up a new field of study in 1896 by his revelation of the radioactivity of uranium. In 1905, Einstein developed his famous formula—$E = MC^2$—which showed that matter and energy could be equated. Thus the basic theory of atomic energy was well established before World War II. In the decade preceding World War II, physicists speculated in their classrooms and in scientific meetings about the limitless amount of energy that might be unleashed if the atom were split. A vast amount of applied research remained to be accomplished and, at the ordinary pace of scientific application, many decades would have passed before the reality of atomic energy

---

[18] *Research and Development* (Washington, D.C.: Industrial College of the Armed Forces, 1963), p. 39. Much of the material for these observations relied on Chapter V (pp. 39–55) of this volume.

emerged. Under the stimulus of war, the time gap between theory and practice was telescoped. In a relatively few years, and with the expenditure of $2 billion, the atomic bomb was created.

The relation of surgery and clinical medicine to war parallels that found in physics: the exposition of theory during peacetime and its application in war. Characteristically, wars have supplied a great laboratory for the application on a mass scale of medical-surgical techniques articulated during interwar periods. It may well be, in fact, that surgery was born when, as a result of injuries sustained in combat, primitive man searched for treatments to staunch the flow of blood, heal fractures and soothe bruises. In the sixteenth century, one of the most famous military surgeons was Ambrose Paré. His contribution, which stressed the healing powers of nature, lay in the treatment of war wounds by methods learned from observations in military actions and from the drawing of careful empirical conclusions. The theories on infection in wounds, developed by Louis Pasteur (1822–1895) and Joseph Lister (1827–1912), were applied extensively in military hospitals, especially after the pioneer work of Florence Nightingale, who established the first military hospital (with a female nursing staff and hospital administration) during the Crimean War. The impact of war on surgical techniques was, however, most evident in the periods 1914–1918 and 1939–1945. The constant demand of war for the improved treatment of wounds resulted in the development by French surgeons of a method known as *debridement*—cutting away the infected edges of wounds, thus converting infected wounds into clean ones. A Spanish surgeon during the Spanish Civil War perfected a method of encasing war wounds in plaster splints—the Trueta–Orr Method. The most dramatic advances made by surgery during World War II were again in the treatment of wounds and the control of surgical infections, as the result of improvements in anesthesia and the use of sulfa drugs and penicillin, coordinated into a group effort, as necessitated by the requirements of war. A tremendous wartime project in governmental and commercial laboratories solved the problems involved in the cultivation and production of penicillin on a quantity basis. Finally, plastic surgery made great strides in both world wars, as did the methods of collecting, distributing and administering blood for transfusions.

If war accelerated the application of medical-surgical innovations, in other respects it retarded the science of medicine. War interrupted the diffusion of knowledge throughout the world community. Physicians found it difficult to report in international journals the results of their practices and investigations. The German surgeon, Kuntschner, by way of illustration, conceived the idea of placing a metal splint inside a broken bone and designed a long pin for this purpose. Kuntschner's technique in many cases eliminated the need for traction. Nevertheless, it could not be employed by Allied surgeons until after the war. Similarly, Axis surgeons lacked the opportunity to apply to their patients the fruits of Allied research. Domestically, too, the state of wartime transportation forced the curtailment of medical conventions and the dissemination of knowledge by this means.

Finally, the Second World War stimulated applied research, but basic research was almost completely halted. With the fate of the nation at stake, there was little disposition to pursue studies merely for the purpose of understanding the laws of nature. Moreover, scientific personnel who had been transferred from basic to applied research to satisfy the needs of war would, in many instances, never return to their peacetime pursuits. The situation was worse still in those countries where the effects of war were more pronounced.

UNECONOMIC ALLOCATION OF RESOURCES

War selects those industries vital to its cataclysmic purposes, concentrates great exertions on their development, and slights endeavors of lesser strategic value. Because of the intricate web of interdependence wrought by specialization and the division of labor, modern war exercises a pervasive sway over the economy, ensnaring every segment of agriculture, industry, trade and finance. It breeds, as a consequence, vertical and horizontal distortions within the market structure. To reconversion falls the task of restoring the balance, an assignment not always performed successfully without severe hardships. A few citations will suffice to show how the survival values of war economics depart from the premises of pacific economic intercourse.

In each of the major American wars, agricultural output, already excessive in times of peace, had to expand further to meet the pull of wartime demand. The farmers of the Civil War and World War I periods increased production, despite a diminution in the number of agricultural workers, by bringing additional land under cultivation (financed through credit), rather than by the medium of improved farming techniques. The American agriculturist, accordingly, emerged from both wars in a rather tenuous financial position, burdened with debt and sensitive to the certain price deflation of peacetime markets. His plight was surely a depressant factor in the primary postwar recession of 1921–22. For different reasons, British agriculture in two world wars offers another example of how the urgency of war alters the distribution of production factors. Because of the overriding need to conserve shipping space, the British farmer had to shift from the output of meat and dairy products to grain and fodder. He was thus impelled, at the conclusion of hostilities, both to lower his scale of operation and to reorient output once again toward meat and dairy products. Conversely, the expansion of grain production in the Western Hemisphere, artificially stimulated by war, made Britain even less self-sufficient in grains.[19]

Modern war in particular accelerates the consumption of natural resources. The imperative need to attain heavier and more destructive firepower faster than the enemy creates an unprecedented call for instruments of destruction made of metal. Munitions requiring minerals were nonexistent in the Stone Age. They comprised less than 25 per cent of the national industrial output during the Franco-Prussian War of 1870. In World War II, however, they were responsible for more than 75 per cent of the industrial effort. The demand for strategic and critical materials for this second global encounter averaged approximately two and one-half times the 1935–39 re-

19 Krooss, pp. 476–478; Rostow, p. 154; Ashworth, pp. 46–70.

quirements.[20] Equally to the point, the coal industry of Great Britain during World War I consumed so much of its remaining easily accessible deposits that it henceforward would sell only at high cost, to the detriment of other British industry and its own export position.[21] Not only does modern war impel its participants to squander their natural inheritance in a profligate manner, but the shortages of natural resources, occasioned by the disruption of international trade, force the belligerents to engage labor and capital in the production of costly substitutes. During the closing months of World War II, while the Japanese were converting rubber factories to make a substitute for petroleum, the United States was busily converting petroleum into rubber by a similar industrial process!

The collapse of the delicate framework of international trade caused by World War I left permanent scars on British industry and commerce. Some industries, such as textiles, which lacked an adequate supply of raw materials and shipping space for their produce, had to contract their output without reducing their capacity, and to stand by while neutrals and more favorably situated belligerents absorbed their foreign markets. Others, such as steel and shipbuilding, enlarged their capacities in order to fulfill special war needs and were able to escape the postbellum onus of idle plant and equipment only if new foreign markets came to light. Although Britain was not herself directly invaded, her economy suffered a severe depletion of physical capital during the course of World War I. About 40 per cent of the merchant fleet, over seven million tons of shipping, was lost and had to be replaced if the country was to retain her traditional role on the high seas. More serious in the way of capital loss was the general failure to make good the depreciation of capital assets, except where the immediate wartime usefulness might have been impaired.[22]

THE SECOND INDUSTRIAL REVOLUTION HYPOTHESIS

So profound were the innovations of World War II technology that many economists professed to see in them the beginnings of a "second industrial revolution." This new "takeoff" supposedly differed qualitatively from the first industrial revolution in two major respects. Military factors per se played hardly any role at all during the first industrial revolution, and during the approximately 150 years that intervened from the first industrial revolution to the present day, military requirements had very little impact on industrial development. Secondly, in the struggles that preceded the first industrial revolution the powers of the state were greatly curtailed. The rising industrialist class progressively reduced the sphere of state influence in the economic life of the community.

Actually, the "second industrial revolution" had its genesis in the lessons of World War I—in the realization, especially by the defeated Germany, that in modern war the mobilization of military manpower and equipment, if it was to be effective, had to be backed by the mobilization of all economic

---

[20] George A. Lincoln, William S. Stone, Thomas H. Harvey, *Economics of National Security* (Englewood Cliffs, N.J.: Prentice-Hall, 1950), pp. 137–139.
[21] Ashworth, p. 290.
[22] *Ibid.*, pp. 286–288.

resources in the community. Efficient military mobilization was not enough; it needed to be accompanied by an equally efficient industrial mobilization. Hence, by World War II, the governments of the major powers had prepared the ground so that military personnel might join hands with civilian scientists for the design of new weapons and other devices to counter the scientific parries of the enemy. As it turned out, this scientific research, while serving military purposes in the first instance, nevertheless did not serve them exclusively, since it became one of the decisive factors in the "second industrial revolution." Accordingly, by contrast with the first industrial revolution, the state played a primary and dominant role in the "second industrial revolution." As late as 1963, some 15 per cent of United States defense outlays were for research and development, and somewhere between 50 and 60 per cent of total research and development expenditures were financed by defense agencies.[23] The "second industrial revolution" hypothesis therefore contends that the main source of technical revolution today lies in the military sphere and the military revolution of our times is now the dynamic factor in economic development.

Apart from advances in the field of medicine, the two primary accomplishments of war-sponsored research lay in the control of nuclear energy and the adoption of electronically operated machinery. The development of nuclear energy as a new source of power placed the military several jumps ahead of the civilian economy in the practical application of atomic physics. It is contended that as a result of the "scientific cold war" this lead will widen.

> If as a result of processes similar to those which lead to the creation of the hydrogen bomb our scientists succeed . . . in mastering the use of nuclear energy for peaceful purposes, thus making a decisive step forward in the generation of energy, then it will once again be the military sphere which went ahead and was followed at some considerable remove by the industrial and economic spheres.[24]

The second aspect, the production of electronically controlled machinery or automation, makes possible a further qualitatively unique substitution of machine for manpower. The way in which automatic controls developed from wartime research is explained by John Diebold:

> During World War II, the theory and use of feedback was studied in great detail by a number of scientists both in this country and in Britain. The introduction of rapidly moving aircraft very quickly made traditional gun-laying techniques of antiaircraft warfare obsolete. As a result, a large part of scientific manpower in this country was directed towards the development of self-regulating devices and systems to control our military equipment. It is out of this work that the technology of automation as we understand it today has developed.[25]

[23] Richard N. Nelson, "The Impact of Arms Reduction on Research and Development," *American Economic Review,* LIII, 2 (May, 1963), 435–446.

[24] Sternberg, pp. 115, 111–195; Norbert Wiener, *The Human Use of Human Beings* (Boston: Houghton Mifflin, 1950), pp. 187–189; Earl of Birkenhead, *The Professor and the Prime Minister* (Boston: Houghton Mifflin, 1962).

[25] Sternberg, p. 115.

Militarily-oriented research proceeds forced draft [i.e., encouraged innovation] in nuclear energy, automatic controls, and now into the great potential of space travel.

It is, of course, far too early to assess the implications for economic welfare of the modes and processes of the "second industrial revolution." Some of the theoretical work on atomic energy, automatic devices, and space travel was accomplished in the interwar period, and it may be plausibly claimed that war only accelerated the realization of things that were already inherent in the evolution of industrialism. Furthermore, breakthroughs from government-sponsored military research may border on the spectacular, but it cannot be claimed that the military use of these innovations is for the material benefit of humanity. Knowledge is one thing; its use may be quite another.

Economic progress implies the use of appropriate scientific and technological knowledge to augment the flow of goods and services. That is not the motivating factor in the research behind the "second industrial revolution." In fact, the artificial allocation of funds to this type of research could actually hamper economic progress. It concentrates on programs of special military concern, but the allotment of resources to particular segments of the industrial system so as to support these specialized projects may unduly deprive other vital sectors (housing, local transportation, and so forth) of the capital assets essential for balanced economic growth. It may even thwart the ultimate purpose of scientific investigation, by overemphasis on the immediate and useful to the detriment of speculative knowledge. Lastly, feats of technological innovation in the military sphere do not provide assurance of their successful or even ultimate application to civilian production. A different set of criteria obtain. Industrial maturation is a long-term evolutionary process, with inventions phased in after analysis of comparative profit margins, the amortization of committed capital, and the types and kinds of financing available. In the military sector, it is usually enough that a new machine is more efficient than an old one, cost considerations being given a lower priority. For industry, however, the new machine must not only be more efficient than the old one, it must also be more profitable. These circumstances act as a brake on the pace at which industry will absorb atomic energy, automation or similar innovations; they are the market's means for assuring balanced growth and orderly economic development.[26]

On the other hand, it is well to remember the trend toward expanding government involvement in economic affairs, and the fact that government, with its great financial resources, is in a unique position to take the fullest advantage of the basic modification in the inventive process: the transition from the "heroic" stage of invention by the self-educated mechanic, building laboriously by trial and error, to the organized group research of the modern laboratory. The government, rather than business or the universities, possesses the wherewithal to finance research facilities, and to supply the necessary equipment for a battery of scientists tackling a defined problem. From the felicitous confluence of finance and patriotic motivation, one would anticipate quick returns in the subjects of chosen interest and, where these

26 "Automation and Technological Change," Hearings before the Subcommittee on Economic Stabilization of the Joint Committee on the Economic Report, Congress of the United States (Washington, D.C.: Government Printing Office, 1955), p. 9.

demonstrate an adaptability to the civilian sector, the results should indeed excite much wonderment.

THE INDIRECT EFFECTS: WAR AND INSTITUTIONAL CHANGE

In *The Process of Economic Growth,* W. W. Rostow ventured the conclusion that, on a strictly economic calculation, war slowed the rate of economic progress for Great Britain but may also have induced social and political changes that assisted long-run economic development.

> Governments have made in war political concessions they would not make in peace. Many of the great shifts in social and political power in the course of British history are intimately tied to the pressures and the processes imposed by war. War did not create these shifts, but it powerfully affected their timing and the rate at which they took place. And these shifts in the social structure and the political balance of power in Britain may well have strengthened what are referred to earlier . . . as the propensities relevant to the process of economic development.[27]

For British history, at least, Rostow believes that these social and political changes worked in a positive direction economically.

The case can be argued cogently both for and against, but the present state of knowledge inhibits a definitive resolution of the question. Man's history is a partially told story, and considerable ambiguities attend the effort to reconstruct the indirect consequences of war on earlier societies and non-Western civilizations. Without doubt, some wars (such as the Indian Wars to clear the American continent, the American Civil War, and the French Revolution) helped to eradicate the debris of archaic social customs and institutions and thereby to hasten economic growth. In other instances (such as the Franco-Prussian War of 1870 and World War I), war either evoked an atavistic reversion to more primitive institutional arrangements, or propagated enmities that impeded the proliferation of commerce and industry. Briefly put, there are wars and wars. Depending upon their causation and the intensity of violence, a number of conflicts have accelerated what hindsight has proven to be desirable social and political adjustments; others, quite the contrary.

CONCLUSION

Against the background of these observations on the historical impingement of war on demographic and natural resources and institutional arrangements, what can be said, in conclusion, about the relationship of war to economic progress?

The preponderance of evidence supports the judgment that war, on balance, does not correlate positively with economic progress. Settlement by arms not only causes a great net waste of resources; it also retards industrial development and the division of labor. The illusion of progress remains, for

[27] Rostow, p. 165.

the intensity of mortal combat spurs men and nations to great exploits in the areas that are deemed essential to military prowess. But it is not balanced growth nor advancement in speculative knowledge that the God of War seeds; it is merely the accelerated application of the already known for immediate purposes. The scientific feats emanating from government-sponsored research, which have been heralded as launching a "second industrial revolution," do not indicate that it will inevitably be further military research that will insure economic progress.

> Indeed, the case can be made that in recent years the growth of military and space R and D has significantly retarded the growth of civilian R and D. . . . There is considerable feeling among R and D directors that the growth of defense R and D, by bidding up salaries and by taking the cream of the new science and engineering graduates, has tended to reduce significantly the quantity and quality of R and D undertaken in civilian-created laboratories. . . . In any case, a significant increase in R and D resources could be used in the civilian sector, with large benefit to society. In many of the civilian industries very little R and D is presently directed toward improving products and processes. . . . Increased R and D spending undoubtedly would yield high returns in many of these industries. The civilian economy would benefit especially from increased long-range research and experimentation with advanced technological possibilities of the sort that research teams presently employed by defense industries have conducted so successfully. The freeing of these highly trained research resources for application to civilian technology would hold great promise for increasing the welfare of the American people.[28]

Pure and applied research are the prerequisites to economic growth in an industrial society. If we accept the hypothesis of Professor Schumpeter that a steady stream of new products and processes begets the expansion phase of the trade cycle, then we may look with the confidence of historical precedent to private industry to supply the want. This does not preclude, however, government-endowed research, for there exist areas of public interest for which the resources of private corporations and universities are insufficient to muster the equipment and personnel required for mastery of the problem. Space research at this stage, for instance, must rest upon government subsidy. In other words, as a result of the transformation in the organization and financing of research and development, scientific projects carried on by government have a definite function in assisting progress in living standards. This does not *ipso facto* imply a military orientation.

Our historical survey of the subject clearly underscores the conclusion that the dire economic effects of belligerency vary proportionately to the degree of participation. Land warfare on the European continent carried the most destructive aftermath, for it exposed the population, industry and resources of the engaged nations to immediate peril. The land powers of France, Germany, and Russia afford us the best examples of the economic calamities wrought by war; England and Holland represent the reverse side of the

28 Nelson, p. 445.

coin. Up to the twentieth century, both the latter nations exerted a potent diplomatic pressure on continental affairs, while simultaneously restricting their military commitment. Although more or less continuously at war from 1585 to 1665, Holland nevertheless grew in prosperity, largely because of two fortuitous circumstances. Firstly, sea trade was a vital component of Dutch commercial fortunes, and war at times enabled the small nation to grasp opportunities not normally open in the ebb and flow of peacetime trade. Secondly, Holland enjoyed an isolation of sorts, based upon a natural water frontier, formed on her southern border by the Rhine and Meuse rivers. Geography conferred even stronger advantages upon Great Britain. Behind the water barrier of the English Channel and blessed as the country was with an abundance of natural resources, a flourishing high-seas and coastal trade simulated industry, which was free of the ravages of continental land warfare.[29]

The military and diplomatic history of Holland and England contains important lessons, germane even to the twentieth century, in which the thought of another "splendid isolation" seems utterly ludicrous. Nevertheless, under the assumption of a nuclear stalemate, and where the configuration of geography and the balance of power permits, dominant naval and air power offers to their possessor instruments of policy that minimize the economic disadvantages that war imposes on human progress. Isolation from world politics is a mere fantasy, impossible as it is unworthy; nevertheless, removal from land warfare presents itself as a viable political objective, compatible with the geographic and power position of the United States in an era of intercontinental ballistic missiles. We have here an important joining of military and economic policy. For the strategy which eschews, where feasible, commitment to land warfare will, in the long run, if not promote, at least not detract as much from the advancement of material well-being.

Peace and war alternate in human history as they do in the human spirit. Superficially, the initiating motives that induce civilized man to wield the sword are innumerable: quarrels over creeds, dynasties and commercial rivalries, and unabashed greed for loot. But it is about the nationalist passion that two world wars have taught Western man to worry most in this century. The discords of nationalistic rivalry demand no elaboration. Suffice it to say, they are apt to be with us in any foreseeable future; for, even should the extant conglomeration of small states regroup into larger regional units, might not this new form of national feeling become as explosive as its more parochial predecessors? Giants may wrestle as well as pygmies; if they do, the consequences are likely to be worse than the Balkanized type of clash that sputters and sparks, now in one corner of the world and then in another. The ultimate *raison d'être* of armed conflict, we must sorrowfully admit, derives from human nature and will not be wished away by mere tinkering with political institutions. As long as man inhabits the globe, he will do battle in one cause or another, and it will be incumbent upon economists to interpret the significance of this fact for the material well-being of society.

. . . .

[29] Nef, pp. 72, 88, 101, 109–111, 160–165, 327–328, 376.

STATISTICAL TABLES

TABLE 1   BASIC STATISTICAL DATA ON AMERICA'S MAJOR WARS

War	Duration Years	Duration Months	Men engaged (in thousands)	Casualties	Estimated original cost (millions of dollars)	Veterans benefits to 1967 (millions of dollars)	Estimated total cost to 1967 (millions of dollars)
American Revolution	8	—	184–250	10,600	$ 100	$ 70	$ 170
War of 1812	2	7	287	6,800	112[3]	49	161
Mexican War	1	5	79	17,400	98[4]	64	162
Civil War (Union Forces Only)	4	1	2,213	646,400	3,065[5]	8,567	11,632
Spanish-American War	—	4	307	4,100	445[6]	5,256	5,700
World War I	1	7	4,744	320,700	33,000[7]	39,854	72,854
World War II	3	8	16,354	1,078,200	381,000[8]	76,767	457,767
Korean conflict	3	1	5,764	157,500	53,600[9]	12,863	66,463
Vietnam conflict (To December 31, 1968)	9[1]	5	1,771	233,200[2]	110,000[10] (to July, 1970)	(NA)	(NA)

NA Not available.
1 The Vietnam conflict is assumed to have begun when the first U.S. troops were killed in combat in July, 1959.
2 Killed, wounded, or injured from hostile-forces action from January 1, 1961, to December 31, 1968
3 Expenditures by Departments of the Army and Navy, 1812-16.
4 Expenditures by Departments of the Army and Navy, 1846-48.
5 Expenditures by Departments of the Army and Navy, 1861-65.
6 Expenditures by Departments of the Army and Navy, 1898-99.

7 From John B. Clark, *The Costs of World War I to the American People* (New Haven, 1931), pp. 278-82.
8 Major National Security Expenditures, 1941-46.
9 Assumes 5,764,000 men served an average of 19 months at $2,835 personnel costs per man per year, $2,723 operation and maintenance costs per man per year, and procurement costs totaling one-third the increase over previous year. Averages were determined by dividing total costs by total personnel.
10 Special Vietnam expenditures, 1954 through fiscal 1970.

TABLE 2   DEFENSE PURCHASES OF GOODS AND SERVICES OF
THE FEDERAL GOVERNMENT AND RELATION TO GNP, 1945–1968

| Calendar year | National defense purchases of goods and services | |
	Amount (billions of dollars)	Percent of GNP
1945	$ 75.9	35.5%
1946	18.8	8.9
1947	11.4	4.9
1948	11.6	4.5
1949	13.6	5.3
1950	14.3	5.0
1951	33.9	10.3
1952	46.4	13.4
1953	49.3	13.5
1954	41.2	11.3
1955	39.1	9.8
1956	40.4	9.6
1957	44.4	10.0
1958	44.8	10.1
1959	46.2	9.6
1960	45.7	9.1
1961	49.0	9.4
1962	53.6	9.6
1963	55.2	9.5
1964	55.4	8.9
1965	55.6	8.4
1966	60.6	8.1
1967	72.4	9.2
1968 (Aug.)	79.0	9.3

TABLE 3   BUDGET OUTLAYS FOR NATIONAL DEFENSE FUNCTIONS, 1962–1969

Cost category, program, or agency	1962	1963	1964	1965	1966	1967	1968 est.	1969 est.
Total	51,462	53,429	54,514	50,790	58,464	70,093	76,489	79,789
Department of Defense, military	46,815	48,255	49,760	46,173	54,409	[1]67,466	[1]73,694	[1]76,658
Military personnel	13,032	13,000	14,195	14,771	16,753	19,787	21,800	22,793
Active forces	11,530	11,386	12,312	12,662	14,407	17,054	18,850	19,623
Reserve forces	607	599	674	725	755	902	890	905
Retired pay	894	1,015	1,209	1,384	1,591	1,830	2,060	2,265
Operation and maintenance	11,594	11,874	11,932	12,349	14,710	19,000	19,800	22,260
Procurement	14,532	16,632	15,351	11,839	14,339	19,012	21,470	23,445
Army	(NA)	2,371	2,315	1,764	2,671	4,390	5,120	5,708
Navy	(NA)	6,396	5,804	4,778	5,075	6,074	6,710	7,554
Air Force	(NA)	7,673	6,959	5,101	6,414	8,096	9,075	9,483
Other[2]	(NA)	192	273	197	179	452	565	700
Research, development, test, and evaluation	6,319	6,376	7,021	6,236	6,259	7,160	7,200	7,800
Military construction	1,347	1,144	1,026	1,007	1,334	1,536	1,565	1,450
Family housing	–	427	580	619	647	482	520	570
Civil defense	90	203	107	93	86	100	93	89
Other[3]	–99	–1,401	–452	–741	281	532	1,412	–1,601
Military assistance[4]	1,756	2,400	1,972	1,980	1,728	[1]865	[1]525	[1]455
Atomic energy program	2,806	2,758	2,765	2,625	2,403	2,264	2,334	2,546
Defense-related activities	92	24	172	136	–62	–14	114	241
Stockpiling of strategic and critical materials	33	22	16	16	16	19	19	23
Expansion of defense production	11	–57	91	60	–152	–102	22	146
Selective Service System	35	34	41	43	54	58	61	64
Emergency preparedness activities	13	25	24	17	20	11	12	8
Miscellaneous[5]	–7	–1,396	–154	–124	–14	–490	–180	–112

– Represents zero. NA Not available.
[1] Relevant interfund and intragovernmental transactions and applicable receipts from the public have been deducted to arrive at totals.
[2] Marine Corps and Defense agencies.
[3] Revolving, management, military trust, and other funds.
[4] Includes trust funds.
[5] Adjustments and net lending; for details, see source.

TABLE 4 GEOGRAPHIC DISTRIBUTION OF DEFENSE CONTRACTS: FOUR PERIODS

State	World War II defense contracts to June 1945		Korean defense contracts July 1, 1950-Dec. 31, 1956		Missile age defense contracts 1959-60		Vietnam defense contracts 1967-68	
	Position	Percent of total contract awards	Position	Percent of total contract awards	Position	Percent of total contract awards	Position	Percent of total contract awards
New York	1	11.0%	2	14.6%	2	11.4%	3	9.1%
Michigan	2	10.9	3	6.4	9	3.3	13	2.5
California	3	8.7	1	16.4	1	24.0	1	17.7
Ohio	4	8.4	4	6.1	6	4.4	7	4.4
New Jersey	5	6.8	5	5.3	5	5.0	9	3.2
Pennsylvania	6	6.6	7	4.3	10	3.2	6	4.5
Illinois	7	6.1	6	4.8	14	2.1	12	2.6
Indiana	8	4.5	*	*	16	1.7	14	2.4
Connecticut	9	4.1	*	*	7	4.2	4	5.9
Massachusetts	10	3.4	9	2.7	4	5.3	8	4.1
Texas	11	3.1	8	3.8	3	5.8	2	10.3
Washington	14	2.3	*	*	8	4.0	19	1.5
Missouri	15	1.8	10	2.3	13	2.2	5	4.9
1st 10 – % of total		70.5%		66.7%		70.6%		73.1%

* Not among the top 10. Data otherwise unavailable.

World War II: War Production Board, Summary of War Supply and Facility Contracts by State, Industrial Area and County (November 1, 1945), Table I.

Korea: Senate, Committee on Armed Services, Hearings, Military Procurement, 86th Cong., 1st Sess. (1959), p. 322. These data are available for only the top ten states.

Missile Age: Fiscal 1959-60 – Department of Commerce, Statistical Abstract 1961, p. 238.

Vietnam: Fiscal 1967-68 – Department of Defense, Prime Contract Awards by State.

1 Also among the top twenty for 1967-68 are:

10th	Georgia	2.9%
11th	Florida	2.8
15th	Maryland	2.1
16th	Virginia	1.9
17th	Minnesota	1.7
18th	Tennessee	1.5
20th	North Carolina	1.3

TABLE 5 DEFENSE CONTRACT AWARDS AND PAYROLLS—STATES, 1965–1967
[In millions of dollars. For years ending June 30. Data for contracts refer to awards made in fiscal year specified; expenditures relating to those awards may extend over several years.]

State	1965			1966			1967		
		Estimated annual payroll			Estimated annual payroll			Estimated annual payroll	
	Contract awards[1]	Military person-nel[2]	Civil ians[3]	Contract awards[1]	Military person-nel[2]	Civil ians[3]	Contract awards[1]	Military person-nel[2]	Civil-ians[3]
Total	26,631	7,781	6,774	35,713	8,432	7,212	41,817	9,350	8,044
Alabama	165	130	228	282	155	233	297	184	233
Alaska	74	138	57	72	155	52	86	166	56
Arizona	177	105	48	248	111	52	250	139	61
Arkansas	39	54	29	96	55	29	127	58	33
California	5,154	983	1,046	5,813	1,099	1,189	6,689	1,150	1,328
Colorado	250	163	100	256	188	106	210	223	116
Connecticut	1,180	23	23	2,052	18	27	1,936	20	32
Delaware	38	43	8	37	41	9	52	50	10
District of Columbia	244	142	230	328	192	191	358	186	209
Florida	633	362	166	767	361	189	799	384	213
Georgia	662	396	224	799	437	259	1,148	532	287
Hawaii	72	183	121	64	181	155	65	176	171
Idaho	12	31	3	20	25	3	15	22	4
Illinois	422	219	200	920	245	205	1,064	304	221
Indiana	605	41	83	1,068	49	97	898	52	116
Iowa	134	8	4	248	8	5	279	9	6
Kansas	229	173	32	313	154	34	399	179	40
Kentucky	43	172	79	70	201	94	124	289	109
Louisiana	256	128	44	303	170	47	656	199	57
Maine	69	65	10	51	64	11	57	61	13
Maryland	584	254	343	843	256	326	870	327	366
Massachusetts	1,179	153	172	1,336	161	184	1,422	139	193
Michigan	533	105	83	918	105	90	1,034	104	103
Minnesota	260	24	13	498	26	15	651	26	18
Mississippi	152	105	42	162	131	46	115	143	50

TABLE 5   DEFENSE CONTRACT AWARDS AND PAYROLLS—STATES, 1965–1967
[In millions of dollars. For years ending June 30. Data for contracts refer to
awards made in fiscal year specified; expenditures relating to those awards
may extend over several years.] *(cont'd)*

State	1965			1966			1967		
		Estimated annual payroll			Estimated annual payroll			Estimated annual payroll	
	Contract awards[1]	Military person- nel[2]	Civil ians[3]	Contract awards[1]	Military person- nel[2]	Civil ians[3]	Contract awards[1]	Military person- nel[2]	Civil ians[3]
Missouri	1,061	104	114	1,113	152	143	2,278	178	166
Montana	69	50	6	14	54	8	78	57	10
Nebraska	43	101	25	80	90	28	103	83	30
Nevada	19	40	18	32	36	20	29	37	19
New Hampshire	52	41	62	110	36	60	163	29	65
New Jersey	820	166	171	1,090	217	181	1,235	227	243
New Mexico	84	111	75	86	94	80	80	96	88
New York	2,229	174	342	2,819	183	282	3,262	168	313
North Carolina	288	344	63	449	373	77	448	439	87
North Dakota	49	59	8	83	70	9	17	76	9
Ohio	863	111	333	1,589	133	321	1,603	135	354
Oklahoma	120	161	169	158	176	196	157	210	226
Oregon	40	26	23	90	23	24	99	20	25
Pennsylvania	989	77	510	1,665	78	511	1,649	77	528
Rhode Island	86	38	56	132	44	64	198	44	71
South Carolina	82	185	99	176	263	117	181	243	130
South Dakota	21	34	9	23	37	9	9	38	10
Tennessee	197	90	45	502	91	44	538	90	49
Texas	1,447	798	399	2,292	938	448	3,547	1,068	515
Utah	191	24	139	170	27	170	179	28	203
Vermont	32	2	–	81	2	1	100	1	1
Virginia	473	444	540	426	476	570	665	590	623
Washington	546	211	157	444	203	174	606	250	197
West Virginia	90	3	7	149	3	8	140	3	9
Wisconsin	203	22	12	365	20	15	384	17	23
Wyoming	8	25	4	11	25	4	33	24	5
Undistributed	3,363	140	–	4,000	–	–	4,435	–	–

– Represents zero.
[1] Awards of $10,000 or more for supplies, services, and construction. Figures reflect impact of prime-contracting on State distribution of defense work. Often the State in which a prime contractor is located is not the State in which the subcontracted work is done.
[2] For shore based personnel only.
[3] Direct hire employees only.

TABLE 6   DISTRIBUTION OF DEFENSE EMPLOYMENT AND
LABOR FORCE BY STATE, JUNE 1966

State ranking[1]	Percentage distribution			Number (in thousands)	
	Defense-generated employ-ment[2]	Labor force	Military person-nel	Defense-generated employ-ment	Military person-nel
(1)	(2)	(3)	(4)	(5)	(6)
1. California	17.0	9.5	13.5	405.0	246.6
2. Texas	5.8	5.1	11.3	139.6	206.9
3. New York	5.7	10.1	1.8	138.0	33.2
4. Pennsylvania	5.4	6.0	.8	129.8	14.9
5. Virginia	5.2	2.1	3.6	125.6	66.3
6. Ohio	3.7	5.3	1.1	88.7	19.8
7. Maryland	3.6	1.7	2.6	85.3	47.5
8. Massachusetts	3.6	3.1	1.5	85.2	28.2
9. New Jersey	3.4	3.5	2.7	80.3	48.8
10. Connecticut	3.3	1.6	.2	78.9	4.2
11. Florida	3.0	2.9	3.8	73.3	69.2
12. Missouri	2.9	2.5	2.1	69.8	38.9
13. Georgia	2.9	2.1	6.0	69.2	109.4
14. Illinois	2.5	6.0	3.3	60.3	60.3
15. Washington	2.2	1.5	2.6	51.5	47.6
16. Alabama	2.0	1.6	1.7	48.1	32.1
17. Indiana	1.8	2.6	.5	43.6	9.8
18. Oklahoma	1.6	1.2	2.1	38.6	37.9
19. Michigan	1.5	4.1	1.0	36.0	18.3
20. Utah	1.5	.5	.2	35.7	4.5
21. District of Columbia	1.4	.5	3.9	32.8	70.5
22. Tennessee	1.3	2.0	1.2	29.9	21.9
23. North Carolina	1.2	2.5	5.1	29.1	92.7
24. Colorado	1.1	1.0	2.2	25.6	40.5
25. Kansas	1.1	1.1	1.9	25.6	34.8
26. Mississippi	1.0	1.0	1.5	23.9	28.0
27. South Carolina	1.0	1.3	3.3	23.2	60.2
28. Hawaii	1.0	.3	1.6	22.8	28.7
29. Minnesota	.9	2.0	.3	21.5	5.1

State ranking[1]	Percentage distribution			Number (in thousands)	
	Defense-generated employ-ment[2]	Labor force	Military person-nel	Defense-generated employ-ment	Military person-nel
(1)	(2)	(3)	(4)	(5)	(6)
30. Arizona	.8	.7	1.1	19.3	20.7
31. Kentucky	.7	1.4	2.8	16.7	51.9
32. New Mexico	.6	.5	1.0	15.1	18.7
33. Louisiana	.6	1.6	2.2	14.6	40.1
34. Wisconsin	.6	2.3	.2	14.6	3.4
35. Rhode Island	.6	.5	.5	13.8	9.5
36. New Hampshire	.6	.3	.3	13.5	5.2
37. Iowa	.4	1.5	.1	9.9	1.6
38. Alaska	.4	.1	1.6	8.8	29.2
39. Arkansas	.3	.9	.5	8.1	9.2
40. Maine	.3	.5	.5	7.2	10.8
41. Oregon	.3	1.1	.2	6.6	3.6
42. Nebraska	.3	.8	.7	6.5	12.4
43. West Virginia	.3	.8	.0	6.4	.5
44. North Dakota	.2	.3	.7	4.2	12.2
45. Nevada	.1	.2	.3	3.3	6.3
46. Delaware	.1	.3	.4	3.0	7.1
47. Vermont	.1	.2	.0	2.6	.3
48. South Dakota	.1	.3	.3	1.9	6.2
49. Montana	.1	.4	.5	1.7	9.4
50. Wyoming	.0	.2	.2	1.3	4.0
51. Idaho	.0	.3	.2	.9	4.0
Undistributed	3.9		2.2	90.4	39.4
Total	100.0	100.0	100.0	2,387.3	1,832.5

[1] Arranged in descending order based on State's percent of defense-generated employment.
[2] Includes defense generated employment in prime plants and civil service employment at DOD installations.

TABLE 7   DEFENSE DEPENDENCY BY STATE, JUNE 1966

State ranking[1]	Work force (in thousands)	Defense-generated employment (in thousands)	Percent defense dependency 3 ÷ 2
(1)	(2)	(3)	(4)
1. Alaska	90.4	8.8	9.7
2. Utah	390.5	35.7	9.1
3. Hawaii	273.3	22.8	8.3
4. District of Columbia	396.0	32.8	8.3
5. Virginia	1,638.6	125.6	7.7
6. Maryland	1,307.3	85.3	6.5
7. Connecticut	1,236.8	78.9	6.4
8. California	7,459.0	405.0	5.4
ʼ9. New Hampshire	274.0	13.5	4.9
10. Washington	1,217.7	51.5	4.2
11. New Mexico	357.4	15.1	4.2
12. Georgia	1,684.9	69.2	4.1
13. Oklahoma	961.2	38.6	4.0
14. Alabama	1,273.1	48.1	3.8
15. Rhode Island	372.3	13.8	3.7
16. Missouri	1,965.9	6.98	3.6
17. Texas	4,024.6	139.6	3.5
18. Massachusetts	2,432.1	85.2	3.5
19. Arizona	544.4	19.3	3.5
20. Colorado	778.8	25.6	3.3
21. Florida	2,264.3	73.3	3.2
22. Kansas	834.6	25.6	3.1
23. Mississippi	786.3	23.9	3.0
24. New Jersey	2,753.7	80.3	2.9
25. Pennsylvania	4,747.3	129.8	2.7
26. South Carolina	998.8	23.2	2.3
27. Indiana	2,019.5	43.6	2.2
28. Ohio	4,153.3	88.7	2.1
29. Tennessee	1,584.5	29.9	1.9

TABLE 7   DEFENSE DEPENDENCY BY STATE, JUNE 1966   *(cont'd)*

State ranking[1]	Work force (in thousands)	Defense-generated employment (in thousands)	Percent defense dependency 3 ÷ 2
(1)	(2)	(3)	(4)
30. Maine	375.4	7.2	1.9
31. New York	7,965.0	138.0	1.7
32. Nevada	189.9	3.3	1.7
33. North Dakota	267.7	4.2	1.6
34. Vermont	166.5	2.6	1,6
35. Kentucky	1,126.2	16.7	1.5
36. North Carolina	1,994.0	29.1	1.5
37. Minnesota	1,591.3	21.5	1.4
38. Illinois	4,730.0	60.3	1.3
39. Delaware	226.7	3.0	1.3
40. Arkansas	685.4	8.1	1.2
41. Michigan	3,187.9	36.0	1.1
42. Louisiana	1,302.5	14.6	1.1
43. Nebraska	650.0	6.5	1.0
44. West Virginia	620.9	6.4	1.0
45. Wyoming	144.6	1.3	.9
46. Oregon	826.4	6.6	.8
47. Iowa	1,194.9	9.9	.8
48. Wisconsin	1,787.5	14.6	.8
49. South Dakota	262.9	1.9	.7
50. Montana	263.7	1.7	.6
51. Idaho	277.7	.9	.3
Undistributed		90.4	
Total United States	78,658.0	2,387.3	
U.S. average			3.0

[1] Arranged in descending order based on percent of defense dependency.

TABLE 8   DEFENSE-ORIENTED INDUSTRIES—EMPLOYEES, VALUE ADDED,
AND SHIPMENTS AND RECEIPTS, BY INDUSTRY, 1965
[Employees in thousands, value in millions of dollars. Covers approximately
6,275 establishments accounting for over 88 percent of all shipments and receipts
in defense-oriented industries. Totals include industries
not shown separately. "N.e.c." means not elsewhere classified.]

Industry code[1]	Industry	Employees	Value added by manufacture	Value of shipments and receipts		
				Total	Government[2]	Nongovernment
(X)	Total	3,859	54,577	105,987	28,785	77,202
19	Ordnance, except complete guided missiles	79	871	1,557	1,162	395
28	Chemicals and allied products	77	1,804	3,254	762	2,492
2819	Inorganic chemicals, n.e.c.	61	1,557	2,847	639	2,208
2911	Petroleum refining	103	3,374	16,861	636	16,224
3069	Rubber, products, n.e.c.	116	1,333	2,406	163	2,243
33	Primary metal industries	303	4,108	10,819	814	10,005
3323	Steel foundries	62	699	1,051	60	992
3351	Copper rolling and drawing	38	572	2,014	49	1,964
3352	Aluminum rolling and drawing	54	662	2,441	176	2,265
3357	Nonferrous wire drawing, etc.	54	931	2,649	130	2,519
34	Fabricated metal products	261	3,239	6,013	395	5,618
3441	Fabricated structural steel	58	636	1,408	72	1,337
3443	Boiler shop products	54	603	1,261	105	1,156
3452	Bolts, nuts, rivets, and washers	50	689	1,170	74	1,096
3494	Valves and pipe fittings	76	1,033	1,669	94	1,575
35	Machinery, except electrical	636	9,646	16,449	1,347	15,101
3519	Internal combustion engines	58	904	1,743	143	1,600
3531	Construction machinery	111	1,672	3,332	140	3,193
3541	Metalcutting machine tools	56	818	1,257	54	1,203

TABLE 8 DEFENSE-ORIENTED INDUSTRIES—EMPLOYEES, VALUE ADDED,
AND SHIPMENTS AND RECEIPTS, BY INDUSTRY, 1965
[Employees in thousands, value in millions of dollars. Covers approximately
6,275 establishments accounting for over 88 percent of all shipments and receipts
in defense-oriented industries. Totals include industries
not shown separately. "N.e.c." means not elsewhere classified.] *(cont'd)*

Industry code[1]	Industry	Em- ployees	Value added by manu- facture	Value of shipments and receipts		
				Total	Gov- ern- ment[2]	Non- govern- ment
3561	Pumps and compressors	65	940	1,636	102	1,535
3562	Ball and roller bearings	55	764	1,230	83	1,147
3571	Computing and related machines	111	2,041	3,175	397	2,778
36	Electrical machinery	1,092	13,571	21,732	6,874	14,859
3613	Switchgear and switchboards	51	710	1,133	48	1,085
3621	Motors and generators	97	1,135	1,942	227	1,715
3661	Telephone, telegraph apparatus	101	1,349	2,239	116	2,123
3662	Radio, TV, communications equipment	328	4,101	6,439	4,954	1,484
3679	Electronic components, n.e.c.	169	1,692	2,699	529	2,170
3694	Engine electrical equipment	39	596	1,027	52	975
37	Transportation equipment	923	11,917	20,197	15,085	5,112
3721	Aircraft	291	3,834	7,092	5,229	1,863
1925	Complete guided missiles	139	2,129	3,128	3,044	84
3722	Aircraft engines and parts	177	2,440	4,076	3,150	926
3723,3729	Aircraft propellers and parts, and equipment, n.e.c.	156	1,985	3,001	2,286	715
3731	Shipbuilding and repairing	123	1,137	1,960	1,285	675
38	Instruments and related products	234	3,897	5,822	784	5,038
3821	Mechanical measuring devices	58	859	1,273	123	1,150
3861	Photographic equipment	65	1,675	2,375	310	2,065

X Not applicable. [1]Standard Industrial Classification code. [2]Comprises products shipped to, or receipts for work done for, Federal agencies, their contractors, subcontractors, and suppliers.

TABLE 9   EXPENDITURES FOR RESEARCH AND DEVELOPMENT, 1955–1967
[In millions of dollars]

	1955	1959	1961	1963	1965[3]	1967[4]
1. U.S. total[1]	$6,270	$12,520	$14,500	$17,350	$20,470[1]	$23,800
Federal Government[2]	3,490	8,035	9,215	11,190	13,070	14,930
DOD	2,630	4,183	6,618	6,849	6,628	7,112
NASA	74	145	744	2,540	4,555	5,310
AEC	385	877	1,111	1,335	1,241	1,272
Others	219	597	807	1,264	1,367	1,921
2. Federal Government as percent of U.S. total	55.5%	64.0%	63.4%	64.3%	63.9%	60.1%
3. Defense-related agencies as percent of Federal Government	85.6%	65.0%	92.4%	95.6%	90.0%	91.9%

[1] Includes all research and development performed in the United States from whatever source.
[2] The sum of DOD, NASA, AEC, and Others.
[3] Preliminary.
[4] Estimated.

TABLE 10   CONCENTRATION OF RESEARCH AND DEVOLOPMENT OBLIGATIONS FOR
EDUCATIONAL INSTITUTIONS, BY STATES, FISCAL 1964

Rank	DOD	NASA	AEC
1. Massachusetts	28.8%	7.0%	3.0%
2. Maryland	13.3	.9	.4
3. New York	11.6	3.3	3.3
4. California	8.1	69.1	39.0
5. Illinois	4.4	2.4	2.4
6. Pennsylvania	3.9	1.8	.6
7. Michigan	3.8	1.6	1.6
8. Ohio	2.7	.6	.5
9. District of Columbia	1.9	.5	.1
10. Colorado	1.8	.4	.3
11. Indiana	1.6	.4	.6
12. Texas	1.4	1.2	.5
13. New Mexico	1.3	1.1	20.4

TABLE 11 OBLIGATIONS BY THE DEPARTMENT OF DEFENSE FOR RESEARCH
AND DEVELOPMENT AT 50 UNIVERSITIES AND COLLEGES
RECEIVING THE LARGEST AMOUNTS, 1964
[In thousands of dollars]

Institution Name	State	Rank	DOD	Army	Navy	Air Force	Defense Agency
Mass. Inst. of Technology	Mass.	1	46,819	3,965	18,807	21,928	2,119
University of Michigan	Mich.	2	14,736	5,413	1,284	4,966	3,073
Stanford University	Cal.	3	12,815	1,824	5,214	4,573	1,204
Columbia University	N.Y.	4	9,194	1,489	4,459	3,184	36
University of Illinois	Ill.	5	7,612	2,524	1,704	1,343	2,041
U. of Cal. Los Angeles	Cal.	6	6,871	397	5,221	1,106	147
U. of Cal. Berkeley	Cal.	7	5,424	439	3,140	1,592	253
Univ. of Pennsylvania	Pa.	8	5,304	1,473	673	961	2,197
University of Texas	Tex.	9	5,281	571	3,502	1,208	0
Ohio State University	Ohio	10	5,256	466	253	4,185	0
University of Chicago	Ill.	11	4,615	774	1,702	1,374	765
Harvard University	Mass.	12	4,539	705	1,425	1,010	1,399
Carnegie Inst. Technology	Pa.	13	4,519	130	334	340	3,668
Cornell University	N.Y.	14	4,358	510	680	452	2,570
California Inst. of Tech.	Cal.	15	4,232	348	1,673	2,211	0
New York University	N.Y.	16	4,019	1,750	1,239	1,030	0
Illinois Inst. of Tech.	Ill.	17	3,852	2,069	352	1,431	0
University of Denver	Colo.	18	3,773	488	81	3,204	0
Johns Hopkins University	Md.	19	3,732	1,098	757	1,867	0
Princeton University	N.J.	20	3,709	561	1,863	1,285	0
Northwestern University	Ill.	21	3,461	332	843	722	1,564
Polytechnic Inst. Brooklyn	N.Y.	22	3,254	113	1,411	1,730	0
University of Maryland	Md.	23	3,089	1,001	210	1,324	514
Duke University	N.C.	24	2,946	2,341	169	436	0
Brown University	R.I.	25	2,746	325	647	389	1,385

TABLE 11   OBLIGATIONS BY THE DEPARTMENT OF DEFENSE FOR RESEARCH
AND DEVELOPMENT AT 50 UNIVERSITIES AND COLLEGES
RECEIVING THE LARGEST AMOUNTS, 1964
[In thousands of dollars] *(cont'd)*

Institution Name	State	Rank	DOD	Army	Navy	Air Force	Defense Agency
University of Colorado	Colo.	26	2,709	2,163	152	394	0
University of Dayton	Ohio	27	2,643	0	0	2,643	0
U. of Cal. San Diego	Cal.	28	2,455	0	29	2,426	0
University of Miami	Fla.	29	2,174	467	1,605	102	0
New Mexico State Univ.	N.M.	30	2,157	1,546	343	268	0
University of Pittsburgh	Pa.	31	2,080	886	340	680	100
Syracuse University	N.Y.	32	2,046	337	382	1,327	0
University of Washington	Wash.	33	1,986	199	1,381	406	0
Purdue University	Ind.	34	1,981	477	10	694	800
Yale University	Conn.	35	1,813	274	530	1,009	0
Northeastern University	Mass.	36	1,685	98	12	1,575	0
Univ. of Southern California	Cal.	37	1,617	121	462	1,034	0
George Washington Univ.	D.C.	38	1,526	395	926	205	0
Univ. of N.C. at Chapel Hill	N.C.	39	1,441	211	74	605	551
Pennsylvania State Univ.	Pa.	40	1,214	381	89	744	0
Texas A. & M. University	Tex.	41	1,204	233	808	163	0
University of New Mexico	N.M.	42	1,199	0	150	1,049	0
University of Oklahoma	Okla.	43	1,193	533	36	624	0
U. of Wis. Madison	Wisc.	44	1,102	358	278	466	0
University of Iowa	Iowa	45	1,077	0	947	55	75
U. of Minn. Mnpls.-St. Paul	Minn.	46	1,076	0	764	312	0
Indiana University	Ind.	47	1,075	153	342	580	0
University of Virginia	Va.	48	1,030	295	643	92	0
Tufts University	Mass.	49	1,021	303	88	630	0
University of Utah	Utah	50	1,021	333	69	618	0

TABLE 12   PRIME MILITARY CONTRACT AWARDS 1960-1967
TO TOP 25 U.S. COMPANIES FOR FIRMS TOTALING MORE THAN $1 BILLION
IN THIS 7-YEAR PERIOD
[In millions of dollars]

Fiscal year	1961	1962	1963	1964	1965	1966	1967	7-year total	Percent of total sales
1. Lockheed Aircraft	1,175	1,419	1,517	1,455	1,715	1,531	1,807	10,619	88%
2. General Dynamics	1,460	1,197	1,033	987	1,179	1,136	1,832	8,824	67
3. McDonnell Douglas	527	779	863	1,360	1,026	1,001	2,125	7,681	75
4. Boeing Co.	920	1,133	1,356	1,365	583	914	912	7,183	54
5. General Electric	875	976	1,021	893	824	1,187	1,290	7,066	19
6. No. American-Rockwell	1,197	1,032	1,062	1,019	746	520	689	6,265	57
7. United Aircraft	625	663	530	625	632	1,139	1,097	5,311	57
8. American Tel. & Tel.	551	468	579	636	588	672	673	4,167	9
9. Martin-Marietta	692	803	767	476	316	338	290	3,682	62
10. Sperry-Rand	408	466	446	374	318	427	484	2,923	35
11. General Motors	282	449	444	256	254	508	625	2,818	2
12. Grumman Aircraft	238	304	390	396	353	323	488	2,492	67
13. General Tire	290	366	425	364	302	327	273	2,347	37
14. Raytheon	305	407	295	253	293	368	403	2,324	55
15. AVCO	251	323	253	279	234	506	449	2,295	75
16. Hughes	331	234	312	289	278	337	419	2,200	u
17. Westinghouse Electric	308	246	323	237	261	349	453	2,177	13
18. Ford (Philco)	200	269	228	211	312	440	404	2,064	3
19. RCA	392	340	329	234	214	242	268	2,019	16
20. Bendix	269	286	290	257	235	282	296	1,915	42
21. Textron	66	117	151	216	196	555	497	1,798	36
22. Ling-Temco-Vought	47	133	206	247	265	311	535	1,744	70
23. Internat. Tel. & Tel.	202	244	266	256	207	220	255	1,650	19
24. I.B.M.	330	155	203	332	186	182	195	1,583	7
25. Raymond International●	46	61	84	196	71	548	462	1,568	u

u – unavailable.
● Includes Morrison-Knudsen, Brown & Root, and J. A. Jones Construction Co.

TABLE 13   U.S. MILITARY PERSONNEL IN SOUTH VIETNAM
AND THE COST OF THEIR SUPPORT, 1954–1968

Date	Number[1]	Estimated cost[2] (millions of dollars)
1954–60 (average)	650	16
1960	773	19
1961	1,364	33
1962	9,865	246
1963	16,575	414
1964	23,300	583
1965	184,314	4,607
1966	385,300	6,094
1967	487,300[3]	20,557
1968	538,500[3]	24,989 est.

[1] As of December 31st.
[2] It cost an estimated $25,000 to keep one U.S. soldier in Vietnam for one year in 1966. This $25,000 figure has been used as the assumed cost of keeping one G.I. in Vietnam for one year during the years 1954-65. After 1965, cost data are actual expenditures. See testimony of Robert N. Anthony, Assistant Secretary of Defense, in *Economic Effect of Vietnam Spending*, I, pp. 2-30.
[3] Approximately 76,500 men in addition to those listed above were serving off-shore or in Thailand during 1967 and 1968.

Region and Country	Gross national product (GNP)[1]	Defense Expenditures[2]	Percent of GNP	Public education expenditures[3]	Public health expenditures[3]
		(millions of U.S. dollar equivalents[4])			
North America					
United States	*$628,700	*$51,323	8.2	$30,400[5]	$10,000[5]
Canada	43,480	1,678	3.9	2,600	1,300[5]
Europe					
France	* 86,000	* 4,918	5.7	2,950	1,000
Germany, West[6]	* 99,270	* 4,888	4.9	3,500	3,800
Italy	* 49,500	* 1,789	3.6	1,700	800
Norway	* 6,200	* 220	3.5	325	100
United Kingdom	* 91,370	* 5,562	6.1	3,700	3,100
Warsaw Pact countries					
Czechoslovakia	([7])	5,000	4.8	([7])	([7])
Germany, East	104,000[8]	6,000[9]	5.8	2,700	2,200
Hungary	104,000[8]	6,000[9]	5.8	2,700	2,200
Poland	104,000[8]	6,000[9]	5.8	2,700	2,200
Soviet Union[10]	300,000	30,000–	10.0	20,000	8,000
Other European countries					
Austria	* 8,460	* 135	1.6	425	150
Spain	* 17,700	* 516	2.9	1,000	200
Sweden	* 17,200	* 826	4.8	800	400
Yugoslavia	* 7,755	* 403	5.2	400	100
Latin America					
Argentina	* 11,200	* 251	2.2	225	50
Brazil	* 14,660	* 570	3.9	400	120
Cuba	2,700	200[11]	7.4	90[11]	50[11]
Dominican Republic	850	35	4.1	30	20
Guatemala	* 1,246	* 11	0.9	20	10
Mexico	* 17,450	* 130	0.7	350	75
Peru	* 3,180	* 111	3.5	130	50

Region and Country	Gross national product (GNP)[1]	Defense Expenditures[2]	Percent of GNP	Public education expenditures[3]	Public health expenditures[3]
		(millions of U.S. dollar equivalents[4])			
Far East					
China, Mainland[11]	70,000	4,000	5.7	2,800	500
China, Republic of	* 2,290	* 218	9.5	60	20
Japan	* 68,000	* 836	1.2	3,000	700
Korea, North	2,500[11]	200[11]	8.0	50[11]	15[11]
Korea, Republic of	* 2,745	* 123	4.5	90	30
Thailand	* 3,330	* 86	2.6	90	25
Vietnam, North	1,800[11]	300[11]	16.5	60[11]	20[11]
Vietnam, Republic of	* 1,900	* 267	14.1	50	20
Near East					
Israel	* 3,111	* 372	12.0	200	50
Jordan	* 410	* 59	14.4	15	5
Saudi Arabia	1,240	* 113	9.1	75	15
United Arab Republic	4,050	300	7.4	215	75
South Asia					
India	* 43,000	* 1,800	4.3	1,000	250
Pakistan	* 9,450	* 287	3.0	200	50
Africa					
Algeria	2,200	70	3.2	190	40
Nigeria	* 4,120	* 48	1.2	100	30
South Africa, Republic of	* 10,400	* 375	3.6	225	75

[1] Data marked with an asterisk have been roughly adjusted to concepts outlined in the *UN Yearbook of National Accounts Statistics*. For additional information, see *Statistical Methods and Concepts*, page ii.

[2] Data marked with an asterisk have been adjusted generally to concepts and definitions used by the North Atlantic Treaty Organization (NATO). Data exclude expenditures on civilian space programs. For additional information, see *Statistical Methods and Concepts*, page iii.

[3] The quality and comprehensiveness of these statistics vary greatly from country to country. Data generally relate only to central government expenditures. In many countries, provincial and local governments have a major role in education and health.

[4] Generally, in current market prices converted at official exchange rates. For exceptions see *Statistical Methods and Concepts*, page i.

[5] Estimate relates to federal, state, and local expenditures.

[6] Excludes West Berlin. For 1964, West Berlin population estimated at 2,193,000; gross national product estimated at $3.8 billion in current market prices.

[7] Unavailable.

[8] Current market prices converted at rough purchasing power equivalents.

[9] Rough dollar estimates based on share of defense expenditures of gross national product at factor cost.

[10] Financial data relate to purchasing power equivalents. At current market prices, 1964 Soviet GNP estimated at 216 billion rubles, and expenditures on public education and health at about 15 billion and 8 billion rubles, respectively. See *Statistical Methods and Concepts* for additional information.

[11] Estimated data.

SOURCES

TABLE 1   U.S. Bureau of the Census, *Historical Statistics of the United States: Colonial Times to 1957; 1968 Statistical Abstract; 1969 World Almanac.*

TABLE 2   Gardner Ackley, Chairman, *Report of the Committee on the Economic Impact of Defense and Disarmament* (G.P.O., 1965), p. 9.

TABLE 3   Executive Office of the President, Bureau of the Budget, *The Budget of the United States Government.*

TABLE 4   Peck, Merton J., and Frederick H. Scherer, *The Weapons Acquisitions Process* (Harvard University Graduate Business School, 1962), p. 111; Department of Defense, *Prime Contract Awards by State, 1967–1968.*

TABLE 5   Department of Defense, Office of the Secretary, *Prime Contract Awards by State,* June, 1967.

TABLE 6   Department of Defense, Office of the Assistant Secretary, Systems Analysis (Economics).

TABLE 7   *Ibid.*

TABLE 8   Department of Commerce, Bureau of the Census, *Current Industrial Reports,* Series MA 175.

TABLE 9   *1968 Statistical Abstract,* pp. 525–26; Ackley, *op. cit.,* p. 87.

TABLE 10   "Obligations for Research and Development, and R&D Plant, by Geographic Divisions and States, by Selected Federal Agencies, Fiscal Years 1961–64," from the Subcommittee on Science, Research and Development of the House Committee on Science and Astronautics, 88th Cong., 2nd Sess., 1964, pp. 90–91.

TABLE 11   Department of Defense, Directorate for Statistical Services.

TABLE 12   *Ibid.*

TABLE 13   *Economic Effect of Vietnam Spending,* I, p. 195; *1968 Statistical Abstract,* p. 248.

TABLE 14   William Sprecher, "World-Wide Defense Expenditures and Selected Economic Data, 1964," Arms Control and Disarmament Agency, Research Report 66–1 (January, 1966).

PART I

The Cold War
and the National Economy

INTRODUCTION

⟨ NATIONAL defense has absorbed almost 10 percent of United States production (GNP) and nearly 10 percent of our work force since the Cold War began. This is the conventional way of measuring the economic impact of defense spending on a nation's economy. This measurement, however, tends to underestimate the force of the Cold War because it assumes that the major economic impact occurs during the years the war is actually in progress. In fact, the major dollar impact of most modern wars occurs *after* the war ceases, in the form of veterans' benefits, which will increase the price of wars in this century to more than three times their initial cost. This fact should be kept firmly in mind as the reader digests the materials in this section. The conventional measurement of war costs also tends to obscure their relation to other government services. For example, when direct defense expenditures for the years 1946–67 are totaled, they amount to 82 percent of total federal purchases of goods and services for that same period. In other words, during the Cold War the federal government has spent 82 percent of its available purchasing funds (except for benefit payments to individuals and grants to state and local governments, which are not purchases and therefore do not directly use up resources produced by the economy) on war-related government programs. Only 18 percent of all funds spent since 1946 have been used by the federal government to buy goods and services for nonwar programs. Moreover, once these government purchases were made, the economic resources purchased by these defense funds were mostly used up and therefore not available for domestic consumption.

Although very large nationally, the impact of defense spending has varied from state to state. Defense-generated employment in a number of industries has been substantially higher in some states—such as California, Texas, New York, Pennsylvania, and Virginia—than in others. In the missile and space system industry, for example, California has consistently won nearly one-half of the total United States defense contract awards in recent years, and Texas has garnered nearly one-third of all defense awards to the petroleum industry. Concentration is even greater in research and development efforts. Almost 40 percent of all research contracts have gone to California during the past ten years, and approximately one-third of all research being carried out at universities has been done in Massachusetts.

The importance of various states in meeting national defense needs has tended to shift over the last two decades, with some states falling and others rising in importance. Texas is a good example of the latter. In 1945, for example, Texas ranked eleventh in the nation with 3 percent of total defense contract awards. During the Korean War Texas rose to eighth place. With the coming of the missile age, Texas rapidly climbed to third place, and by 1967 the Lone Star State had garnered 9.5 percent of total awards and was surpassed only by California. Most of the growth in Texas' defense industry stems from her rapid buildup in the airframe, aircraft equipment, and ammunition industries. During the same period, on the other hand, Michigan fell from second place to twelfth place as defense requirements shifted from conventional ordinance products easily produced in established manufacturing firms in the older states to the newer missile and electronic firms, which tended to be located in the newer industrial states (such as California and Texas) or in newly rejuvenated ones (such as Massachusetts). Later, owing to the conventional nature of the Vietnam War, the Great Lakes region recovered some of this defense work. These national and regional trends are discussed in the first two selections below.

The economic and social consequences of defense spending is becoming a much debated subject. The central issue is whether the costs of protecting the nation's security are too high. Those who believe that our defense expenditures have not been too high include every administration from President Truman to President Nixon, the overwhelming majority of congressmen during that period, and public opinion in general. Basically, this formidable and diverse group considers our Cold War expenditures a necessary response to deliberate aggression by the Communists, particularly the Soviet Union. This group has sought to make America the strongest military power in the world, and it rejects the thesis that social programs geared to making America strong domestically are an acceptable alternative to military power abroad.

Arrayed against this powerful majority is a small but articulate coterie of professors, a handful of influential politicians, a few journalists, and a vocal—and at times violent—group of dissident students. This group sees the Cold War less as a struggle against the evils of Communist aggression than as a struggle between the conflicting interests of the East and West. And, they argue, even if there is some danger of Soviet aggression, the possibility of nuclear holocaust is now so real that physical security can no longer be purchased at any price. These people argue further that we have overreacted to Communism as an ideology and that this overreaction has been enormously and needlessly costly.

Seymour Melman (Selection 3) is a passionate spokesman for this minority view. Professor Melman is known primarily for his ideas on "overkill." Since there are only about 140 Soviet cities with populations of more than 100,000, and only 370 such cities in the entire "Sino-Soviet bloc," Melman believes that even if 90 percent of our missiles and 75 percent of our bombers were destroyed in a first-strike, the United States would still have many times more nuclear bombs than it would need to destroy these cities. Any capacity in excess of one successfully delivered bomb per city is "overkill." The excerpts below, taken from Professor Melman's book *Our Depleted Society*, describe the economic impact of "overkill" spending. Melman maintains that scientific talent has been "unjustifiably" drawn away from civilian industries into war industries, that our rate of economic growth had been slowed, that our domestic environmental problems have been neglected, and that our colleges and universities have become the instruments of foreign policy rather than institutions for basic research. In addition, Melman maintains that the Apollo program is little more than a "seven-day T.V. spectacular" and that the space race is a "pseudo-challenge."

Joseph Felton and Elisabeth Kernan

(Selection 4), staff members of the Subcommittee on NASA Oversight of the House Committee on Science and Astronautics, disagree with Melman. They maintain that spending for the exploration of space has created the technological know-how to solve the very domestic problems Professor Melman is so concerned about.

Murray Weidenbaum, a foremost authority on the economics of defense spending, is especially interested in the practical alternative uses for resources currently being used in our defense program. He suggests in the final selection that it will be very difficult to convert defense efforts to productive civilian uses, and, in particular, he is dubious about the practicality of awarding government research funds to defense contractors to solve pressing civilian problems.

This chapter raises a number of important questions: Which sections of the country have benefited the most and which the least from defense spending? Has the pattern of defense spending been politically oriented? What price have we paid for being the strongest nation in the world? Could the economy be "managed" without the massive spending required by a Cold War? Could our defense economy really be converted to civilian uses? If so, who would be hardest hit? If not, have we any options other than creating a serious economic depression on the one hand and remaining a "warfare-welfare" state on the other?

THE READINGS

1] The National Impact of Defense Spending

FEDERAL expenditures on goods and services in the combined defense, space, and atomic energy programs have accounted for about 9–10 percent of gross national product (GNP) and 85–90 percent of total Federal purchases of goods and services in the past decade. Expenditures of this magnitude obviously have major impacts on incomes and employment in the country as a whole, and in a variety of regions and industries.

The estimated 6.6 million persons engaged in defense-related work [1] accounted for nearly one-tenth of total employment in the United States in 1963. Of these 6.6 million workers, over half were employed directly by the Federal Government—in the armed forces and in civilian positions with Federal defense agencies. The rest worked either for contractors and subcontractors employed on defense programs in the private sector of the economy, or for firms providing materials and services to defense contractors.

INDUSTRIAL DISTRIBUTION OF DEFENSE WORK

Although defense work is performed by companies in almost every industry, some industries and firms are much more heavily committed than others. New insight on the varying extent of these commitments was provided by a special inquiry made as part of the 1963 Census of Manufactures (Table 1). This inquiry also indicates how subcontracting disburses Government business to some industries where prime contracting is not so important. For example, data on shipments on Government account (during 1963) by six industries with heavy involvement in defense work show that nearly all Government shipments from the shipbuilding and ordnance industries were in response to prime contracts, but that nearly three-fourths of electronic component shipments were on subcontracts.

Defense work is the major business of only a relatively small percentage of U.S. business firms. But some very large firms, and many small ones, have defense agencies as their major customers. A recent analysis of the 34 firms

---

[1] For purposes of convenience, this report frequently uses such terms as "defense" and "defense-related" to include space and atomic energy work, even though much of this work is nonmilitary in purpose. The main reason for including space work in the defense category is that it tends to be carried on by the same industries and firms as military work. This is much less true of atomic energy work. Certain major programs—principally in space and, to a lesser extent, in atomic energy—are by nature not directly sensitive to shifts deriving from defense-related considerations and may actually be areas of opportunity for increased investment in the event that new resources are available.

FROM *Report of the President's Committee on the Impact of Defense and Disarmament* (Washington, D.C., GPO, 1965), chap. 1.

TABLE 1   SHIPMENTS BY SIX DEFENSE-ORIENTED INDUSTRIES, 1963

Industry	Shipments (billions of dollars)[1]			Total Government shipments as percent of total shipments[2]	Subcontract shipments as percent of total Government shipments[2]
	Total	Government			
		Total	Sub-contract		
Total[3]	$37.2	$25.3	$ 5.2	68	21
Aircraft and missile products	15.8	13.9	2.0	88	14
Communication equipment	7.1	4.9	1.3	69	27
Shipbuilding and ordnance (except missiles)	3.0	2.3	.2	77	8
Instruments	2.9	1.5	.6	52	37
Electronic components	2.6	1.0	.8	40	73
Machinery	4.8	.7	.3	16	34

[1] By establishments reporting shipments of more than $100,000.
[2] Based on shipments in millions of dollars.
[3] Includes miscellaneous industries not shown separately.
SOURCE: Department of Commerce, Bureau of the Census.

with the largest defense contracts shows that defense-related work represented 75 percent or more of the total company sales for 9 of these firms; for 9 other firms it represented 25 percent or less of sales.

GEOGRAPHICAL DISTRIBUTION OF DEFENSE WORK

Defense spending in the United States has an uneven geographic distribution. Among the areas proportionately most affected are the Far Western States of Alaska, California, Hawaii, and Washington; the Middle Atlantic States of Maryland and Virginia—and also the District of Columbia; certain New England States, notably Connecticut and Massachusetts; some of the less populous Mountain States, such as Arizona, New Mexico, and Utah, where the Government's defense operations loom large; and some of the Southern and Border States where there are numerous military installations, such as Alabama, Georgia, Kansas, and Oklahoma.

Although full information is not available, good indicators of the areas of greatest concentration are employment and payrolls in the 5 leading defense-related manufacturing industries (ordnance, aircraft, shipbuilding, communication equipment, and electronic components) and in Federal defense agencies. These categories accounted for about 6 percent of total wage and salary payments in the United States during 1963. The military establishments and civilian Government employment connected with defense are also geographically concentrated to a considerable degree, not infrequently in the same general region.

Wages and salaries paid by the major defense-related industries and by the Federal defense agencies in 1963 were of relatively greatest importance in Alaska and Hawaii, where 25 and 20 percent, respectively, of personal income was from these sources. Next in order were Virginia, with 15 percent; California, Maryland, Utah, and Washington, each with 11–13 percent; and Alabama, Connecticut, the District of Columbia, Georgia, and New Mexico, each with 9–10 percent. In the remaining 39 States, such wage and salary payments accounted for less than 9 percent of personal income. In some of the States with the highest percentages—for example, Alaska, Hawaii, and Virginia—most of the defense employment is in Federal defense agencies, rather than in private manufacturing industries that have defense contracts.

Some 66 percent of total payrolls in defense-related activities were disbursed in only 12 States. They were largest in California, where in 1963 they approached $6 billion; in New York and Texas, where they amounted to $1.7 billion each; and in Virginia, where they were $1.4 billion. Payments were also very substantial in some of the other large industrial States, such as New Jersey and Pennsylvania; but the great diversification of industry in those States makes the impact of defense expenditures relatively less.

Certain specific communities have a notably high concentration of defense-connected industrial activities, or are heavily dependent on direct Government payrolls. Examples are the Los Angeles and San Diego areas in California; the Seattle area in Washington; the metropolitan area of the District of Columbia; the Boston area in Massachusetts; Wichita, Kansas; Huntsville, Alabama; and Cape Kennedy, Florida. In a number of smaller localities, military installations generate a large part of the employment and income.

OCCUPATIONAL COMPOSITION OF DEFENSE EMPLOYMENT

The occupations and skills needed to produce goods and services for defense have been greatly affected by changes in the composition of defense procurement in manufacturing processes. A large and increasing proportion of defense workers consists of engineers, scientists, technicians, highly skilled craftsmen, and professional workers. In the 5 major defense-related industries, "nonproduction workers" in 1964 comprised 43 percent of all workers, compared with 26 percent in all manufacturing. As recently as 1958, the proportion of nonproduction workers in the 5 defense industries had been 36 percent.

IMPACT OF DEFENSE ON RESEARCH AND DEVELOPMENT

Over half of all research and development work (R&D) in the Nation is financed by the Department of Defense, the National Aeronautics and Space Administration, and the Atomic Energy Commission. In addition to the work done in Government laboratories, the defense agencies pay for more than half of the research undertaken in industrial laboratories and about three-fifths of the work preformed by universities and other nonprofit institutions. It is recognized, of course, that some of this research has relevance extending beyond narrow defense objectives.

In the industries producing aircraft and missiles, and electrical and communications equipment, which account for more than three-fourths of Government research funds spent in industry, expenditures on R&D exceed 10 percent of sales. (For the rest of manufacturing, R&D outlays do not exceed 3 percent of sales.) Moreover, these industries employ one-fourth of all engineers and scientists in U.S. industry, and well over two-fifths of those primarily engaged in R&D work.

IMPACT OF DEFENSE ON CIVILIAN EXPENDITURES

The real cost to our society of allocating productive resources to defense programs is that these resources are unavailable for nondefense purposes. Thus, the expenditure of $50 billion on defense programs means that the Nation must forego $50 billion of nondefense goods and services. The transfer of productive resources to defense purposes takes place partly by reducing Government spending on nondefense programs and partly by reducing civilian spending on consumer and capital goods through tax rates that are higher than they would otherwise be.

There are, to be sure, tangible and occasionally significant incidental benefits which flow from the defense program to the civilian sector (peaceful uses of military technology, training of personnel, and the "spin-off" of new science-based enterprises). However, there can be little doubt that the Nation could have obtained these same benefits at substantially lower costs and with more certainty if comparable research and training resources had been devoted directly to civilian purposes.

If a reduction of international tensions or an improvement in the efficiency with which defense dollars are used should permit a curtailment of the amount spent for defense, we would, as a society, be better off. The resources released from defense production could then be used to produce goods and services for private or public consumption and investment. Of course, in order to realize these potential benefits, the resources set free would, in fact, have to be effectively transferred to civilian production, rather than wasted in the form of unemployment and underutilization of plant capacity or kept busy only in make-work projects. If the transition were poorly managed, we could not only lose the use of the resources released from defense but also, through the reduction of incomes and purchasing power, lose the services of other resources now used in producing purely civilian goods and services. But there is no need for this to happen. With appropriate public and private policies, a reduction of the defense budget can and should be a source of increased material welfare for all of our citizens.

PAST SHIFTS IN DEFENSE SPENDING

Experience testifies to the ability of the American economy to adjust successfully to major reductions in defense expenditures. However, we can recall that many observers during World War II doubted the ability of the economy to adjust to demobilization without experiencing serious problems of transition, and many feared a return to the depressed conditions of the 1930's. At the time, defense outlays accounted for more than 35 percent of total production (measured in terms of 1945 GNP).

Yet demobilization was extremely rapid, and no sizable unemployment problem developed. Between June 1945 and June 1946, over 9 million men were released from the Armed Forces, more than 3 times the present total of military personnel. Between 1945 and 1946, national defense purchases of goods and services were reduced by 75 percent. This reduction was equivalent to more than 25 percent of the GNP in 1945, nearly 3 times the present percentage of GNP that is represented by defense expenditures. Between 1946 and 1947, defense purchases were reduced by a further 39 percent (Table 2).

Nevertheless, despite the size and pace of the post-World War II demobilization, the average unemployment rate in the immediate postwar years remained below 4 percent of the labor force. While defense spending fell, business investment more than doubled and consumer outlays and nondefense Government programs increased, to fill much of the gap. Hours of work were considerably shortened, and many workers withdrew from the labor force. Vast reservoirs of unfilled needs and purchasing power which had been accumulated during the war created strong markets for all that could be produced. Postwar economic adjustments were also substantially helped by effective governmental policies regarding such matters as contract terminations, property disposal, and veterans' affairs.

The end of the Korean conflict involved a much smaller reduction in defense spending, which in turn started from a much lower peak than at the end of World War II. Tax reductions helped to maintain aggregate consumer income and personal consumption spending. Moreover, there still remained substantial backlogs of consumer and business demand for durable goods and construction. The net result was that the decline in GNP was smaller than the decline in defense spending. By 1955, economic activity had fully recovered, despite further cutbacks in defense spending. Unemployment, after rising to 5.6 percent of the labor force in 1954, declined to 4.4 percent in 1955.

Since the end of the Korean conflict, important changes have occurred in the defense budget. In addition to a sharp reduction followed by a steady rise in the over-all size of the budget, there have been drastic shifts in the pattern of defense procurement. These shifts have produced problems for individual industries not unlike those which would have been faced if there had been a major arms reduction.

For example, the value of production of tanks, conventional ordnance, and commercial types of military hard goods dropped from $11 billion in fiscal year 1953 to about $2 billion in fiscal year 1957, a cut of 85–90 percent in 4 years. The result was a massive loss of defense business for the Middle West where such production had been concentrated; but since the resources set free were not highly specialized, they were reabsorbed in an economy with growing total demand. Subsequently, an increasing proportion of military

TABLE 2   DEFENSE PURCHASES OF GOODS AND SERVICES OF THE
FEDERAL GOVERNMENT AND RELATION TO GNP, 1945–68

Calendar year	National defense purchases of goods and services	
	Amount (billions of dollars)	Percent of GNP
1945	$ 75.9	35.5%
1946	18.8	8.9
1947	11.4	4.9
1948	11.6	4.5
1949	13.6	5.3
1950	14.3	5.0
1951	33.9	10.3
1952	46.4	13.4
1953	49.3	13.5
1954	41.2	11.3
1955	39.1	9.8
1956	40.4	9.6
1957	44.4	10.0
1958	44.8	10.1
1959	46.2	9.6
1960	45.7	9.1
1961	49.0	9.4
1962	53.6	9.6
1963	55.2	9.5
1964	55.4	8.9
1965	55.6	8.4
1966	60.6	8.1
1967	72.4	9.2
1968	79.0	9.3

SOURCES: Treasury Department, Bureau of the
Budget, Commerce Department, Council of Economic Advisers, and *Defense Indicators.*

purchases from private industry was for electronics, propulsion, and other
technologically advanced components of weapon systems rather than for
metal and other fabricated structures. The very fact that many people, to
this day, remain wholly unaware of this significant reorientation of defense
procurement reflects how smoothly the reconversion was carried through.

The experience in the periods following World War II and the Korean
conflict seems to indicate that the U.S. economy—with the proper use of tax,
expenditure, and monetary policy—can in the aggregate successfully cope
with major reductions in defense spending.

However, we must recognize that some of the "conversion" problems that we are likely to face in the immediate future—whether arising from over-all reductions or simply from shifts in composition—may be more difficult to solve than were "conversion" problems in the past. The character of many of the goods procured by the military has become increasingly different from that of nonmilitary goods. Further, there appears to have been some tendency for defense production to become more concentrated geographically and to develop and use more highly specialized resources—human, capital, and natural.

In earlier defense cutbacks, the problem was largely one of reconversion—a return to production of previously produced goods. Many leading defense suppliers knew that the diversion of their facilities and personnel to defense purposes would be a short-run affair. Even so, not all defense-goods manufacturers succeeded in converting to nondefense production after World War II and the Korean conflict. Today, many firms in the defense industries have never produced for nonmilitary markets to any significant degree.

On the other hand, the differences should not be exaggerated. Although there is a considerable localization of prime contracts in a few areas, extensive subcontracting tends to spread defense work geographically to a greater extent than would be judged from prime contracts alone. A large proportion of defense procurement is of items closely similar to civilian consumption items. The view that skills are highly specialized is probably an exaggeration. Although today's defense plants use large numbers of highly skilled workers, they often take on the character of gigantic job shops, in which workers must be able to move from one kind of operation to another. Many light assembly operations in defense production differ from those of nondefense industry principally in the high standards of workmanship demanded—and their workers are consequently quite adaptable to most civilian production of a generally similar character. The technical requirements demanded of engineers and scientists in defense work do, of course, often emphasize requirements different from those of civilian work; but the normal course of the work puts decided emphasis on the ability to adjust to frequent and rapid shifts in requirements.

RECENT CHANGES IN DEFENSE EMPLOYMENT AND PROSPECTS

Recent preliminary reports on fiscal year 1965 expenditures show spending of $46.2 billion for military functions of the Department of Defense, together with $1.2 billion for military assistance abroad, $2.6 billion for atomic energy, and $5.1 billion for space research and technology. These figures along with those for some smaller defense-related programs total $55.2 billion.

Table 3 shows that this total represents a significant decline from the total for fiscal year 1964. Within this total, there has been some expansion in space programs and in peaceful uses of atomic energy which has partly offset the decline in defense expenditure more narrowly defined.

Through economies in the defense budget, and because the large buildups

TABLE 3   FEDERAL ADMINISTRATIVE BUDGET EXPENDITURES FOR NATIONAL DEFENSE,
UNDER VARIOUS DEFINITIONS, FISCAL YEARS 1964–65
[In millions of dollars]

Function	1964	1965[1]	Change, 1964 to 1965
Department of Defense, military	49,760	46,178	−3,582
Military assistance	1,485	1,204	
Subtotal	51,245	47,382	−3,863
Minor defense-related activities	172	137	
Subtotal	51,417	47,519	−3,898
Defense-related atomic energy	1,855	1,367	
Subtotal	53,272	48,886	−4,386
Nondefense atomic energy	910	1,257	
Subtotal	54,181	50,143	−4,038
Space research and technology[2]	4,171	5,094	
Total	58,352	55,237	−3,115

[1] Preliminary expenditures released July 21, 1965.
[2] Includes NASA aircraft technology.
NOTE: Detail will not necessarily add to totals because of rounding.
SOURCES: Treasury Department, Bureau of the Budget, and Atomic Energy Commission.

in defense and space programs during the last few years are basically completed, we are now able to maintain our strong defense posture and move our space activities forward without a repetition of the recent large annual increases in total defense-related outlays. Whether or not total defense-related spending will in the years immediately ahead remain close to that of fiscal year 1965 will depend on a number of factors not now foreseeable.

Any projection will, of course, be markedly affected by any appreciable change—for better or for worse—in the prevailing climate of international relations. In particular, if important agreement were reached in the continuing negotiations over general and complete disarmament or other more limited measures, the projection would be significantly altered.

The recent general stability of total defense spending is itself a significant new development. Except for a slight dip between fiscal years 1959 and 1960, spending for national defense increased every year from fiscal 1956 to fiscal 1964. Including space as well, the total increase in the annual rate between 1955 and 1964 was $17.6 billion, or an average of about $2 billion a year. The pattern of defense and defense-related spending by fiscal years since 1945, both in absolute amount and as a percentage of GNP, is shown in Table 2.

In addition to the recent stability in total defense spending, shifts are occurring in the relative importance of individual programs within the total. Between fiscal years 1963 and 1965, a decline of over one-third is estimated to have occurred in new funding for strategic retaliatory forces (such as

TABLE 4   DEPARTMENT OF DEFENSE OBLIGATIONAL AVAILABILITY
BY MAJOR PROGRAM AREA, FISCAL YEARS 1962–65
[Percent]

Program area	1962	1963	1964	1965[1]
Total obligational availability[2]	100.0	100.0	100.0	100.0
Strategic retaliatory forces	17.7	16.2	14.1	10.4
Continental air and missile defense forces	4.5	3.9	4.0	3.5
General purpose forces	34.3	33.9	34.1	35.6
Airlift/sealift forces	2.4	2.7	2.5	2.9
Research and development	8.3	9.8	10.2	10.0
Reserve and guard forces	3.5	3.5	3.9	4.1
General support	23.8	25.0	26.4	28.1
Retired pay	1.8	1.9	2.3	2.8
Military assistance	3.5	3.1	2.3	2.4

[1] Estimate as of January 1965.
[2] Excludes costs of nuclear warheads.
NOTE: Detail will not necessarily add to total because of rounding.
SOURCE: Department of Defense, Office of the Assistant Secretary of Defense.

ICBM's) as required levels of strength were attained. In contrast, outlays for general purpose forces, such as surface-based Army and Navy equipment, were higher in fiscal year 1965 than in 1963, as were general support activities and retired pay. Some of the major patterns of change within the total defense budget are shown in Table 4.

Fundamental shifts in the broad composition of defense spending—as well as the phaseout of production on particular weapon systems, and the curtailment of operations at particular military bases—will continue regardless of the direction in which the over-all military budget moves. Moreover, they will continue to have important impacts on individual communities, companies, and employees and their families. Shifting geographical patterns of procurement are indicated—although somewhat roughly—by a comparison of prime contract awards by States in fiscal year 1964 with those in fiscal year 1963. The national total fell by only 2.3 percent: in 16 States, there was an actual increase, including a near doubling in Missouri and a near tripling in North Dakota; but, in 15 States, awards decreased by 20 percent or more.

Special attention has recently been drawn to local impacts of defense changes caused by the announcement on November 19, 1964 of the reduction or termination of activities at 95 defense installations, 80 of them in the United States, as part of the cost reduction program of the Defense Department. During the preceding 3½ years, an even larger number of similar actions had been taken, but no single announcement attracted so much attention as that of last November. A number of the communities where these installations are located have faced, or now face, major problems of readjustment, just as other communities face readjustment problems from the shifting character of defense procurement.

Some manifestations of the economic impact of recent defense shifts are already apparent. Reductions in defense work over the past year have put a severe drag on the growth of employment in some States, especially in the West and Northeast. In 1964, unemployment in a few Western States actually increased. Alaska, California, and Washington had unemployment rates that were among the highest in the Nation. California and Washington, as well as Arizona, Nevada, New Mexico, and Utah, report sharp employment reductions in defense-type manufacturing. Some Eastern States, notably Connecticut, Maryland, and New Jersey, also were greatly affected. But the Deep South and Southwest, where much of the space program is concentrated, are still reporting gains in defense-space work; Missouri has shown a large increase in aircraft employment. In other areas, also, defense activity is still expanding. And almost everywhere, the strength of the overall economic expansion has cushioned any drop stemming from the defense sector.

Some indication of the impact on industrial employment of recent shifts in defense procurement may be obtained from an examination of changes in the five defense-related industries—ordnance, communication equipment, electronic components, aircraft, and shipbuilding (Table 5). (Industry employment figures, of course, include both defense and nondefense work.) In the fourth quarter of 1964, total employment in these industries (not seasonally adjusted) was 6.2 percent lower than in the fourth quarter of 1962. Declines had occurred in these industries in 1963 and early 1964, while total employment in industries manufacturing durable goods rose by 4.3 percent. In terms of absolute numbers of workers, the largest decline in employment was in the aircraft and parts industry, with employment down nearly 50,000 between the fourth quarter of 1962 and the fourth quarter of 1964. Nearly as large a decline occurred in the communication equipment industry. In the ship and boat building and repairing industry, employment rose by about 10,000 over the same period, and there was a small rise in the electronic components industry, apparently as a result of increased nondefense business.

A more comprehensive view of the impact of defense cutbacks would be gained if unemployment data for these same five defense-related industries were available. Because they are not available for such detailed industry groupings, changes in accession and separation rates must be used to shed some light on what has been happening.

For example, in the ordnance industry, which includes missiles and space vehicles, the annual average layoff rate ran from a low of 0.7 percent to a high of 1.0 percent a month in the period 1958–62. During most of 1964 the layoff rate ran between 1.0 and 1.7 percent a month, but by December it had reached a low of 0.7 percent. The layoff rate in the communication equipment industry was high during 1963 and the first half of 1964, but subsequently dropped to only 0.8 percent in December 1964. Quit rates tend to move inversely with layoff rates.

The changing composition of defense spending is having an unequal effect not only among different industries and various areas of the country but also among different categories of workers. As already noted, there is a heavy concentration of nonproduction workers—including, particularly, engineers

TABLE 5   EMPLOYMENT IN FIVE DEFENSE-RELATED INDUSTRIES, 1962–65
[Thousands, not seasonally adjusted]

Quarter	Total five defense-related industries	Ordnance and accessories (SIC 19)	Communication equipment (SIC 366)	Electronic components and accessories (SIC 367)	Aircraft and parts (SIC 372)	Ship and boat building and repairing (SIC 373)
1962: III	1,770.9	274.8	448.2	270.3	637.3	140.3
IV	1,791.4	276.6	456.3	270.0	647.3	141.2
1963: I	1,778.6	274.7	451.4	264.4	642.4	145.7
II	1,746.7	271.0	436.1	262.6	631.8	145.2
III	1,730.0	274.1	426.1	261.3	629.8	138.7
IV	1,732.5	276.4	420.5	261.2	636.5	137.9
1964: I	1,701.9	271.9	411.1	258.6	622.9	137.4
II	1,670.8	262.3	401.7	258.5	605.1	143.2
III	1,655.0	250.5	401.6	263.5	596.0	143.4
IV	1,679.5	245.5	408.7	276.1	597.9	151.3
1965: I[1]	1,678.9	242.6	411.9	282.0	595.2	155.9
II[1]	1,713.8	243.1	416.0	290.7	603.1	160.8

[1] Preliminary.
NOTE: Data are based on March 1963 benchmark levels and include defense-related and non-defense work in these industries. SIC numbers refer to Standard Industrial Classification established by the Bureau of the Budget.
SOURCE: Department of Labor, Bureau of Labor Statistics.

and technicians—in the industries producing strategic weapons (missiles, aircraft, electronics). The sizable cutbacks of defense production in these industries, together with the recent stabilization of defense R&D and the impending tapering off of a rapid expansion phase of our space programs, have—for the first time in many years—brought reasonable over-all balance between supply of and demand for technical and scientific personnel. This shift has attracted considerable attention in recent months.

Still, there is no evidence of any substantial unemployment of technical and scientific workers. Over the past several years, the total employment of engineers and technical personnel has continued to expand.

In the early part of 1964, unemployment among engineers appeared to be slightly higher than the very low rates of earlier years. In addition, there was a rise in the ratio of applicants in scientific, engineering, and technical occupations to unfilled openings in these same occupations in major employment centers. This softening of the market was most notable for electrical and aeronautical engineers, and for physicists and mathematicians. Since the first half of 1964, the market seems to have stabilized and even tightened somewhat, with unemployment declining again, and job openings increasing.

2] The Regional Impact of Defense Spending

I F A "DEFINITIVE" history of the post-World War II period in the United States is ever written, few subjects will loom larger in importance than the multifarious efforts of the federal government to maintain and enhance its defense posture in response to the cold war. To accomplish this purpose, 62 per cent of the national budget, or $776 billion, was spent on national defense from 1946 through 1965.[1] The full impact of this very substantial sum is impossible to measure precisely and difficult to imagine meaningfully, but all will agree that whatever its effect on the international "balance of terror," defense spending has been shaping, often dramatically, the growth patterns of several important regions of the United States since the cold war began.

This fact has assumed special significance for the thirteen far western states. Although less than one-sixth of the nation lives in that region, in recent years one-fourth of all Department of Defense (DOD) military and civilian personnel, one-third of all military prime contract awards, including one-half of all DOD research and development contracts, and two-thirds of all missile awards have been let to business firms and other organizations located there. In addition to these awards, expenditures of the National Aeronautics and Space Administration (NASA) in the Far West from 1961 through 1965 amounted to $5,317 million or 48 per cent of the total national expenditures of that rapidly growing administration. If other federal defense-oriented agency expenditures are included, such as expenditures by the Atomic Energy Commission and the National Science Foundation, the proportion of defense spending funneled into the Far West is even larger. Unfortunately, except for 1963, no figures of expenditures by state are available for these agencies.

These heavy federal defense expenditures are in many ways a new development in the history of the Far West. In the past most federal expenditures in that area were, at least in their inception, essentially regional subsidies, i.e., government grants to private enterprise for public purposes without serious concern for a profitable return to the government. For example, land grants to railroads, mail-carrying contracts, irrigation and flood control grants for the development of marginal lands, depletion allowances to mineral producers, grazing rights in national forests, and (indirectly) artificially high prices for silver were and to some extent still are subsidies. Most defense expenditures, however, cannot be classified as subsidies. Procurement actions, where most defense money is spent, are by law required to be made on the

[1] [Includes only official national security expenditures. See *January 1966 Economic Report of the President*, 276—J. L. C.]

FROM James L. Clayton, "The Impact of the Cold War on the Economies of California and Utah, 1946–1965." © Copyright 1965 by the Pacific Coast Branch, American Historical Association. Reprinted from *Pacific Historical Review*, Vol. XXXVI, pp. 449–473, by permission of the Branch. [Footnotes omitted—J. L. C.]

basis of least cost to the government. In spite of continued assertions by some congressmen and journalists that political considerations decide many allocation decisions, no significant departure from this procedure has been proven to date.

Still, despite logical, cogent, and well-known reasons for defense expenditures there is striking regional concentration, especially in research and development efforts. Ninety per cent of all federal research and development programs and, in recent years, over half of all scientific research has been funded by defense agencies. These research grants are the "seed corn" of future production contracts and the very life blood of the science and engineering departments in most distinguished universities. Recognition of this fact has given rise to a spate of congressional fulminations and has turned jealous eyes toward California, which receives by far the most money, and toward the Mountain States, whose share of the defense pie in the late 1950's and early 1960's had been growing more rapidly than any other section of the country.

This article will attempt to measure the more important economic and demographic aspects of the impact of the cold war prior to the Vietnam escalation on two of these far western states: California and Utah. By comparing the impact of defense spending in these two quite different and regionally separated states—particularly on the county level—it is hoped that if there are common patterns of impact in these western states they will be evident. These particular states were chosen for a number of reasons. First, both have been heavily oriented toward defense spending but in different ways since 1946 (and earlier). California received more DOD monies, for example, from 1946 to 1965 than any other state, and defense spending has made a larger contribution to the growth in exogenous income in the state of Utah than for any other state during most of this same period. Second, the impact of defense spending in California is primarily via industry, whereas in Utah it is generated mostly by military installations. This allows different kinds of impact to be compared. Third, the obvious differences in size and importance allow a comparison between a major and relatively minor political subdivision for common patterns. Finally, although there are several studies in depth of the impact of defense spending for individual states, there are few comparative studies and, to my knowledge, none for the far western states.

Before we begin, however, it must be made clear what is meant by defense spending, for there is no clear-cut definition of this much-used term. Nor is there a defense "sector" in the standard industrial classifications. Moreover, most of the data pertaining to this subject are compiled on a national basis and are not broken down by state. Consequently, anyone wishing to measure the impact of defense spending on a particular region must largely devise his own methods of measurement. For the purpose of this discussion "defense spending" will include all expenditures of the DOD for supplies, services, construction, research and development, and payroll data for active duty DOD military and civilian personnel. These expenditures represent over 90 per cent of all monies spent by the DOD. In addition to DOD funds, defense spending as defined here will include expenditures by NASA and the Veterans Administration. Appropriations for the Atomic

Energy Commission, for stockpiling and other similar defense related efforts, are not included because they are either classified, not broken down by state, or otherwise not readily available. The determining factor of what is included was the availability of pertinent expenditure data on a state-by-state basis. Nevertheless, defense spending as used here includes about 85 per cent of the national security sector of the United States budget.

I

Turning to California, it is common knowledge that defense spending has been particularly lavish in that state. From 1951 through 1965, $67.2 billion or about 20 percent of all DOD prime defense contracts for supplies, services, and construction were let there. It is well known, of course, that these prime contracts only reflect the location of final processing or assembly and that the extent of subcontracting is unknown. But for reasons which shall be explained momentarily, it is submitted that, although using prime contracts and the employment generated by such contracts may not be the most accurate method of measurement possible, it is a generally accurate and widely acceptable approach—particularly for a series of years.

The most important reason why California has received more defense contracts than any other state is because California was the nation's foremost aircraft producer when aircraft were needed for defense, and this competence gave the Golden State a decided advantage when, subsequently, missiles and electronics dominated the procurement program. In addition, California business firms and research institutions strongly emphasized experimental and developmental projects which later led to production contracts, while competing states were concentrating on the more lucrative but less foresighted returns of production contracts.

It is virtually impossible to estimate precisely how much of this $67.2 billion was actually spent in California, but on a national basis about half of all DOD prime contracts are subcontracted, and most of these subcontracts tend to remain in the area of the initial grant. Included, of course, within these production contracts are about $20 billion in research and development contracts, most of which undoubtedly stayed in California. Certainly, it is safe to say, therefore, that most of this investment stayed in California. If one adds to this figure the DOD subcontracts California received from prime contractors outside the state, it is conceivable that California received and retained somewhat more than this amount.

From 1961 through 1965 an estimated additional $5.3 billion was spent by NASA in California. This was 41 per cent of NASA's total expenditures during those years. In 1965, 51 per cent of the original NASA expenditure in California was subcontracted as first-tier grants to out-of-state firms, and 44 per cent of the total was received back by California firms as subcontracts originating outside the state, suggesting that more than 90 per cent of the original NASA grant in that year actually remained in or came into the state.

This $67.2 billion in DOD procurement awards and the more recent $5.3 billion in NASA procurement awards have supported a massive defense-related manufacturing industry in California since World War II. When the annual average earnings in the aircraft and parts, ship and boat building, ordnance, and one-half the annual earnings in the electrical machinery industries in California are tabulated from 1946 through 1965, $28.9 billion in wages and salaries have been generated in California by direct defense spending. (See Table I.) When DOD military and civilian payrolls and veterans' benefits are tabulated, the figure for the same period is $73.5 billion, or an annual average of 10.90 per cent of all California personal income (Table II). To get an idea of the magnitude of such a sum, comparisons with national endeavors are helpful. For the same period, this is more than two-thirds of all United States business expenditures for new plants and equipment for durable goods, it is more than all state and local public welfare expenditures, and almost as much as United States foreign assistance, both economic and military, for Europe and the Far East since World War II.

II

Undoubtedly, the most immediate measurable impact of this enormous financial outlay has been the creation of new jobs. Although it is difficult to transfer dollars into jobs, particularly when, as we have seen, there is no defense sector in the standard industrial classification, nevertheless, we do know that from 1950 to 1963, 661,000 new jobs were created in California's manufacturing industries and that more than 60 per cent of these were in the aerospace industries.

The bulk of these new jobs were in the electrical equipment sector (146,000) and the aircraft and parts sector (56,640). Eighty to ninety per cent of these two sectors are defense oriented. The number of new jobs in the aircraft sector increased sharply during the early 1950's, but by 1963 over 120,000 persons had lost jobs in that industry because of the shift to missiles. Contrary to what one would expect, this precipitous layoff among aircraft workers caused hardly a ripple in California's economy generally. For example, although 80,000 persons lost their jobs between 1957 and 1963 in the Los Angeles–Long Beach area, over 90,000 new jobs were created there in the electrical machinery and ordnance sectors. Of course, individuals were hurt and many aircraft workers did not find work in the electronics industry, but the point here is that because of continued defense expenditures in other areas the California economy as a whole was not adversely affected by layoffs in the aircraft industry.

If all the largely defense-related industries are taken into account—aircraft and parts, ordnance and accessories, communications equipment and electronic components, portions of the electrical machinery sector, and ship and boat building and repairing—and to these are added the DOD civilian employees, there were between 201,000 (1948) and 523,000 (1963) employees directly engaged in defense work in California between 1946 and 1965 (Table III). As one might expect, the sharpest increase in defense employment occurred in 1951 and 1952 with the coming of the Korean war, although defense employment has been fairly constant since 1959. In 1963, at its peak,

TABLE I ESTIMATED WAGE AND SALARY DISBURSEMENTS IN DEFENSE-RELATED
MANUFACTURING INDUSTRIES; DOD MILITARY AND CIVILIAN PAYROLLS;
AND VETERANS' BENEFITS IN CALIFORNIA, 1946–65

[In millions of dollars]

	Defense-related manufacturing industries*	DOD		Veterans' benefits§	Amount‖
		Military†	Civilian‡		
1946	300	830	358	93	1,581
1947	327	464	362	431	1,584
1948	305	453	364	452	1,640
1949	360	463	401	463	1,687
1950	373	596	414	425	1,808
1951	692	1,016	654	381	2,753
1952	993	1,325	740	363	3,421
1953	1,161	1,274	724	343	3,502
1954	1,265	1,113	650	360	3,388
1955	1,402	1,109	721	376	3,608
1956	1,716	1,130	751	406	4,003
1957	1,933	1,112	764	429	4,243
1958	1,880	1,152	804	458	4,294
1959	2,092	1,193	837	495	4,617
1960	2,086	1,220	862	525	4,693
1961	2,176	1,241	922	556	4,895
1962	2,401	1,309	975	567	5,252
1963	2,471	1,351	1,012	592	5,426
1964	2,448	1,427	1,071	540	5,486
1965	2,500 est.	1,482	1,047	543	5,572
Total	28,881	21,260	14,433	8,798	73,453

* Average weekly earnings x 52 x the average annual number of employees in the following industries: (a) Aircraft and Parts, SIC 372; (b) Ship and Boat Building and Repairs, SIC 373; (c) Ordnance and Accessories, SIC 19 (average weekly earnings in manufacturing in California were used here because SIC 19 earnings are unavailable); (d) Electrical Machinery, SIC 36, 50% of the total, a formula suggested by George Steiner.

† For 1946-55 from *Personal Income by States Since 1929*, Department of Commerce, Office of Business Economics, 1956; from 1956-65 from the (August) issues of *Survey of Current Business*, Department of Commerce.

‡ For 1946 from "Significance of Military Installations for California's Economic Growth, 1930-52," Bank of America Study, 1955, p. 11. For 1947-62 from Roger Bolton, *Defense Purchases and Regional Growth*, 171-73. For 1963-65 from *Statistical Abstract* (DOD wage and salary disbursements minus military payroll).

§ From Veterans Administration annual reports.

‖ Sum of columns 1, 2, 3, and 4.

defense employment in manufacturing represented 27 per cent of that sector and 8 per cent of the total civilian force. The Census Bureau in its special report on manufacturing for that year, which included thirty industrial cate-

TABLE II   ESTIMATED ANNUAL DEFENSE INCOME IN CALIFORNIA
AS A PERCENTAGE OF PERSONAL INCOME, 1946–65
[In millions of dollars]

	Personal income*	Defense income†	Defense income as percent of personal income
1946	16,048	1,581	9.85
1947	16,637	1,584	9.52
1948	17,621	1,640	9.31
1949	17,866	1,687	9.44
1950	19,760	1,808	9.15
1951	22,740	2,753	12.11
1952	25,196	3,421	13.58
1953	26,984	3,502	12.98
1954	27,661	3,388	12.25
1955	30,356	3,608	11.89
1956	33,154	4,003	12.16
1957	35,468	4,243	11.96
1958	37,339	4,294	11.50
1959	40,944	4,617	11.28
1960	42,910	4,693	10.94
1961	45,608	4,895	10.73
1962	48,980	5,252	10.72
1963	52,431	5,426	10.35
1964	56,264	5,486	9.75
1965	59,476	5,572	9.28
Total	673,454	73,453	10.90

* From *Survey of Current Business*, XLVI: 4 (April, 1966).
† Col. 5, Table I.

gories but excluded government-owned plants, placed the defense employment figure at 407,500, with 54 per cent of these workers in the Los Angeles–Long Beach area and 12 per cent each for the San Jose and San Diego areas. If these direct defense jobs support two additional indirect jobs—a crude but conservative assumption—over a million and a half workers or about one-third of all non-agricultural employees in California in recent years have been dependent on continued defense expenditures.

The extent to which defense spending has generated additional dollars of personal income is controversial, and the estimates vary widely. The most thorough time series study on this subject is Roger Bolton's *Defense Purchases and Regional Growth* (1966). The Census Bureau's special report on the shipments of defense-oriented industries, mentioned above, is the best source for a single year (1963). Including DOD military and civilian wages

TABLE III   ESTIMATED ANNUAL AVERAGE DIRECT DEFENSE-RELATED
EMPLOYMENT IN CALIFORNIA, 1946–65
[Thousands]

	Aircraft and parts (SIC 372)	Ordnance and accessories (SIC 19)	Electrical machinery (50%) (SIC 36)	Ship and boat building and repair (SIC 373)	Civilian employees of DOD*	Total
1946	84	–	10	37	125	256
1947	78	–	10	21	102	211
1948	75	1	11	14	100	201
1949	79	1	11	7	100	198
1950	85	1	15	6	95	203
1951	136	5	22	10	123	296
1952	189	12	28	13	134	376
1953	209	18	34	13	127	401
1954	221	19	33	12	119	404
1955	229	24	38	11	118	420
1956	256	33	48	10	123	470
1957	273	38	59	12	125	507
1958	231	43	62	11	123	470
1959	227	59	77	11	123	497
1960	194	69	87	13	127	490
1961	178	80	94	13	130	495
1962	172	97	107	11	133	520
1963	171	102	105	11	134	523
1964	164	99	97	11	134	505
1965	166	100	98	10	137	511

* Civilian employees of the DOD are estimated here at one-half the total federal government employment in California. Other estimates place it somewhat higher.
SOURCE: *Employment and Earnings Statistics for States and Areas, 1939-1965,* Bureau of Labor Statistics.

and salaries with procurement, Bolton's figures show that from 1951 through 1962 defense spending represented 17.2 per cent of California's personal income and, more importantly, between 20 and 27 per cent of California's growth in exogenous income. Other studies suggest a higher multiplier. Defense spending has not, however, materially altered the state's already high per capita personal income growth rate, although the counties of greatest defense spending concentration show a considerably higher per capita personal income than the state average.

A much clearer picture of the impact of defense spending emerges when one examines its impact on different regions within the Golden State. Fortunately, for the analyst at least, almost all defense expenditures for production and research as well as for NASA awards find their way into four California counties. These counties are Los Angeles, San Diego, Santa Clara, and

Orange. Unfortunately, however, data are not available to determine the number of DOD military and civilian personnel located in military installations in each county, but without question most DOD personnel undoubtedly have been stationed at the naval and marine bases in San Diego, the army base at Ft. Ord near Monterey, and at various installations in the San Francisco Bay area.

On the other hand, the far more important defense *industries,* as opposed to defense *installations,* are largely concentrated in Los Angeles County. Probably over $50 billion in one form or another has been spent there since the cold war began. The $50 billion infusion is the primary reason why the number of employees in manufacturing in Los Angeles County jumped 92 per cent from 1950 to 1962. In spite of cutbacks in the aircraft industry since 1957, employment in that sector rose 60 per cent during this period. Electrical machinery and parts—the heart of the county's booming electronics industry—rose a phenomenal 568 per cent. If sectors other than manufacturing are included it is conceivable that over half of the work force of the Los Angeles area is defense oriented.

Some of Los Angeles County's defense business has spilled over into neighboring Orange County. Orange County's electrical industries employment grew from virtually nothing in 1950 to 31,000 by 1962 and is the major reason that manufacturing employment in Orange County has grown over tenfold since 1950. By 1965 electronics was Orange County's fastest growing industry, having quadrupled its employment since 1957, and could account for about 40 per cent of the county's manufacturing employment.

San Diego and Santa Clara counties have also experienced heavy infusions of defense funds. Manufacturing employment in San Diego grew 276 per cent from 1950 to 1963, with electrical machinery (733%) and aircraft and parts (418%) showing the largest gains. During some years, over 70 per cent of that county's manufacturing employment was directly employed in defense work. Santa Clara County's manufacturing employment rose 444 per cent during this same period, with a 600 per cent increase in electrical machinery. By 1965, these four counties—Los Angeles, San Diego, Orange, and Santa Clara —could account for 57 per cent of all new jobs in ordnance, aircraft and parts, and electrical machinery. It is also interesting to note that, except for Orange County, per capita personal income in these counties in 1960 was considerably higher than for the rest of the state.

III

The impact of defense spending on California's population growth is equally striking. It has long been established that internal migration is the primary reason for rapid regional population shifts in the United States. Based on numbers added, but not including births, Los Angeles County experienced the largest growth of any United States county from 1950 to 1960, adding 1,171,000 persons during the decade. Over 900,000 people came between 1950 and 1955, when over 146,000 new jobs in the aircraft industry alone were created.

In general, California counties with the highest rate of growth in the manufacturing sector have had the greatest net in-migration. From 1950 to 1962, for example, manufacturing employment increased most in Orange, Santa Clara, Riverside, San Mateo, Santa Barbara, and San Diego counties, in that order. Net in-migration was highest during these years in Los Angeles, Orange, Santa Clara, Santa Barbara, Riverside, San Diego, and San Bernardino.

That defense spending was the main factor in this rapid growth can be seen by comparing the defense spending counties with those with the highest in-migration. Again, to illustrate, since 1950 defense spending was most pronounced in Los Angeles, San Diego, Santa Clara, and Orange counties in that order. These four counties accounted for 82 per cent of all new manufacturing jobs in California from 1950 to 1962. It will be recalled that 57 per cent of the new manufacturing jobs were in aircraft and parts, electrical machinery, and ordnance. Clearly, then, defense spending in these four counties has been the primary reason for California's manufacturing employment growth since 1950. When one considers that these four counties also accounted for 64 per cent of the total net in-migration to California during the 1950's, the conclusion seems inescapable that defense spending has been the primary reason for California's rapid population growth since World War II. Other factors, such as an attractive climate and a substantial number of persons seeking retirement in California, have been important as an attractive force, but not of the same magnitude as defense jobs.

Space does not permit careful evaluation of the impact of defense spending on all possible areas. Before leaving the Golden State, however, it should be pointed out that there is a definite relationship between defense spending and the rising importance of California's engineering and technical schools. Defense spending may also be one reason why the number of engineering students in California has increased, while at the same time the number studying engineering in the rest of the United States has declined. Moreover, a number of indirect but ponderable consequences suggest themselves. Since defense spending, by attracting an enormous number of people to Los Angeles, is primarily responsible for the congestion of that area, it is also indirectly and in part responsible for furthering the movement of middle- and upper-income families to the suburbs and the subsequent spiral of spreading slums, rising crime, highway congestion, and smog.

I V

We have observed how massive defense expenditures have contributed to the growth of a large, dynamic, rich, and industrially progressive state located on the west coast. What are the effects of a comparatively modest amount of defense spending on a small, inland, relatively isolated western state with a per capita income traditionally below the national average and without abundant natural resources or a record of innovation? Do factors emerge which suggest that defense spending may have certain predictable economic and demographic consequences wherever it is applied in substantial amounts? Are there any historical insights to be gained from comparing California and Utah's experience, insights which might be tested on other states and regions of the United States? With these questions in mind we turn now to Utah.

The first fact that strikes one's mind upon comparing California's defense complex with Utah's is that, whereas defense spending in California is centered largely in *private* manufacturing plants, in Utah it is concentrated at *government* military installations. According to one authority, no state has such a variety of government supply and repair installations nor such a large per cent of its work force occupied in this type of activity as does Utah. One of the reasons for such a concentration of supply installations in Utah is because the Salt Lake City–Ogden area is equidistant from the leading ports of Seattle, San Francisco, Los Angeles, and San Diego, with an excellent climate for storage purposes and good transportation facilities for distribution to the remainder of the West.

At the close of World War II there were six military supply and repair depots in Utah employing about 10,000 persons. With the coming of the Korean war employment more than doubled at these installations, and since 1956 it has stabilized at about 22,000, with an average yearly payroll of $282 million. Hill Air Force Base, located directly south of Ogden and approximately twenty miles north of Salt Lake City, is by far the most important of these bases, employing almost one-half the total employment in military installations in Utah in 1964. Tooele Army Depot, located a few miles southwest of Salt Lake City, is second with 3,600 employees in 1964.

The second most striking fact one sees in comparing Utah's defense industry complex with California's is that whereas California's defense income as a percentage of personal income has been declining slowly since the Korean war, Utah's defense income grew very rapidly in the late 1950's and early 1960's. Beginning in 1957, the emphasis on missile and rocket fuels began to create a new defense industry in Utah. From 1951 to 1957 most of the defense orders came from the Army or Navy and represented only 0.1 to 0.2 per cent of all DOD contract awards. But, in 1957, in response to impressive Soviet missile innovations, the magnitude of Air Force contracts let in Utah for missile work began to spiral, and the Beehive State's proportion of defense contracts rose rapidly to 1.6 per cent of total DOD awards. By 1963, Utah was receiving $408 million in defense contracts, an absolute gain of 1700 per cent since the Korean war, and the largest gain recorded by any state. (See Table IV.)

The reasons for Utah's defense industry boom are not entirely clear. There seems to be general agreement, however, on the following reasoning: in response to the DOD's now obsolete policy of industrial dispersion, plant managers wanted a location far removed from the defense agglomerations on the west coast and yet easily accessible to all important western markets. Cheap land, isolated testing areas, good weather, a pro-business tax structure, a productive but tractable labor force, and relatively good schools seem to have been the most important location factors. Moreover, the already existing military bases and supply depots—especially Hill Air Force Base near Ogden—were an added attraction. This line of reasoning does not explain, however, why Utah was chosen over say the Denver area, or for that

TABLE IV   Estimated Wage and Salary Disbursements in Defense-related
Manufacturing Industries; DOD Military and Civilian Payrolls;
and Veterans' Benefits in Utah, 1946–65

[In millions of dollars]

	Defense-related manufacturing*	DOD military payroll†	DOD civilian payroll‡	Veterans' benefits§	Amount‖
1946	.3 est.	34	(NA)	5	
1947	.3	7	32	34	77.3
1948	.3	7	45	33	85.3
1949	.3	6	44	34	84.3
1950	.3	11	46	31	88.3
1951	.3	18	77	27	122.3
1952	.4	18	98	23	139.4
1953	.4	18	100	22	140.4
1954	.4	22	84	23	129.4
1955	.8	23	85	25	133.8
1956	1.2	19	87	27	134.2
1957	5.3	17	85	27	134.3
1958	15.6	18	94	28	155.6
1959	38.8	19	97	27	181.8
1960	52.7	21	99	31	203.7
1961	84.3	22	107	34	247.3
1962	115.9	24	119	33	291.9
1963	130.7	25	124	34	291.2
1964	101.6	27	130	35	293.6
1965	80.0 est.	27	139	33	279.0
Total	709.9	383	1,692	566	3,213.1

* Figures for 1947-55 from Utah Ordnance and Transportation employment data, SIC 19 and 37, and the average weekly earnings in manufacturing in Utah X 52 in *Personal Income by States Since 1929;* from 1956-64 from Arrington and Jensen, *The Defense Industry of Utah,* 44; and for 1965 the figure is my estimate based upon the decline of defense-related employment in Utah from Jan., 1965 to Jan., 1966.
† From *Personal Income by States Since 1929,* 1956; and *Survey of Current Business* (August issues).
‡ For 1947-62 from Roger Bolton, *op. cit.,* 171-73; for 1963-65 from *Statistical Abstract.*
§ From Veterans Administration annual reports.
‖ Sum of columns 1, 2, 3, and 4.

matter several excellent sites in Texas, Missouri, and even California itself.

As in California, the proportion of Utah prime contracts subcontracted out-of-state is unknown. But if the experience of Thiokol Chemical Corporation, Utah's largest defense contractor, is typical, Utah retains far less sub-

TABLE V   ESTIMATED ANNUAL DEFENSE INCOME IN UTAH AS A PERCENTAGE
OF PERSONAL INCOME, 1947–65
[In millions of dollars]

	Personal income	Defense income	Defense income as percent of personal income
1947	749	77.3	10.32
1948	809	85.3	10.54
1949	833	84.3	10.12
1950	910	88.3	9.70
1951	1,051	122.3	11.61
1952	1,114	139.4	12.51
1953	1,164	140.4	12.06
1954	1,163	129.4	11.13
1955	1,270	133.8	10.54
1956	1,378	134.2	9.74
1957	1,478	134.3	9.09
1958	1,543	155.6	10.08
1959	1,673	181.8	10.87
1960	1,767	203.7	11.53
1961	1,904	247.3	12.99
1962	2,066	291.9	14.13
1963	2,147	291.2	13.56
1964	2,211	293.6	13.28
1965	2,317	279.0	12.04
Total	28,245	3,213.1	11.35

contracts than does California. From 1960 through May of 1964, for example, 86 per cent of the value of that company's total awards left the state. Nevertheless, it is significant that by 1965 Utah had received an estimated $4,200 billion in *initial* DOD prime defense contracts and military and civilian payroll expenditures since World War II.

If Utah's subcontracts are more diversified than California's, her prime contracts are more concentrated. From 1959 to 1965, 89 per cent of all contract awards over $500,000 were let to firms located in Salt Lake and Box Elder counties. If Weber County is added, 98.6 per cent of all large awards during those years went to these three counties. When employment in 1963 for both defense installations and defense industries is added together, it is clear that one-half of all employees associated with defense spending are working in the Ogden area, one-fifth in the Salt Lake area, and the rest are almost equally divided between Box Elder and Tooele counties. (See Table V.)

TABLE VI   ESTIMATED ANNUAL AVERAGE DIRECT DEFENSE-RELATED EMPLOYMENT
IN UTAH, 1946–64
[Thousands]

	Civilian employees of DOD	Ordnance and accessories (SIC 19)	Aircraft and parts (SIC 372)	Electrical machinery (SIC 36) (50%)	Total
1946	17,800				17,800
1947	13,700				13,700
1948	14,800				14,800
1949	14,500				14,500
1950	14,800				14,800
1951	24,600				24,600
1952	28,000	1			28,001
1953	25,300	2			25,302
1954	20,900	3		74	20,977
1955	20,000			80	20,080
1956	19,500	3	53	122	19,678
1957	18,800	462	438	154	19,854
1958	17,700	1,113	1,345	207	20,365
1959	17,800	2,282	4,017	292	24,391
1960	17,800	3,141	5,695	288	26,924
1961	17,700	3,135	8,663	210	29,708
1962	19,400	4,146	11,695	379	35,620
1963	19,300	4,463	12,046	598	36,407
1964 (March)	19,500	4,034	10,146	788	34,468

SOURCE: Utah Department of Employment Security. BLS breakdowns not available.

v

During this century, non-agricultural employment growth in Utah and the United States was about the same until 1950. From 1950 to 1956, however, Utah's non-agricultural employment rate doubled the national average, and thereafter to 1962 it was four times the national average. This growth is easily explained. From 1956 to 1962, 51,502 new jobs were created in the state. Of these, 18,000 or 35 per cent were in the aerospace industries. Assuming each new aerospace position generated one additional supporting job, then 36,000 or 70 per cent of this employment increase was caused directly and indirectly by defense spending.

In 1962 at the peak of Utah's defense boom, an estimated 35,600 were working either at defense installations or in defense plants (Table VI). Some authors, by including somewhat more than one-half of the electrical equipment sector, estimate defense employment as 42,000 or 12.1 per cent of total Utah employment. In either case this was probably the highest percentage of the work force directly employed in defense-related activity of any state in the United States in that year. Including DOD military and civilian personnel, these jobs may have supported an additional 40 to 80 thousand jobholders, or 30 to 40 per cent of Utah's non-agricultural work force, on the basis of job acceleration formulas mentioned earlier. It should be noted, however, that Utah's missile industry has been of less significance to the state than was the rapid industrial expansion of World War II. At that time 25,000 new jobs were added to the manufacturing sector, whereas less than 20,000 manufacturing jobs were created from 1956 to 1962.

Utah was probably the nation's most defense-oriented state in 1962, because production contracts and research contracts peaked at the same time. Research contracts going to Utah rose from $13 million in 1958 to $119 million in 1962. This represents a rate of growth of 833 per cent, and was the second fastest rate of growth in the nation among those states receiving $50 million or more of research contracts. Production contracts rose from $76 million in 1958 to $299 million in 1962, the third fastest rate of growth in the nation among those states receiving $100 million or more of production contracts (Table VII).

Since 1963, however, Utah's defense industries have been cutting back their labor forces. In 1964 over 4,000 persons in the missile industry lost their jobs, but since that time employment in Utah's defense industries seems to have stabilized itself.

Contrary to California's experience, defense spending has had a profound effect on personal income in the Beehive State since the Korean war. From 1930, Utah consistently had a lower per capita personal income than the nation and several other western states. This was partly because Utah has one of the highest birth rates in the nation and a very high proportion of its young people in school. But during the period of sharply increasing defense expenditures (1957–1962), Utah's per capita personal income rose $394 compared with $148 for the nation. This represented a rate of per capita personal income growth which was considerably faster than for any other intermountain state. By 1962, about one-third of Utah's personal income was dependent on defense. The most rapid rise in personal income within the state occurred in the two counties with the greatest concentration of new defense jobs—Salt Lake and Box Elder. The next largest increase occurred in the Weber-Davis region where most of Utah's DOD military and civilian employees are concentrated. Since 1963, however, because of defense cutbacks, Utah's rate of personal income growth has been slower than in all but a few other states.

The impact of defense spending on other Utah industries is considerably less than in California. Leonard Arrington and George Jensen have shown that purchases by Utah's military installations from other Utah establishments have been small, primarily because these installations are supply depots rather than manufacturing plants. Moreover, the proportion of purchases in Utah by the defense manufacturing plants is also small, largely

TABLE VII   CHANGES IN MILITARY RESEARCH AND PRODUCTION CONTRACTS FROM
1958 TO 1962 IN THE TEN STATES WITH HIGHEST PERCENTAGE OF INCREASE

Research		Production	
Rank	Percent of change	Rank	Percent of change
Wisconsin	1,335	South Dakota	769
Utah	833	West Virginia	454
West Virginia	482	Utah	293
Florida	148	Colorado	176
Colorado	135	Tennessee	130
Washington	100	Florida	108
California	64	Virginia	102
Massachusetts	56	Minnesota	90
New Jersey	46	Massachusetts	78
Maryland	40	Louisiana	72

* Only states with $50 million or more in research contracts and $100 million or more in production contracts.
SOURCE: *Five-Year Trends in Defense Procurement*, 27 and 17.

because most of the needed hardware is not produced within the state. As a consequence "spin-off" jobs created by defense spending in Utah are only about two-fifths as many per initial defense job as in California.

VI

Defense spending in Utah, unlike California, has had only a modest effect on Utah's population growth pattern. Net migration figures measured by the vital statistics method (births minus deaths equal natural increase, and the difference between natural increase and actual or estimated census figures in any given year is the net migration) indicate Utah lost through out-migration about 60,000 persons from 1910 to 1940. From 1940 through 1946, using the same method, this pattern was reversed, and Utah gained approximately 9,000 new residents. By comparison, California gained over two million new residents. From 1947 to 1954 Utah reverted to her traditional pattern of out-migration, losing an estimated 16,000 persons, but thereafter until 1964 Utah experienced a net in-migration of about 18,000, unquestionably owing to the establishment of the missile industry.

Of the factors affecting Utah's migrational patterns, defense spending is clearly the most significant. In fact, from 1940 to 1964 there is a very high mathematical correlation between direct defense employment changes and school enrollment changes. In general, when defense spending has been substantial, Utah has experienced a net in-migration; when defense spending has been cut the state has lost population. Indeed, for the past 55 years, defense expenditures *alone* have made it possible for Utah to attract outside residents in significant numbers.

Most of these newcomers went to Salt Lake, Davis, and Box Elder counties, settled in the better residential areas, built expensive homes, and raised considerably the personal income and median education levels wherever they went. Of Thiokol's salaried employees, 80 per cent were recruited from out of state; the same is true of Brigham City and to a lesser extent of Ogden.

The most marked impact of defense spending on a local community probably occurred in Brigham City, located north of Ogden and the city closest to Utah's largest defense plant. Over 5,000 people migrated to this small northern Utah community, doubling the assessed valuation of the city and skyrocketing many building lots to ten times their previous value. The quality of local government was raised, the culture diversified, and the Mormon point of view was less frequently taught in the local schools (after complaints were made). Hundreds of small dairy and chicken farmers quit the land for higher pay at Thiokol, credit was liberalized, personal debt increased markedly, and optimism abounded. In 1964, by way of contrast, because Thiokol had rapidly cut back its labor force, uncertainty hung over the city, unfinished new homes stood vacant, and the ambitious once again began moving to greener pastures.

Finally, defense spending has had a special effect on southeastern Utah. The AEC subsidies to the uranium industry touched off a vast mineral search in San Juan and Grand counties in the early 1950's. Hundreds flocked to that remote region, doubling and tripling population in some villages. When it became evident that these towns could not handle such an influx, the federal government granted them additional funds for water mains and other improvements. Similar subsidies were granted Weber and Davis counties, where two-thirds of the state's federal aid to impacted school districts has gone.

CONCLUSIONS

The impact of defense spending in California and Utah since 1946 has been enormous. It amounts to an estimated $73 billion directly, probably more than $100 billion in California if indirect income is included, and possibly as much as $4 billion in Utah. In both instances these expenditures were made for essentially non-political reasons, contrary to widespread and, particularly, eastern popular opinion. In each state defense expenditures were highly concentrated in four urban-industrial counties, but the money spent there raised considerably the average income of the state as a whole. More important, defense spending has been the primary reason for the extraordinarily rapid expansion of industry and population in California since World War II and the more temporary growth of industry and in-migration to Utah during the late 1950's and early 1960's. Without these massive outlays, California's manufacturing growth since World War II would probably have been about one-third, other things being equal, and her net in-migration about one-half its present level. Under the same circumstances the Beehive

State very probably would have reverted to her "traditional" pattern of out-migration.

A comparison of California's and Utah's experience suggests furthermore that the impact of defense spending will be considerably larger where defense monies are funneled into manufacturing plants than where the money is spent on military bases and depots. Large, sophisticated, industrial states moreover may already have established an insurmountable lead in competence compared with smaller, developing states. This was, for example, evident when California's competence in aircraft production gave her the edge nationally in missile production. It is becoming even more apparent in relation to space research administered by NASA. Whereas Utah might compete to a very modest degree with California in missiles contracts, she has received virtually no contracts for space research. In neither case, however, is it inevitable, as was commonly feared in the 1950's, that sharply reduced defense spending necessarily brings a spiral of unemployment and instability beyond the locale of direct investment.

If California's and Utah's experiences are typical of other western states (or any state for that matter), one can say that once defense money is invested in an area—for whatever reason—it tends to stabilize there. Like ice on a pond, defense spending tends to freeze on the top layer of the industrial-urban complex and to concentrate in one corner of the pond. In the instant study defense spending was concentrated in only four counties in each state. Reductions in defense spending can and do depress the local economy of small states and especially isolated communities, but new defense programs seem to replace cutbacks more often than not in larger states. In neither case, however, is there a clear-cut correlation between spending and multipliers, either up or down.

Finally, whether defense spending in California and Utah has lessened the likelihood of disarmament, limited national educational and public welfare goals, drawn scientists away from peaceful pursuits, or in other ways changed our way of living are questions beyond the scope of this paper. What I have attempted to show here is that these massive defense budgets, although only the most recent of a long history of federal expenditures, are a new but far more potent historical development in the Far West which has already produced momentous economic and demographic change. Indeed, if the impact of defense spending in California and Utah is typical of what has happened in the other strongly defense-oriented western states (Alaska, Hawaii, Colorado, Arizona, and New Mexico), and if it is also at least comparable to the moderately defense-oriented western states (Washington, Nevada, Montana, and Wyoming), then it is entirely possible that defense spending will loom as the single most important economic and demographic factor in the history of the Far East during the past two decades.

3] The Negative Consequences of Defense Spending

DURING A 1962 Senate-committee discussion on how the United States uses its technical talent, Senator Hubert Humphrey burst forth with this critique:

> In Germany, 85%—85 cents out of every research dollar is private, and less than 15 per cent goes into military and space. Eighty-five cents of that goes into the civilian economy, so that today the German plant competition for world markets of civilian goods is being automated, modernized, equipped in the latest and best fashion, and new products are developing, while we are developing new wrappings. We are the greatest packagers in the world. We package them beautifully. We have an artistic capacity second to none in cellophane wrappings, foils, and so forth, but the German is developing the thing inside the package.
>
> In Japan, it is about 85 to 15 again. That is a rough estimate. Eighty-five cents out of every research dollar is private and going into the civilian economy, with huge capital investments going into the Japanese civilian economy.
>
> In England, which also has a low rate of economic growth, as does our country, 60 cents out of every research dollar is governmental and goes into military and space, atomic energy, and 40 cents out of that research dollar goes into the private sector. . . .
>
> This poses some problems here . . . the fact is that scientific manpower, technological and scientific research, moneys and the facilities, attract capital, because that is where the money is to be made; that is where the new product is to come from; that is where you need the new plant, the new facility. . . .
>
> What is happening to our civilian economy as we plow more and more of our scientific personnel, our brains, into the military and into space and into atomic energy for military purposes? Where are we going to end up in this trade competition with these Belgians and these Dutch, who are clever, and the Germans who are very clever, who are spending more money for civilian aspects and will develop products cheaper, better, and more serviceable? Our rate of economic growth is nothing to be proud of. Look at the Italians, who put very, very little money into military—very, very little. We are paying the cost of their military expenditures. They put 90 cents of their research dollar into the civilian economy. They talk about a miracle of Italian economy. It proves that if you put enough brains to work on something with money, you get it done.

FROM *Our Depleted Society* by Seymour Melman. Copyright © 1965 by Seymour Melman. Reprinted by permission of Holt, Rinehart and Winston, Inc.

Humphrey's worry about the nation as a whole is underlined by the troubles of firms which cannot find needed research talent. These are civilian industries—the part of American industry that has not shared in the cost-hardly-matters affluence of the defense contractors.

On August 9, 1963, the *Wall Street Journal* reported:

> . . . Top research men in industry reason this way: Frantic bidding, by space and military contractors, for scientists and engineers is creating a big shortage for industry. This scarcity, along with the skyrocketing salaries it is provoking, is bringing almost to a halt the hitherto rapid growth of company-supported research. This development hampers efforts to develop new products and processes for the civilian economy.
>
> And it's not just the moon race they question. In general, they wonder about the wisdom of the nation's continually increasing concentration of research effort on Government-sponsored projects.
>
> Samuel Lebner, vice president of Du Pont Company, puts it this way: "Government research programs serve as a brake on research in the private sector." Even if corporations had unlimited money to spend, they could not find the personnel to expand research indefinitely, Mr. Lebner says.

> . . . The space program alone could gobble up nearly all of the 30,000 new professional workers expected to enter research this year if Commerce Department calculations are correct. Personnel working on Government research contracts rose 317% to 190,000 between 1954 and 1961, while industry increased its private research payrolls only 30% to 130,000.
>
> While the need for technical manpower is expanding, the growth in supply is slowing. The demand for new engineers alone now runs close to 60,000 a year, but only about 33,700 will be graduated this year, down from as many as 38,134 in 1959. While accurate figures are not available, the situation appears to be nearly as acute in the physical sciences such as chemistry and physics.
>
> Not surprisingly, many companies report they are falling far short of their goals in their recruiting drives.
>
> Xerox Corporation which is trying to expand its research and development in line with booming sales of its office copiers, fell short of its 1962 goal by about one-third and so far this year is lagging by about the same amount. Du Pont says it probably will get only 75% to 80% of the 1,100 new technical graduates it is seeking this year. Adds the research manager of a major oil producer: "Like most companies, we haven't met our goals. The growth rate in our department has been up and down with the availability of technical personnel and right now it's down."
>
> Many companies also are faced with the problem of holding present staffs against recruiting for Government projects. "A major space contractor put a lab right next to one of ours in Los Angeles and hired

away 20% of our staff at a 15% premium," complains Borg-Warner's
Mr. Collier. . . .

. . . Minneapolis-Honeywell Regulator Co. says unfilled openings for
technical specialists have forced delay of its study of the nature of flame,
which it considers vital to its basic heat control business. According to
Mr. Lebner of Du Pont, in recent months three of the company's 12
industrial departments have said "they can't push as rapidly as they're
being urged because they don't have the people." Joseph C. Wilson,
President of Xerox, says lack of personnel last year meant "we didn't get
to start some projects we wanted to."

   Not all companies attribute slower growth in research and development directly to unfilled jobs. Many say big expansions can't be justified
at this time by the profit possibilities from research. Part of this concern
over profit potential reflects rising research costs, stemming primarily
from the bidding up of salaries. . . .

These criticisms come from firms with major reputations and large and
continuing budgets for research and development. DuPont, Xerox, and
Minneapolis-Honeywell, are the sort of firms that normally serve as magnets
for high-grade research talent. These are not the complaints of small firms.

The rationing of engineers and scientists into military and allied activities
takes place by means of systematic salary differentials that were disclosed in
June, 1963, by the American Society of Mechanical Engineers. A survey of
engineering salaries showed that for an engineer with 10 years' experience,
machinery-producing industries pay $9,300 on the average, while the aero-
space industries pay $11,500, on the average.

By 1963, two out of three research scientists and engineers were working
directly or indirectly for the space or defense agencies of the Federal
Government.

What has been the impact of this concentration? From 1940–52, there was
a continuous relationship between growth in research performed by industry,
and growth in Gross National Product. From 1952 onward, there was a
sharp break with the previous pattern. Although spending for research rose
steeply after 1952, there was a sharp drop in the related rate of growth in
total goods and services produced. The reason for this is that an overwhelming part of the research increase was for military and space programs.
Spending in these spheres differs fundamentally from spending in the civilian
area of the economy, because the military goods and services, whatever worth
may be attached to them, do not contribute to further production.

Even though those doing military research use their pay to function as
consumers, the product of their working time, once created, does not, like
civilian products, become an input for further production. Therefore, as
research became more and more militarily oriented after 1952, there was
no parallel rate of general economic growth.

Officers of the Federal Commerce Department have become sensitive to
the technological side of the industrial depletion process. They know that

Japan and Europe, free of the space and defense effort borne by the United States, are gearing their technical resources to industrial needs. Sitting in technological backwaters, as a result, are entire U.S. industries like textiles and apparel, food processing, building and construction, machine-tool, forging, and the machinery industry generally.

By 1963 some of President Kennedy's associates were aware of technological deficiencies in major civilian industries. Dr. J. Herbert Holloman, Assistant Secretary of Commerce, found that:

> Switzerland, Sweden, Japan, and West Germany each spend a larger percentage of their resources (labor force or Gross National Product) on Research and Development that aids the civilian economy than does the United States. Furthermore, . . . in West Germany, the number of scientists and engineers engaged in Research and Development that benefits the civilian economy is a much larger fraction of the labor force than is the case in the United States.
>
> At present, only the largest firms in the largest industries can afford to maintain the technical capability that leads to new products, processes and improved productivity. In many other important industries, the individual firms are so small and the profit margins so limited that it is next to impossible for them to hire and support the technical staff which would be needed to develop and apply new, complex technology for their industry.
>
> Such segments of the economy are the textile, lumber, leather, wood and clay products, machine-tools, foundries and casting, and the railroads industry. These segments have not supported or performed much Research and Development, and, consequently are neither well-situated to participate in the advances in technology generated by the other Research and Development efforts (industrial as well as military), nor to maintain their relative economic strength internationally. These industries have often been vulnerable targets for foreign competition.

How did this happen? Research and development spending in the United States totaled $6.4 billion in 1955, and grew to $20 billion by 1964. Out of the Gross National Product for 1964, $20 billion was expended for research and develpoment and $15 billon of that was an expenditure of the Federal Government. The figure indicates that without formal planning Research and Development have been undergoing a process of nationalization.

This growth period has been characterized mainly by the expansion of the military and space programs. In 1964, five government departments in the table accounted for 96% of all Federal research spending. In the Federal Government, during the period 1950–65, research and development expenditures by the Department of Defense grew tenfold, from $652 million to $7 billion. In the space field, the growth from 1950 to 1965 was hundredfold, from $54 million to $5 billion. The Atomic Energy Commission budgeted $221 million for research and development in 1950, and $1.5 billion in 1965. Other research and development activities grew during this period.

FEDERAL RESEARCH AND DEVELOPMENT BUDGETS, 1940–65

[In millions of dollars]

Fiscal Year	Department of Defense	National Aeronautics and Space Administration	Atomic Energy Commission	Department of Health, Education, and Welfare	National Science Foundation	Office of Scientific Research and Development
1940	26	2		3		
1945	513	24	859*	3		114
1950	652	54	221	40		
1955	2,630	74	385	70	9	
1960	5,654	401	986	324	58	
1965 (est.)	7,107	4,990	1,557	796	204	

* Manhattan project.

While the proportional change in the nonmilitary fields is significant, the magnitude of sums spent is drastically different. Thus, research for health, education, and welfare grew from $40 million, in 1950, to $800 million, in 1955. Expenditures by the National Science Foundation, established to sponsor research, especially in basic science and related fields, grew from $1 million in 1952, to $204 million in 1965. By 1965, however, about 90% of the Federal Government's outlays for research and development lay in the military and related fields.

While the Government's budgets for military and allied research have been booming, there has been no parallel proportionate growth in the number of trained people available. A House of Representatives Committee on Government Research in 1964 noted: "It is significant that the number of individuals capable of performing this urgent development increases by only 7% annually, while the annual growth in Federal research and development expenditures has averaged 15%." This contrast measures the rationing pressure that has been exerted on the research and development manpower sources of the country through the growth of government expenditures in these fields.

The growing concentration of engineering talent in government-directed defense and space programs is sharply revealed by the impacts on technological developments in many fields. This subject was explored by an eminent committee of the Engineers' Joint Council in its report on "The Nation's Engineering Research Needs, 1965–1985." Published in 1962, this report has a table of contents that reads like an analysis of the relatively depleted sectors of technology in American society.

First, the committee noted that there is a significant imbalance in the national technical effort. Many industries have been left without resources for developing their technology either in terms of products or production methods.

Second, the committee found that there has been relatively little increase in research on energy and raw material resources. (I am told by colleagues in electrical engineering that it is hard to find university teachers for fields like power engineering, which have been left aside while electronics burgeoned.) Research into urban environmental problems has been substantially neglected. The same is true for national and metropolitan transportation systems. In that context, for example, the depletion of the railroad system is particularly notable. The engineering of hospital and medical services has not been developed, although a reasonable understanding of the problem indicates that many economies can be made, and are even essential, if competent medical care is to be provided for all citizens. For example, there is no excuse for nurses spending a substantial part of their work time in essentially unproductive activity.

Educational services have been neglected. The technological problems of developing nations receive fragmentary attention in various universities. Furthermore, the EJC report notes that many possible applications of engineering to biological systems are yet to be explored.

Finally, they note that there are problems of engineering education and technical information involving, for example, how to operate many large libraries as the number of books and journals rises at a geometric rate.

The EJC, in its detailed report on how research and development resources are used in the United States, drew this conclusion:

> The needs of people and society are not given sufficient attention in the allocation of research and development funds. Non-defense agencies do not have research and development programs that relate broadly to their entire mission or that reflect the enormous impact of technology on the lives of people and social organizations. It has been far easier to win support for an $80-million-dollar program on high energy physics, than $10 million dollars for research and development on national transportation problems. It has been far easier to win support for a $30-million-dollar program in atmospheric sciences than $5 million dollars for research and development on problems of aid to the developing countries. The need-oriented problems associated with the impact of technology on society and the revolution of rising expectations do not conform to the patterns associated with man's scientific knowledge of the physical world. Yet, orderly empirical engineering developments have been possible in the absence of a comprehensive theoretical science. Need-oriented research and development programs could make contributions to the alleviation of problems raised by the spread of technology in the modern world.

. . . .

The space program, featuring a manned landing on the moon (the Apollo program), is a major demonstration of how Cold War pressures operate on science and technology. The manned moon landing will cost between $20 and $40 billion—let us say $30 billion. From the standpoint of scientific return, little is expected from this effort. The space program includes launching

a series of satellite vehicles around the moon as well as various instru-
mented, unmanned lunar landings that will produce a long array of scientific information. The incremental contribution of the manned landings to
science will be "geological exploration"—though prior unmanned vehicles
are scheduled to take core samples of the moon crust and return them to
earth. Why then a $30 billion manned landing?

The record discloses that the decision by President Kennedy to race for a
lunar landing was a political decision for a political purpose, and had little
relation to purely scientific considerations. The Space Science Board, established by the National Academy of Science in 1958, gave manned lunar
landing low priority in a schedule of space-science activities.

After the disastrous Bay of Pigs adventure and subsequent Soviet space
flights, President Kennedy gave the man-to-the-moon project political priority. Since then about 75% of the $5.2 billion 1964 space budget has been
used in pursuit of this program.

From the standpoint of science there has been a warping effect from this
decision, as defined by the report on *The Integrity of Science:*

> In general, scientific observations required for the planning of the
> manned landing are not assigned higher priorities than other studies
> which are of greater scientific interest but not essential to the develop-
> ment of the technology needed for the Apollo project. Therefore, the
> pattern for development of scientific research in space has been altered
> significantly by the essentially political decision to undertake the Apollo
> program.
>
> This procedure is seriously at variance with important precepts of
> scientific experimentation and technology. The preferable order of
> events is: basic scientific investigation, technological application based
> on the resultant basic knowledge, social use of the technological inno-
> vations. In the Apollo program this sequence has been reversed, so that
> a program for a particular technological achievement has been commit-
> ted, even as to the date of its accomplishment, in advance of the orderly
> acquisition of the related basic knowledge. The Apollo program, in its
> present form, does not appear to be based on the orderly, systematic
> extension of basic scientific investigation.

We are also, all of us, sponsoring a gamble with the lives of the men
aboard. However much money, talent, and time is devoted to doing things
the best-known way, it remains that an estimated 22,000 separate acts must be
carried off without flaw in performing the projected manned earth-moon-
earth journey. Even a very small percentage of error could produce tragedy.

There are now substantive reasons for doubting that man can survive
after space flight over an extended period. Professor Marcel Florkin of Liege
University, a member of the international scientific Committee on Space
Research, announced on December 23, 1964, that the consensus among
scientists was that weightless flight by man would be impossible for more
than five or six days. He indicated that Soviet scientists had produced
photographs showing abnormalities in human cell division attributable to

the sustained weightlessness some of their astronauts have experienced. Normal cell division is a vital life process, and abnormal division can be lethal. In Project Apollo the astronauts landing on the moon will be weightless for less than three days on each leg of the journey. A third man, in a moon-orbiting vehicle while his colleagues land, would be weightless about a week.

The Space Science Board, on November 17, 1964, issued a new policy recommendation on research in space. With respect to manned moon exploration the Board wrote:

> Aware of the parallel criteria of scientific and intellectual importance *and* of significance to the national interest, the Board summarizes its recommendations on the primary national objectives in the field of space science for the 1971–1985 period as follows: *Exploration of the planets with particular emphasis on Mars*
>
> (a) This objective includes both physical and biological investigations, and especially the search for extraterrestrial life.
>
> (b) The experimentation should be carried out largely by unmanned vehicles while the solution of difficult biomedical and bioengineering problems proceeds at a measured pace so that toward the end of this epoch (1985) we shall be ready for manned planetary exploration.
>
> (c) Alternatives to the Mars and planetary exploration goal—(i) extensive manned lunar exploration (possibly including lunar base construction) and (ii) major manned orbiting space station and laboratory program—are not regarded as primary goals, because they have less scientific significance. However, both have sufficient merit to warrant parallel programs but of lower priority.

Professor Polykarp Kusch of Columbia University and Nobel Laureate in Physics, commented on the Apollo crash program from the standpoint of classically understood requirements for competent inquiry:

> It is my belief that the present space program attempts too much too fast. There is not enough time for profound thought, for imagination to play over the demanding problems that occur. Someone has said to me, in a discussion of the space program, that the attempts that are being made to explore space are similar to those that would have been made had the physicists of the prewar era attempted a program of research involving a billion-volt proton accelerator. The scientific ideas that allow us presently to build such machines had not yet appeared; conceivably that machine could have been built, but only with very much greater difficulty than present machines propose. The important problems that have engaged in mind and efforts (sic) of the generation of physicists now in their prime were too dimly understood to allow the kind of effective inquiry currently undertaken. Much of the auxiliary gear that is central to the observation of high energy phenomena had not yet been invented. Finally, the extraordinarily effective guidelines that the theorists of physics develop had not yet begun to appear. (June

10, 1963, to the U.S. Senate, Committee on Aeronautical and Space Sciences.)

Meanwhile, spending $5 billion a year in one set of projects stirs up the economy of the localities that are directly involved. The space agency estimates that 20,000 firms and 300,000 people eventually will be involved in the project: $2 billion each year in direct salaries alone. Already 130,000 men are working on the spacecraft program itself; 20,000–40,000 substantial homes have been built near the $150 million Houston, Texas, Manned Space Center.

In 1962 Dr. Hugh L. Dryden, Deputy Director of NASA, stated that by 1970 one fourth of American scientists and engineers would be engaged in space activities. Skeptics may note that in July, 1964, a random sample of 2,000 members of the American Association for the Advancement of Science showed 12% of them receiving Federal support related to space activities. Meanwhile the space program appetite for technical talent cannot be satisfied—even at the cost of depleting many American activities. With relatively high-paying jobs as a lure, space contractors have been attracting foreign scientists and engineers. About 43,000 scientists and engineers have come to the United States since 1949, thereby imposing our priorities on other nations.

Why this massive space effort? James E. Webb, Director of the National Aeronautics and Space Administration has declared:

> Far more is involved in the Apollo program than the propaganda or prestige value of insuring that an American is first to set foot on the moon. Rather, we are concerned with the strength and the image of the United States as the acknowledged leader in all areas of science and technology.
>
> Exploration of the moon has been selected as the focal point of our present efforts in space partly because, by its very nature, it commands worldwide public interest. But it also has been selected because it is the first major objective in which we have an excellent chance of being first, because it promises to add to our knowledge of the laws of nature, the forces mankind strives to understand and use, the origin of the universe, and because its accomplishment requires mastery of a broad spectrum of science and technology on which a growing capability to operate in space and increase efficiency on earth must rest.
>
> Those who view the lunar program simply as a "propaganda" effort fail to grasp that not only our prestige, but our capacity for constructive international leadership, our economic and military capacity for technological improvement, depend upon our ability to achieve acknowledged superiority in science and technology, and to use this capability in our own behalf and that of our allies.
>
> With a billion people already allied against us, and the uncommitted and emerging nations weighing events that will affect their own future welfare, the United States must present the image of a can-do nation, with which they can confidently align their futures.

Two sets of issues are at stake here: first, the meaning of the space program for science; second, the political significance of the effort. The space agency's 1964 budget for basic research was about twice the budget of the National Science Foundation—whose responsibility for encouraging science is broadly defined. While the space agency's spending for basic research will surely produce new knowledge in the fields that are tackled, it remains that the space projects, as defined, set constraints to what the agency is interested in. These constraints are automatically understood both by the agency's administrators and by the scientists who apply for grant funds. Consequently, the scientists, seeking success in their applications for funds, ask themselves: What is NASA interested in? Asking that question is a distortion of the priority that free inquiry needs. For the integrity of science the investigator must be free to ask: What do I think is the next research step for unfolding new knowledge in a field that is interesting to me and to other scientific colleagues?

On the political side, concern for America's total strength should take into account the depleting effects caused elsewhere by the concentration of talent and capital in defense-space work. The manned lunar landing as a mark of constructive international leadership may be gauged against alternatives such as acting to reduce hunger or developing and building good quality mass-produced housing that is desperately needed at home and abroad. A Civil Rights bill or murder without punishment in the American South are more influential than space shots in affecting the judgment of most of mankind about the moral or political merits of American society.

There is little warrant for the prediction that the Apollo project could be decisive politically—in winning "the battle for the minds of men." American political positions in Asia and Africa are not controlled by the success of space projects. Soviet decisions to move toward profit incentives in industry and agriculture have little to do with rank in an international rocket weightlifting contest. The movement of Eastern European countries toward greater autonomy and less Soviet control is not determined by the crash program for lunar landing.

In my judgment the "space race" altogether is a form of pseudo-challenge. It is an evasion of the substantive issues which deeply concern most of the people of the earth: How can one organize and act for rapid economic development, so that the potentials of science and technology can be realized for man? Which social order best combines efficiency with human freedom?

How shall we look to ourselves after spending $30 billion on an operation that we shall see as a seven-day TV spectacular? It will be spectacular, and we can only admire the display of technical ingenuity and the bravery of the astronauts. But will it be worth $30 billion? Won't we and many millions of people throughout the world wonder: What sort of society is this that could devote so much wealth to so trivial a purpose?

Dr. Warren Weaver, distinguished mathematician and former president of the American Academy of Science, has drawn up this shopping list as an alternative to spending $30 billion on the Apollo program:

	Cost ($ billions)
10% yearly salary raise for 10 years to all U.S. teachers	9.8
$10 million to each of 200 small colleges in U.S.	2.0
Complete 7-year fellowships to train 50,000 scientists and engineers, at $4,000/man/year	1.4
$200 million to create 10 new medical schools	2.0
Build and endow complete universities, with liberal arts, science, engineering, medical and agricultural faculties, in each of 53 nations	13.2
Establish 3 new foundations, like the Rockefeller Foundation	1.5
For public education on science	.1
(or the cost of a manned lunar landing)	= $30.0

Serious doubts about the wisdom of the space race have not been restricted to some leading scientists or particular political parties. Democrats have affirmed that being first in productive achievement on earth is more significant—politically and humanly—than being first on the moon. When the 1964 NASA budget was under consideration in the Congress, a staff paper of the Senate Republican Policy Committee asked:

> Is it more important to have a man on the moon than to conquer cancer which will take the lives of over 40 million Americans now living?
> Is being first more important than insuring an adequate water source for our great metropolitan centers?
> Is a fistful of lunar dust meaningful to the 17 million Americans who, we are told, go to bed hungry each night?

President Kennedy, too, touched on this problem, when he wrote in his Economic Report to the nation for 1963, that the United States has "paid a price by sharply limiting the scarce scientific and engineering resources available to the civilian sectors of the American economy."

4] The Positive Consequences of Defense Spending

WE, AS AMERICANS, have the highest standard of living in the world. We take for granted the quantity and quality of the food we eat and the clothes we wear. We work a relatively short work week, yet we are able to purchase homes, automobiles, televisions, and an amount of luxuries that defy

FROM *The National Space Program—Its Values and Benefits,* Staff Study for the Subcommittee on NASA Oversight, U.S. House, 90th Cong., 1st Sess. (GPO, 1967), pp. 6–9.

number or description. We have an educational system where any American, if capable, can receive a college education at little or no cost. We have relatively inexpensive transportation, mail service, and a host of other services which make our daily life more enjoyable.

It has not always been thus, nor is it likely to remain so unless we as a Nation continue to move forward. For in this land of plenty there are trouble spots on the horizon. Some of our cities are rapidly becoming areas inhabited only by the very rich and the very poor and the concentration of people in and around cities is constantly increasing. We are polluting our streams, rivers, and the very air we breathe. And under the constant stress of an ever-increasing population, we are rapidly using up our national resources of timber and croplands and replacing them with ever-expanding lanes of concrete and asphalt.

During recent hearings before a subcommittee of the Senate Government Operations Committee, New York Mayor John Lindsay estimated that it would require an expenditure of $50 billion to remedy the urban problems confronting New York City. Other mayors and Governors testifying before the subcommittee expressed similar thoughts.

As recently as December 1966, Detroit Mayor Jerome P. Cavanagh, president of the National League of Cities, pleaded in a speech before the league's 43rd Annual Congress of Cities "for the rebirth of the American City." Criticizing space and defense spending, Cavanagh indicated that this money could be better spent on urban redevelopment.

No thinking person would question that something must be done to eradicate the blight settling upon our urban areas. However, robbing the future to pay the for the present is not the answer. Nor is money alone the answer—even amounts running into the many billions of dollars. Also needed are more jobs, more housing, better education, and better transportation, and this in turn demands that we create new industries, new technology, and new know-how.

THE SYSTEMS APPROACH

Currently under study by the administration is a proposal to create a quasi-public corporation modeled along the same lines as the Communications Satellite Corp. which would attract and marshall private resources to invest in cities. Testifying before the Ribicoff subcommittee on December 5, 1966, Walter P. Reuther, president of the United Auto Workers, called for the creation of a nonprofit corporation which would conduct intensive research into how to utilize modern technology to make cities a better place to live.

On a much larger scope, a number of bills were introduced during the 89th Congress to create a National Commission on Public Management whose task it would be to study the scope of Government activity with an eye toward applying the "systems" approach to problems like pollution, crime, traffic management, education and other areas of Federal activity.

In introducing his bill, Representative Frank J. Horton said: "The kind of data and planning I am speaking of, while it is today employed by the Department of Defense, the National Aeronautics and Space Administration, and a few other executive bodies, is not presently applied to even a fraction of the public management problems which require such comprehensive approach."

NASA's demonstrated ability to manage programs involving many thousands of people and the flow of literally millions of components to the launch pad as evidenced by every successful mission should find application in solving many of the complicated and large scale problems of today.

ECONOMIC BENEFITS OF NASA PROGRAM

A recent report of the U.S. Department of Labor on "Technological Trends in Major American Industries" discusses the nine broad areas of technological innovation which will have the greatest impact upon our world of tomorrow. Those areas are—

(1) Computerization of data processing;
(2) Greater instrumentation and process control;
(3) Trend toward increased mechanization;
(4) Progress in communication;
(5) Advances in metalworking operations;
(6) Developments in energy and power;
(7) Advances in transportation;
(8) New materials, products, and processes; and
(9) Managerial and related techniques.

All of these trends cannot be traced to the space program itself, but they can be traced to a considerable degree to the Federal support of research and development which in fiscal year 1967 is approaching the $16 billion level. These funds are making the advances in technology and new knowledge which will have implications for many years to come.

In the case of NASA, advances in the fields of communications, weather detection, navigation, and earth resources planning will have the most immediate impact upon the lives of everyone. Further out in time, some people are talking about using the weightless vacuum of space for industrial research, medical research, manufacturing, and even tourism. In fact, the 13th annual meeting of the American Astronautical Society to be held in Dallas, Tex., in May 1967 will be devoted to the "commercial utilization of space." Similar meetings of the American Institute of Aeronautics and Astronautics and the National Academy of Sciences to be held in 1967 also will be devoted to the practical applications of space technology.

EFFECT UPON COMMUNITIES

While this report will be devoted in large measure to the future of space research, it must also be remembered that the NASA program has a tremendous impact upon our present economy. As of June 30, 1966, NASA employed 35,708 personnel, and it has been estimated that over 400,000 additional personnel are employed on the space program by the various industrial contractors. When one considers each person as a member of a family unit and then adds the many people that provide supporting services to a community of this size—the food store personnel, the gas station attendants, teachers, bus drivers, construction workers, bankers, each himself a member of a family unit—it would not be surprising to say that perhaps well in excess of 2 million people are dependent upon the space program for their source of livelihood and standard of living.

It might also be pointed out that 94 percent of the $5 billion in NASA procurements during the year ending June 30, 1966 went to private industry, and another 4 percent went to educational and other nonprofit institutions. Every State in the Union and the District of Columbia participated in NASA's prime contract awards of $25,000 or over. This represents 1,565 business firms, 189 universities, and 52 other nonprofit organizations. Five percent of the awards were placed in labor surplus areas located in 17 States, and 6 percent of the awards went directly to small businesses.

Subcontracting effected a further distribution of prime contract awards. Eighty-eight of NASA's major prime contractors reported that their larger subcontract awards on the NASA program had gone to 2,017 different subcontractors, over 60 percent of which were outside the State in which the prime contractor was located.

In summary then, the national space program does have, and will continue to have, a powerful influence upon the economy of the United States. It provides jobs, new technology, and new knowledge. If the United States is able to maintain the technological pace it has set in recent years, there is no reason why it cannot solve some of the problems coming upon the American scene and be able to give all Americans a higher standard of living.

5] The Consequences of Disarmament

T HIS STATEMENT analyzes the portions of the American economy which are heavily dependent on defense work and indicates some of the opportunities for and obstacles to transferring defense industry resources to civilian applications.

SUMMARY

(1) The conversion of defense industry resources to peacetime pursuits would present both a tremendous opportunity as well as a problem of major proportions.

(2) The heart of the adjustment problem would center on four industries, the bulk of whose sales go to the Government: ordnance, aircraft, ship construction, and electronics.

(3) The adjustment problem would be compounded because these four

FROM Murray L. Weidenbaum, "The Transferability of Defense Industry Resources to Civilian Uses," in *Convertability of Space and Defense Resources to Civilian Needs: A Search for New Employment Potentials*, Subcommittee on Employment and Manpower, Committee on Labor and Public Welfare, U.S. Senate, 89th Cong., 2nd Sess. (GPO, 1964), pp. 848–55. Used by permission.

industries cluster in a few regions—notably the west coast—where they represent a major part of the industrial base of these areas.

(4) Moreover, the resources used by these industries for defense work are extremely specialized, relatively minor portions of either the people or the facilities have ever been "converted" to civilian work in the past.

(5) With few exceptions, the large specialized defense companies have not been successful in utilizing their technical capability to penetrate civilian markets.

(6) Hence, Government actions which have been suggested to assist defense contractors in commercial diversification to offset a defense cutback may be of limited effectiveness.

(7) In view of the concentration of the Nation's R. & D. in these companies, attention might be given to transferring some of these resources to other parts of the economy with possible long-term benefits for the "under-researched" industries.

(8) The Federal Government could encourage all private industry to increase its demand for R. & D. through such mechanisms as a tax credit, joint financing, loans and loan guarantees, and technical assistance.

(9) A long-range national program to encourage the development of alternate demands for any potentially surplus defense industry resources would require: (a) developing public policy on utilizing the resources that would become available, and the respective roles of industry and Government, (b) assigning responsibilities to the various Government agencies involved, defense as well as nondefense, and (c) developing mechanisms, such as those suggested, for carrying out these responsibilities both in the private sector as well as the public sector.

INTRODUCTION

> But while strongly insisting on the great advantages of peace, and the reduction of military and naval expenditure, it is quite as essential to assure that so long as present conditions last, a well-organized and effective system of defense is a necessary part of State expenditure—to maintain a due balance between the excessive demands of alarmists and military officials, and the undue reductions in outlay sought by the advocates of economy, is one of the difficult tasks of the statesman.—C. F. Bastable, "Public Finance," 1895.

This paper is based on the assumption—which may be hypothetical—that a major shift will occur in the size and/or composition of the defense budget. I am not recommending any specific budget levels, other than those necessary to maintain the national security.

If a major reduction in defense spending is consistent with the national security, it would represent both a tremendous opportunity and also a yet unsolved problem of major proportions.

It is quite simple to take, for example, a hypothetical reduction in defense spending of, say, $10 billion and point out that these funds could be used to double the annual expenditure level in the United States on men's and boys' clothing, or to give each household a brand new refrigerator, or to permit a reduction in Federal income taxes of $200 for each taxpayer.

However, human wants are insatiable. A "wish list" of alternatives to defense expenditures might readily encompass most categories of public as well as private demand. The real problem is on the supply side—the limitations to resource mobility and the barriers that a business firm faces in entering or even in trying to leave individual sectors or industries of the economy.

This statement presents some information concerning the supply side—dealing with the lack of mobility in the sector of our Nation's economy devoted to producing goods and services for the defense program.

I will then examine what I interpret to be some of the hard questions involved in determining the alternatives to defense expenditures; namely, what are the practical alternate uses for the resources currently devoted to the defense program? What basic modifications of public policy are required?

THE SPECIALIZED NATURE OF DEFENSE RESOURCES

As a first step in analyzing the specialized nature of defense resources, it is helpful to examine the degree of concentration of defense work in the private economy. Seventy-two percent of the value of the military prime contracts awarded in the fiscal year 1962 went to 100 companies and institutions. Within this amount, seven major industry groups account for over nine-tenths of the value of the contracts awarded—aircraft, electrical and electronic equipment, oil refining, automobiles, construction, rubber, and shipbuilding, in that order.

Fifty-six of the hundred companies are engaged directly in aircraft, missile, and space work, or in electronics and research and development work closely related to aircraft and missile programs. Ten of the hundred are suppliers of aviation gasoline and other petroleum products. Seven each are automotive, shipbuilding, ammunition, and service companies; five are construction firms; and one is a rifle producer.

Of greater significance is the relative importance of defense work to each of these industries and to the companies in these industries. For example, although the oil companies rank high as defense suppliers, military sales only account for about 10 percent of the industry's output and a reduction in defense sales would involve only marginal adjustment problems. In contrast, for four industries, defense work represents from one-half to all of the output. The conversion problems here would clearly be of a totally different order of magnitude. It is likely that the heart of the adjustment problem would center on these industries: ordnance (including missiles), aircraft, shipbuilding, and electronics.

Table 1 is an attempt to show the dependence of individual companies in these and related industries on defense-space orders. Because the proportion of company sales to the Government is not reported by many defense contractors, an approximation method has been used. Essentially, the table shows the amount of prime contracts received from the Department of Defense and the National Aeronautics and Space Administration by the 35 companies with the largest volume of such contracts. The combined defense-space orders of each of these companies is then expressed as a percentage of their sales for their last fiscal year, to provide a rough approximation of the importance of this business to these firms.

The limitations of this approach need to be kept in mind, particularly the fact that the production orders received in a given year normally result in sales in subsequent years. Nevertheless, the data in table 1 show that some major defense contractors derive the bulk of their business from commercial sources, while others are primarily dependent on Government work. Clearly, companies like A.T.&T., Ford, and General Motors devote a relatively small portion of their efforts to defense-space work, while North American Aviation, Republic, and McDonnell are heavily committed.

The adjustment problem would be compounded by the fact that the four cited industries cluster in a few regions of the country and represent a major part of the industrial base of these areas. In seven States the employment in the above four defense-related industries accounts for one-fifth or more of total manufacturing employment, and for a much larger share of the post-war employment growth: Kansas, Washington, California, New Mexico, Connecticut, Arizona, and Utah, in that order.

The concentration is far greater in individual metropolitan areas such as Los Angeles, San Diego, Wichita, and Seattle.

Another aspect of the problem is the very specialized nature of the resources used by the major defense supplying companies. In contrast with the situation during World War II, and even with that during the Korean conflict, a far greater share of defense production today is performed in highly specialized facilities which have been specifically built for the purpose, often at the initiative of the Military Establishment which still retains title to the factories and the equipment in them.

For example, four-fifths or more of the equipment of the armies that took the field at the outbreak of World War I consisted of standard peacetime goods produced in ordinary peacetime production facilities. By 1941, almost one-half of the total material needs of warfare consisted of special-purpose equipment. However, the bulk of this was still material that could be produced by converting ordinary peacetime facilities. Currently, about 90 percent of the material needs of defense consists of specialized equipment which is produced in special facilities built for the purpose.

Moreover, the companies involved were set up for, and their experience is limited to, the design and production of military weapon systems and related aerospace vehicles. As a consequence of the technical requirements of military work, these companies have tremendous numbers of scientists and engineers, compared to the commercial-oriented industries. The typical defense company hires four or five times the number of scientists and engineers than the most technically oriented commercial company to support the same volume of sales.

The National Science Foundation reports that aircraft and missile companies alone employ more scientists and engineers on research and development work than the combined total of the chemical, drug, petroleum, motor vehicle, rubber, and machinery industries.

Company	(1) Defense contracts	(2) NASA contracts	(3) Total (1) + (2)	(4) Company sales[1]	(5) Ratio of orders to total sales (3)/(4)
75 to 100 percent:					
Republic Aviation Corp.	$ 332.8	$ 6.9	$ 339.7	$ 295.8	100.0%
McDonnell Aircraft Corp.	310.9	68.5	379.4	390.7	97.11
Grumman Aircraft Engineering Corp.	303.6	24.6	328.2	357.1	91.91
Lockheed Aircraft Corp.	1,419.5	5.0	1,424.5	1,753.1	81.27
AVCO	323.3	1.4	324.7	414.3	78.37
North American Aviation, Inc.	1,032.5	199.1	1,231.6	1,633.7[2]	75.39[3]
Hughes Aircraft Corp.	234.2	9.2	243.4		
50 to 74 percent:					
Collins Radio Co.	150.1	3.7	153.8	207.8	74.01
Thiokol Chemical Corp.	178.3	.8	179.1	255.8	70.02
Raytheon Co.	406.6		406.6	580.7	70.02
Newport News Shipbuilding & Dry Dock Co.	185.0		185.0	267.3	69.21
Martin Marietta Corp.	802.7	1.8	804.5	1,195.3	67.31
Boeing Co.	1,132.8	15.6	1,148.4	1,768.5	64.94
General Dynamics Corp.	1,196.6	27.9	1,224.5	1,898.4	64.50
Curtiss-Wright Corp.	144.6		144.6	228.7	63.23
United Aircraft Corp.	662.7	34.1	696.8	1,162.1	59.96
Douglas Aircraft Co., Inc.	365.6	68.4	434.0	749.9	57.87
25 to 49 percent:					
American Machine & Foundry Co.	187.3		187.3	415.4	45.09
General Tire & Rubber Co.	366.1	66.4	432.5	959.8	45.06
Northrop Corp.	152.5	1.3	153.8	347.5	44.26
Hercules Powder Co.	181.6		181.6	454.8	39.93
Sperry Rand Corp.	465.6	2.2	467.8	1,182.6	39.56
Bendix Corp.	285.9	19.4	305.3	788.1	38.74
FMC Corp.	160.4		160.4	506.5	31.67
Pan American World Airways, Inc.	146.7		146.7	503.9	29.11
0 to 24 percent:					
International Telephone & Telegraph Corp.	243.6	2.2	245.8	995.5	24.69
General Electric Co.	975.9	23.0	998.9	4,792.7	20.84
Radio Corporation of America	339.6	20.2	359.8	1,742.7	20.65
Westinghouse Electric Corp.	246.0	3.4	249.4	1,954.5	12.76
International Business Machines Corp.	155.5	12.6	168.1	1,925.2	8.73
American Telephone & Telegraph Co.	467.7	10.8	478.5	11,742.4	4.07
Ford Motor Co.	269.1		269.1	8,089.6	3.33
General Motors Corp.	449.0	1.4	450.4	14,640.2	3.08
Standard Oil Co. of New Jersey	180.1		180.1	9,537.3	1.89

[1] Net sales for fiscal year ending during 1962.
[2] Not available.
[3] Estimated from other sources to be in excess of 75 percent.
NOTE: In some cases, it appears that the ratio of defense-space orders to total sales in fiscal year 1962 is not an accurate indicator of the actual ratio of military-space sales to total sales.
SOURCE: M. L. Weidenbaum, Stanford Research Institute, November 1963.

On the assumption that the work performed bears a definite relationship to the source of the funds, a rough approximation can be made as to the number of scientific personnel on defense-space work.

The National Science Foundation reports that 58 percent of the R. & D. expenditures of private industry were financed by the Federal Government in 1962 and that 90 percent of these are contributed by the Department of Defense and the National Aeronautics and Space Administration. Hence, approximately 52 percent of total industry R. & D. (58 percent times 90 percent) is performed for defense-space purposes.

Applying this proportion to the 339,400 engineers and scientists doing research and development work in American industry, as of January 1963, yields the conclusion that 52 percent, or 176,500 were engaged on projects funded by defense-space programs.

Let us examine the extent to which the specialized resources of the defense companies have been utilized in producing goods and services for the commercial economy.

THE LOCKED-IN NATURE OF DEFENSE RESOURCES

Since the end of World War II, many major defense contractors have sought to diversify their operations into commercial lines of business. The motives were numerous and varied over time—to compensate for a declining military market, to offset the fluctuations in military budgets, to enter more profitable areas, and to adjust for shifts within the military market.

These companies attempted to utilize the technological capabilities developed in the course of their military work to design and produce a great variety of commercial items. These included—among many, many others—aluminum sport boats, prosthetic devices, stainless steel caskets, heavy duty land vehicles, adhesives, wall panels, welding equipment, gas turbine engines, and cargo-handling systems. These efforts literally ranged from canoes to computers to coffins.

With one major exception, these diversification attempts have each been relatively small in comparison with military equipment. The exception, of course, is transport aircraft for the commercial airlines. The large jetliners, the DC–8's, the 707's, and the 880's, have each involved large numbers of scientists, engineers, and other employees, and the resultant unit sales prices are comparable with many military products. However, the profit performance on these jet programs has been extremely poor. The losses incurred have both depleted the venture capital available to seek other commercial businesses and have reduced the enthusiasm of other defense companies to diversify.

Other than the few firms selling to the airlines, the large defense suppliers, especially in the aerospace field, have reported commercial sales of 1 or 2 percent, or even less, over the years. The list of abandoned commercial ventures is a long and constantly growing one. The surviving efforts continue generally at marginal levels—either actually losing money, barely breaking even, or showing profit results considerably below military levels.

A variety of reasons is usually given for the inability of the large specialized defense companies to utilize their resources in commercial endeavors

—their lack of marketing capability and their inability to produce large numbers of items of low unit price.

These weaknesses are not necessarily handicaps in defense and space work, where other capabilities are more important. For example, the lack of commercial marketing capability of these firms results from their preoccupation with meeting the rigorous technical requirements of the military customer. Their inability to produce large volumes at low cost also reflects their unique capability to design small numbers of large-scale systems of great technical complexity.

Even if we examine companies that have divisions producing weapon systems as well as commercial product divisions, we find little transference of either personnel or product ideas from military to commercial work—within the same company. A company's commercial departments may be hiring engineers, while simultaneously a military department may be laying off experienced technical personnel. Many knowledgeable persons contend that the environment of military weapon system design and production is fundamentally different from, and hence the experience is rarely useful in, commercial enterprises. In the former, technical advance is often the prime and essential output, while in the latter, price is a critical parameter. A new model of refrigerator at half the price of current types may have a large market even if it suffers from significant reductions in quality. The second best missile, in contrast, may hardly be a bargain. The comparison, of course, is oversimplified, but it illustrates the different nature of product innovation characteristic of commercial competition as compared to technological competition in the military field.

A large majority of the technical personnel who leave a company doing defense work go to other firms similarly engaged on defense contracts. There is some movement of professional and technical personnel from universities and other industries to defense work, but relatively little movement in the opposite direction. Differences in pay scale and degree of challenge in the work are often cited as barriers to movement from military to commercial or other work.

It may be helpful to note that, for a typical company producing aircraft and missiles, engineers and related technical personnel no longer constitute merely a single important but limited department, but may exceed in actual numbers the total of factory or "blue collar" employment. In good measure, the major military contractors have become primarily large aggregations of R. & D. resources.

The alternate utilization of these resources, in the event of a substantial reduction in defense requirements, would present an important issue of public policy.

CHANGES IN PUBLIC POLICY

There are two major categories of public policy which may be relied upon to help transfer defense industry resources to nondefense pursuits. One category of Federal programs and policies covers various attempts to aid defense contractors in diversifying into commercial markets. The other consists of efforts to transfer the R. & D. and other resources of defense contractors to companies and organizations in other parts of the economy. Both of these types of actions would, of course, be enhanced by effective application of general monetary and fiscal policies which would maintain the overall levels of demand, income, and employment in the Nation.

Given a cutback in defense spending there is a variety of actions which, it has been suggested, the Federal Government could undertake to help defense contractors diversify. These include awarding them large amounts of nondefense R. & D. contracts or even establishing new requirements for nondefense goods which these companies could produce and sell to the Government.

Also, under existing military contracts, the Department of Defense could do several things which would currently increase the commercial capability of defense contractors, such as treating commercial product planning as an allowable cost on military contracts. This would provide a financial inducement to defense contractors to perform initial commercial studies while still engaged in defense work.

Defense industry executives state that there are major civilian pursuits where their massive engineering competence is needed and could be employed. Examples cited include large-scale construction, mining of the ocean floor, sea farming, further air and space travel, integration of transportation systems, revitalizing of the merchant marine, improved communications and weather forecasting, nuclear electric power salt water conversion, air traffic control systems, air and water pollution control, urban development, and programs of technical assistance to developing countries.

Government actions designed to aid the individual defense companies in converting to civilian activities may be the most direct and effective way of absorbing potential unemployment in the defense industries and of meeting the short-run requirements of economic stability. However, does sole reliance upon this course of action provide the best longrun reorientation and utilization of the resources currently employed in the defense sector? Is this approach to short-run economic adjustment consistent with maximum longrun economic growth and progress?

Faced with the difficulties encountered by the select business organizations which produce military weapon systems to penetrate commercial markets, it may be questionable public policy to invest very large amounts of Government funds in motivating such endeavors. In view of the tremendous concentration of R. & D. in these companies, attention might well be given to the desirability and possibility of transferring some of these resources to other parts of the economy. Such action could have tremendous long-term benefits for the currently "under researched" industries.

In contrast to the oft-voiced claims of private affluence amidst public poverty, research and development may be an important case of the reverse situation. The bulk of the R. & D. performed in the United States at the present time—65 percent in 1962—is done pursuant to contracts with or grants from the Federal Government. Moreover, the portion represented by privately initiated and funded R. & D. has declined during the past decade, from 47 percent in 1954 to 35 percent in 1962.

Along these lines, it seems to be clear that the demonstration effect on private industry of the massive Government expenditures on R. & D. may have already passed. The growth of company-funded R. & D. appears to have slowed down during the last few years, despite continued expansion in military and other Federal R. & D. outlays. Compared to annual increases of 33 percent in 1956 and 10 to 11 percent during 1959 and 1960, company-funded R. & D. rose 3 percent in 1961 and 6 percent in 1962.

Hence, there seem to be relatively small pent-up private demands for the R. & D. resources currently devoted to the defense program. We cannot expect that a major reduction in military R. & D. expenditures will automatically lead to any significant increase in private outlays for R. & D.

However, to the extent that the cost of R. & D. to an individual business firm can be reduced, private industry would increase its demand for R. & D. Mechanisms for so reducing the cost of R. & D. include (1) a tax rebate similar to the tax credit recently enacted to encourage business firms to increase investment in producers durable equipment, (2) an aid program similar to the mining exploration program of the Department of the Interior whereby the Government pays part or all of the cost, but is reimbursed out of the proceeds of the results—if the R. & D. leads to profitable production, and (3) loan and loan guarantees similar to those of the Small Business Administration and the Export-Import Bank.

Several operational questions would arise, of course. What is the elasticity of private demand for R. & D.? Even if it is made a free good, will the demand rise sufficiently to offset a major defense cutback?

Many of these and other alternatives would involve a number of Government departments and agencies, and both the legislative and executive branches. These various alternative courses of action raise serious questions of national policy. Would the concern of the Federal Government with commercial product development be an acceptable extension of the role of government in the American economy? Would some important characteristics of a private enterprise economy be sacrificed?

If, as a nation, we are to come up with useful, acceptable and timely answers to questions like these, public discussion and consideration needs to begin. In the event of a significant decline in defense spending, it would appear that the resultant surplus of valuable resources, particularly R. & D., would call for a broad long-range national program to encourage the development of alternate demands.

The major elements of such a program include:

(1) Developing public policy on (*a*) the utilization of the resources that would become available and (*b*) the respective roles of private industry and Federal, State, and local governments.

(2) Assigning responsibilities to the various Government agencies involved —Treasury, Commerce, Labor, the Council of Economic Advisers, the Office of Science and Technology, the Arms Control and Disarmament Agency, as well as the Department of Defense.

(3) Developing mechanisms for carrying out these responsibilities, such as some of those suggested above, which would operate in the private sector of the economy as well as in the public sector.

PART II

The Impact of the Cold War
on the Institutional Framework

INTRODUCTION

⟨ The length of the Cold War, its enormous cost, and the strong personality and unusual brilliance of Robert McNamara—who served longer as Secretary of Defense than any of his predecessors—introduced changes of such a magnitude in our defense policy that they effected basic changes not only in our governmental structure but also in our traditional market economy itself.

Some of these basic structural changes are primarily the result of McNamara's policies. Seldom has a cabinet member attained so much influence and aroused so much controversy. The most basic change, aside from shifting our defense posture from one of massive retaliation to one of a more flexible response to crises, was McNamara's introduction of the principles of "cost-effectiveness" and long-range budgeting into government institutions. Former Secretary McNamara describes this innovation in layman's terms below. Note in particular his belief that significant waste is inevitable in our defense expenditures, and his assumption (at that time) that our ability to meet challenges to our national security was unlimited. It should also be pointed out that McNamara's thinking on cost-effectiveness, in light of subsequent criticism of this method, would probably be more circumspect today.

The new system of cost-effectiveness emphasized the necessity of evaluating military budget requests in terms of function rather than service. This made it possible to compare the costs and ad-

vantages of the Navy's Polaris missiles with the Air Force's Minuteman missiles and B–52 bombers. Developed by McNamara's advisors and introduced in 1961, this system, called PPB (Planning, Programing and Budgeting), applied the Pentagon's experience in systems analysis to virtually all federal programs. Some congressmen openly opposed these innovations, exclaiming that the defense department now knows the "cost of everything and the value of nothing."

Russell Murray, Deputy Assistant Secretary of Defense for General Purpose Programs (Systems Analysis) under Secretary McNamara, explains the origin and development of cost-effectiveness and systems analysis. Note in particular Murray's observation that analytical techniques are not applicable to all decisions; some require judgment or cannot be quantified. Moreover, analytical techniques involve as much art as they do science. Defining terms and deciding what measurements to use also often rest on questions of judgment.

The second basic institutional change brought about in part by the Cold War has been the movement toward a new economic era. As Robert T. Averitt has shown,[1] our major firms are now separating themselves from their mother industry and from the domestic economy by diversifying their product base and seeking foreign markets. These major

[1] See *The Dual Economy: The Dynamics of American Industry Structure* (New York: Norton, 1968).

firms engage in extensive planning; they often administer prices; and many of them participate in government at the highest levels. These firms form an economy outside the framework of our traditional market economy, with its emphasis on supply and demand. A substantial percentage of these firms have been created by defense contracts. For example, between 1947 and 1962 eighteen new firms joined the list of the hundred largest industrial firms in the United States. One third of these new giants, that is, six, were defense contractors.[2]

This nonmarket characteristic of defense-oriented firms is described below by Merton Peck and Frederick Scherer. They explain why a market system cannot exist in the weapons industry. Instead a new kind of government–business relationship has emerged since 1945, one in which neither government nor business plays its traditional market role.

This new kind of economy raises a number of important questions: If supply and demand no longer influence many major industrial corporations and most of the defense corporations in the United States and if our antitrust laws are not more vigorously applied than in the past, who will ensure that these massive corporations act in the public interest? Since the livelihood of most of these defense corporations depends upon a strong anti-Communist stand by our government, will the influence of these defense corporations on political issues be a wholly benign one? Finally, the Secretary of Defense now has greater control over the economy than anyone except the President himself. Is this too much power for an official not directly responsible to the people?

2 U.S. Senate, Committee on the Judiciary, *Economic Concentration, Part I, Overall and Conglomerate Aspects,* 1964, pp. 208–10.

THE READINGS

1] How Defense Decisions Are Made

WHAT I WANTED TO talk to you about is the problem of decision-making in the Defense Department, and the way we are trying to approach the problem.

The Department of Defense is responsible for spending nearly 10 per cent of the national income of this country. It employs 3.7 million Americans directly, in and out of uniform, and millions more indirectly in every aspect of our economic life. It absorbs over half of every tax dollar, as it has done for over a decade.

All of this is well enough known. If anything, the potential dangers of this so-called "military-industrial complex" have been overstated rather than understated in recent months. But at the risk of repeating the obvious, let me point out once again that this unavoidably vast establishment exists for one purpose and one purpose only: to act as the servant of United States foreign policy. Our responsibility is to provide this nation with the means to safeguard its legitimate interests and to meet its commitments at home and around the world. The Defense Department exists to serve that purpose, and to serve none other.

Yet, although it is easy enough to say in a few words what our purpose is, the translation of this purpose into decisions on force levels, on contingency war planning, on weapons developments—and cancellations—on reorganizations, on all the range of decisions which shape our defense establishment, cannot be readily or easily deduced from the general principles. You probably remember General Marshall's shrewd remark: "Don't ask me to say we agree in principle; that just means we haven't agreed yet."

What I want to do is to outline, as best I can in a single talk, how we are trying to translate these general principles, on which all Americans would agree our defense policy should be based, into specific decisions that will effectively carry through those general principles. These specific decisions will inevitably and properly remain the subject of searching, even harsh, criticism. We are, after all, dealing with issues which could affect the very life of this nation, indeed the life of a great part of this planet. We cannot and do not claim infallibility. Only the future can tell when and where we have been right, when and where we have been wrong. We can only do our best to approach these problems as sensibly and realistically as we know how.

Let me start with two points which seem to me axiomatic. The first is

FROM Robert S. McNamara, "Decision Making in the Defense Department," in *Vital Speeches of the Day,* June 1, 1963, pp. 508–12. Delivered before the American Society of Newspaper Editors, Washington, D.C. Used by permission.

that, at least within any range of defense spending that is likely to appear at all desirable in the foreseeable future, the United States is well able to spend whatever it needs to spend on national security. The second point is that this ability does not excuse us from applying strict standards of effectiveness and efficiency to the way we spend our defense dollars.

Last fall, while we were preparing for the fiscal 1964 budget decisions, the separate requests for funds of the three military departments totalled over $67 billion. The budget as finally submitted to the Congress totalled nearly $54 billion, a cut of over $13 billion. This was still $2 billion more than the current defense budget, and $10 billion more than when we took office in 1961. We have been criticized both for overruling the military in cutting the Service requests, and for spending too much money, presumably in failing to cut the Service requests far enough. Sometimes, to my continuing surprise, we are criticized in both counts by the same people.

The fact is that we could, as a nation, afford to spend more than we are proposing if that were judged to be in our national interest. Our national security does not need to be compromised to keep defense spending down. Where we have cut, the cuts have not represented decisions to compromise national security in the name of frugality. For our children will hardly admire us for our frugality if it is achieved at a price they will have to pay in blood and suffering. And where we have added to defense spending, those additions have not been based on the naive notion that the bigger our defense budget is, the safer we will be. National security in this age of hydrogen bombs and intercontinental missiles is more complicated than that.

The facts are that national security in these times cannot be purchased by military spending alone, however generous a scale, and that the task of assuring that our military spending truly serves the national interest is more complicated than it has ever been in the past. And more urgent. The test we have to apply, over and over again, is whether a particular expenditure for a specific purpose is really in our national interest.

Every dollar we spend inefficiently or ineffectively is not only an unnecessary addition to the arms race which threatens all mankind, but an unfair burden on the taxpayer, or an unwise diversion of resources which could be invested elsewhere to serve our national interests at home or abroad, or a dollar that could, even if kept in the military budget, be invested in something that would better strengthen our military posture. The fact that we cannot be poor enough to grudge the price of our own survival does not mean we are rich enough to squander our resources in the name of national security.

I do not mean to suggest that we can measure national security in terms of dollars—you cannot price what is inherently priceless. But if we are to avoid talking in generalities, we must talk about dollars: for policy decisions must sooner or later be expressed in the form of budget decisions on where to spend and how much.

When we took office, we saw three major tasks before us. First, we had to accelerate the strengthening of our strategic nuclear force, a task which involves not merely increases in the size of the force, but major improvements in its survivability and in the provisions to maintain responsible command

and control at all times. We had a firm base from which to work. My predecessor, Tom Gates, had already given strong support to such programs as Minuteman and Polaris, which are designed to ride out any conceivable attack, so that they do not have to be launched on short or ambiguous warning. But we felt further impetus was needed. We have, for example, increased by 50 per cent the programmed rate of Polaris procurement, and doubled our production capability for Minuteman. We have increased by 50 per cent the portion of B-52 bombers on 15-minute ground alert. The kind of flexibility that these programs provide is absolutely vital. Overall, in the last 24 months we have doubled the number of warheads in our strategic alert forces. And during the same period we have increased by 60 per cent Nato's tactical nuclear forces in Western Europe.

Second, major increases in our non-nuclear capabilities were urgently needed. Accordingly, we increased the number of combat-ready Army divisions by 45 per cent. We augmented by 30 per cent the Air Force capability for tactical air support of combat operations. We have increased our procurement of combat supplies and equipment, to correct serious imbalances and inadequacies that had developed over the years. We have increased nearly six-fold our special forces, made up of highly trained men who can not only deal with guerrilla warfare, but more important, can train the peoples under terrorist attack to defend themselves.

The third major effort cannot be so easily defined. What it involves is a broad effort to improve the effectiveness and efficiency of the defense establishment. It is this effort that I want to talk about most, partly because it is the most controversial—really the only one of these three efforts which has been widely controversial—partly because it is, by its nature, very diffuse, involving a wide variety of largely independent efforts, which cannot properly be summed up in a few sentences.

.   .   .   .

It is only in the third area, the problem of increasing the effectiveness and efficiency of our military establishment, that controversy has developed. Not that there was much disagreement about the need: for years everyone who has thought seriously about the Department of Defense has felt that major improvements were needed. The solutions offered ranged from drastic proposals for complete unification of the armed forces to vague suggestions about "cutting the fat out of the military budget."

Thus, there was a national consensus here that reforms were in order. But there was no consensus on just what should be done. And there was an additional and inevitable human problem. For these reforms would necessarily take the shape of changes in the traditional ways of doing things, and limitations on the customary ways of spending defense money. It is inevitable that people will take more easily to suggestions that they should have more money to spend, as in the improvement of our nuclear and non-nuclear capabilities, than to suggestions that they must spend less, or that they must abandon established ways of doing things. Yet the very substantial increases in the budget which we felt necessary added a further strong incentive, if any were needed, to move ahead on these problems of increasing efficiency and effectiveness.

The first and most important thing to notice about the effort in this area is what it is *not*. It is *not* an effort to save dollars at the expense of military effectiveness. What we are trying to do can be divided into two parts: the first is essentially a series of management reforms of the kind you will find in any well-run organization, an effort which is in large part covered by the formal Five Year Cost Reduction Program we set up in July 1962. The common characteristic of reforms in this part of the effort is that they have very little, if anything, to do with military effectiveness, one way or the other. They neither increase nor decrease our military effectiveness; they merely save money by introducing more efficient methods of doing things.

To give a small example of what I mean, we found that the various elements of the Department were using slightly different forms for requisitions —16 in all. As a result, nearly every time a piece of property was transferred from one part of the Department to another, a new requisition form had to be typed out, tens of thousands of forms per year. By establishing a common requisition form and system, we eliminated tens of thousands of man-hours of labor formerly wasted in having clerks retype the forms. This will save us about $20 million a year when the change becomes fully operative.

The creation of the Defense Supply Agency to handle the purchase of common supplies for the Department saved $31 million this year in overhead costs alone, and these annual savings will grow in succeeding years. I need not dwell on such colorful, but relatively minor accomplishments as the consolidation of the 18 different types and sizes of butcher smocks, the 4 kinds of belt buckles, and the 6 kinds of exercise bloomers.

We estimate that actions initiated this year will ultimately save nearly $300 million through increased use of competitive, as opposed to noncompetitive procurement; over $300 million through shifts from cost-plus-fixed-fee contracts to fixed or incentive price contracts; over $300 million through better management of inventories; nearly $300 million through closing or reducing operations at 330 installations, freeing 45,000 men and 280,000 acres of land, and so on down the line. The total savings which will ultimately be realized from actions taken so far in the cost reduction program will be over $1.9 billion.

Our target by fiscal year 1967 is saving $3.4 billion a year, each year, every year, through reforms in the procurement and logistic areas alone. So we are not talking about trivial sums of money. And my own judgment is that we are still only scratching the surface. I believe that we should eventually be able to surpass our own present goal of $3.4 billion annual savings, and I emphasize that we are talking about *annual*, not one-time savings. Several years ago there was talk of saving $8 billion per year by unifying the Armed Services. I think that through vigorous pursuit of the cost reduction effort we can save the same kind of money that had been envisaged through unification of the Services without the serious disadvantages of a single Service.

As I have said, most of this formal cost-reduction program has little or nothing to do with military effectiveness, one way or the other. It merely saves large sums of money.

The second, and really the more important, part of the effort does bear directly on military effectiveness. Although dollar savings are sometimes an important by-product, here the essential point is to increase military effectiveness. For example, we found that the three military departments had been establishing their requirements independently of each other. I think the results can fairly be described as chaotic: the Army planning, for example, was based primarily on a long war of attrition, while the Air Force planning was based, largely, on a short war of nuclear bombardment. Consequently, the Army was stating a requirement for stocking months of fighting supplies against the event of a sizable conventional conflict, while the Air Force stock requirements for such a war had to be measured in days, and not very many days at that. Either approach, consistently followed, might make some sense. The two combined could not possibly make sense. What we needed was a coordinated strategy seeking objectives actually attainable with the military resources available.

We are moving with all reasonable speed towards a properly balanced force structure. I say with all reasonable speed because there would be enormous practical difficulties in trying to get this job done overnight. But we are moving as fast as we sensibly can to balance men against supplies; deployable divisions against sea and airlift capability to handle those divisions; ground combat units against tactical air squadrons to support those units.

A realistic reappraisal of our needs resulted in a reduction of stated requirements by $24 billion, but also in a doubling of the division-months of combat equipment actually on hand. The fact is that in the past so-called requirements bore almost no relation to the real world: enormous requirements bore almost no relation to the real world: enormous requirements existed on paper, often almost entirely disembodied from the actual size and nature of the procurement program. There were gross inventory imbalances: the Army, for example, while in general far short of its stated requirements, had 270 per cent of its requirement for 105 mm. towed howitzers, 290 per cent of the requirements for 4.2 inch mortars; we had ten times as many 2.75 inch rockets as were required. By taking a more realistic look at the whole requirements picture, we were able, for example, to save $150 million on Sparrow missiles for the Navy and Air Force, $163 million on Army .50 caliber machine guns.

The new form of budget for the first time grouped together for planning purposes units which must fight together in the event of war. The Navy strategic force, the Polaris submarines, are considered together with the Air Force Strategic Air Command; Navy general purpose forces are considered together with the Army and Marine divisions and the Air Force Tactical Air Command. This kind of reform provides substantial improvement in the effectiveness of our military establishment. Even where it does not lead directly to lower expenditures, it is economical in the true sense of the word; that is, it gives us the maximum national security obtainable from the dollars we do spend. We can imagine many different kinds of wars the United States must be prepared to fight, but a war in which the Army fights independently of the Navy, or the Navy independently of the Air Force, is not one of them. Quite obviously, the coordination of the planning of the four Services makes eminently good sense on the narrowest military grounds.

So I would repeat: it is a mistake to equate our efforts towards improving effectiveness and efficiency solely with a desire to save money. That is very important. But military effectiveness is even more important. Money savings are what is easiest to talk about: for it is easy to explain something in terms of saving X hundreds of millions of dollars, and complicated to get into the details of planning and logistics, and the like. But the fact is that the total effort is aimed *both* at saving money and improving military effectiveness. And it is the latter, improving the effectiveness of our military establishment, which is the first priority, for it is the latter which directly affects national security.

Where the situation becomes more complicated is when decisions must be made on requested force level increases or development or procurement of new weapons.

The first thing to remember is that adding a weapon to our inventory is not necessarily synonymous with adding to our national security.

The second thing to remember is that even if we were to draft every scientist and engineer in the country into weapons development work, we could still develop only a fraction of the systems that are proposed. We must pick and choose very carefully among the proposals to get the ones on which we should actually proceed. This process of choice must begin with a requirement for solid indications that a proposed system would really add something to our national security. Even then, we still have to pick and choose, but we cannot even seriously consider going ahead with a full-scale weapons system development until that basic requirement has been met.

The whole subject of Research and Development management deserves a separate speech. Department costs alone on typical major weapons systems today average upwards of $1 billion. Over a billion dollars was spent on the atomic airplane, which was little closer to being a useful weapon when we cancelled it, shortly after taking office, than it had been half a dozen years earlier. Eighty million was spent on the Goose decoy missile, essentially a pilotless aircraft that the enemy would confuse with our B-52s. But the device, once launched, could not be recalled. Since the B-52s have to be launched on ambiguous warning to avoid being destroyed on the ground, the non-recallable decoys were obviously incompatible with the B-52s. These are a few examples of the sort of thing we hope will happen less often in the future.

The RS-70 is an example of a weapon which, it seems to me, fails to meet the basic requirement for a major systems development; a solid indication that the weapon, if developed, would add significantly to our national security. It happens to be a particularly expensive weapon: to develop, procure, and operate a modest force of these planes would cost us at least $10 billion. Yet considering the weapons we already have, or will have by the time the RS-70 could be operational, it is very hard to see how this weapon would add to our national security.

The whole debate on the RS-70, in fact, has tended to be conducted in terms which have very little to do with the facts of the situation. There is a lot of talk about missiles versus bombers. I have no feeling about missiles versus bombers as such. If bombers serve our national interest, then we should be interested in bombers; if missiles, then we should be interested in missiles; if a mix, then we should be interested in the mix. As General LeMay observed: "If kiddie cars will do the job, we will use them." But the question is really not about bombers versus missiles, because the RS-70 is not a bomber in anything like the traditional meaning of the term. The RS-70 would carry no bombs. It would attack its target with a very complex air-launched missile system from distances of hundreds of miles. Now there are various platforms from which to launch missiles. We can launch them from hardened silos in the ground; we can launch them from submarines under the sea; we can launch them from aircraft. The question is not bombs versus missiles. We are all agreed it must be missiles. The debate is about alternative launching platforms and alternative missile systems. And the particular launching platform and missile system proposed in the RS-70 program just is not an effective means to accomplish the missions proposed to be assigned to it.

Skybolt was a somewhat different story. The Skybolt development was begun in 1959 to meet a very specific need. This was to clear a path for our bombers by knocking out the enemy's air defenses. The defense suppression role is vital: unless it is performed, the bombers cannot get through to their targets. One reason that it is now agreed that by the 1970s the traditional manned bomber will be obsolete is that by then we anticipate it will be more costly to suppress air defenses in order to carry out an effective bombing attack than it will be to attack the target directly with missiles. Even now, bombers are of limited value unless we have something that can go in ahead and clear a path for them. That means a missile.

The Hound Dog had been developed for that job, but the Skybolt, it was planned, would do it much better. Two important things have happened during the Skybolt development that changed this judgment: First, the development itself fell far short of its goals: Skybolt turned out to be much more expensive than had been anticipated; it would be less accurate than had been anticipated; it would take longer to achieve acceptable levels of reliability than had been anticipated. Second, we had been successful in developing other weapons that were still on the drawing board when Skybolt was proposed. What all this added up to was that while the defense suppression role remained vital, Skybolt was no longer vital. In fact, it became clear that by using the already developed Hound Dog plus some additional Minutemen, already developed, we could do the defense suppression job for about $2 billion less than we could by continuing to go ahead on Skybolt as if nothing had changed since 1959.

These two illustrations, the RS-70 and Skybolt, point up some of the fundamental considerations that must enter into defense policy decisions. Does the proposal really add something significant to our national security? If the proposal does serve an important need, does it do so as well as other alternative means of reaching the same end? Do the assumptions on which you based your preliminary decisions several years ago still hold true?

Let me note also another reason for restraint in pushing ahead uncritically on proposed new weapons of doubtful importance. As weapons systems grow more complex, more expensive, and more difficult to maintain in a high state of military readiness, it is essential that we limit as far as possible the number of new systems that we bring into operation; for we want to be as sure as possible that we can depend on every system to operate when it is really needed. A basic fact of life is that under the chaotic conditions of combat you do not get anything like the efficiency of weapons systems that you get on a test range. Relative simplicity is a most desirable characteristic of a weapons system, or of a combination of systems.

One of the difficulties in the past has been the tendency of planners, concentrating on a particular proposed system, to forget that every additional bit of complexity you add to your operation tends to degrade the overall efficiency of the operation. Eventually you reach a point where the advantage of adding a new system is outweighed by the effect of the additional complexity. We have accumulated some disturbing evidence about the effect of proliferation of weapons systems in the recent past on the operational dependability of those systems. We don't want to put ourselves in the position of the camera bug who weights himself down with so much specialized equipment for every contingency that he actually gets poorer results than a more lightly equipped competitor. And let me add that not only do the proliferation and complication of weapons reduce dependability, but they are also major factors contributing to enormous excess inventories of parts and equipment—excesses which today amount to over $12 billion.

These considerations had a great deal to do with the TFX decisions. On that issue, the really difficult decision was not the choice of contractor, but the cancellation of the Services two-plane program and the substitution of a single aircraft to serve both the Air Force and the Navy. After extended discussion and great controversy, both the civilian and military leaders now agree such a program will meet the military requirements. It will yield a saving of approximately $1 billion. The choice of a contractor for such an aircraft was a subsidiary decision. Both contractors presented acceptable designs, each capable of meeting the military requirement, and with little to choose between them on the basis of performance. The choice of contractor, therefore, could be determined by the civilian authorities who are charged by law with making such decisions, on considerations of ultimate cost and program risk.

What I have been suggesting in these illustrations is that the question of how to spend our defense dollars and how much to spend is a good deal more complicated than is often assumed. It cannot be assumed that a new weapon would really add to our national security, no matter how attractive the weapon can be made to seem, looked at by itself. Anyone who has been exposed to so-called "brochuremanship" knows that even the most outlandish notions can be dressed up to look superficially attractive. You have to consider a very wide range of issues—the missions our forces must be prepared to perform, the effects of a proposed system on the stability of the military situation in the world, the alternatives open to us for performing the missions required.

You cannot make decisions simply by asking yourself whether something might be nice to have. You have to make a judgment on how much is enough.

2] Major Procedural Innovations Introduced by the Cold War

I AM NOT ENOUGH of a historian to speak authoritatively as to the exact moment when systems analysis techniques were introduced into the defense business. But it is clear that the kind of questions addressed by systems analysis activities have been around for some time. For example, in Richard Hough's book *Dreadnought* there appears the following extract from a report by Lieutenant Commander Sims to President Theodore Roosevelt at the turn of the century, concerning American battleship construction policy:

> The final conclusion is, that for the sum that it would cost to maintain the twenty small battleships, we would maintain a fleet of ten large ones that would be greatly superior in tactical qualities, in effective hitting capacity, speed, protection, and inherent ability to concentrate its gunfire, and have a sufficient sum left over to build one 20,000-ton battleship each year, not to mention needing fewer officers and men to handle the more efficient fleet.

Though battleship construction policy is not our problem today, the whole tone of that quotation—the framing of the issue, the relationship between cost and effectiveness—has a remarkable ring of familiarity for today's systems analyst.

With the advent of World War II, the demand for activities in the general area of systems analysis grew sharply, and the groundwork was laid for its growth in the post-war period. Though the area of interest in World War II was narrowed by the urgencies of the situation, the intent was really no different than it is today. At that time, the emphasis was naturally on maximizing the effectiveness of existing forces; whereas, in the post-war era, the analysis could consider longer-ranged alternatives with significant differences in cost applications. Systems analysis began to expand from consideration of what we could do with what we might elect to have on hand in the future. Throughout this period, assuring the efficient utilization of resources in the DOD became progressively more difficult as a result—to coin a phrase—of mushrooming technology. The bewildering array of entirely feasible alternative forces which our scientists can offer today has enormously complicated our problems of choice. There is hardly a military task which cannot be accomplished in a multitude of ways—and many capabilities which we take for granted today have been wholly impossible over most of the span of military history. We cannot hedge against this array of possibilities by simply buying them all. To attempt to do so would only lead to squandering of resources on partially completed programs. Choices have

FROM Russell Murray II, "Systems Analysis and Cost Effectiveness," *Defense Industry Bulletin* (September, 1966), pp. 1–2.

to be made, and the aim of systems analysis is to help in making those choices correctly.

Just what systems analysis consists of is difficult to put into a few words, for it really is a blend of many things, and it draws on many of the formal disciplines. We do find, however, that economics is one of the most useful of the disciplines, since the core of systems analysis work centers on the economic problem of the efficient allocation of resources. Charles Hitch and Roland McKean, in their book *Economics of Defense in the Nuclear Age,* had this to say on the subject:

> The economic problem is to choose that strategy, including equipment and everything else necessary to implement it, which is most efficient (maximizes the attainment of the objective with the given resources) or economical (minimizes the cost of achieving the given objective)—the strategy which is most efficient also being the most economical.
>
> Strategy and cost are as interdependent as the front and rear sights of a rifle. One cannot assign relative weights to the importance of the positions of the front and rear sights. It does not make sense to ask the correct position of the rear sight except in relation to the front sight and the target. Similarly one cannot economize except in choosing strategies (or tactics or methods) to achieve objectives. The job of economizing, which some would delegate to the budgeteers and comptrollers, cannot be distinguished from the whole task of making military decisions.

Much of the systems analysis work in the Defense Department utilizes an approach that is familiar to the engineer, the mathematician, the statistician and other professions. But one thing which it does not do is substitute for the decision maker. On the contrary, the whole aim is to present the decision maker with the clearest possible picture of what his choices really are—what each will do, when it will do it, and what it will cost. It also attempts to point out the uncertainties—to show what it would mean if uncertain key assumptions were changed, and to give a feeling for which factors are critical and which are not. To sort out those issues, to bring them into the open, to establish a forum for discussion along orderly lines, systems analysis has been found a useful tool in the Defense Department.

Systems analysis was formally introduced in DOD in 1961 when Charles Hitch, formerly the head of the Economics Department at The Rand Corporation, was appointed Comptroller. Within his organization, a systems analysis office was established at the level of a directorate. In 1962, this group had expanded and its head, Dr. Alain Enthoven, was appointed a Deputy Assistant Secretary of Defense. With additional demands being placed on this group, and with analysis being applied to an increasingly wider scope of the Defense activities, in 1965 the systems analysis office, together with the existing cost estimation facility, was split from the Comptroller's office and established as a new office at the level of Assistant Secretary of Defense—this level, of course, reporting directly to the Secretary of Defense.

The Office of the Assistant Secretary of Defense (Systems Analysis)—OASD (SA)—is organized into five sections: one for strategic programs; a second for general purpose programs; a third for resource analysis (including cost estimation and manpower requirements); a fourth for economic analysis; and a fifth for command, control, communications and intelligence.

The office is closely integrated with other activities within the Office of the Secretary of Defense. For example, for expert advice and analysis of technological matters, we rely on the Office of the Director of Defense Research and Engineering. For matters relating to production scheduling possibilities and procurement policies, we rely on the Office of the Assistant Secretary of Defense (Installations and Logistics). And, of course, we work very closely with the Services and the Joint Chiefs of Staff. I would like to refer briefly to this relationship.

A portion of the analytical work done in DOD does take place within OASD(SA) proper. However, by far the largest fraction of the analytical effort is conducted by, or under the aegis of, the Services and the Joint Chiefs of Staff. In any program as overwhelmingly large as that of DOD, the opportunities for analysis are far beyond the physical capacity of OASD (SA), and our function is not to conduct all, or even an appreciable fraction, of the analyses that affect our defense planning. Rather, one of our major functions is to suggest to the Secretary of Defense those areas in which analysis would be profitable, i.e., areas adapted to analysis. The Secretary then considers our recommendations and, from time to time, requests the Services or the Joint Chiefs of Staff to conduct analyses. At that point, our function becomes one of working closely with the study organizations. If we can, we will work with the groups in selecting proper figures of merit and criteria, and we will try to help with the choice of assumptions. Above all, we will try to make sure that the analyses are directed along lines which will be responsive to the Secretary's needs.

In some instances, these analyses will be conducted by the military staffs. In others, they will be contracted out to organizations such as Rand, the Center for Naval Analysis, the Research Analysis Corporation, or the Institute for Defense Analysis. Though not all studies require it, it is generally at this stage that inputs of various kinds are solicited from industry and, in some cases, industry may conduct specialized studies for the various Services. I will have more to say later about the role I believe industry can play in this process.

When these studies are submitted to the Secretary of Defense, OASD(SA) participates in their review. In this function, we examine the studies in detail, and inform the Secretary as to our feelings as to their validity, what new information has been uncovered, what that implies for the future, and what we would recommend in that light—with respect both to changes in defense planning and the need for any further analyses.

I think you should be able to appreciate from this that the use of systems analysis techniques in DOD has come of age. It now has become a way of life.

3] Major Market Innovations Introduced by the Cold War

THE CONSEQUENCES of uncertainty for the organization and administration of the weapons acquisition process will be discussed throughout
this study. At this point we can, however, examine in a preliminary fashion
the most general consequence: the uncertainties connected with weapons
acquisition preclude the development of a market system in anything approaching the usual meaning of that term.

THE ESSENTIALS OF A MARKET SYSTEM

To examine this proposition let us first summarize the essential features
of a market system, as indicated both in the economic literature and in the
actual pratices of American business.

The seller normally takes the initiative in deciding to produce a product,
raising the capital required for its development, and determining its price.
Buyers then decide whether to purchase that particular finished product or
one offered by a competing seller. These buyer decisions determine whether
the firm will sell its products profitably. This interaction between buyers
and sellers at the point of sale constitutes a market.

A market transforms the apparent anarchy of sellers' independent actions
into a highly effective system of social organization in two ways. The market
is first of all an information system. If a product fares poorly with consumers
in competition with other products, this is a signal for a seller to revise its
price or its product. Second, the market is a reward and punishment system. Prices are determined by competition, not by the cost incurred or a
"fair" level of profit. Those sellers with better than average performance in
reducing costs or anticipating consumer desires receive an above-average return, while those with poorer than average performance lose money and
eventually leave the market. The lure of above-average profits and the fear
of bankruptcy serve as carrots and sticks to induce sellers to achieve efficiency
and to satisfy consumer wants. In this process, the competition between
sellers ensures reasonable prices, and as a further protection, the entry of
new sellers in response to high profits or the exit of existing sellers in response to losses serves to keep profits in line with costs, uncertainties,
and capital requirements for each product. In these two ways, providing
information and furnishing incentives, a market guides the activities of individual sellers toward meeting consumer desires. And at least in the Amer-

FROM Merton J. Peck and Frederic M. Scherer, *The Weapons Acquisitions Process: An
Economic Analysis* (Boston, 1962), pp. 55–64. Copyright © by Harvard University Graduate
School of Business Administration. Used by permission. [Footnotes omitted—J. L. C.]

ican economy, the wants of the consumer are considered the ultimate test of society's needs.

Thus, a market system decentralizes decisions on what to produce and what the price should be among many buyers and sellers. In this way the impersonality of the market is substituted for the rigidities and arbitrariness of centralized planning. Furthermore, a market provides a very workable system of incentives, for as Adam Smith noted nearly two hundred years ago, a market system harnesses self-interest into a social harmony. "It is not from the benevolence of the butcher, the brewer, or the baker that we expect our dinner," said Smith, "but from their regard to their own interest."

In practice, of course, a market system has its limitations. Yet changes in public policy of the last decades have been largely directed toward modifying the market system, rather than to its overthrow. All in all, a market system has been one of the factors underlying the impressive performance of the American economy.

A market system exists only in a more or less atrophied form for the weapons acquisition process. Even though the weapons industry contains its share of entrepreneurial personalities, the buyer (that is, the military service) generally decides whether a new weapon is needed and in this sense takes the initiative on new products. Furthermore, by making progress payments on development contracts and by furnishing government-owned plant and equipment, the buyer finances most development outlays. The seller does not offer a finished product which the buyer can either accept or reject. Rather, the government pays development costs before it knows what the ultimate performance of the product or its desirability relative to other products will be. The government can, and frequently does, change, reduce, or cancel the project before its completion.

Finally, the price of a weapon system is not determined by market competition. Instead, the price is largely determined by reimbursement of costs actually experienced plus a fee bargained for in advance. This is most obvious in the case of cost-plus-fixed-fee contracts, but in practice the prices on other types of weapons contracts are based largely upon the contractor's actual or anticipated costs rather than a market price. This is to be expected, since market prices usually do not exist in weapons acquisition simply because most weapons are unique to a much greater degree than, say, different brands of toothpaste or soap.

The absence of competitive pricing does not, however, imply the absence of competition among defense contractors. Indeed, a considerable part of this study is devoted to describing the operation of intercontractor competition. Yet however pervasive this competition, it is not the price competition that occurs in a market situation.

Thus, even though there are some manifestations of a market system, the weapons acquisition process falls considerably short of the essentials of such a system: initiative vested largely with the sellers with an ultimate consumer veto; and an automatic system of incentives insuring that sellers will serve the consumer and be rewarded accordingly, not by an administrative device, but through the competitive determination of a market price.

THE IMPOSSIBILITY OF A MARKET SYSTEM
FOR WEAPONS ACQUISITION

It is not only that a market system does not now exist in the weapons acquisition process. We can state the proposition more strongly. A market system in its entirety can never exist for the acquisition of weapons. To economists schooled in the virtues of the market system as a solution to the problems of economic organization, this is a regrettable conclusion. Nevertheless, an examination of four conditions typical in the development of weapons supports such a view.

First, individual weapons projects require such large expenditures that the private financing of their development is virtually impossible. Of the 12 weapons projects we studied, the least costly had a development cost of about $60 million; the median development cost was about $400 million; and the three largest had a development cost of over a billion dollars. Relatively few commercial projects are comparable in size to the expenditures involved in the smallest of these weapons projects.

Nylon, color television, and the jet airliner are usually cited as representative of the largest of the commercial developments, although in the latter two cases government funds had helped in the development of predecessor projects. DuPont's nylon development costs have been variously estimated at from $27 to $45 million, which at today's prices would be at least twice that in sum. For color television RCA, the leading manufacturer, stated it had invested more than $100 million over the last decade. For the jet transport, Boeing, one of the leading manufacturers, is estimated to have spent about $165 million in development costs and inventory losses. The limits of private financing are further indicated by industry's reaction to developing a commercial supersonic transport. This billion dollar project was considered feasible by business executives only if government aid were available.

If we take these largest of commercial new product projects as representing the upper limit of private development financing, it is apparent that a good many weapons projects lie beyond this limit. Even with the smaller weapons projects, the prospects for private financing are not encouraging. Granted that there are companies such as General Motors and duPont which could finance a half-billion dollar project, such isolated examples can hardly be the basis of organizing the weapons aquisition process. Instead, by financing weapons development the government must play the combined role of investor and buyer. In a market system not only are these two functions separated, but it would be a radically different type of economic organization if, for example, each prospective automobile buyer had to contribute to its financing some years in advance of the purchase.

Second, the prospect of a "commercially organized" weapons acquisition process is further reduced by the existence of the unique uncertainties described in the previous chapter. Private investment would be subject to the risks of obsolescence, changes in strategic planning, and changes in government policy, as well as to the possibility of unforeseen technical difficulties.

In 1954 it was such uncertainties, combined with the billion dollar invest-ment requirements, that gave pause to members of the Strategic Missiles Evaluation Committee considering the Atlas program for the government. If this same group in addition had to consider the reactions of stockholders and investors, the decision might well have turned out very differently. At least, with government funds the risks were distributed among the general body of taxpayers. The Atlas decision was, of course, an extreme case, but the same kind of situation occurs to a lesser degree in the decision to initiate smaller weapons projects.

Let us assume, however, that despite the large capital requirements and great uncertainties, private financing would be forthcoming for a weapons program. There would remain a third obstacle to a market system: the problem of determining the product characteristics desired by the buyer. Numerous decisions are required during the development of a weapon as to its technical and operational characteristics and as to the relative importance of early availability vs. higher performance. The seller might make "market surveys" by contracting various individuals in the service. But the prefer-ences expressed might well be in conflict with one another, and without official machinery to resolve these conflicts, the best the seller could do would be to make his own assessment of the strategic situation and proceed ac-cordingly. Alternatively, with an official body to make such decisions for the service, we might find the buyer's participation in the seller's internal deci-sions somewhat like that which presently exists. This would lessen the initiative for product decisions by the seller, an important characteristic of a market system.

Finally, the determination of a weapon system's price would hardly cor-respond to that in a market system. The government is generally the only buyer, so that it has the bargaining power of a monopsonist (single buyer). As we shall see in subsequent chapters, the government has some possibilities of substitution among various weapons not only of the same type, such as between two air defense missiles, but also among different types, such between an air defense missile and a manned interceptor aircraft. Never-theless, most weapons are sufficiently unique so that the seller (selected by the government) has some of the bargaining power of a monopolist. The situation then would be analogous to the industry-wide bargaining between labor and management, where neither party can survive without the other. And here frequent stalemates over contract terms are only resolved under government pressure, This kind of pricing situation is not that of a competitive market.

For these reasons, we would argue that a complete market system is an impossibility in the weapons acquisition process. Such an approach has few advocates, despite the recurrent vague talk about a "free enterprise" ap-proach to weapons procurement. Stripped of generalities, such phrases usually turn out to introduce such diverse proposals as higher profits for defense contracting, more freedom from government supervision for defense contractors, or a larger share of defense business for small firms. While there may be merit in each of these proposals, it should be clear that none of them creates free enterprise in the sense of a market system.

CONTRACTING IN THE WEAPONS ACQUISITION PROCESS

It can be argued, however, that we have made the wrong comparison. Instead of taking a market system as a commercial prototype, we should have taken a contracting system, particularly since the weapons industry prefers to call itself a "contracting" industry. There is little literature as to what this term means, but it should be apparent that the distinguishing feature of "contracting" is that the buyer and seller agree upon the purchase before the product exists. Such agreements frequently involve advance payments. "Contracting" describes most transactions in a few commercial industries such as building construction, electric power generators, and some other types of custom-made machinery.

There are, however, two quite different types of contracting situations. At one extreme is the contract for a product or task that can be clearly specified in advance and for which various competitors can submit fixed-price bids. Much of the more routine construction falls into this category. In its economic essentials, such a situation is not radically different from a market system, for there can be price competition and the buyer knows in advance what he will receive. (In practice, as anyone who has built a house knows, these situations are often not quite that simple, but at least there is an agreement that furnishes a framework in which to adjust subsequent disputes.)

At the other extreme is the contract with cost reimbursement provisions covering tasks that cannot be specified in detail. This situation is quite different from a market system. Professor Tybout succinctly characterizes this kind of relationship as follows:

> The cost-plus-fixed-fee contract is the administrative contract par excellence. For the market mechanism, it substitutes the administrative mechanism. For the profit share of private entrepreneurs, it substitutes the fixed fee, a payment in lieu of profits foregone. And for the independent private business unit, it substitutes the integrated hierarchical structure of an organization composed of an agency . . . and its contractors.

Contracting for weapons is largely of this cost-plus-fixed-fee type. Indeed, all the weapons we studied were developed under cost reimbursement contracts.

It is not surprising that this should be so. As we have seen in the preceding chapter, the possibility of unforeseen technical difficulties precludes accurate estimation of cost in advance, so both parties are reluctant to agree to a fixed price at the outset. Technical uncertainties as well as frequently changing military requirements preclude detailed advance specification of the weapon system product.

In these contracts, the services attempt to control costs through a detailed audit of expenditures, a set of definitions as to what constitutes allowable costs, and formal approval of product design changes. A corps of auditors, plant representatives, and engineering change administrators attempts to serve as a limit upon costs, rather than the need to meet competitive prices.

Likewise, the services attempt to make the major development decisions, and often they may pass in detail upon the specific technical features of the weapon. This kind of administrative control over both cost and the product means that service officers participate in what would be regarded elsewhere as internal business activities.

The commercial world also has examples of this type of cost reimbursement contracting. We have studied one such situation in detail. Because it is a close commercial parallel to weapons contracting, a highly condensed version of the project history follows:

> In 1955 the Consolidated Edison Company of New York, one of the largest electrical public utilities in the United States, entered into a fixed-price contract with the Babcock & Wilcox Company for the development and construction of a 235,000-kw atomic energy power generating station. This relationship involved major technological uncertainties. Not only was the commercial use of atomic energy virtually unexplored at that time, but it was decided to develop for the first time a reactor core burning thorium rather than uranium. Despite the uncertainties, it was felt that thorium would be in more generous supply and possibly more economical than uranium.
>
> Because the development efforts encountered various technical difficulties, the level of costs rose to make the amount of the fixed price unrealistic. Consolidated Edison did not choose to hold Babcock & Wilcox to the original contract, but instead supplanted the original contract with a cost-plus-no-fee contract. At the same time, Consolidated Edison exerted detailed supervision over Babcock & Wilcox, auditing all their invoices, approving all engineering changes, and authorizing any variations that might affect the level of cost. This was a highly detailed control by the buyer of the contractor's activities.
>
> The resulting relationship between Consolidated Edison and Babcock & Wilcox was very much like the relationship between the services and their weapons contractors. The fundamental factor underlying this relationship was the difficulty of estimating costs and developing firm specifications in a situation of substantial technological uncertainty. This example suggests that when the underlying conditions are the same, the nature of "contracting" in the commercial world is often not radically different from that in the weapons acquisition process.

To characterize a relationship in a cost-plus-fixed-fee situation as administrative, however, does not mean that elements of a market system may not play some role. For example, General Motors and other large companies have found the administrative task sufficiently difficult that they have established an artificial interdivisional market mechanism. In this system, each division as a profit center buys from other divisions at market prices and sells at other prices. The profitability of the division serves as an index of the effectiveness of divisional management in reducing costs and providing products accepted by the "market," much as if they were independent firms.

In this way, some of the difficulties of centralized administration are overcome through the use of a synthetic market system. Still this is hardly a complete laissez-faire market system.

The services likewise have attempted to reproduce some of the automatic incentives of a market system through various contractual devices. Yet the feasible opportunities in this area fall considerably short of the creation of a complete market system.

THE PROBLEM OF BUSINESS-GOVERNMENT RELATIONSHIPS IN A NON-MARKET SYSTEM

We can now state more fully the basic problem of government-business relations in the weapons acquisition process. We have chosen to rely upon private business firms for the development of weapons, and in this respect we have followed the private enterprise approach. This approach has several advantages. First, such a policy serves to overcome the government's difficulties in recruiting able technical and managerial talent and the built-in inflexibility of government organizations described in the next chapter. Second, it permits using the talents of existing companies engaged in commercial activity. Third, management by central direction of such a diverse and large activity as weapons development would be well nigh impossible.

What is lacking is a market system to ensure that private firms in pursuit of their objectives are serving what the government as buyer considers to be its interests. In the most fundamental sense, the question underlying this study is whether, through modifications in existing policies and institutions, the initiative and interest of the individual corporation can be more effectively harnessed to serve the interests of national security. . . .

PART III
The Impact of the Cold War on Research and Development

INTRODUCTION

◖ Prior to World War II, annual federal research and development (R and D) expenditures totaled about $100 million. World War II increased our R and D budget about ten times, to an annual average expenditure of about $1 billion. The Cold War, however, has raised the World War II figure sixteen times, and we are now spending *sixteen hundred times* more money on federal research than we did prior to World War II! Approximately 90 percent of these funds have been spent by three agencies (the Department of Defense, the National Aeronautics and Space Administration, and the Atomic Energy Commission) for purposes that relate directly or indirectly to defense. This figure represents about one-sixth of the national budget, and more dramatically, about 70 percent of all research expenditures in America. Furthermore, R and D expenditures are expected to rise considerably under the Nixon Administration, which, concerned about a "security gap" during the campaign, has promised to expand our weapons systems, which are the most costly in our history.

In October, 1966, the Subcommittee on Employment, Manpower, and Poverty of the Senate Committee on Public Welfare held hearings to determine the effect of these massive R and D funds upon our scientific manpower and the development policies of our universities and industries. These hearings led a majority of the committee to arrive at four general conclusions about the impact of federal R and D expenditures:

(1) There is a marked and persistent concentration of R and D funds in certain states and in the large corporations and better known universities. (2) R and D funds act as a powerful magnet, drawing highly trained scientific and technical manpower to the areas, corporations, and universities in which these funds are expended. These funds are therefore an important factor in the growth of these areas or institutions. (3) The present distribution of R and D funds harms the national interest, the committee felt, by concentrating our most competent scientific minds in certain regions of the country—especially California, Texas, southern New England, and the Middle Atlantic states. Finally (4) further congressional study, a broader distribution of research funds, and a national search for research talent are strongly recommended. The section of the committee's report on the amount and the distribution of federal research funds is reprinted below.

The second selection discusses the impact of government research on industrial growth. Its author, John H. Rubel, Assistant Secretary of Defense when this piece was written and now Senior Vice President of Planning and Development at Litton Industries, is understandably more optimistic in his conclusions than the Senate subcommittee above. Rubel maintains that R and D is "the most fruitful source" of long-term industrial growth; that defense spending has always been the chief vehicle for expanding R and D growth; that the immediate benefits of federal R and D outweigh its enormous cost; and that it is too early to judge how valuable this R and D investment might turn out to be in the long run. Finally, Rubel believes that rather than cutting back on defense-oriented R and D, we should expand our *non*defense R and D efforts.

A contrary view is presented in the next selection by Robert Solo. Solo is less sure that R and D is the key to technological growth, and in fact he contends that R and D as presently constituted probably hampers the economy. Using three measurements—output per man-hour, our GNP, and the number of patents filed—Solo shows that there is no positive correlation between our rate of economic growth and the level of R and D expenditures. Moreover, Solo believes that the rate of spillover has been declining since World War II because the civilian and military economies are becoming less and less alike, so that a substantial advance in military weapons is of little use in solving civilian problems. Even where problems are similar, only a small part of the scientific information generated by the DOD is unclassified and hence available for application in the civilian economy.

In the final selection of this chapter, H. L. Nieburg describes the importance of defense contracts as a "social management tool." The influence of these contracts as social management tools, he maintains, actually rivals the government's power to tax and to spend for the general welfare. These defense contracts have introduced a "new kind of economic federalism." Instead of a free-enterprise system, we are moving towards a "government-subsidized private-profit system," he declares, ". . . which resembles traditional private enterprise and the corporate state of fascism."

Several questions are worth pondering: Is defense R and D a burden or a prop to the economy? Is its distribution fair? [1] Is the $8200 million allocated for federal R and D defense expenditures (1970) contrasted with the $22 million R and D expenditures for crime research a wise division of government financial resources? According to Senator Stuart Symington (Democrat, Mo.), some $23 billion has been invested in unworkable or obsolete missiles. Does the "state of the art" justify such an expenditure? How much security is there in "bristling missiles standing tall around deteriorating cities," as Senator Mike Mansfield (Democrat, Mont.) maintains? On the other hand, would the United States be as advanced technologically today if it had not been for these R and D funds? Would we have the same degree of ability to manage and develop the highly complex systems we now have? And is there *really* a refutable answer to the justification, "better safe than sorry"?

---

[1] In 1964, for example, California received 40 percent of all prime R and D awards, including 63 percent of all awards to non-profit institutions (except educational institutions) and 40 percent of all R and D awards given to business firms. California also received 69 percent of all R and D awards by NASA and 39 percent of AEC R and D awards that year.

THE READINGS

1] The Distribution of Federal Research and Development Funds

A. DEFINITIONS

IT IS IMPORTANT to distinguish the various categories of research. Basic research is defined for our purpose as a search for understanding of the laws of nature "without regard to the ultimate application of the results." Applied research, on the other hand, is carried on "with practical objectives in mind," general though the objectives may be. Distinctions between basic research and applied research, obviously, can become quite fine in specific cases.

Development is defined as "the systematic use of knowledge directed toward the design and production of useful prototypes, materials, devices, systems, methods, or processes." Development applies the results of research to the eventual end product, and in this way, is distinct from both basic and applied research. It is often described as involving more engineering than science, and in any event, it accounts for the great bulk (an estimated 61 percent in fiscal year 1967) of research and development costs.

Though not actually considered a part of research and development proper, a fourth component, research and development plant and equipment, is often included in assessing total costs of the research and development effort.

This includes funds for land purchases and facilities modification, but not for salaries and routine maintenance. Whenever funds for research and development plant are included in statistics mentioned in this report, such inclusion will specifically be noted.

B. REGIONAL BOUNDARIES

The regional boundaries used for reporting geographic distribution of Federal funds for research and development are those [of the Census Bureau].

C. THE OUTLAYS OF FEDERAL RESEARCH AND DEVELOPMENT FUNDS

Federal funds for research and development and research and development plant have increased drastically since 1940, both as an absolute figure

---

FROM *The Impact of Federal Research and Development Policies upon Scientific and Technical Manpower,* Committee on Labor and Public Welfare, U.S. Senate, 89th Cong., 2nd Sess. (1960), pp. 6–21. [Footnotes omitted—J. L. C.]

and as a percentage of the total budget. (See table 1.) Federal obligations for research, development, and research and development plant for fiscal year 1967 are estimated at $15.9 billion, of which almost $2 billion is for basic research, $5.3 billion for basic and applied research, $9.8 billion for development, and $0.8 billion for research and development plant.

There were 28 Federal agencies which reported obligations for research and development. As table 2 indicates, however, only a few of them make substantial contribution to the overall research and development effort. Obligations for research and development amounted to $14.8 billion in 1965, an estimated $15.9 billion in 1966, and a proposed $16.1 billion in 1967. Four agencies—the Department of Defense, National Aeronautics and Space Administration, Atomic Energy Commission, and Department of Health, Education, and Welfare—accounted for 95 percent of the total during each of these 3 years. Another 4 percent of the total in each year came from four other agencies, the Department of Agriculture, National Science Foundation, Department of the Interior, and Federal Aviation Agency. Details of major characteristics of Federal funding for research and development appear in appendix A.

D. DISTRIBUTION

Research and development is now a $21 billion business in the United States. Of this total approximately 70 percent, or $16 billion, is funded by the Federal Government. The Federal share, in fact, is dominant in almost every phase of the program. In 1963, 65 percent rather than the present 70 percent of funds expended on research and development came from the Federal Government. At that time 60 percent of research and development funds in industry and 70 percent in universities and other nonprofit organizations came from the Federal Government, 60 percent of basic and applied research and 70 percent of development were also financed with Federal funds.

The subcommittee has found the geographic distribution of these funds to be markedly uneven. In both 1963 and 1964, approximately 78 percent of Federal research and development funds—totaling $12.5 billion in 1963 and $14.6 billion in 1964—were obligated in only 12 States and the District of Columbia. Of these States, California was overwhelmingly the major recipient, with 35 percent of the total in each year. New York and Maryland followed, at about 8 percent and 5 percent respectively. Then came Texas, Massachusetts, and Pennsylvania each with about 4 percent; the District of Columbia, Florida, New Jersey, and New Mexico, each at about 3 percent; and Missouri, Ohio and Alabama, each with approximately 2 percent. The remaining 38 States divided 22 percent of the total of Federal research and development funds; and 30 of the 38 States, in fact, received considerably less than 1 percent each.

The same unevenness is also shown in a regional reporting. Table 3 shows the regional distribution of Federal research and development funds for 1963 and 1964. The Pacific division was the leading recipient, again by an

TABLE 1   FEDERAL OBLIGATIONS AND EXPENDITURES, FISCAL YEARS 1940–67[1]

[In millions of dollars]

Fiscal years	Total Federal budget expenditures	Research, development, and research and development plant[2]		
		Obligations	Expenditures	Expenditures as percent of budget
1940	$ 9,055	([3])	$74	0.8%
1941	13,255	([3])	198	1.5
1942	34,037	([3])	280	0.8
1943	79,368	([3])	602	0.8
1944	94,986	([3])	1,377	1.4
1945	98,303	([3])	1,591	1.6
1946	60,326	([3])	918	1.5
1947	38,923	$691	900	2.3
1948	32,955	868	855	2.6
1949	39,474	1,105	1,082	2.7
1950	39,544	1,175	1,083	2.7
1951	43,970	1,812	1,301	3.0
1952	65,303	2,914.	1,816	2.8
1953	74,120	3,361	3,101	4.2
1954	67,537	3,039	3,148	4.7
1955	64,389	2,745	3,308	5.1
1956	66,224	3,267	3,446	5.2
1957	68,966	4,389	4,462	6.5
1958	71,369	4,905	4,990	7.0
1959	80,342	7,116	5,803	7.2
1960	76,539	8,074	7,738	10.1
1961	81,515	9,601	9,278	11.4
1962	87,787	11,060	10,373	11.8
1963	92,642	13,650	11,988	12.9
1964	97,684	15,310	14,694	15.0
1965	96,507	15,731	14,875	15.4
1966 (estimate)[4]	106,428	17,069	15,963	15.0
1967 (estimate)[4]	112,847	16,650	16,152	14.3

[1] National Science Foundation. Federal Funds for Research, Development, and Other Scientific Activities, fiscal years 1965, 1966, 1967. Vol. XV (NSF 66-25), 1966, p. 4. (Hereafter referred to as NSF 66-25.)

[2] Beginning in fiscal year 1953, amounts include pay and allowance of military personnel in research and development for both obligations and expenditures.

[3] Not available.

[4] These estimates are based on amounts shown in the Budget, 1967, subject to subsequent administrative action. Data for 1967, moreover, do not reflect congressional action.

NOTE: Data for fiscal year 1952 and subsequent years are based on surveys of the National Science Foundation. Prior data were prepared by the Bureau of the Budget. Since the NSF surveys began, agencies have, when necessary, submitted revised data to maintain historical comparability of reporting.

TABLE 2   CHANGES IN FEDERAL OBLIGATIONS FOR RESEARCH, DEVELOPMENT, AND
RESEARCH AND DEVELOPMENT PLANT FROM THE BUDGET, 1965,
TO THOSE REFLECTING SUBSEQUENT CONGRESSIONAL ACTION AND
ADMINISTRATIVE DECISIONS, BY AGENCY, FISCAL YEAR 1965 (ESTIMATED)[1]
[In millions of dollars]

Agency	The budget, 1965	Subsequent congressional and administrative decisions	Actual change	Percent change
Total	$16,104	$16,601	+$497	+3%
Department of Agriculture	196	232	+36	+18
Department of Commerce	87	86	−1	−1
Department of Defense	7,341	7,250	−91	−1
Department of Health, Education, and Welfare	981	1,002	+21	+2
Department of the Interior	128	128		
Atomic Energy Commission	1,504	1,677	+173	+12
Federal Aviation Agency	63	115	+52	+83
National Aeronautics and Space Administration	5,399	5,736	+337	+6
National Science Foundation	295	267	−28	−9
Veterans Administration	40	41	+1	+3
Other agencies	70	68	−2	−3

[1] National Science Foundation. Federal Funds for Research, Development, and Other Scientific Activities, Fiscal Years 1963, 1964, 1965. Vol. XIII (NSF 65-13), 1965, p. 187. (Hereafter referred to as NSF 65-13.)
NOTE: Detail may not add to totals because of rounding.

overwhelming margin, receiving more than the next three leading divisions combined.

Table 4 presents a breakdown of Federal research and development funds by geographic division and by eight selected agencies, which account for over 97 percent of the total Federal research and development effort. The dominance of the Pacific division can be seen here. Three agencies, the DOD, AEC, and NASA, which together account for about 90 percent of the Federal effort, devote significant shares of their respective totals to the Pacific region. The actual percentages given for 1963 remain substantially the same in the estimates for 1964 and 1965.

Information on geographic distribution of Federal funds for research and development takes on meaning in comparison with other characteristics of States and regions. For instance, table 5 belies the assertion that the Federal funds are evenly dispensed when compared with population. For the New England and the South Atlantic regions, the correlation between percentage of population and percentage of funds is quite close. But disparities exist for the other regions, and for two of the regions they are huge. The Pacific region has only 11.8 percent of the population, yet 37 percent of the funds. The disparity is just as large in the other direction for the east north cen-

TABLE 3   DISTRIBUTION OF FEDERAL RESEARCH AND DEVELOPMENT OBLIGATIONS OF
SELECTED AGENCIES, FOR ALL PERFORMERS, BY GEOGRAPHIC DIVISION,
FISCAL YEARS 1963 AND 1964[1]

Geographic division	Fiscal year 1963	Fiscal year 1964 (estimated)
Total (millions of dollars)	$12,250	$14,316
	Percent distribution	
New England	6%	5%
Middle Atlantic	15	15
East North Central	7	6
West North Central	3	4
South Atlantic	14	14
East South Central	3	4
West South Central	5	7
Mountain	9	8
Pacific	38	37
Other (including territories)	1	2

[1] NSF 65-13 op. cit., p. 55.
NOTE: Percent detail may not add to 100 because of rounding.

tral region, which has only 6 percent of the funds, yet the largest (20.2) percentage of the population.

It is sometimes objected that instead of a straight population funds ratio, it would be more realistic to compare the percentages of scientists and engineers in each of the regions with the percentage of the Federal funds going there. Yet even here wide disparities are obvious, as table 6 brings out.

Again, the Pacific region is markedly favored, with only 15 percent of the Nation's scientists yet 37 percent of the Federal funds. The Middle Atlantic and, again, the East North Central appear to lose out. The former has 22 percent of the scientists but only 15 percent of the funds; the latter has 17 percent of the scientists and only 6 percent of the funds.

In general the same disparities remain when one considers the percentages of engineers in each region. It was noted earlier that our statistics on engineers were imperfect but it is certain that any correction would not be able to eradicate the disparities obvious in the Middle Atlantic region and in the Pacific and East North Central regions in particular. The paper submitted to the subcommittee by Dr. Sidney Sonenbloom of the National Planning Association used other indicators such as labor force, industrial employment, personal income, and per capita income. The Daddario subcommittee compared distribution with payment of Federal taxes and with distribution of scientists. All such comparisons show the same marked and disturbing disparities.

TABLE 4   DISTRIBUTION OF FEDERAL RESEARCH AND DEVELOPMENT OBLIGATIONS FOR ALL PERFORMERS BY GEOGRAPHIC DIVISION AND SELECTED AGENCY, FISCAL YEAR 1963[1]

Geographic division	Department of Agriculture	Department of Commerce	Department of Defense	Department of Health, Education, and Welfare	Department of the Interior	Atomic Energy Commission	National Aeronautics and Space Administration	National Science Foundation
Total (millions)	$160	$51	$7,264	$636	$92	$1,074	$2,831	$143
				Percent distribution				
New England	2	2	7	11	5	2	2	14
Middle Atlantic	8	10	17	20	13	20	7	18
East North Central	12	3	7	14	3	8	4	16
West North Central	10	1	1	6	8	1	8	4
South Atlantic	33	62	13	28	18	3	14	18
East South Central	6	(2)	2	3	6	8	6	1
West South Central	9	3	3	3	6	1	12	5
Mountain	8	16	9	2	21	32	1	7
Pacific	12	2	40	12	20	24	47	16
Others (including territories)	1	(2)	2	1	(2)	(2)		(2)
Agency as percent of Federal total	1	(2)	59	5	1	9	23	1

[1] NSF 65-13, p. 57.
[2] Less than 0.5 percent.
NOTE: Percent detail may not add to 100 because of rounding.

TABLE 5   A COMPARISON OF EACH REGION'S PERCENTAGE OF THE POPULATION
AND ITS PERCENTAGE OF RESEARCH AND DEVELOPMENT FUNDS[1]

Region	1960 percentage of Nation's population	1964 percentage of research and development funds (estimated)
New England	5.9%	5%
Middle Atlantic	19.0	15
East North Central	20.2	6
West North Central	8.6	4
South Atlantic	14.5	14
East South Central	6.7	4
West South Central	9.5	7
Mountain	3.8	8
Pacific	11.8	37
Other (including territories)	(NA)	2

[1] Compiled from data in NSF 65-13.

TABLE 6   A COMPARISON OF REGIONAL DISTRIBUTION
OF FEDERAL FUNDS FOR RESEARCH AND DEVELOPMENT
WITH DISTRIBUTION OF SCIENTISTS AND ENGINEERS[1]

Region	Federal research and development funds—1964 estimate (percent)	Employed scientists in National Register (percent)	Employed engineers, 1960 census (percent)
New England	5%	7.0%	7.2%
Middle Atlantic	15	22.1	21.8
East North Central	6	16.6	21.9
West North Central	4	6.3	5.9
South Atlantic	14	13.8	10.8
East South Central	4	3.4	3.6
West South Central	7	8.5	7.0
Mountain	8	5.7	3.7
Pacific	37	15.3	18.1
Other (including territories)	2	1.4	(NA)

[1] National Science Foundation, "Scientific and Technical Manpower Resources" (NSF 64-28),
1964 (hereafter referred to as NSF 64-28).
NOTE: Percent detail may not add to 100 because of rounding.

A breakdown of the performers of Federal research and development work reveals that the bulk of the work, almost two-thirds, is done by industry.

Within industry, the distribution of Federal research and development funds remains quite unbalanced. Table 8 presents that percentage of Federal funds awarded to each region as reported by contractor for 1963. The distortion here is ever greater than that of the overall research and development picture. The Pacific region received 37 percent of the total Federal investment in industrial research and development, more than seven other regions combined. Again, it can be noted that the Pacific area, with 37 percent of the funds, has but 11.8 percent of the population, whereas the West South Central region, for example, with almost 10 percent of the population, has but 7 percent of these funds. The share of Federal funds flowing to five other regions also is less than their share of the national population.

An additional, significant unevenness occurs in the distribution of funds between big business and small business firms. By the standards of the Small Business Administration, a firm employing less than 1,000 employees is regarded as small. Mr. Eugene P. Foley, then administrator of the SBA, testified that of 11,800 firms doing research and development, 90 percent are small. Yet this 90 percent receives only 5 percent of the research and development total. Those firms having work forces in excess of 5,000 men number only 3 percent of the 11,800 firms. Yet this 3 percent receives 86 percent of the research and development total. This concentration can be explained in part by the fact that 80 percent of the scientists and engineers engaged in industrial research and development work for the large firms, those with more than 5,000 employees. The small firms, correspondingly, employ only 11 percent of the total number of scientists and engineers in industry.

The Department of Defense, as the largest single performer of Federal research and development serves as a good illustration of the difficulties faced by small business in the research and development area. The Department of Defense awarded $5,114,637,000 in research and development contracts to extramural, industrial performers in 1964. The Department notes that 61.3 percent of the U.S. business firms with which it contracted were small; it notes that of its 370 major business contractors, over one-third (136) were small. These facts are significant, but surely the most important one for the small businessman is that of this total of $5.1 billion, only $190 million—less than 4 percent—was awarded to small business firms.

Table 7 gives an impressive indication of the high concentration of defense research and development funds, with 10 leading Department of Defense business contractors accounting for over $3 billion of the $5.1 billion total. In other words, approximately 60 percent of the Department of Defense research and development awards to business went to merely 10 firms. The remaining 1,270 business firms on the Department of Defense contract list were left with 40 percent of the total.

In addition, the DOD stated that while its procurement offices "have the further responsibility . . . to recommend set-asides for small businesses, in-

TABLE 7   TEN LEADING DOD CONTRACTORS, FISCAL YEAR 1964[1]

Rank	Contractor	Amount (thousands)
1	North American Aviation, Inc.	$568,163
2	General Dynamics Corp.	432,855
3	Lockheed Aircraft Corp.	324,022
4	Western Electric Co.	318,264
5	Boeing Co.	313,473
6	Martin Marietta Corp.	281,391
7	General Electric Co.	216,263
8	Aerojet General Corp.	215,916
9	United Aircraft Corp.	201,924
10	Pan American World Airways, Inc.	136,275
	Total	3,008,546

[1] Compiled from *Impact of Federal Research and Development Policies on Scientific and Technical Manpower,* Subcommittee on Employment and Manpower of the Committee on Public Welfare, U.S. Senate, 89th Cong., 1st Sess., 1965, pp. 453-57.

cluding the research and development procurements, where such preferences can be justified and competition obtained," the set-aside procedures are not usually utilized for research and development. Thus, even where specific provision has been made for small business, the Department of Defense, the largest Federal purchaser of research and development, fails to make use of authority intended to spread the present concentration.

In this regard, of course, it is essential to bear in mind that small businesses receive a greater part of their research and development through subcontracts from big businesses. However, the subcommittee believes the flow of subcontracts is by no means sufficient to offset the overwhelming effects of the concentration of prime contracts with big business.

F. EDUCATIONAL INSTITUTIONS

It is generally agreed that because of the importance of education to national prosperity, strength, and security, the funds awarded to educational institutions have a long-range significance far in excess of the face value of the awards. In this light, then, the $1.5, $1.7 (estimated), and $1.8 (estimated) billion distributed to educational institutions of higher education in 1963, 1964, and 1965 respectively take on a special significance.

The geographic distribution of the $1.7 billion, to use 1964 as an example, is more nearly even than that for industry, but there are some disparities. As table 8 brings out, the Pacific region receives 31.3 percent of the total and again is the most favored region. California alone, which invariably outpaces the rest of its region by far, in this case receives a full 29.1 percent of the national total. The east south-central region and the west south-central region form an eight-State area that receives a very small share of the total.

TABLE 8 PERCENT DISTRIBUTION OF RESEARCH AND DEVELOPMENT OBLIGATIONS FOR EDUCATIONAL INSTITUTIONS, BY GEOGRAPHIC DIVISIONS AND STATES, FISCAL YEAR 1964[1]

NEW ENGLAND	
Maine	0.1
New Hampshire	.2
Vermont	.2
Massachusetts	11.0
Rhode Island	.4
Connecticut	1.2
Subtotal	13.1

MIDDLE ATLANTIC	
New York	8.4
New Jersey	1.9
Pennsylvania	3.4
Subtotal	13.8

EAST NORTH CENTRAL	
Ohio	1.9
Indiana	1.2
Illinois	7.2
Michigan	2.8
Wisconsin	1.3
Subtotal	14.3

WEST NORTH CENTRAL	
Minnesota	1.3
Iowa	1.1
Missouri	1.0
North Dakota	.1
South Dakota	.1
Nebraska	.2
Kansas	.4
Subtotal	4.1

SOUTH ATLANTIC	
Delaware	.1
Maryland	4.3
District of Columbia	1.0
Virginia	.6
West Virginia	.1
North Carolina	.9
South Carolina	.1
Georgia	.7

SOUTH ATLANTIC–continued	
Florida	1.0
Subtotal	8.9

EAST SOUTH CENTRAL	
Kentucky	.3
Tennessee	.7
Alabama	.5
Mississippi	.2
Subtotal	1.8

WEST SOUTH CENTRAL	
Arkansas	.2
Louisiana	.6
Oklahoma	.5
Texas	1.8
Subtotal	3.1

MOUNTAIN	
Montana	.1
Idaho	.4
Wyoming	(2)
Colorado	1.0
New Mexico	5.3
Arizona	.4
Utah	.5
Nevada	.8
Subtotal	8.5

PACIFIC	
Washington	1.1
Oregon	.6
California	29.1
Alaska	.3
Hawaii	.2
Subtotal	31.3
Territories	.2
Unallocated	.9
Total	100.0

[1] Abstracted from U.S. Congress, House. Obligation for research and development, and research and development plant by geographic divisions and States, by select Federal agencies, fiscal years 1961-64. Subcommittee on Science, Research, and Development of the Committee on Science and Astronautics, 88th Cong., 2d sess., 1964, committee print, pp. 90-91.

[2] Less than one-tenth of 1 percent. Percentages may not add to total because of rounding.

TABLE 9   DISTRIBUTION OF FEDERAL SUPPORT TO UNIVERSITIES AND COLLEGES,
BY GEOGRAPHIC DIVISION AND TYPE OF SUPPORT, 1965[1]
[In millions of dollars]

Geographic division	Total Federal support	Academic science				Other educational activities
		Total	Research and development	Research and development plant	Other	
U.S. total	$2,273.4	$1,730.1	$1,075.6	$126.2	$528.4	$543.2
		Percent distribution				
U.S. total	100.0	100.0	100.0	100.0	100.0	100.0
New England	9.9	11.2	12.6	5.3	9.5	6.1
Middle Atlantic	18.7	19.9	20.1	29.5	17.0	15.1
East North Central	18.4	18.4	19.1	14.1	17.8	18.5
West North Central	7.5	7.3	6.3	6.9	9.5	8.3
South Atlantic	13.1	12.0	11.0	11.8	14.2	16.5
East South Central	4.1	3.7	3.0	2.8	5.2	5.4
West South Central	6.6	6.1	5.6	2.5	7.8	8.3
Mountain	4.9	5.0	4.7	7.5	5.0	4.7
Pacific	16.2	16.1	17.2	19.3	12.9	16.6
Puerto Rico	.6	.6	.4	.2	1.0	.7

[1] National Science Foundation, "Federal Support for Academic Science and Other Educational Activities in Universities and Colleges, Fiscal Year 1965," (NSF 66-30), 1966, table VII, p. 25. SOURCE: National Science Foundation, "Federal Support for Academic Science and Other Educational Activities in Universities and Colleges, Fiscal year 1965," NSF 66-30, 1966, table IV, p. 16.

The unevenness in this instance, then, does exist, but it is somewhat less marked than in previous cases.

The unevenness is greatly reduced if one considers only the geographic distribution in fiscal year 1965 of those funds to educational institutions for research and development ($1 billion) and excludes those funds to Federal research centers managed by universities ($0.9 billion). Table 9 reveals that the Pacific region here ranks behind both the middle Atlantic and east north-central regions, while the east and west south-central regions have increased their shares.

Although on this basis there appears to be lessened geographic concentration of funds, there still exists appreciable concentration. Of a total of $1.7 billion Federal academic science support during fiscal year 1965, the first 10 institutions received 25 percent and the second 10 received 16.5 percent. These figures do not include the Federal funds to Federal research centers operated by colleges and universities. Federal obligations to 24 such contract centers amounted to $0.9 billion in fiscal year 1965, virtually all of which was for research and development. The Jet Propulsion Laboratory, managed by the California Institute of Technology accounted for about 27 percent, with the next largest center being the Lawrence Radiation Laboratory, also operated by the University of California, which received about 17 percent. Still, in 1948 only 32 percent of funds to educational institutions went to the leading 20 recipients, including contract research centers. Another effect on today's 20 universities that is also a critical matter is their dependence on Federal support, for Federal money comprises from 32 to 85 percent of their budgets. As Dr. Robert L. Edwards, president of Clemson University, noted: "Several of these universities, as a result, find themselves in the position of looking to the Federal Government as their single most important income source.

G. INTRAMURAL

The intramural work is that carried out directly by laboratories of Federal agencies. Intramural obligations for fiscal year 1965 amounted to $2.8 billion. The geographic distribution of these funds is shown in table 10. Again, the Pacific region is a leading recipient, but this time the South Atlantic, with 35.7 percent of the funds, is the top region. This figure reflects the amount of funds awarded to the Washington area, particularly in Maryland (14.8 percent) and the District of Columbia itself (11.9 percent). The west north central region, through this set of percentages, is revealed as surprisingly poor in federally owned and run research centers.

H. DISTRIBUTION BY FIELD

Table 11 presents total Federal research obligations by field of science from 1956 to 1965. The table reveals the heavy emphasis that has been placed on the physical sciences, particularly the physical sciences proper and the engineering sciences. They have regularly accounted for roughly two-thirds of the total research effort. The geographic concentration of total research and development funds is thus paralleled by an equally significant concentration by field of science in total research.

I. THE BASIS FOR THE OUTLAYS

As will be discussed, it is the opinion of the subcommittee that research and development awards have important effects on the Nation's manpower and its regions. Why does the money go where it goes? There are two extreme views as to the proper basis for agency decisions in this field. One is that money should go only where the best competence to perform exists. This criterion rules without regard to the long-term effects the award will have on the development of science, business, and education in the region. The other extreme is that only the long-term effects on development should be determining. Perhaps the clearest example of the former are Department of Defense awards in 1964 of only 1 percent of its research and development funds in the east south-central region, an area with 7 percent of the population, and 5.5 percent of its funds in the east north-central region, an area

TABLE 10   PERCENT DISTRIBUTION OF RESEARCH AND DEVELOPMENT OBLIGATIONS
FOR INTRAMURAL PERFORMERS, BY GEOGRAPHIC DIVISIONS AND STATES,
FISCAL YEAR 1965[1]

NEW ENGLAND

Maine	0.1
New Hampshire	.1
Vermont	(2)
Massachusetts	2.6
Rhode Island	.6
Connecticut	.8
Subtotal	4.3

MIDDLE ATLANTIC

New York	1.2
New Jersey	4.2
Pennsylvania	3.9
Subtotal	9.4

EAST NORTH CENTRAL

Ohio	5.2
Indiana	.4
Illinois	.4
Michigan	.8
Wisconsin	.2
Subtotal	7.0

WEST NORTH CENTRAL

Minnesota	.3
Iowa	.2
Missouri	.2
North Dakota	.1
South Dakota	.1
Nebraska	(2)
Kansas	(2)
Subtotal	.8

SOUTH ATLANTIC

Delaware	(2)
Maryland	14.8
District of Columbia	11.9
Virginia	3.9
West Virginia	.1
North Carolina	.2
South Carolina	.1
Georgia	.5
Florida	4.2
Subtotal	35.7

EAST SOUTH CENTRAL

Kentucky	0.2
Tennessee	.5
Alabama	4.5
Mississippi	.4
Subtotal	5.7

WEST SOUTH CENTRAL

Arkansas	(2)
Louisiana	.3
Oklahoma	.1
Texas	3.2
Subtotal	3.7

MOUNTAIN

Montana	.1
Idaho	.1
Wyoming	.1
Colorado	.9
New Mexico	5.8
Arizona	1.4
Utah	.8
Nevada	.2
Subtotal	9.4

PACIFIC

Washington	.4
Oregon	.2
California	20.8
Alaska	.2
Hawaii	.1
Subtotal	21.8
Territories	.1
Offices abroad	.1
Unallocated	2.0
Total	100.0

[1] U.S. Congress, House. Obligations for research and development, and research and development plant by geographic divisions and States, by selected Federal agencies, fiscal years 1961-64, and op. cit., pp. 38-39.

[2] Less than one-tenth of 1 percent. Percentages may not add to total because of rounding.

TABLE 11 Obligations for Total Research by Field of Science,
Fiscal Years 1956–65[1]
[In millions of dollars]

Field of science	1956	1957	1958	1959	1960	1961	1962	1963	Estimate	
									1964	1965
Total, all fields	879	953	1,069	1,430	1,961	2,647	3,302	4,070	4,571	5,087
Life sciences, total	220	300	345	424	518	638	822	937	1,084	1,186
Medical sciences	121	177	216	271	343	444	605	674	786	852
Biological sciences	56	67	70	89	107	130	146	186	215	247
Agricultural sciences	44	56	59	64	68	63	71	76	83	87
Psychological sciences	(2)	(2)	(2)	26	39	52	57	72	97	115
Physical sciences, total	628	616	683	914	1,335	1,779	2,167	2,882	3,198	3,536
Physical sciences, proper	254	270	321	431	563	914	1,079	1,354	1,546	1,680
Engineering sciences	363	335	348	467	747	818	1,024	1,441	1,551	1,743
Mathematical sciences	12	12	14	16	24	46	64	87	101	113
Social sciences	31	37	41	31	35	45	63	80	103	127
Other sciences	(2)	(2)	(2)	35	34	134	193	99	89	124

[1]NSF 65–13, op. cit., p. 187.
[2]Not available.
SOURCE: National Science Foundation.

with over 20 percent of the population. In fact, 25 States combined received less than 3 percent of Department of Defense research and development funds in 1964. Perhaps the clearest example of the latter is the legislation that established one land-grant college for every State. In this the criterion is straight-forward: the long-term effects are so important that each geographic unit must receive its share.

The stated basis for almost all of the Federal research and development and research and development plant awards has been "competence." The Department of Defense statement that follows is typical of the major performer position.

> The policy of the Department of Defense in awarding research, development, test, and evaluation contracts is based on competence—that is, the ability of the contractor to do the best job at the lowest possible cost. The Department of Defense mission is the defense of the United States and the support of its foreign policy. Success in research and development is dependent on excellence in science and technology, and innovative approaches closely related thereto. Under these circumstances, competence is the only sound basis for determining where Defense research and development is to be carried out.

In NASA's view, "the responsive bidder capable of performing the contract which bids the lowest price must be awarded the contract regardless of where it is located."

There are, of course, modifications of this rule. In addition to the Department of Agriculture program, the Department of Health, Education, and Welfare states that through its Office of Education and through the Public Health Service it has instituted a series of programs embodying the principle that all regions of the country should have the opportunity to develop centers of excellence. The Department of Commerce notes that its Area Redevelopment Administration and the successor Economic Development Administration have been vitally concerned with the impact of a contract on the region when making an award.

The National Science Foundation provides an example of concern with building the Nation's resources for scientific research. The NSF has its major impact on educational institutions proper, which received $118 million of its $167 million in awards in 1964. In the words of its Director, Dr. Leonard J. Haworth, its role "relates primarily to . . . the maintenance of a vigorous and healthy scientific and technological base for the country as a whole." Such a role at least implies a concern with geographic concentration and with the stagnation of science in certain areas of the Nation. The NSF has embarked on a science development program designed to promote significant improvement in science in educational institutions which have a sound base on which to build. Table 12, which includes not only NSF research funds, but its funds for training and facilities as well, shows that this distribution of NSF funds is fairly even.

All of the witnesses, including those from the largest Federal agencies, agreed that factors reflecting the needs of specific areas should be considered

TABLE 12   DISTRIBUTION OF NATIONAL SCIENCE FOUNDATION GRANT AND CONTRACT AWARDS BY GEOGRAPHIC DIVISION, FISCAL YEAR 1964[1]

Geographic division	Total (millions)	Total (percent)
Total	$ 338.9	100%
New England	39.7	12
Middle Atlantic	56.8	17
East North Central	52.1	15
West North Central	21.5	6
South Atlantic	44.4	13
East South Central	6.6	2
West South Central	24.9	7
Mountain	32.1	9
Pacific	57.4	17
U.S. possessions and foreign	3.4	1

[1] Compiled from NSF 65-13.

when two or more firms of "equal" competence submitted "equally good" proposals. That geographic and other factors should control in such cases, in the words of Mr. Earl D. Hilburn, Deputy Associate Administrator of NASA, "may very well be valid." But NASA had no examples to offer, as indicated by the conversation immediately following between Mr. Hilburn, his aide, Dr. Smull, and Senator Nelson.

> MR. HILBURN. . . . If we judge the two firms' technical proposals to be equal, then I believe that geographical consideration should, and, in fact, do receive consideration in the ultimate selection.
> SENATOR NELSON. Do you have any examples of when that was done?
> MR. HILBURN. I could not quote any specific examples offhand——
> SENATOR NELSON. Mr. Smull, would you know of any examples where the geographic factor was given consideration?
> DR. SMULL. My activities are largely with the educational institutions, so I could not cite a case of this.

At the very least, it can be said that save for a few specific programs and a correspondingly minor portion of the research and development funds, there is scant attention paid to factors other than immediate competence. There is little attempt even to determine those cases and contracts on which other factors could be given consideration. And, as will be seen in practice, the criterion of "competence" itself is by no means a guide to the understanding of existing patterns of distribution.

2] Military R&D: The Most Fruitful Source of Long-term Growth

IT IS THE purpose—the excellent and, I trust, fruitful purpose—of this conference to explore the impact of Federal expenditures for research and development upon industrial growth. The topic is timely and important. It is inseparable from the larger subject of "economic growth" which is attracting more political, public and policy attention than ever before. The trends of the past two decades continue to accelerate, with technology exploding in new directions as never before and the role of the Federal Government in supporting it increasing. And yet—curious and even puzzling as it is—we are faced with major areas of economic stagnation throughout our Nation precisely when national income, research and development activity, and Federal support of science and technology are at an all time high. Research and development supported by and for industry seems to be receiving less support and to be attracting and retaining fewer top-notch scientists and engineers as Federally-supported R&D competes with R&D in the private sector. Many believe that efforts in the private sector are retarded by those in the public sector, and that spillover from military and space programs, however useful it may be in some specific cases, is increasingly inadequate to compensate for the shift away from private support of R&D aimed at private goals. And it appears that the shift to large-scale application-type projects may be eroding the quality and adequacy of scientific research in the U.S. by attracting many of the best scientific investigators away from research. All these are policy issues of deep and current interest to officials and citizens concerned with national security, economic growth, the utilization of our scientific, technological and managerial resources, and many related considerations. It is the purpose of this paper to set forth some general views concerning these issues, to outline the scope and trends of Federally-supported R&D, and to discuss how we might usefully define the term "industrial growth" as a basis for further and deeper study.

While I have not set out to establish or to prove any single thesis, there are a few points that I have tried to make, without attempting, in this short space, to demonstrate or support them in a thoroughgoing way. They include:

1. First: it is important to make careful distinctions, and to agree upon definitions, especially about what is meant by "industrial growth." Does "growth" mean new products, increasing diversity of products, cheaper products, better quality? Does "growth" mean more companies, or bigger ones, or higher profits? Does it mean increasing our capacity and potential to produce, or does it concern only what is actually consumed? It could mean

FROM a March, 1963, speech before the National Security Industry Association by John H. Rubel, then Assistant Secretary of Defense and currently Vice President at Litton Industries. Used by permission.

many or all of these, and more, but the most convenient and familiar statistical measures of economic growth reflect only the magnitude of total consumption and production. Yet, figures for total GNP, for example, tell us nothing about the qualitative features of industrial and economic development, and furthermore, there is no correlation (that I have discovered) between current expenditures for research and development and measured economic growth.

2. As a corollary, one must not place undue emphasis on merely statistical measures of economic activity in thinking about how research and development affects "industrial growth." What we are able to measure or have measured with respect to the support of research and development activities and their impact upon and correlation with other economic activities is undoubtedly much less important and significant than what we have not measured. The scientific and technological explosion is not just a matter of more productivity or more product, and neither is industrial growth. Both are part of an evolving revolution in the structure, perceptions and capacities of modern society. Their interaction is dynamic, however imperfectly the dynamics of that interaction can be quantified. Some headings under which "industrial growth" needs to be considered in relation to the impact of Federal expenditures for R&D are discussed in Section III.

3. And finally, to coin a useful solecism, we must be careful that we do not lose sight of the invisible. What is least noticed may, in the long run, be most important; our perceptions of the proper, the useful, the valuable, and the good may, as they change with the passage of time, discover a veritable treasure of scientific and technological methodology and results from which to draw, supported under the aegis of military, space and other Federal programs which, for many reasons, we are unable to utilize or perhaps even to perceive today. It took a long time to apply the discovery of anaesthetics; of the germ theory of disease; of penicillin; (not to mention the lag of decades usually associated with the wide application of new industrial processes following their initial introduction). Similar factors may be at work, and probably are, even now; one must provide for that likelihood in thought and action.

I. SOME GENERAL CONSIDERATIONS

A. *Interest in and attitudes toward Federally-Supported Research and Development:* If the Federal Government were to propose to produce 10% of the automobiles, or to make 10% of the clothing, or to raise and distribute 10% of the food consumed in the United States, I would expect to hear some public discussion. In fact, of course, any such proposal is unthinkable and even the suggestion seems beside the point. It is completely foreign to our conception of the way in which our national economy and our national life should be conducted.

As a matter of fact, however, the Federal Government does support not merely 10% but nearly 70% of all research and development being done in the United States today (at least insofar as expenditures are a measure of R&D effort). Only a little more than twenty years ago, the Federal Govern-

CHART 1   GROWTH OF FUNDS FOR R&D
1941–60

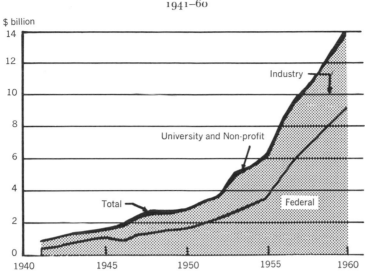

SOURCES: NSF, DOD.

ment supported practically no research and development outside a few of its laboratories. (The first chart illustrates this trend.) In the last four years alone, the Federal Government has increased appropriations for research and development by over $6.0 billion, more than doubling the level of Federal support for research and development during this short period. This increase in the level of support alone is greater than all agricultural subsidies combined.

And, yet, somewhat surprisingly, few or none of these vast aggregations of program and project efforts, nor the unprecedented rate at which Federal support for them has increased have been the subject of very much debate in the Congress, or for that matter, in any other forum.

There are probably several factors that explain this somewhat surprising absence of general interest or debate concerning the Government's research and development programs. Part of the explanation stems from the readiness of the public and the Congress generally to accept expenditures for national defense with comparatively little debate, convinced that they are probably essential to national survival, that it is "better to be safe than sorry."

Moreover, it is widely stated and believed that expenditures for defense research and engineering, and now for the exploration of space, will benefit the private sector, not only because direct expenditures are made with industry for these undertakings but because of the technological "fall-out" or "spillover" that is said will result from them.

And, perhaps most important of all is the fact that about 66% of the funds spent for Federally-supported research and development are expended by industry. In this sense, the principles of private enterprise are not violated by these Federal undertakings. Research and engineering, which is regarded as a business expense in the private sector, now represents enormous business opportunities to firms furnishing R&D services and material to the Government.

Whatever emphasis they may be given, or however intermingled they may be, these factors add up to a marked transformation in the attitude of American citizens toward expenditures by the Federal Government. They do not seem to be widely regarded as an important or onerous burden that adds to taxes, but almost as a shifting and focusing of readily expandable resources upon needed or wanted objectives.

But although these comments suggest wide support for Federal expenditures for R&D, based in part upon the conviction that they are not only necessary but desirable for collateral reasons, the expenditures are not uniformly distributed in any respect. They are sharply concentrated in a comparatively small number of technical areas and industries (see Chart 2), and heavily focused on highly specialized objectives and technologies, many of which have little or no direct, near-term application in the private sector. It is not apparent, in short, that policies have been or could be adopted which would point these efforts, or some of them at least, toward objectives which might better serve national needs in the private sector, or which might more directly or demonstrably affect economic and industrial growth.

B. *Focussed effort, spillover and teams:* Nobody concerned with the security of the United States would question for a moment the great importance of research and development sponsored by the Defense Department aimed at the evolution of new knowledge, new technologies and new weapons systems. It would be impossible, of course, to make an iron-clad case that every R&D project and program supported by the Defense Department was essential for national defense. In fact, in FY 1964, approximately $5.8 billion of the defense budget for research and engineering (out of a total of $7.9 billion) is planned for programs and projects for which no decision to produce or deploy a weapons system has been made.

For there is no argument that in principle it makes sense to support research and development efforts at a very high level: experience shows that we can expect with confidence that such efforts will maintain our military technology close to the forefront of the possible, and it is perfectly obvious that an advanced and developing military technology is essential to the maintenance of a strong military posture in today's world. I think it is generally believed, too, that, having established the national goal of accomplishing a manned lunar landing and return we will be successful as a nation in accomplishing that objective. It can be done; a national policy decision has been made (and accepted) to do it; therefore, it will be done.

In short, nobody seriously questions that the deliberate application of research and development efforts is virtually certain to lead to the attainment of the objectives sought, providing only that an ample technological and scientific base is maintained and that sound judgment is applied in selecting particular projects and objectives. In this sense—that ultimate goals have been attained, despite set backs and rising costs—very few major undertak-

CHART 2   COMPARISON OF GROWTH OF R&D FUNDS
WITH GROWTH OF GNP AND FEDERAL BUDGET

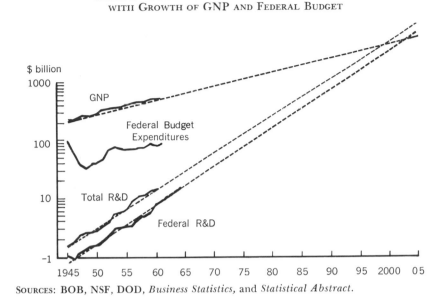

SOURCES: BOB, NSF, DOD, *Business Statistics,* and *Statistical Abstract.*

ings in the military or space field have failed. Many such "successes" would have been considered catastrophic failures if undertaken in the private sector, if only because they would have brought financial ruin to their supporters before their continued evolution could have led to "success." In fact, the history of several privately-supported jet transport developments comes close to illustrating the point. Unsubsidized private attempts to develop a supersonic transport would probably prove it.

But many of the most spectacular technological attainments of all time have been made in the last few years through this process of deciding to undertake the projects and then organizing and funding them as necessary to get them done. The technique of organizing and directing vast team efforts on an interdisciplinary, multi-industry base has emerged as a new power, a new social instrument, out of the military and space programs of the past two decades. It is precisely this powerful and relatively new technique of large-scale organization focussed upon major project objectives that most sharply distinguishes military and space endeavors from R&D in the private sector.

Yet, spillover, as I have noted earlier, is often used as an argument by advocates of Federal expenditures for major programs and projects. Why? The argument would almost seem to be self-defeating. For if one believes that the deliberate application of effort toward a specified goal is the way to reach it, and if one has such goals in mind for the private sector, then surely it would make sense to organize programs and projects in the private sector needed to attain those goals. And if one really believes in the efficacy and value of spillover, why not alter our policies by 180 degrees and undertake those projects in the private sector, depending upon spillover to support the advance of military and space requirements?

The answer seems obvious. Spillover is too uncertain, too inefficient, and too long in coming to satisfy near-term needs of the sort that must be met by, for example, the Department of Defense. And specialized defense and space needs simply require the specialized developments required to meet them.

But above all, the ground rules differ in an essential and distinguishing way. The Federally supported projects are, in essence, limited only by technology and "requirements." Funding constraints may affect this project or that for a time, or dictate a technical compromise here or there, but for the most part, progress is limited by what is possible. If trained operators are required, they are trained. If new installations are needed, they are furnished. If new supply lines, new communication systems, new factories must be set up, they are. The environment necessary to accept and to utilize these technology-limited undertakings is created for them. Back in the laboratory it is "performance," not cost, that counts. Thus are removed constraints that govern developments in every other phase of modern life, especially R&D in the private sector. Undertakings there, whether to improve a process or develop a product, are "socially limited," not "technology" or "performance limited."

Economic factors are foremost but they are by no means the only important "social limitations" imposed in the private sector. There are many others. They include the definition of "needs" by the public, both individual needs which collectively create demands for goods and services, and collective needs which reflect community aspirations and perceptions. They include the complex of rules and traditions which govern the role and objectives which private industrial concerns can adopt on their own—when not serving, that is, as an instrumentality for the accomplishment of Federal programs. In any case, and this is my principal point here, we are not able to choose between large-scale military and space projects on the one hand, and any other large-scale undertakings aimed at objectives of a wholly different sort on the other. The social mechanisms for harnessing and directing modern, large-scale, inter-disciplinary, inter-industry R&D resources for other purposes simply do not exist.

Perhaps this new-found ability to combine a great diversity of scientific and technical skills and disciplines to make a massive assault on very large-scale problems will turn out to be a social innovation of even greater consequence in the long run than the scientific and technical innovations on which most of our attention is generally focussed. This may be the "spillover" of greatest national and social consequence, once it can be used. There is no doubt that the development of this new capability has endowed us as a nation with new powers, and with a new sense of power. The question remains open: how can this new social invention be used outside the space and defense sector to which it is presently so largely confined?

III. INDUSTRIAL GROWTH

Here I wish to propose a description (an outline, not a definitive description) of the chief headings under which "industrial growth" may be understood.

To begin with, we must distinguish at once between "measured growth" and "true growth" as I pointed out at the start. If "industrial growth" is considered just another input to "measured economic growth" then there will be little or no correlation between growth and expenditures for R&D. Chart 10 illustrates this point. And, moreover, what correlation there is will be very difficult to pinpoint with confidence or accuracy.

Now, measured product is increased by increases in productivity per worker. Undoubtedly technology contributes to that very greatly, although other factors, such as "scientific factory management," may have made very large contributions, too. If by "industrial growth" we mean input to measured economic growth, then increases in productivity will be the chief factor of interest insofar as R&D contributions (or the withdrawal of these by competing programs in the public sector) is concerned. In my opinion such a definition is much too narrow. It simply fails to provide a vehicle for discussing the qualitative as well as the quantitative features of "industrial growth": although, as I have stated earlier, industrial and economic growth in a most important sense, signifies the transformation of culture and social activity to permit the creation and acceptance of the fruits of modern science and technology. Mere gadgetry has nothing to do with growth seen in this perspective.

To illustrate: suppose we had only four industries in America—food, transport, housing and clothing—would we be satisfied with a form of industrial growth that only made these industries more efficient, but never saw new ones or new products evolve? I think not. Change which includes the invention of new products and the obsolescence of old ones is certainly included, or should be, in our concept of what is meant by "industrial growth." It will be difficult to measure it—I have no measures of it at all, though some undoubtedly could be discovered or acquired—but that does not diminish the importance of change, and of other factors too.

To repeat: granted that the creation of new end products, or of new industries, does not of and by itself contribute to increased productivity or to measured economic growth per se. (It may turn out, of course, that new intermediate products and techniques appear which stimulate greater productivity and diversity of economic activity in other areas and other forms. In fact, government support may facilitate the introduction of these when they are not at first economically competitive in the private sector.) But certainly the absence of new developments, new techniques, new companies would suggest a degree of immobility and even stagnation inconsistent with a common-sense concept of "industrial growth."

In this sense, of course, the rocket industry created by the military and space programs of the nation would comprise an element of "industrial growth." Its utility outside the military and space sector is very small and it

CHART 10   RATIO OF NUMBER OF R&D SCIENTISTS AND ENGINEERS
IN INDUSTRY TO GNP

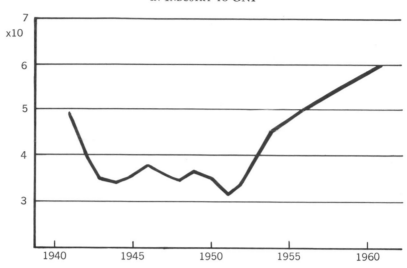

SOURCES: NSF, DOD, and *Business Statistics*.

may remain small. Those who think of economic and industrial growth in terms of activities and products useful for consumption in a form which promotes the higher aspirations of an advancing culture will not consider such an industry much of a contribution to "growth". But neither are tail fins. In any case, viewed from an over-all national standpoint, the creation of new companies, new industries and new products, in whatever sector, comprise elements of "industrial growth." Their utility is another question: it concerns the matter of "values" I have discussed in earlier sections.

I have summarized five chief headings under which one might measure "industrial growth" according to the definition I have adopted here (Chart 11). The first of these headings is "productivity."

But as I have suggested, "industrial growth" here defined is also to be measured, at least to a degree, by the extent to which new products are introduced. By new products I have end-use items particularly in mind.

The development of new technologies and new devices is also a measure of industrial growth. An industrial base from which no new technologies or new devices emerged would be exhibiting stagnation of a sort with or without increases in productivity that stemmed from other sources; and many of these intermediate devices and technologies, may later lead to increases in productivity.

The introduction of new techniques, including scientific and managerial techniques, is also (again, to a degree) a measure of industrial growth and a factor in promoting industrial growth in other areas as well.

And finally, one may measure industrial growth in part by the extent to which new industries are introduced.

In the middle column I have given examples to illustrate each of these

CHART 11 INDUSTRIAL GROWTH

Chief parameters which measure industrial growth	Examples of each from private and public sectors	Principal impact of government (especially defense) R & D expenditures
Productivity	Introduction of electrical machinery; automation; "scientific" factory management	Accelerated impact of automation: greatly increased cost of R & D
New products (end items)	TV; Pyroceram; nuclear submarines; rocket engines	Creates many new, highly specialized "products", but few having direct civilian application
New technologies and devices	Transistors; etched circuitry; masers; infra-red; radar	Greatly accelerated rate of development and exploitation
New techniques (scientific and managerial)	Systems engineering; operations analysis	Some techniques (e.g. PERT) finding wide acceptance; others (e.g. systems engineering) not yet widely used outside the military-space sector
New industries	Data processing; electronics; solid propellants	Most new industries depend heavily on military-space support for their existence

headings drawn from both the private and the public sectors. Productivity has been enormously increased in our country and other industrialized nations through the introduction of electrical machinery; by the introduction of automation in a variety of forms; and by the application of principles of "scientific" factory management (which owed much to engineers but nothing to science and little to technology) to name three examples. In the right hand column I have noted one or two examples under each of these headings to illustrate the principal impact of government expenditures for research and development, with particular emphasis on defense research and development.

Thus, for example, there seems to be a little or no doubt that automation has been applied in a refined form and on an accelerated time scale largely owing to the great stimulation it received during and immediately following World War II. The concepts inherent in automatic control devices and the bulk of all feed back theory that was placed in use in World War II had been available for many years before. The reduction-to-practice of these techniques on a very large scale disseminated knowledge and educated engineers at a hitherto unprecedented rate. In a sense it made automation a part of what one might call our "technical consciousness." The very rapid flow of engineers and scientists from war work back to non-defense work at the end of World War II probably had a great deal to do with the rapid dissemination of that new knowledge throughout non-defense industry.

Apropos of productivity, one may note that many of the indices which I have presented earlier seem to indicate that the cost of performing research and development per technical man year has gone up and may increase further. It may be argued that the output per technical man is not increasing at a corresponding rate; that, in other words, the productivity per technical man, insofar as it is measured by dollars, has been going down. Experience and the opinions of others, sampled somewhat randomly, tends to support this view. More general considerations advanced by Price do too.

There is additional, but not conclusive evidence to support this inference. Chart 5 shows the total number of patent applications per year per engineering and scientific worker in America. To the extent that patents represent the creation of new devices and new technologies, it would appear that the per capita productivity of the scientific and engineering community concerned with research and development has declined rather than increased as a consequence of large government expenditures for research and development. But the number of publications, as measured by abstracts, has risen on a per capita basis in recent years, and could suggest that, if the publication of papers measures R&D productivity, it is increasing.

I appreciate the fact that statistics of this kind are highly arguable. There may be reasons for thinking that many of the best ideas are not patented at all and many of the papers are worthless. Besides, it is very difficult to patent some of the greatest achievements of modern engineering and science; patents are really a little old fashioned as a way of measuring the significance of technological progress as represented by, say, the Polaris or the Minuteman System. In any event, I have not endeavored to prove a case but only to suggest that those trends we are able to measure do not point to increases in productivity, and some may suggest the reverse, in the research and development field, especially if one uses criteria classically applied in the private sector.

Let us return now to Chart 11. The balance of it is essentially self-explanatory. In every one of the areas that I have noted, government expenditures for research and development have had a profound effect. In some cases the effect has begun to be felt outside of those industries which receive the bulk of the direct support for government research and development. In other cases, very little of that sort of "spillover" is to be observed.

We can summarize this part of the presentation as follows:

1. A very large fraction of government research and development expenditures have led to the creation of new industrial organizations. The revolution in government support of research and development has also been a revolution of method and of approach, especially the creation of interdisciplinary, inter-industry teams under central management to tackle enormously complex tasks.

2. It is obvious that a vast segment of industry does not share directly, and probably shares very little even indirectly, in the techniques and the approach to problems which have stemmed and are stemming from the military and space programs that account for the bulk of federally supported research and development.

CHART 12 TWO MEASURES OF OUTPUT PER SCIENTIST
AND ENGINEER ENGAGED IN R&D

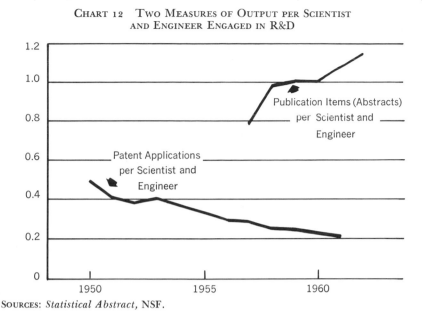

SOURCES: *Statistical Abstract,* NSF.

3. It is also clear that these R&D expenditures often serve comparatively narrow purposes. They may be, and hopefully in all important cases they are, necessary purposes. But although necessary, they may, from a national standpoint, be more costly or of less general utility than we have tended to assume. The purposeful broadening of the objectives that are served by federally supported research and development activities would appear to be clearly in the national interest, and certainly in the national security interest.

.   .   .   .

3] Military R&D: A Drag on the Economy

IN THIS ARTICLE I want to analyze some leading issues concerning economic growth and development in the United States. The main questions I shall consider, and my answers to them, can be summarized very briefly as follows:

Do our rising expenditures on research and development ensure faster economic growth? Despite a popular impression to the contrary, the

FROM Robert A. Solo, "Gearing Military R&D to Economic Growth," *Harvard Business Review,* vol. XL (November–December, 1962), pp. 49–54. © 1962 by the President and Fellows of Harvard College; all rights reserved. [Footnotes omitted—J. L. C.]

answer seems to be *no*. In fact, the present pattern of R & D outlays
in the United States may even be reducing the rate of economic growth.
*Are the scientific and technological advances made in space and military
R & D easily transferable to private industry?* While there are many
examples of successful transference, the process is becoming increasingly
difficult. Not only is space and military research growing farther apart
from industrial research in a technical way, but communication between
the two sectors is becoming more unmanageable.

*What organizations can help transmit the benefits of military and space
R & D to private industry?* Government agencies, universities, and industrial corporations themselves all have critical roles in this task, but
each group has a long way to go to fulfill its promise.

*How can the great potentials in scientific research be utilized for eco-
nomic growth as well as for progress in space and military programs?*
Increasing the payoff is an immensely difficult but vital task for social
engineering. The output of government-sponsored R & D must be
geared to the needs of civilian industry (not to the detriment, but to the
ultimate gain, of military-space programs). Also, industrial companies
must become more responsive to the opportunities offered.

DISAPPOINTING GROWTH

In the American Assembly's study, *Outer Space,* Leonard Silk, the distinguished author of *The Research Revolution,* writes as follows:

> There can be little doubt that the most important element in economic
> growth is in expansion of scientific and technological knowledge. . . .
> In our own time some economists have reached the conclusion that
> technological advance has accounted for about 90 percent of the rise
> in productivity—output per man-hour—in the United States since the
> latter part of the 19th century. The implications of these findings are
> of outstanding importance. . . . They mean that the greatest emphasis
> in any program for long-term economic growth must focus on techno-
> logical progress and the factors that promote or obstruct it.

Silk goes on to argue that the advances in information and technology
resulting from the U.S. space programs will stimulate progress significantly,
"in electronics, metals, fuels, the life sciences, ceramics, machinery, plastics,
instruments, textiles, thermals, cryogenics, and, most important, . . . basic
research in all the sciences." His viewpoint—and many people share it—
could be restated as a syllogism:

---

1. Economic growth is generated through technological advance.

2. Technological advance derives from new scientific and technical
knowledge.

3. New scientific and technical knowledge is the consequence of R & D.

4. Hence, an increase in R & D must accelerate the rate of economic growth.

This might seem, indeed, a self-evident truth. But alas—like many another such truth—it fares badly when measured against the evidence. EXHIBIT 1–A shows the annual rate of change in output per man-hour since 1894, and, also, R & D expenditures as a ratio of national income since 1920. Output per man-hour is used as the index most likely to reflect the benefits of R & D. It cannot be equated with economic growth but is one of the best indicators. And certainly it is the best general measure of technological advance, since it eliminates the statistical effect on gross national product (GNP) of population increases and variations in the level of employment. The arguments in this article, however, could be supported by other measures of the rate of growth.

What does the comparison tell us? Since the 1920's—when it first emerged as a significant element in the American economy—the rise in expenditures for R & D (absolutely, and as a proportion of the total) has been quite phenomenal. Nevertheless, as EXHIBIT 1–A shows, the rate at which output per man-hour has increased appears to waver about the same old norm. Indeed, after 1953, while expenditures for R & D skyrocket, the rate of increase in output per man-hour slumps. In any case, no positive correlation whatsoever is evidenced between the national rate of economic growth and the national level of R & D expenditures. Much the same conclusion must be reached if we look at other economic indicators—for instance, the rate of increase in GNP (see EXHIBIT 1–B).

What is the significance of this finding? It does *not* mean that individual companies have not benefited from R & D, or that great industries have not been created because of it. Clearly they have. Nor does it mean that there have not been benefits to national economic growth from federally sponsored R & D. Most certainly there have been. But it may mean that some other, unspecified barriers to growth have been rising, and have balanced out the mounting benefits of R & D. However, it will be shown later that R & D, as it is currently constituted, can itself be a drag upon, as well as a stimulus to, growth, and, hence, that the detriments to growth implicit in R & D itself may not have been sufficiently offset by its benefits.

The evidence *does* show that the effect of the national R & D effort on economic growth cannot be taken for granted. To posit on a priori grounds the relevance of R & D to higher industrial productivity is not enough. R & D activity must be examined to determine how, in fact, it is (or might better be) geared into the processes of technological advance and economic growth.

IS R & D A DRAIN

In the mythos of science, R & D is the horn of plenty out of which all the "goodies" of health and wealth must necessarily flow. Would that it were! Simply stated, R & D is the planned, organized approach by professionals to the solving of certain sorts of problems. The problems may be those of a civilian industry, seeking better techniques or products which, if found, would raise the value of real per capita output; in such a case, R & D might be called growth-oriented.

There are other problems, too, which absorb R & D efforts, such as seeking the means of diagnosing a virus infection, reducing the size of an atomic warhead, or shielding instruments from radiation in orbital flight, which are not those of civilian industry, and whose successful solution need not raise productivity and accelerate economic growth. Such R & D is not growth-oriented; and this means that the great bulk of the national R & D effort is not growth-oriented. Most of it focuses on the problems of outer space and weaponry. To be more specific:

In 1960–1961, out of a total R & D expenditure of $14,040 million, approximately $9,220 million was spent by the federal government. More than 90% of that amount was expended by the Department of Defense, the National Aeronautics and Space Administration, and the Atomic Energy Commission.

A very substantial part of the $4,490 million of company-financed R & D in 1960–1961 was also oriented toward space and military technologies.

That great and spectacular gains have been made in science and in certain types of technology through such R & D is not to be denied. Nor is the inherent importance or necessity of space and military achievement at issue. What is at issue is the relationship of this military and space-oriented R & D to the achievement of higher productivity in nonmilitary industry, i.e., to the production—with the same input of human effort—of more of those goods and services which are the "stuff" of economic growth.

Ought we to expect economic growth as a result of R & D which is not oriented toward the achievement of such growth? Turn the tables and suppose that all R & D expenditures were "growth-oriented," i.e., focused on problems of economic growth—e.g., efforts to create new products and lower the real costs of home construction, road construction, urban organization, communication, transportation, mining, metal fabrication, textiles, clothing, agriculture, and so on. Would one expect, as a consequence of such growth-oriented R & D, to put a man on the moon? To develop an atomic bomb? To find a cure for cancer? Hardly. Conversely, advances in space, military, and other nonmilitary technologies need not accelerate economic growth. While such achievements might yield many industrial benefits, they might well, in the end, actually *deter* the advance of industrial technologies and *reduce* the rate of economic growth.

Contrasting Trends

There are two sides to every coin. On the other side of higher wages and higher profits is higher prices and higher costs. On the other side of a cut in imports is a decline in exports. And on the other side of an increase

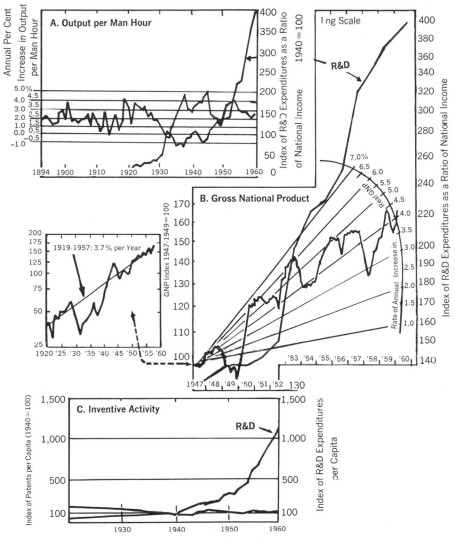

SOURCE: EXHIBIT 1-A—J. W. Kendrick, *Productivity Trends in the United States*, National Bureau of Economic Research (Princeton, Princeton University Press, 1961), p. 333, Table A-xxii; *National Economic Projections* (Washington, D.C., National Planning Association, 1961), p. 105, Table 16; Vannevar Bush, *Science, The Endless Frontier* (Washington, D.C., U.S. Government Printing Office, 1945), p. 80; Research and Development Board, Department of Defense, *Research and Development Expenditures in the United States and Cost of Research and Development Performed by Government, Industry, and Colleges & Universities—1941-52* (Washington, D.C., U.S. Government Printing Office, April, 1953); National Science Foundation, *Reviews of Data on Research and Development* (Washington, D.C., U.S. Government Printing Office, September 1961, April 1962).

EXHIBIT 1-B—Robert Theobald, *Profit Potential in the Developing Countries* (New York, American Management Association, Research Study # 53, 1962), p. 31.

EXHIBIT 1-C—Patent Data from *Science*, May 12, 1961, pp. 1464–65. Resident population data from U.S. Bureau of the Census, *Statistical Abstract of the United States: 1961* (Washington, D. C., U.S. Government Printing Office, 1961).

in space and military R & D is a decrease in the trained, creative brainpower available for civilian industry.

The increase in space and military R & D may be a diversion from and, consequently, may be at the expense of R & D oriented toward economic growth. And although the ratio of R & D expenditures to national income has increased greatly since 1953, the corresponding trend of growth-oriented R & D seems actually to have been downward. This conclusion is based on the following reasoning:

(1) Growth-oriented R & D can be estimated by deducting from total R & D expenditures those by the military and space agencies, and by the Veterans Administration and the Department of Health, Education, and Welfare (for medical research), and a proportion (estimated at 30% of the R & D expenditure of the military and space agencies) of company-financed R & D, considered as oriented toward the space and military technologies.

(2) An index of growth-oriented R & D as a ratio of national income, *at constant prices,* can then be developed, with research costs adjusted with a deflator developed by the (former) Operations Research Office.

(3) While very much subject to correction, the resulting index of growth-oriented R & D seems a sufficient measure at least of the direction of change. From 1953, the index varied as follows: 1953, 100; 1954, 104; 1955, 107; 1956, 98; 1957, 88; 1958, 94; 1959, 93; 1960, 97. While growth-oriented R & D declined, an index of the residual, consisting essentially of space and military R & D—similarly deflated for price change—increased as follows: 1953, 100; 1954, 103; 1955, 112; 1956, 163; 1957, 192; 1958, 201; 1959, 216; 1960, 233.

Diversion of Brainpower

Not only does space and military R & D divert research power from its growth-oriented counterpart, but R & D per se can draw creative resources from alternative forms of inventive and innovative activity.

Postwar R & D, considering its magnitude and the depth of its organization, constitutes a truly novel phenomenon in the U.S. economy—a new approach in the coordinated organization of scientific inquiry, invention, and innovation. The approach is new, but scientific inquiry, invention, and innovation did go on before. Through the advent of R & D, those who were, or who might have been, restless, probing industrialists, innovating entrepreneurs, or inventors tinkering in their shops became, instead, engineers on project teams, heads of research divisions, scientists in laboratories, or subcontractors with the task of developing a component for a complex weapons system. Something is given to one side, but lost from the other. A clue as to the degree to which creative resources have been drained away from the older forms of inventive activity is offered in the patent statistics. EXHIBIT 1–C shows R & D expenditures per capita and patents applied for per capita in the United States since 1920.

When technologically creative activities are individualized and market-directed, they are, logically, more patent-focused than when organized as team research—where individual reward no longer specifically depends on patent protection. If, therefore, the increase in R & D does draw away or divert creative brainpower from another kind of individualized, inventive activity, then, it could be hypothesized, an increase in R & D spending would result in a decline in patents per capita. This is precisely what has happened, as shown in EXHIBIT 1–C. In spite of the tremendous increase in R & D expenditures and, presumably, of the deployment of a larger proportion of the population for technologically creative activities, the number of patents applied for declined, both absolutely and per capita.

Since the earlier, unorganized, individualized form of inventive and innovative activity was almost entirely involved with nonmilitary industry, and since, in the new R & D, concentration is on military and space technology, the onset of massive R & D expenditures signals not only a change in the manner of organizing creative brainpower but, also, a shift in its locus. As this occurs, a dynamic element is drained from (or denied to) the civilian sector, and the price that is paid is in the economic growth that this element might have generated. Thus, more space and military R & D can mean, and perhaps has meant, less economic growth. The argument, in brief, is this:

(1) Those with the capacity to grapple successfully with problems of high complexity, those who have an experimental bent and creative genius, are limited in number (fixed, indeed, at any point in time).

(2) If most of their efforts and energies are concentrated on advancing the space and military technologies, then these same efforts and energies are denied to the civilian sector.

(3) This means that the potential for technological advance in industry and for economic growth is narrowed.

(4) *However*, the consequent diminution in the potential rate of economic growth might be offset where these space and military achievements, as well as the R & D outputs that went into them, yield additional benefits for nonmilitary industry. In short, against the diversion of creative brainpower away from the problems of civilian industry must be matched the "spillover" of concepts, knowledge, techniques, products, and processes developed on space and military R & D, but also useful to nonmilitary industry. (Spillover here refers only to the technological advances and consequent higher productivity derived by nonmilitary industry from space and military R & D.)

My argument then does not intend to denigrate, but rather to emphasize, the importance of spillover. This is a phenomenon which need not occur and, certainly, which need not occur spontaneously. But we must increasingly depend on it in the United States (given the massive increase in space and military R & D expenditures) in order even to maintain our rate of growth.

.   .   .   .

4] A New Kind of Economic Federalism

AMERICAN society has shown considerable resilience in adapting to rapid change. When need arises, an existing institution leaps to meet it, becoming quite a different institution in the process. In recent years the industrial corporation, which "began life as a sort of legal trick to spread the ownership of industrial equipment over a lot of people," has evolved into a routine and immensely powerful method of organizing large undertakings. But the relationship between individuals and corporations has been greatly modified by the overshadowing concentration of corporate power. Government has ceased to be merely a passive arbiter of "the rules of the game" and is forced to become an omnipresent force for balancing the competition for values and controlling the dynamics of social change.

Government has become the economy's largest buyer and consumer. The government contract, improvised, ad hoc, and largely unexamined, has become an increasingly important device for intervention in public affairs, not only to procure goods and services but to achieve a variety of explicit or inadvertent policy ends—allocating national resources, organizing human efforts, stimulating economic activity, and distributing status and power. The government contract has risen to its present prominence as a social management tool since World War II, achieving in two decades a scope and magnitude that now rival simple subsidies, tariffs, taxes, direct regulation, and positive action programs in their impact upon the nature and quality of American life. This evolution has occurred quietly and gradually through a series of improvised reactions to specific problems. Its central role has been achieved without public consideration of far-reaching social and political implications. Even today there is precious little consciousness of the trend; political leaders tend to see each contract as an isolated procurement action, overlooking the general pattern. Just as federal grants-in-aid to state and local governments have (since 1933) become principal means for national integration of divided local jurisdictions, so federal contracting with private corporations is creating a new kind of economic federalism.

The implications of grants-in-aid have acquired some clarity: state taxation still takes care of traditional functions, while new and greatly expanded activities devolve upon local bodies through national decision-making, the states operating more and more as administrative districts for centrally estab-

Reprinted by permission of Quadrangle Books from *In the Name of Science* by H. L. Nieburg, copyright © 1966 by H. L. Nieburg. [Footnotes omitted—J. L. C.]

lished policies. Here, decision-making is nationalized under the constraints of public attention and democrtaic politics. On the other hand, economic federalism based upon contracts holds implications that are far from clear. To some degree, the forms and effects of contracting evade the forums of democracy, obscuring the age-old conflict between private and public interests. Mobilized to serve national policy, private contractors interpenetrate government at all levels, exploiting the public consensus of defense, space, and science to augment and perpetuate their own power, inevitably confusing narrow special interests with those of the nation.

Explicit authority for the U.S. government to conduct its business by contract is not found in the Constitution but has historically been accepted as a means of achieving explicitly constitutional objectives. There is ample precedent, such as the use of railroads for troop movements, or General McClellan's arrangements with the Pinkerton Detective Agency for espionage against the Southern Confederacy.

What is new is the persistence and growth of government-industry contract relationships under which, in the words of David E. Bell (then director of the Budget Bureau), "numbers of the nation's most important business corporations do the bulk of their work with the government." The Martin Company, for example, does 99 percent of its business with the government. Bell asked: "Well, is it a private agency or is it a public agency?" Organized as a private corporation and "philosophically . . . part of the private sector," yet "it obviously has a different relationship to governmental decisions and the government's budget . . . than was the case when General Motors or U.S. Steel sold perhaps 2 or 5 percent of their annual output to government bodies." Except in time of war, the government traditionally has not been the dominant customer for any private firm. The contract state of the postwar world must be viewed as a drastic innovation full of unfamiliar portents.

Grandiose claims are heard on all sides for the "unique contribution" that the contract mechanism has made in preserving "the free enterprise system" at a time when it could have been damaged. Atomic energy has been cited as an example of the new collaboration: "Without contracts, it would be government-owned and operated. With contracts, one person in sixteen in the industry works for government; the other fifteen work for contractors." An aerospace journal cites space technology as "the fastest moving, typically free-enterprise and democratic industry yet created," achieving these values "not on salesmanship" (that is, traditional quality/cost competitiveness) but "on what is needed most—intellectual production, the research payoff." Lyndon B. Johnson, while Vice President, argued: "If we want to maintain credibility of our claim to the superiority of a free political system—and a free private enterprise system—we cannot seriously entertain the thought of precipitating now so massive a disillusionment as would follow a political default on our commitments in space exploration."

The government contract has made it possible to perform new tasks deemed essential without direct additions to the size of federal government, thus preserving the alleged rights of private property and profit. But these huzzahs ignore the real ambiguity of the system that is emerging—neither "free" nor "competitive," in which the market mechanism of supply/demand (the price seeking the level which best serves overall productivity and social needs) has been abolished for key sectors of the economy, its place taken by the process of government policy and political influence. Instead of a free enterprise system, we are moving toward a government-subsidized private-profit system.

KEY TO THE KINGDOM

Unlike older government-fostered industries, the new contractor empire operates without the yardsticks of adequate government in-house capability or a civilian market in areas where research and development has become *the* critical procurement and the crux of the system. As described in the 1962 Bell Report: The companies involved "have the strongest incentives to seek contracts for research and development work which will give them both the know-how and the preferred position to seek later follow-on production contracts." Favored corporations that win R&D work thereafter exploit a number of special advantages: They may achieve sole-source or prime contractor status, which eliminates competition and dilutes all cost and performance evaluation. The open-end, cost-plus nature of the contract instrument, the lack of product specifications, official tolerance of spending overruns, all of which increase the total contract and fee (in a sense rewarding wasteful practices and unnecessary technical complication), permit violation of all rules of responsible control and make possible multiple tiers of hidden profits. The systems-management or prime contractor role enables favored companies to become powerful industrial brokers using unlimited taxpayer funds and contract awards to strengthen their corporate position, cartelize the contract market, and exert political influence.

In less than a decade the area surrounding Washington, D.C., has become one of the nation's major R&D concentrations. Every large corporation has found it necessary to establish field offices in proximity to NASA, the Pentagon, and Capitol Hill. Most of these new installations emphasize public relations and sales rather than research and development. The Washington area now ranks first in the nation for scientific personnel (per 1,000 population), although the major product is company promotion and politics rather than science.

The gross figures provide an index of the economic impact: the 1966 federal budget called for $23.7 billion in new obligational authority for defense and space—$11.4 billion for Defense Department procurement of hardware and control systems, $6.7 billion for R&D; $5.26 billion for NASA (virtually all R&D), and an additional $272 million for space-related R&D conducted by the Weather Bureau, the National Science Foundation, and the Atomic Energy Commission. Over 90 percent of this flows to the highly concentrated aerospace industry. Another $3.3 billion was budgeted for other kinds of R&D, making a total of $27 billion. The 1967 budget allocated more than $30 billion to aerospace. Space, defense, and R&D together now comprise the single most substantial allocation of federal funds, towering over all other programs. In the mid-1960's, government R&D (excluding related procurement) stabilized between 2 and 3 percent of the GNP. Cumulative missile/space spending in the decade which began in 1955 amounted to over $100 billion (Defense Department, $84 billion; NASA, $18 billion), and the remainder of the sixties will add at least an additional $125 billion. Virtually every department and agency of the federal government is involved to some extent in R&D contracting, although the Defense Department and NASA account for more than 96 percent.

The first result of this staggering outpour has been the artificial inflation of R&D costs which has enabled contractors to raid the government's own in-house resources. Officials in the lower reaches of the government bureaucracy (both civilian and military), charged with administration of contracts, find themselves dealing with private corporate officials who often were their own former bosses and continue as companions of present bosses and congressional leaders who watchdog the agencies. A contract negotiator or supervisor must deal with men who can determine his career prospects; through contacts, these industrial contractors may cause him to be passed over or transferred to a minor position in some remote bureaucratic corner, sometimes with a ceremonial drumming before a congressional committee.

The military cutbacks that characterized the Eisenhower years were accompanied by expanding military budgets, a paradox explained by the systematic substitution of private contractors to carry out historically in-house activities. This trend was heralded as a move back to "free enterprise." Government installations and factories built in World War II were sold to industry, usually at a fraction of the taxpayers' investment. Others were leased at low fees to contractors who were then given government business to make the use of these facilities profitable. In some instances government built new facilities which it leased at nominal fees. Such facilities were permitted to be used, without cost, for commercial production as well.

The splurge of mobilizing private contractors for government work occurred as a part of the unprecedented growth of the Air Force. As an offspring of the Army, the new branch lacked the substantial in-house management, engineering, and R&D capability that the Army had built into its arsenal system. The Air Force sought to leapfrog this handicap in competing for jurisdiction over new weapons systems, turning to private contractors to correct the defect. In its rapid climb during the fifties, the Air Force fostered a growing band of private companies which took over a substantial part of regular military operations, including maintaining aircraft, firing rockets, building and maintaining launching sites, organizing and directing other contractors, and making major public decisions. In the area of missilery, junior officers and enlisted men were subordinated to the role of liaison agents or mere custodians.

This had several bonus effects, enabling the Air Force to keep its military personnel levels down in conformity with Defense Department and administration policies, while building an enormous industrial and congressional constituency with a stake in maintaining large-scale funding of new weapons systems. The Air Force's success over her sister services during the Eisenhower years established the magic formula that all federal agencies soon imitated. It set in motion a rush to contract out practically everything that was not nailed to the floor and, in the process, it decimated the government's in-house management, engineering, and R&D capability; inflated the costs of R&D through futile contests for supremacy among contractors financed by contract funds; and as a consequence reduced as well the scientific and engineering resources available to the civilian economy and to the universities.

The Army learned an important lesson in its struggle with the Air Force during the Thor-Jupiter controversy—that its extensive in-house engineering-management capability was a positive *disadvantage* in mobilizing congressional and public influence to support military missions and budgets. Private industry had provided the Air Force with a potent weapon in Congress for outflanking the Army during all the years of strategic debate over missile development and the role of infantry forces in a nuclear world. In part, the Air Force lobbying instrument of the 1950's contributed importantly to overdependence by the nation on nuclear weaponry and massive retaliation as the primary security doctrine, while the complete range of subnuclear military capabilities was allowed to wither. This lesson was inscribed on the Army-Navy skin by the budget-paring knife of the Eisenhower administration and led to gradual weakening of the arsenal system. In the sixties all the military services and NASA sought to parade bankers, captains of industry, local business leaders, and politicians through the halls of Congress and the White House as lobbying cadres in every new engagement.

The old research triad—government, industry, university—has virtually disappeared. In its place is a whole spectrum of new arrangements, such as the so-called "systems-engineering and technical direction" firms operated on a profit or non-profit basis (for example, General Electric is employed by NASA to integrate and test all launch facilities and space vehicles, while Bellcomm, a subsidiary of American Telephone and Telegraph, is employed for engineering and management of all NASA operations; Aerospace Corporation plays a similar role for the Air Force). In between are the major corporations, universities drawing a majority of their research budgets from government, non-profit institutions conducting pad-and-pencil studies of strategic and policy matters for government agencies, and government laboratories operated by industry or by universities.

Knitting the complex together is an elite group of several thousand men, predominantly industrial managers and brokers, who play a variety of interlocking roles—sitting on boards of directors, consulting for government agencies, serving on advisory committees, acting as managers on behalf of government in distributing and supervising subcontracts, moving between private corporations and temporary tours-of-duty in government. Private corporations have contracts to act as systems engineers and technical directors for multi-billion-dollar R&D and production activities involving hundreds of other corporations. Instead of fighting "creeping socialism," private industry on an enormous scale has become the agent of a fundamentally new economic system which at once resembles traditional private enterprise and the corporate state of fascism. A mere handful of giants (such as North American Aviation, Lockheed, General Dynamics, and Thompson-Ramo-Wooldridge) holds prime contracts over more than half the total R&D and production business. In dealing with their subcontractors and suppliers, these corporations act in the role of government itself: "These companies establish procurement organizations and methods which proximate those of the government. Thus large prime contractors will invite design competition, establish source selection bids, send out industrial survey teams, make subcontract awards on a competitive or a negotiated basis, appoint small business administrators, designate plant resident representatives, develop reporting systems to spot bottlenecks, make cost analyses of subcontractor operations, and request monthly progress and cost reports from subcontractors."

They are in the position of deciding whether or not to conduct an activity themselves or contract it out, and they may use their power over a subcontractor to acquire his proprietary information, force him to sell his company to the prime, or make or break geographical areas and individual bankers, investors, and businessmen. They may themselves create "independent" subcontractors in order to conceal profits, to keep certain proprietary information from the government, or for other purposes. Generally, they can and do use their decision-making power to stabilize their own operations, expanding or contracting their subcontracts in accordance with the peaks and troughs of government business, thus protecting their economic strength at the expense of smaller and weaker companies, seeking to assure their own growth and standing among the other giant corporations by mergers, acquisitions, and investments in the flock of companies dependent upon them for government largess.

The same top three hundred companies that perform 97 percent of all federal R&D also perform 91 percent of all private R&D. Most of the private R&D is a means of maintaining the inside track for new awards in anticipated areas of government need. Since these same companies do all or most of their business with government, the so-called "private" R&D is paid for by the government in the form of overhead on other contracts. For example, the U.S. is still paying for Douglas Aircraft's investment in developing the DC-3 thirty years ago. A congressional committee noted the trend:

> At the moment a small number of giant firms in a few defense and space-related areas, with their facilities located principally in three states, and engaged almost exclusively in the application of existing engineering the physical knowledge to the creation of new products and processes, receive the overwhelming preponderance of the government's multi-billion dollar research awards. . . . Clearly, if the resulting technical discoveries are permitted to remain within these narrow confines rather than be disseminated widely through the society, a disproportionate amount of the benefits will be channeled into the hands of the few and further economic concentration will take place.

Prime contractors are becoming brokers of the managerial elites that control American industry, their power limited only by self-restraint and political necessity. Congressman Carl Hebert, after a 1961 investigation, declared his amazement at "the daring of these individuals," recalling that during World War II "the brokers became so prevalent in Washington that they wore badges," and the only office space they had was "under their hats."

That was twenty years ago, "and yet we find the same practice not only not halted but increasingly becoming exposed as we go along these days."

Government itself continues to enhance the power of the primes by accentuating the trend toward fewer and bigger contracts. Peter Slusser, an aerospace securities specialist, noted in 1964 the increasing concentration of procurements within a hard core of big contractors. It appears, he said, that the industry may eventually be dominated by a few firms, much as the automobile industry is today. Further, there will be a concentration within the concentration. "It seems to us," he asserted, "that this concentration ratio will probably continue among the larger companies." The House Select Committee on Small Business reported that while defense procurement increased by $1.1 billion in 1963, small business awards declined by $268 million. NASA doubled its prime procurements while the small business share dropped from 11.7 to 8.5 percent. The congressional Joint Economic Committee reported that a hundred companies and their subsidiaries accounted for 73.4 percent of total federal procurement value in 1964; the number of companies receiving annual awards of more than $1 billion has been steadily narrowing. Six companies belonged to that exclusive club in 1964; their combined NASA and defense work: Boeing, $2.3 billion; North American Aviation, $1.9 billion; Lockheed, $1.4 billion; McDonnell Aircraft, $1.4 billion; General Dynamics, $1.1 billion; and General Electric, $1.03 billion. North American alone, whose vending machine business made Bobby Baker a millionaire, held 28 percent of all NASA procurements.

EROSION OF PUBLIC CONTROL

The dominant centers of corporate power have largely usurped the government's evaluation and technical direction responsibilities. Frank Gibney, one of the early consultants to the House Space Committee, observed that "the spectacle of a private profit-making company rendering national decisions makes the old Dixon-Yates concept look as harmless as a Ford Foundation Research Project." The government's Bell Report of 1962 expressed concern at the erosion of its ability to manage its own affairs and to retain control over contracting, which ". . . raises important questions of public policy concerning the government's role and capability and potential conflicts of interest." The proliferation of quasi-public corporations, both profit and non-profit, springing from the soil of R&D spending (such as Bellcomm, Aerospace Corporation, or Comsat Corporation), symbolizes the bewildering innovations of the Contract State. Congressmen throw up their hands trying to understand their relations to these new organizations under the traditional dichotomy between private and public enterprise.

Nageeb Halaby, former head of the Federal Aviation Agency, insisted that the private airlines fund at least 25 percent of costs of developing a supersonic transport: "I think we have a half-free enterprise industry now, and I don't want to see it any more under government control than it already is. This is going to take some risk and . . . some ingenuity in figuring out how the government helps a relatively free enterprise to remain so, at a profit." The industry itself insists that the SST will be profitable in commercial service but demurs from investing in a small share of the developmental cost, claiming that government is obliged to do the whole job in the name of national prestige. GE Board Chairman Ralph J. Cordiner worries about the future course of the American system, the secret of whose "drive and creativity" lies in maintaining "many competing points of initiative, risk, and decision." As we move into the frontiers of space, he declares, "many companies, universities, and individual citizens will become increasingly dependent on the political whims and necessities of the federal government. And if that drift continues without check, the United States may find itself becoming the very kind of society that it is struggling against."

Labor joins its voice, decrying those sectors of industry that in the name of preserving free enterprise call for ever-greater farming-out of government responsibility: "It is purely charlatanism to claim that the government is in any form in competition with private industry because the government researches and develops and manufactures products for its own exclusive use. . . . It is competing only with the right of private industry to make a profit at the expense of the American taxpayer. But this is competition of a different color."

The arrangements of the Contract State may, in the words of Don K. Price, avoid the problems that come with the growth of bureaucracy, but "encounter them again in more subtle and difficult forms. . . . If public ownership is no guarantee of unselfishness, neither is private ownership." President Eisenhower, who came to office as a believer in the American business community and with a commitment to get rid of "unfair" government competition, ended his term of office with a forceful warning that private corporations (hired for the government's work) were tending to subordinate public to private weal, using strategic positions and influence for economic and political aggrandizement at the expense of democracy and the public interest.

There is no doubt that the flow of billions of federal dollars into narrow areas of the economy tends to create a self-perpetuating coalition of vested interests. With vast public funds at hand, industries, geographical regions, labor unions, and the multitude of supporting enterprises band together with enormous manpower, facilities, and Washington contacts to maintain and expand their stake. Pork-barrel politics and alignments with federal agencies and political leaders provide a powerful political machine to keep the contract flow coming.

The pattern is already in the process of filtering down to state and local governments. In the name of preserving and utilizing the "unique" systems-engineering and management capability that NASA publicists claim as one of the space program's major benefits to the civilian economy, underemployed aerospace industrial teams are now pushing for contracts in such areas as urban traffic management and water conservation. Governor Pat Brown of California has led the way. The only way to approach such problems, he declared recently, is from the systems-management viewpoint. Waste-management facilities will be built with or without the aerospace industry, he told a congressional committee, but the new capability holds great promise. The state has already retained Aerojet-General for preliminary studies.

An aerospace trade magazine commented: "The governor's effort to put aerospace talents to work on these problems is an imaginative one. Other states and the federal government are watching the experiment with interest."

If the method of work follows the pattern cut for the federal government, the aerospace firm will win a major contract by hiring some civil engineers (including some from the state agencies already responsible in the area) to write a persuasive proposal. Once the contract is awarded, the corporation will hire away from the state government, the universities, and other on-going operations all the technical people required, paying them greatly augmented salaries for work they were already doing under the traditional arrangements.

The first product will be an integrated state plan with engineering details, specifications, and cost estimates (always optimistically low at this stage). The company will then move for a prime contract to conduct the work, performing some of it itself and subcontracting some of it to the local builders and architects who possess knowledge and experience because of work they have already done for the state on a piecemeal basis. The contractor will cut across the cleavages of state, county, and municipal jurisdiction, insuring everyone a reasonable return while retaining for itself two tiers of profit: one from its own work, the other added to that of the subcontractors. In time the systems teams, having emasculated state and local technical resources in these fields, will by judicious use of contract money build a political machine in the state legislature—relegating to their own managerial cadre (and the investment brokers who control their corporate paper) a large share of the decision-making authority of the State of California.

Later, as the contract arrangements acquire stability, the prime contractor may begin a process of mergers and acquisitions among its sub-contractors, directed at building the resources of the company and in the process eliminating competition and much of the cost yardstick. The result will be a new concentration of economic power in these areas of activity which will increasingly give the corporation sole-source status. Like the conventional political party, the corporation will have acquired the ability to allocate state resources, to dispense job and financial patronage, and to insure profits for its investors from the tax resources of state government.

Aerojet-General completed its preliminary waste disposal study in late 1965, recommending a ten-year program to be conducted by systems-management techniques at a cost of billions.

The California experiment may achieve the positive goal of building or imposing a consensus for state-wide planning and technical, rather than political, logic in solving large-scale problems. The traditional political parties have so far failed to achieve this goal. But it must be asked: Cannot social consensus and rational planning be achieved without the abdication of traditional political and governmental processes? The slower progress of traditional politics is preferable to a system that evades democratic controls and may eventually spread its grip into all areas of public policy.

In essence, the same questions may be directed at the full-blown Contract State nurtured by the federal government. Adherence of the R&D contract cult to the shibboleths of free enterprise may be a cloak to conceal the fact that the sharks are eating the little fishes and that a kind of backhanded government planning, in which they participate and from which they benefit, has come to replace free enterprise. In spite of such temporary stimulants as tax-cutting and the multiplier effect of missile-space spending, the civilian economy maintains a faltering pace of growth. The aerospace industries, on the other hand, ride high on unprecedented profits and diversify their holdings, biting deep into the most succulent portions of the civilian production machine in a new wave of economic concentration. In order that their "unique capability" not be wasted, defense firms are now moving into "systems management" of Job Corps camps and national conservation programs.

The politics of corporate finance have accelerated concentration not only in the government contract market but also in the civilian market, both of which are now thoroughly interpenetrated and interlocked. The aerospace giants have built huge conglomerate empires that span both markets, and the old respectable firms are playing major roles as public contractors. Among the top hundred prime aerospace contractors are such household names as General Electric, General Motors, AT&T, Westinghouse, Chrysler, Ford, Socony-Mobil, Firestone, Philco, Goodyear, and so on. Many of the aerospace companies are mere façades and legal fictions having no individual existence but representing entities of financial and/or political convenience. In a 1965 House Judiciary Committee report, the five largest aerospace firms were cited as flagrant examples of corporate interlock. Douglas has fifteen directors interlocked with managements of seventeen banks and financial institutions, one insurance company, and twenty-eight industrial-commercial corporations (including Cohu Electronics, Giannini Controls, and Richfield and Tidewater Oil Companies). Not uncommon is the pattern by which each company holds stock in its nominal competitors (McDonnell Aircraft holds a large block in the Douglas Company "as an investment"). A study of seventy-four major industrial-commercial companies found that 1,480 officers and directors held a total of 4,428 positions. The anti-trust subcommittee staff concluded that management interlocks today are as prevalent as they were in 1914 when the Clayton Act, prohibiting interlocking directorships, was passed.

POINT OF NO RETURN?

The quasi-governmental mercantilist corporations, maintained in a position of monopoly power through royal franchises, were anathema to the classical liberals. Thomas Hobbes compared them to "worms in the entrails of man," and Madison in *The Federalist* dealt at length with the problems of limiting their growth. At the end of the nineteenth century Henry Adams emphasized the origin of the corporation as an agency of the state, "created for the purpose of enabling the public to realize some social or national end without involving the necessity for direct governmental administration."

During the second half of the nineteenth century the corporation proved a powerful vehicle for mobilizing and organizing productive resources to achieve rapid economic growth made possible by burgeoning technology. Its very success, the efficiencies of bigness, and the inevitable politics of corporate empire-building thrust into American skies the spires of monopoly power. Since that time sectional and economic interests have shifted and changed, the social and technological landscape has vastly altered, and government has emerged as guarantor of social interests against the claims of private power. Government contracting on its present scale has added another dimension. Business and industry have always been close to the centers of political power, but never before in peacetime have they enjoyed such a broad acceptance of their role as a virtual fourth branch of government—a consensus generated by the permanent crisis of international diplomacy. Sheltered by this consensus, government has accepted responsibility to maintain the financial status of its private contractors as essential to U.S. defense and economic health. Cost competitiveness, the traditional safeguard against corporate power and misallocation of national resources, has been suspended by R&D contract practices.

NASA and the Pentagon use their contracting authority to broaden the productive base in one area, maintain it in another, create more capability here or there for different kinds of R&D, create competition or limit it. Under existing laws they may make special provisions for small business and depressed areas and maintain contracts for services not immediately required in order to preserve industrial skills or reserve capacity for emergency needs. All of this represents national planning. But without recognition of planning as a legitimate government responsibility, planning authority is fragmented, scattered among federal agencies and Congress, and the makeshift planning that results serves the paramount interests of the most powerful political alignments. In place of forward planning responsible to the broad national community, the nation drifts sideways, denying the legitimacy of planning, yet backhandedly planning in behalf of narrow special interests whose corridors of power are closed to public control.

The result is severe distortion in the allocation of resources to national needs. For almost three decades the nation's resources have been commanded by military needs, consolidating political and economic power behind defense priorities. What was initially sustained by emergency comes to be sustained, normalized, and institutionalized (as emergency wanes) through a cabal of vested interests. The failure of nerve on the part of these interests to redirect this magnificent machine toward a broader range of values denies the nation what may be the ultimate basis of diplomatic strength and the only means to maintain the impetus of a mature economy, namely the fullest enjoyment by all of our people of the immense bounty of equity and well-being almost within our grasp.

The shibboleths of free enterprise perpetuate a system by which, one by one, the fruits of the civilian economy fall into the outstretched hands of the aerospace group. The so-called "Great Consensus" assembled by President Johnson is based on the paradox of support from great corporate giants as well as from labor and the Liberals. The civilian economy and home-town industry have been systematically neglected in the vicious circle of government contracts and economic concentration, leading the small businessman, vast numbers of middle-management, white-collar workers, and professional groups to embrace the simple formulas of Goldwater conservatism, directing the anxieties generated by incipient stagnation against the targets of autocratic organized labor and government spending for welfare and foreign aid. The exploitation of the myths of free enterprise have deflected attention from the feudal baronies of economic power and the tendency of the administration to attack the symptoms of growing inequality of wealth without disturbing the steepening slope itself.

The dynamics of the Contract State require close scrutiny lest, in the name of national security and the science-technology race, the use of the nation's resources does violence not only to civilian enterprise but also to the body politic. In place of sensational claims about the ability of the American system to meet the challenges of new tasks and rapid technological change, it is necessary to judge the appropriateness and adequacy of national policies that increasingly raise a question concerning the relation between government and private contractor: who is serving whom?

The R&D cult is becoming a sheltered inner society isolated from the mainstream of national needs. More and more it departs from the reality principles of social accounting, insulated against realism by the nature of its contract relations with government and its political influence. The elementary principle of economics applies: whatever is made cheaper tends to grow proportionately. Massive government subsidies to R&D facilitate its expansion beyond the point of rational response to international politics; it becomes a self-perpetuating pathology, intensifying the regressive structure of the economy and making further pump-priming exertions necessary.

As the arms race slows and is sublimated in space and science, as world politics break the ice of bi-polarity and return to the troublesome but more flexible patterns of pluralism, it becomes important that great nations achieve positive values. Military power, though essential, remains essentially a limited and negative tool. Economic and social equilibrium at maximum resource use may hold the key to ultimate international stability, prestige, and national power. Federal expenditures are a response to national needs and aspirations in all areas of public responsibility. The needs and aspirations are limitless, while the resources to satisfy them are relatively scarce. Many rich societies have withered because they allocated their resources in a manner that precipitated the circular pathology of inequity and instability. "Neither Rome's great engineering skills, its architectural grandeur, its great laws, nor, in the last analysis, its gross national product, could prevail against the barbarians."

The problem of bringing the Contract State under democratic control is but a new phase of a continuing challenge in Western industrial societies. The legal fiction that holds economic and political institutions to be separate and distinct becomes ever less applicable as economic pluralism is swallowed up by corporate giantism. The myths of economic freedom tend to insulate the giants from social control, protecting their private-government status and threatening the political freedom of the majority. The tension between private and public decision-making can be a self-correcting process when its causes are visible and understood, and when public authority is not wholly captive to the pressures of narrow interest groups. The process is delicately balanced, and there are points of no return.

PART IV

The Culmination of the Cold War: Vietnam

INTRODUCTION

⟨[The Vietnam conflict has been the longest war in American history, and excepting only World War II, it has also been our most expensive war. Through fiscal 1970 the United States will have allocated $107 billion for the Vietnam War, a figure that is twice the cost of the Korean conflict, three times the cost of World War I, and more than thirty times the cost of the Civil War. If we then include veterans' benefits and assume a rate of costs similar to that for the past three major wars (in which ultimate veterans' costs totaled at least three times the original cost of the war), then the Vietnam conflict will eventually cost well over $300 billion. This figure approximately equals the total national debt now held by the public.

The most thorough study to date on the economic impact of the Vietnam conflict came out of the Joint Economic Committee hearings of April, 1967.[1] Excerpts from these hearings are printed below as a unit. The first selection in this unit is Senator William Proxmire's description of the purpose of the hearings. Many congressmen felt inadequately informed at that time about the costs of the war—especially about why costs were escalating at such a rapid rate—and the immediate purpose of these hearings was to explain why these costs were climbing so rapidly. Proxmire's declaration is followed by an exchange between Senator Stuart Symington and Robert N. Anthony, Assistant Secretary of Defense, on

how the Department of Defense figures costs in Vietnam. This exchange emphasizes both the extraordinary complexity of determining costs in advance and the attitude of officials in the Department of Defense at that time that the economy could adjust to *any* level of defense spending. In the next selection Robert W. Eisenmenger, Vice President and Director of Research, Federal Reserve Bank of Boston, concentrates on what would happen if the Vietnam conflict should end suddenly. His basic conclusion is that there would be little real economic or social disruption, provided that tax cuts or increased federal spending accompanied decreased military spending. Following this selection is an analysis by Roger Bolton, an economist at Williams College, who demonstrates how the Vietnam conflict has tended to funnel money away from the Pacific Coast states and toward the Great Lakes region. Finally, an exchange between Senator Proxmire and Wassily Leontief, professor of economics at Harvard, shows the reader a cost-benefit analysis of that war. Leontief's testimony shows that in 1967 the war cost a 2 percent reduction in the real standard of living of the average American and an 11 percent reduction in the satisfaction of public needs.

The Vietnam conflict has focused considerable attention on the allocation of manpower to fight the war. Walter Oi of the University of Washington argues that the draft is inequitable, that its cost is too high, and that a volunteer army

[1] Further hearings were held in June, 1969.

would be cheaper. Harold Wool, Director of Procurement Policy at the Department of Defense, defends the present system. Both authors emphasize the fact that war has many inequities and unforeseen side effects.

The third selection in this section is a very incisive analysis by Murray L. Weidenbaum, formerly at Washington University in St. Louis and currently the Assistant Secretary of the Treasury. He is one of the most knowledgeable writers today on the economics of defense spending and reviews step by step how the Vietnam buildup has affected the American economy as a whole. Weidenbaum emphasizes that even the most perceptive leaders of this nation were not fully aware of the economic implications of this buildup. As a result, public officials were uncertain as to which policies to follow, and their decisions were "too slow and too late."

Part IV closes with two selections on the ABM (antiballistic missile) debate. This debate, brought about largely because of the Vietnam crisis, represents the first time in recent history that the Senate has refused to take at face value the recommendations of the Pentagon and the congressional committees oriented toward the military establishment. The ABM debate also presents striking evidence that two schools of political and economic thought have recently developed in the United States. One school—exemplified by President Nixon's defense of his decision to approve the ABM system (Selection 2c-1)—looks outward and rests on the idea that Communism is a death-struggle conspiracy against the "free world." The other school—represented by Senator William Proxmire (Democrat, Wis.) (Selection 2c-2)—looks inward and argues that the main threat to free institutions lies in the unchecked power of the military, the deterioration of our cities, the stagna-

tion of our educational system, and the pollution of our environment. The first school seeks overwhelming military power to deter Communist aggression. The other seeks "social justice" and better economic conditions. Seldom does either side attack the other's basic assumption: only rarely does the first school argue that civilian needs are secondary to military needs, and, conversely, advocates of the second school seldom rebut the position that Communism is in fact aggressive and expansionistic. Hence little is settled and argument continues.

The final selection (2c-3) is an astute analysis of congressional opinion by *Congressional Quarterly,* which was published in their *Weekly Report* two days after the anti-ABM forces lost by only two votes. The basic ideological differences followed closely the positions presented below by President Nixon and Senator Proxmire. Three other important political factors should also be noted however: (1) Of those Republican senators opposing the ABM system, only two represent states west of the Mississippi River. Of those Democratic senators opposing the ABM, only one is from the Deep South. Conversely, of those senators in either party favoring the ABM system, only one represents a large eastern state. Clearly, the ABM issue is one that pitted the large eastern states against the South and West and aligned southern Democrats with conservative western Republicans. (2) Forty-seven percent of those Democrats who opposed the ABM system are up for re-election in 1970. If that election favors the party out of power—as is usually the case in nonpresidential election years—the anti-"military establishment" forces might be able to consolidate their power and ultimately defeat ABM deployment. If the country votes conservatively, then the surge to check the military that we have seen in the past few years will be thwarted. (3) The ABM issue also pitted the older senators against the younger senators. The average age of those senators who favored the ABM was 60. The average age of those opposed was 50. Almost all senators over 65 favored the ABM, but only 3 senators (of 10) under 45 did.

Many questions are raised in this chapter, but perhaps the most fundamental one is whether we should have intervened in South Vietnam or just let the country be taken over by Ho Chi Min, and whether, assuming Congress would have been willing to do so, we should have spent the $300 billion the war has cost us thus far on domestic needs instead. If one answers that we should have let Vietnam go Communist, then where do we draw the line against Communist-inspired revolutions? If the answer is to continue to assist the South Vietnamese government, where do we draw the line on the sacrifices required of our own people?

THE READINGS

1] The Cost of the Vietnam Conflict

a] THE PURPOSE OF THE JOINT ECONOMIC COMMITTEE HEARINGS ON THE ECONOMIC EFFECT OF VIETNAM SPENDING.

[Senator Proxmire] Our present purpose is to obtain clarification on three basic questions:

First, is Congress being adequately informed on the rate of change of defense expenditures right now? That is, are they going up, as some interpret, or are they going down, as others interpret?

Second, what impact on our manpower and resources is the Vietnam war now having? I cannot recall any time in our history when the Congress has attempted to assess the full economic impact of a war. In this sense, we may be pioneering, in this inquiry, in a most important aspect of economic policymaking, because we all know the immense and significant and often changing impact that wars have had in the past on our economy that undoubtedly this war is having.

Third, if the President is successful in terminating Vietnam hostilities, are adequate contingency plans available for conversion of the "wartime" uses of our resources into peaceful pursuits.

b] HOW THE DOD FIGURES WAR COSTS

.　.　.　.　.　.　.　.　.　.　.　.　.　.　.　.

CHAIRMAN PROXMIRE. Thank you, Senator Jordan.

Senator Symington?

SENATOR SYMINGTON. Thank you, Mr. Chairman.

Mr. Anthony, let me commend the way you present your position. But I would like to know how much you think this war is costing. Prior to the last appearance of Secretary McNamara I asked the staff of the Senate Appropriations Committee about the cost of the war. They estimate around $2.5 billion a month—total, $30 billion.

I asked the Secretary of Defense how long he felt the cost of the war could

---

FROM *Economic Effect of Vietnam Spending*, Joint Economic Committee, U.S. Congress, 90th Cong., 1st Sess., I (1967), p. 1.

FROM *Economic Effect of Vietnam Spending*, Joint Economic Committee, U.S. Congress, 90th Cong., 1st Sess., I (1967), pp. 17–20.

continue on the basis of $2.5 billion a month without affecting, perhaps in serious fashion, the American economy. His answer, as I remember it, was, first, he thought it was nearer $2 billion a month than $2.5 billion. Secondly, he felt the costs could continue forever.

I am interested in the cost of this war. It seems nobody has come up with the normal cost accounting you would have in a large industrial, or in other branches of Government [*sic*].

You surprise me when you say, "At first glance defense expenditures may not seem to constitute a major factor in our economy." That is some statement.

At second glance, however, apparently you think it is. Have you been to Vietnam?

MR. ANTHONY. No, sir.

SENATOR SYMINGTON. One goes around Cam Ranh and the other installations and watches the billions of dollars that are being shelled out for that type and character of construction. When you read the amount of money involved, to say it may not constitute a major factor in our economy, is hard to understand.

It is the largest single expenditure in our economy, is it not?

MR. ANTHONY. Most certainly. I would not debate anything. My sentence is a lead-in to the paragraph which goes on to say that defense expenditures are, of course, very important; that is the main point I am trying to make.

SENATOR SYMINGTON. I have had longstanding differences with the Pentagon on this GNP ratio analysis.

You say, "Our expenditures related to Southeast Asia amounting to $19.4 billion during the current year constitute only approximately 2½ percent of the gross national product."

Are you telling this committee that the cost of the war, under sound accounting principles, now amounts to only 2½ percent of the gross national product of the United States?

MR. ANTHONY. As I have discussed with you before, Senator Symington, we do not have a cost accounting system for the Vietnam conflict. I think you and everyone agrees that one does not set up a cost accounting system for a war.

SENATOR SYMINGTON. I do not quite understand what you mean by that statement. Do you mean we do not have a system designed to find out what is the true cost of the war?

MR. ANTHONY. We do not have an accounting system, a system of debits and credits that has a set of books called Southeast Asia in which we put as debits for all the amounts of money tagged with Southeast Asia.

SENATOR SYMINGTON. I know you only have single entry bookkeeping, without assets on one side and liabilities on the other. As the chairman pointed out earlier, at times you have been pretty far off; but is there no place where you check how far off you are, or are not, when you estimate the actual cost of the war?

MR. ANTHONY. No, sir, and I would be glad to expand on that a little bit if you find this an undesirable thing.

Let me explain what the figures that we have tried to put in the statement do mean. They really result from requests that you and others made last summer that we try to come up with an estimate of the cost of the war. Now, there were two essential approaches we could take to that. One is what is called an allocated cost approach in which we would try, for example, to include a part of Secretary McNamara's salary, and all of the other allocations associated with the costs. We decided that was not really the better approach and was not the one you were interested in.

SENATOR SYMINGTON. Could you let me interrupt there? I want to listen, but want to be sure I understand.

Cost consists of material, labor, and overhead. Overhead can be divided into variable and fixed. You can establish your variable overhead, and can take a percentage of fixed overhead. That being true, inasmuch as the heat is so much on the Congress about the heavy cost of the war, is it not possible to estimate material costs and variable overhead—labor cost is obvious. If you want to split part of your fixed overhead, fine.

But it seems to me the basic elements of cost especially when you are working on a resultant basis—not extrapolation—it disturbs me that here are three different estimates of the costs of this war: One from the Senate Appropriations Committee, $30 billion a year. Another from the Secretary of Defense several months ago, closer to $2 billion a month. Then you have a figure here of some $19 billion.

I know the trials and tribulations of costing any product, but I do think that somewhere, sometime, somehow, the American people should know the cost of this war. We are not getting it in the Appropriations Committee, nor in the Armed Services Committee. You would say $19 billion?

MR. ANTHONY. Certainly I would, and I think my figures are not inconsistent with Secretary McNamara's because when he was talking, I am sure he was rounding to the $2 billion a month. We are here using the same figures. His estimates of the cost of the war are the estimates my people work out.

Continuing my description of how we developed cost figures, I think I was saying that this allocated cost approach is not the figure you want. We do not, for example, see any great point in trying to depreciate the ships and other major equipment items that are involved, even if we could.

Instead, we went to an incremental cost approach. I think this is what you had in mind when you said labor, material, and variable overhead.

We have tried to estimate incremental costs associated with Southeast Asia. This cost is certainly greater than the cost, say, of the people that are in Southeast Asia, because our whole support establishment has expanded because of Southeast Asia.

SENATOR SYMINGTON. That is what I wanted to ask. As example, take the tremendous expansion on Guam, also the large expansion on Okinawa, both incident to B–52 operations. Are they all in the $19.1 billion figure?

MR. ANTHONY. Yes, sir.

SENATOR SYMINGTON. Are the costs incident to the transferring of troops from Germany, retraining of pilots? Are such costs also in the $19.1 billion figure?

MR. ANTHONY. They are in there. They are intended to be in there. We do not build it up in that amount of detail, but they are in there as part of the operating costs, which is what you are now talking about.

What we did was to take the 1965 operating costs, adjust that for price changes that have occurred since 1965, net out other known changes in non-Southeast Asia programs, and say the remaining costs in succeeding years were Southeast Asia related. I think therefore, we are automatically picking up the kind of things that you mentioned even though our system does not go into Guam and split the costs on Guam between non-Southeast Asia costs and Southeast Asia costs. The system just plainly does not work in this way.

SENATOR SYMINGTON. These expenditures are what you are talking about?

MR. ANTHONY. No, the figure of $21.8 billion that I give you for 1968 is a cost figure.

Actually in the buildup phase many different types of figures float around because obligations, expenditures, and costs are three different concepts, quite different concepts, and in the buildup phase they are radically different numbers. In a level-off phase, they all are about the same. So when I say $21.8 billion—if you will permit me to round it to $22 billion—$22 billion is really pretty close to obligations, expenditures, and costs for Southeast Asia.

SENATOR SYMINGTON. For the period of?

MR. ANTHONY. One year.

SENATOR SYMINGTON. Ending next June 30?

MR. ANTHONY. June 30, 1968. Our cost figure for fiscal year 1968 is $21.8 billion. Our cost figure for fiscal year 1967 is $19.5 billion. Our expenditure figure for fiscal year 1967 is $19.4 billion.

SENATOR SYMINGTON. Then for the fiscal year 1968, starting next July 1 you estimate that the total cost of the war in Vietnam will be about $22 billion.

MR. ANTHONY. Incremental costs, yes.

SENATOR SYMINGTON. What does that word mean?

MR. ANTHONY. The same as what you meant, I think, when you tried to define the term.

Maybe I am professorial in this, but I never would give a figure for the word "cost" without some kind of a modifier to it. The word "cost" is absolutely meaningless taken by itself. Here, I think we are both talking about incremental costs in the sense of the costs that are incurred for Southeast Asia that would not be incurred were there not Southeast Asia. Is that not the concept you have?

SENATOR SYMINGTON. I have one more question. The Secretary of Defense defends the cost of the Vietnamese war as not being punitive on the economy on the grounds it is not an increasing percentage of the gross national product.

Now, we have labor problems going on. It would appear there may be some major increases in costs, increases incident to labor demand and therefore very possibly increases in prices. That will increase the gross national product automatically, will it not?

MR. ANTHONY. Yes, sir.

SENATOR SYMINGTON. But you still feel, regardless of the international position, that if the gross national product increases and the percentage of increased cost of the Defense Department does not increase in percentage of the GNP that figure in itself demonstrates it is not punitive to the economy; correct?

MR. ANTHONY. I would prefer that economists, who are much more versed in this subject than I, talk about this.

My impression is that the effect on the economy depends heavily on the rapidity of an increase and not the absolute amount at any level. That is, the economy can adjust to any level; the difficult time, the time of strain, is when you are building up rapidly to a new level.

I should also say, Senator—I should have said earlier when I gave you the figure for 1968, that this figure was in terms of current prices. I did not try to build in the inflationary factors that you just mentioned.

SENATOR SYMINGTON. Do you think this philosophy would justify—and I ask this with great respect—claims on the part of some people in this country as well as in other countries, that we are promoting a war economy to maintain economic stability?

MR. ANTHONY. Not at all, no, sir.

SENATOR SYMINGTON. Thank you.

. . . .

c] THE REGIONAL IMPACT OF THE VIETNAM WAR

. . . .

[Mr. Bolton]

The more recent increases for Vietnam have also changed the geographical distribution of defense demand, partially reversing the trends of the later fifties and early sixties. The war is the more conventional type, and the needs for ordnance, vehicles, and combat supplies have grown much more rapidly than for missiles, ships, and electronics. Inspection of Defense Department data on commodity classification of prime contracts in fiscal years 1965 and 1966 shows very large increases in 1966 in the relative importance of vehicles, weapons, ammunition, food, textile and clothing products, and several different categories of equipment and supplies of ordinary types. These increases in the percent of contracts imply very large increases in dollar amounts, because the national total increased by more than one-third in 1966 over 1965. The increase for ammunition is especially striking. The absolute dollar value of contracts for ammunition increased by more than $2 billion. There were, on the other hand, declines in the share of contracts going for missiles, ships, and construction (in this country) so large that the absolute dollar value in these programs declined. The amount for missiles had already fallen sharply in fiscal years 1964 and 1965, and figures from direct surveys by the Defense Department of large missile manufacturing

FROM Statement of Professor Roger Bolton in *Economic Effect of Vietnam Spending*, Joint Economic Committee, U.S. Congress, 90th Cong., 1st Sess., I (1967), pp. 154–56.

plants show declines in employment of about a third between 1963 and 1966.

Along with this change in commodity pattern has come a change in the regional distribution of procurement. All the major census regions received more prime contracts in fiscal year 1966 than in 1965, but the increase varied greatly in size. The increases for the Mountain and Pacific regions, for example, were quite small and their fractional share of the total fell greatly. Despite the large increase in the national total, increases were relatively even faster in the East North Central, South Central, and New England regions.

CHAIRMAN PROXMIRE. What is the east north central region? What States does that include?

MR. BOLTON. Ohio, Indiana, Michigan, Illinois, Wisconsin.

CHAIRMAN PROXMIRE. Thank you.

MR. BOLTON. Other areas of the country had increases roughly in pace with the national total. Although prime contracts do not indicate the true regional distribution of all defense production, because of the subcontracting across regional lines, they are nevertheless very important indicators. A very large part of the contract value is produced in the State the prime contractor is located in.

Inspection of data on prime contract value classified by both commodity and State, clearly shows the regional effect of the new emphasis on conventional equipment. Relative to the total change for the State, increased ammunition contracts were large for many Midwestern States, for Tennessee, New Jersey, Texas, California, and some States in the South. New England benefited greatly from weapons contracts; and the Midwest from vehicle procurement. Helicopter contracts loomed large in Pennsylvania and Connecticut; and aircraft engines in Connecticut, Massachusetts, New Jersey, Ohio, and Indiana. Textile and clothing products were important for many Southern States and several New England ones. Various miscellaneous kinds of equipment and supplies, such as military building supplies, production equipment, photographic equipment, and construction equipment were contracted for in large quantities in all the East North Central States, and some Southern ones. The wide variety of items for which large contracts were placed in the traditional Manufacturing Belt of Ohio, Indiana, Illinois, Michigan, and Wisconsin is particularly striking.

These have been indications of the procurement picture. There are also data on changes in civilian and military payrolls. Between June 1965 and June 1966, about three-quarters of the increase in civilian employment at Defense Department installations took place in nine States: California, Virginia, Maryland, Texas, Utah, Georgia, Oklahoma, Pennsylvania, and Missouri. In the same period, the States in which there were the largest increases in military personnel assigned, and thus the States where they spend at last some of their pay, were Texas, California, Georgia, Illinois, Hawaii, New Jersey, Missouri, Virginia, and South Carolina. In civilian and military payrolls, then, the Midwest has not participated nearly as much as it has in procurement. Their regional description has followed the traditional lines of concentration on the south and west.

.   .   .   .

d] A COST-BENEFIT ANALYSIS OF THE VIETNAM WAR

.   .   .   .

CHAIRMAN PROXMIRE. What are the total real costs of our Vietnam hostilities? You lived through the Russian revolution. You saw the Chinese revolution. My staff informs me you will soon be going to Greece as a neutral observer. With your broad theoretical economic background and your broad practical experience, will you attempt to place our Vietnam commitments in broader perspective in the "short and long run," as you economists say?

MR. LEONTIEF. Yes. Mr. Chairman; as I said in my statement, we are engaging here in a cost-benefit analysis of the Vietnamese war. The question I myself would like to ask is this: Of the two sides of the ledger spread before us on my graphs, which represents the costs and which the benefits?

I suppose, as things go now, the benefits are the war in Vietnam. At least, the State Department acts as if these were benefits. What then are our costs? Our costs are a nearly 2-percent reduction in the standard of living of the average American, and a nearly 11-percent, $12-billion cut in funds allocated to the satisfaction of all kinds of urgent public needs. These are the direct immediate prices that we pay for the benefits which this country allegedly derives from the Vietnamese war.

It is my own personal opinion that, in addition to this, we are paying other terrifically high costs which ultimately will also be translated into material burdens that we will have to carry for years to come. As you know, this is a war supported by the people whose support, under ordinary circumstances, we wouldn't wish to have at all, and which, on the other hand, has alienated, throughout the world, those people whose support we badly need.

.   .   .   .

We will have to cut down on consumption, we will have to cut down on social services, we will have to cut down on education, and so on, to produce more planes and more munitions and to send more boys to Vietnam.

CHAIRMAN PROXMIRE. What you are using here is what is called input-output analysis?

MR. LEONTIEF. Yes, I do.

CHAIRMAN PROXMIRE. And what would be the total employment displacement under alternatives one and two over here?

MR. LEONTIEF. Displacement might amount to possibly one-million people having to shift into different jobs. It might be still larger because our computations tend to underestimate the amount of displacement in that we count as displacement only movements out of one into another of the 80-odd sectors in terms of which these figures are presented. But within each sector there are many subdivisions. Shifting out of one department of the steel

---

FROM Statement by Professor Wassily Leontief in *Economic Effect of Vietnam Spending,* Joint Economic Committee, U.S. Congress, 90th Cong., 1st Sess., I (1967), pp. 253–54.

industry into another might be quite a displacement for a worker, although statistically it does not appear as such. The same, of course, applies to shifts between regions.

e] THE NATIONAL IMPACT OF ENDING THE VIETNAM WAR

IMPACT ON FIRM AND INDUSTRY

MR. EISENMENGER. . . . I have been asked to testify this morning about fluctuations in military spending for Vietnam and their impact on firms, industries, small isolated communities, and large metropolitan areas. I imagine I was invited because the Research Department of the Federal Reserve Bank of Boston has supported numerous studies which analyzed the impact of various defense closings on local communities in New England. In addition, I have recently written a book which discusses the problems of economic adjustment in New England since World War II.

As most of you probably know, with the exception of the coal mining areas and some of the depressed agricultural areas, primarily in the South, probably no major section of the country has experienced such a radical transformation of its economic base in the last 20 years as has New England. When World War II ended and outmoded machinery was no longer needed to satisfy swollen wartime demand, the region's antiquated textile industry collapsed and laid off 180,000 employees over a period of 15 years. In many metropolitan areas unemployment was serious. For example, during 1948 the unemployment rate averaged between 13 and 25 percent in Lawrence, New Bedford, Fall River, and Providence-Pawtucket. Even as late as 1958 the unemployment rate averaged more than 10 percent in these same cities and was 15 percent or more in many of the smaller textile cities.

Today, the unemployment rate in New England as a whole is only 3.3 percent, well below the national average of 3.6 percent. Only two of our large textile cities now have serious unemployment problems. Thus, given enough time, it would appear that even the most depressed communities can make a strong comeback. We may ask ourselves, however: Is it necessary for communities to go through such a long, hard readjustment process before they regain economic balance?

What would happen if the Vietnam war should end suddenly and national defense spending were cut by 20 percent or more? Would many of the country's large economic areas have the same agonizing readjustment problems that New England's textile communities faced after World War II? No one can answer this question with 100 percent assurance, but I am reasonably confident that a very substantial defense cutback would not bring

FROM Statement of Robert W. Eisenmenger, Vice President and Director of Research, Federal Reserve Bank of Boston in *Economic Effect of Vietnam Spending,* Joint Economic Committee, U.S. Congress, 90th Cong., 1st Sess., I (1967), pp. 147–50.

similar problems to many metropolitan areas in the United States. The problems of the older textile cities in New England were considerably different from those of most metropolitan areas which depend heavily on defense spending today.

I have four reasons for saying the situation is different now:

1. New England's depressed textile towns had a very slow economic and population growth rate long before most of their economic base collapsed with the textile industry. To a surprising extent, in contrast, most defense-dependent areas have been growing very rapidly for many years. For example, the Los Angeles population increased by more than 45 percent between 1950 and 1960. More than three-quarters of this total gain was accounted for by net in-migration from other parts of the country. More recent figures show a 10.5-percent increase in population in Los Angeles between 1960 and 1964, almost half of which was accounted for by migration. The figures for Harford County, Conn., another defense-dependent area, are somewhat similar. Between 1950 and 1960 there was a population increase in Hartford County of 28 percent. About two-fifths of this percentage increase was accounted for by net in-migration.

My main point is this. Even if large military cutbacks occurred, these exploding areas might merely see a decline in their rate of growth and consequently, in their rate of in-migration. As a result, the areas' industries might well be able to absorb the existing labor supply without major difficulties. This is not to say that there would be no problems in the transition period. The housing industry and some of the service industries which expanded in anticipation of a continuation of a rapid rate of growth would likely have an over-capacity problem for a number of years, but it is difficult to envision the kind of problems that faced the stagnant textile communities in New England.

2. New England's depressed postwar mill towns also differed very substantially from most of today's larger metropolitan areas in that their economic health depended largely on one stagnant industry—textile manufacturing. Furthermore, most of their nontextile firms were also in slow growing industries.

Two years ago, looking at metropolitan areas where defense spending is of major importance, the National Planning Association made a study of the possible impact of defense cutbacks on Baltimore and Seattle-Tacoma. The NPA was reasonably optimistic about Baltimore where 15 percent of the total civilian employment was defense-related, because Baltimore has a diversified economy with many firms in growing industries. The NPA study suggests, therefore, that even a substantial military spending cutback, if offset at the national level by tax cuts or increased spending, would bring little economic and social disruption to Baltimore.

The N.P.A. study was slightly more pessimistic about Seattle-Tacoma where 24 percent of the total civilian employment was defense-related and military personnel accounted for 6 percent of total employment. Here again, however, there was no suggestion that defense conversion would create the kind of problems that plagued New England's textile communities for so many years. The study foresaw unemployment of only 2 to 7 percent of the work force. While the N.P.A. did point out that many scientists and engineers at the dominant Boeing plant would be displaced, these professional employees are among the most mobile members of our society. In addition, the N.P.A. expected that the rising national demand for commercial airliners and the area's growing service industries would prevent major economic disturbances.

3. Even during World War II, New England's textile towns could not have been considered the Nation's most prosperous communities. The case is different, however, for today's defense-dependent metropolitan areas. Professor Weidenbaum of Washington University in St. Louis has found that as of 1963 the regions with the highest per capita incomes were receiving the bulk of the defense contracts and that low-income regions were obtaining only a small share. He concluded, therefore, that a reduction in war spending and an equivalent increase in other types of Government spending would inevitably work to the advantage of the lower income sections of the country.

My examination of military procurement data indicates that the distribution of defense contracts has changed very little since Professor Weidenbaum made his study in 1963. There is one important exception to this generalization. *The proportion of defense contracts allocated to California has declined significantly in the last few years.* But, on the whole, the defense contracts are still directed predominantly to the high-income manufacturing centers in the United States. Thus, with a big increase in defense spending, these areas have developed labor shortages. I am sure, for example, that the rapid rise in defense spending in 1966 and 1967 explains the extreme labor shortage which we now have in Hartford, New Britain, and New Haven, Conn., and in Manchester, N.H. A reduction in defense spending would help alleviate some of these problems by reducing labor shortages in high-income areas and bringing additional income to low-income communities.

4. One of the obvious characteristics of military procurement is that it must be concentrated in geographical areas where the average skill level of the labor force is very high. The Battelle Memorial Institute has shown, for example, that engineers and technical workers constitute only 11 percent of the work force of electronics manufacturers producing consumer products. The corresponding figure for military and space products is 33 percent. In contrast, semiskilled and unskilled labor make up 63 percent of the work force in the consumer products sector of the electronics industry, while the figure for the military and space sector is only 27 percent. For these reasons, the defense products manufacturers tend to locate in areas where the labor force has diverse and above-average skills. But it is in just these areas that the labor force is most mobile and most able to change jobs if shifts in Government spending bring about an abrupt change in employment requirements. These high-skill areas differ substantially from the textile communities in New England. As of 1960, for example, the median number of years of schooling of the adult male population in New Bedford and Fall River was 8.6, compared to a statewide average of 11.3 in Massachusetts.

All in all, I conclude that most of our large metropolitan areas would undergo relatively minor disruptions if there were a cutback of only 20 percent in defense spending. The smaller metropolitan areas or isolated rural communities which are linked to military spending in various ways present a different case, however, and I will now turn to them.

.   .   .   .

2] The Domestic Impact of the Vietnam Conflict

a] THE CONSEQUENCES OF CHANGING COMMITMENTS

I. INTRODUCTION

THIS STUDY traces the expansion of the U.S. defense effort resulting from the changing American commitment in South Vietnam, analyzes the impact on the U.S. economy, and examines the resultant questions of domestic economic policy.

Several *key points* emerge from this study: (1) *persisting uncertainty as to the nature and extent of the United States commitment*, (2) *a lack of general understanding of the speed with which a military buildup affects the economy*, (3) *confusion in interpretation and delay in the release of budget information in 1966*, and (4) *resultant basic problems in national economic policy*. The final section of this study deals with the process of economic adjustment to peace in Vietnam.

A. Some Historical Perspective

Until comparatively recently, expenditures for national security were a minor factor in American economic activity. In the half century prior to 1930, such outlays normally equaled less than one percent of the Gross National Product (GNP), except for the World War I period. From 1931 to 1939, military outlays averaged 1.3 percent of GNP. Since World War II, however, the Cold War and the Korean and Vietnam conflicts have raised security programs to a relatively high level even in the absence of hostilities. Immediately prior to the Vietnam buildup, purchases by the Department of Defense were about 8 percent of the total output of the Nation. The proportion was of course higher during World War II (peak of 48 percent) and the Korean War (peak of 12 percent).

The most recent levels of military demand reflect an extended period of Cold War, interspersed by incidents leading to limited conflicts, such as Korea and Vietnam, and temporary thaws and defense cutbacks, such as in 1957–58 and in 1963–64. An abrupt change in the nature of the external

FROM "Impact of Vietnam War on American Economy" (Background paper prepared by Murray L. Weidenbaum) in *Economic Effect of Vietnam Spending*, Joint Economic Committee, U.S. Congress, 90th Cong., 1st Sess., I (1967), pp. 193–215. [Footnotes omitted.— J. L. C.]

environment—a sudden intensification of war or a cold war thaw—and in this country's reaction to it, might well cause another major shift from the present proportion of resources devoted to security programs. Unlike many other categories of demand for goods and services, the level and composition of national security expenditures are relatively independent of influences in the private economy. Yet, these military demands heavily influenced the private economy.

The impact of defense on the economy depends not only on the level and rate of change of spending. The availability of resources and the state of peoples' expectations affect the timing and extent of the impact on prices, production, and economic growth. Heavy reliance on deficit financing during World War II, in contrast to the emphasis on tax financing during the Korean War, produced different results on consumer income and spending both during and after the war.

Even before the Vietnam buildup, military spending had been dominating the Federal Budget. Such spending accounts for over 85 percent of all Federal Government purchases of goods and services. In real terms (when the dollar figures are adjusted to eliminate changes resulting from inflation) virtually all of the increase in direct Federal purchases of goods and services during the past two decades has been accounted for by defense programs. The aggregate of all other purchases by the Federal Government is at about the same real level as in 1940. The large increases in Federal spending for civilian purposes have been transfer payments and grants, which do not show up in the GNP as Federal purchases of goods and services. Hence, the rise in the Federal share of GNP from 6.2 percent in 1940 to 10.3 percent in 1964 was accounted for almost entirely by military and related security expenditures. On this basis, it can be seen that these security-related expenditures have been the primary factor in the expansion of the Federal Government as a purchaser and consumer of goods and services.

B. The U.S. Commitment in Vietnam

An evaluation of the impact of the Vietnam war on the U.S. economy requires first a review of recent developments in South Vietnam itself and of the changing nature of the U.S. involvement. The nature and extent of the American commitment in South Vietnam was continually unfolding during the period 1963–66. This, of course, created fundamental difficulties both in forecasting U.S. military expenditures and in analyzing their impact on the American economy.

It is the essence of present-day limited war for one side to be uncertain of the future actions of the other. However, in the hitherto conventional conflicts such as the role of the United States after Pearl Harbor, there was little uncertainty as to the extent of our own participation in World War II—the maximum effort which could be supported by the economy. Vietnam, in contrast, and to some extent Korea, are examples of conflicts in which our uncertainties have included both our own as well as enemy actions.

1. *The Diem Coup in 1963.*—From 1954 through early 1963, the U.S. role in South Vietnam was limited to providing training and military ad-

visory activities. Fewer than 1,000 members of the U.S. armed forces were stationed in South Vietnam during the period 1954–1960. This number rose slightly in 1961, to 1,364. During 1962, an expansion occurred to almost 10,000 (see Table 1). In early 1963, the situation seemed relatively stable. In February, Secretary McNamara stated, "The drive of the Vietcong supported by the North Vietnamese against the established government in South Vietnam has been blunted . . . There are a number of factors that are favorable, a number of indications that the South Vietnamese are stronger in relation to the Vietcong than they were a year ago."

However, later in the year Buddhist agitations against Diem increased markedly. Combined with the continued deterioration of Diem's governmental support, these events culminated in his death and the overthrow of his government in November 1963. There followed a very substantial increase in Vietcong activity and a weakening of the fabric of the South Vietnam society. In commenting on this period, Secretary McNamara stated that, "the political control structure . . . has, in certain cases, practically disappeared following the November 1 coup . . ."

Nevertheless, the position of the Administration remained, in the words of the Secretary of Defense, "This is a Vietnamese war, and in the final analysis it must be fought and won by the Vietnamese." Several weeks after the coup, the Secretary announced that, upon completion of certain training missions, "small numbers of the U.S. personnel will be able to return by the end of this year." About 1,000 U.S. soldiers were returned to the U.S. during that period.

2. *The Vietcong Initiative in 1964.*—In 1964, the Vietcong stepped up their rate of attack, especially against the rural population. During the year, they killed an estimated 436 hamlet chiefs and other government officials at all echelons and kidnapped an additional 1131. To put that in perspective on the basis of relative populations, we can multiply the figures by 12 and think of 18,800 mayors, governors, and legislators in the United States being murdered or kidnapped in the space of one year. Also, it was reported that the Vietcong were using weapons of higher calibre than previously noted and that these weapons were being supplied by the North Vietnamese. These included 75 millimeter recoilless rifles and large stocks of machine guns and ammunition of Chinese manufacture.

By the end of 1964, the number of U.S. troops in South Vietnam had risen to 23,300. Even so, the U.S. involvement was still only that of support. The military budget presented in January 1965 actually projected a small decline in total U.S. defense spending for the fiscal year ahead. However, the Tonkin Gulf Resolution approved by Congress in August 1964 authorized all necessary measures "to repel any armed attack against U.S. forces and . . . to prevent further aggression in Vietnam."

3. *The North Vietnamese Infiltration in 1965.*—A significant change in the nature of the conflict occurred in 1965—the intensification of infiltration of arms and personnel into South Vietnam. The increase in infiltration gave the Vietcong increased capability, enabling them both to operate in larger units and to increase the number and intensity of attacks.

The resulting expansion in the U.S. role in Vietnam is explained by the

TABLE 1   U.S. MILITARY PERSONNEL IN SOUTH VIETNAM

Date	Number
1954-60 (average)	650
Dec. 31, 1960	773
Dec. 31, 1961	1,364
Dec. 31, 1962	9,865
Dec. 31, 1963	16,575
June 30, 1964	21,000
Dec. 31, 1964	23,300[1]
June 30, 1965	103,000[1]
Dec. 31, 1965	184,314
June 30, 1966	322,000[1]
Dec. 31, 1966 (estimated)	455,000[1]

[1] Total of U.S. military personnel in southeast Asia.
SOURCE: U.S. House of Representatives, Committee on Appropriations, *Department of Defense Appropriations for 1967*, Part 1, p. 378; *1968 Budget*, p. 77.

following dialogue between a member of the House Appropriations Committee and Secretary McNamara in April 1965:

Question: "Is our stepped-up effort there, our direct intervention and air strikes, motivated to some extent by the feeling that time is of the essence?"

Answer: "Our increased effort is motivated by the fact that the North Vietnamese were greatly increasing their infiltration of men and equipment into South Vietnam. We recognized if they continued that they will just overwhelm the nation."

In February 1965, the United States Air Force began bombing targets in North Vietnam. The decline in total uniformed personnel of the U.S. Army halted in March. In April, the U.S. buildup of troops in South Vietnam rapidly accelerated. In May, the Administration asked for and Congress quickly approved a $700 million military supplemental appropriations bill for the fiscal year 1965.

The estimated ratio of 4 Vietnamese military forces to 1 Vietcong was considered highly unfavorable for successful South Vietnam prosecution of guerrilla warfare, particularly in view of the ratio of at least 10 to 1 found necessary for successful anti-guerrilla operations in Malaysia, the Philippines, and elsewhere. Accordingly, a major expansion of U.S. armed strength in South Vietnam was underway in 1965, reaching a total of 184,314 by the end of the year. This represented an expansion of sevenfold over the previous year.

During the monsoon season of 1965 the Vietcong attempted to cut South Vietnam in half and thus bring about a signal victory. The sharply-increased U.S. capability was instrumental in blunting this drive. This led the Secretary of Defense to state in November 1965, that ". . . we have stopped losing the war."

4. *The Reliance on U.S. Combat Forces in 1966.*—By early 1966, the U.S. forces were conducting the bulk of the offensive military actions against the

Vietcong. This can be inferred from Secretary McNamara's analysis of the four major types of military operations against the Vietcong during that period. A schematic presentation based on his Congressional testimony follows:

Type of military operation	Purpose	Primary responsibility
Search and destroy	Destroy known or suspected Communist forces and their base areas. Excludes seizing and holding territory permanently.	United States and other free world forces and strike elements of South Vietnamese Armed Forces.
Clear and secure	Permanently eliminate Communist forces from specified areas. Includes conducting pacification measures.	South Vietnamese forces.[1]
Reserve reaction	Relieve Provincial capitals and district towns under Communist attack and reinforce friendly forces when needed.	South Vietnamese forces.[1]
Defense of Government centers.	Protect Provincial capitals, district towns, and key Government installations.	South Vietnamese forces.

[1] With assistance from U.S. forces and other free world forces.

During 1966, the regular Army, Navy, Marines and Air Forces of South Vietnam numbered about 320,000, and were primarily responsible for the more passive missions, such as pacification and defense. Total U.S. forces in South Vietnam exceeded 300,000 in 1966, the bulk of them assigned to the active "search and destroy" mission.

It should be noted that various paramilitary forces also are available to South Vietnam. According to recent estimates, these include approximately 150,000 in regional forces, 150,000 in popular forces, and 110,000 in national police, armed combat youth, and civilian irregular defense groups.

Clearly, during 1966 the nature and extent of U.S. involvement in Vietnam were altered fundamentally. Subsequent chapters will trace through the consequences of these changes on the U.S. military budget and the economy.

5. *An Overview. It is clear that the U.S. role in Vietnam changed from support to combat when the South Vietnamese government and armed forces no longer could withstand the combined onslaught of the Vietcong and massive infiltration of North Vietnamese equipment and manpower.*

It is futile to speculate as to anyone's ability to have precisely forecast these developments prior to their occurrence. In any event, *the uncertain nature of future developments in Vietnam continually clouded the public and private analyses of their unfolding impact on the U.S. Budget and the American economy.*

A historical review—admittedly an armchair analysis—is undoubtedly easier now than any contemporaneous effort. Two types of statements by the Department of Defense increased the difficulty: (1) extremely firm statements on the limited nature of the U.S. role which did not turn out to be that limited and (2) optimistic statements which were technically accurate but which nevertheless tended to mislead regarding future prospects.

For example, on various occasions in 1963 and 1964 the policy was expressed that the war was to be fought not by U.S. troops but by Vietnamese, a policy position that later became inconsistent with the changed military and political situations. Indications of this can be found in the following excerpts from a series of quotations, which Secretary McNamara presented to Congressional committees early in 1966 in connection with press reports concerning "the reliability of my statements with respect to the outlook in South Vietnam."

January 27, 1964. "This is a Vietnamese war, and in the final analysis it must be fought and won by the Vietnamese."

May 6, 1964. "We can provide advice; we can provide logistical support; we can provide training assistance, but we cannot fight the war itself."

And then, after U.S. troops were engaged in combat on a large scale:

August 9, 1965. "They [South Vietnamese forces] are bearing the brunt of the fighting; they will continue to bear the brunt of the fighting."

The relatively optimistic appraisals of the outlook was retained from 1963 to 1965, as reflected in the statements of the Secretary of Defense (taken from the same report).

July 19, 1963. "The military operations in South Vietnam have been proceding very satisfactorily and this is true no matter what method you apply to them. We are quite pleased with the results."

November 21, 1963. ". . . we are equally encouraged by the prospects for progress in the war against the Vietcong."

December 21, 1963. "We reviewed in great detail the plans of the South Vietnamese and the plans of our own military advisers for operations during 1964. We have every reason to believe they will be successful."

May 14, 1964. "The path to victory will be long and it will take courage and imagination for both the Vietnamese and for our forces who are assisting them to assure success, but I firmly believe that the persistent execution of the political-military plans which the Government of Vietnam has developed to carry out that war with our assistance will lead to success."

November 10, 1964. "So I think that today, as compared to a month or two ago, we can look ahead with greater confidence."

May 9, 1965. "I think in the last eight weeks there has been an improvement." In response to the question, then you, yourself, are more optimistic? "Yes, I am. . . ."

However, by 1966, a new note of caution had entered into official statements. In February, the Secretary of Defense testified to the House Appropriations Committee that "we must assume that the number of North Vietnamese Regular Army troops in South Vietnam will continue to increase substantially in the months ahead . . ."

In January 1967, he stated at a joint hearing of the Senate Appropriation and Armed Services Committees, "I do not know of any war of any substantial size that anyone has ever been able to predict the end of it accurately, and we cannot do it here."

To repeat, the purpose of reviewing these statements is to demonstrate and underscore the difficulties in analyzing the impacts of these developments on the American economy at the time they were occurring.

·   ·   ·   ·   ·   ·   ·   ·   ·   ·   ·   ·   ·

III. THE U.S. MILITARY BUILDUP FOR VIETNAM

A. The Expansion of U.S. Military Spending for Vietnam

The relatively minor American involvement in Vietnam during the 1954–63 period was hardly visible in the U.S. military budget. However, applying the average annual cost per U.S. soldier ($23,000) to the number of American troops in South Vietnam during that time yields a rough order of magnitude of the demand on U.S. resources.

On that basis, the American commitment was costing about $15 million a year during 1954–60 and rose to somewhere around $18 million in the fiscal year 1961. In contrast, total U.S. defense spending was $43,227 million in fiscal 1961. By the crude estimating technique used here, U.S. defense spending in South Vietnam was around $31 million in fiscal 1962, $227 million in fiscal 1963, and $381 million in fiscal 1964, still quite minor amounts compared to the military budget totals.

An official estimate is available for "special support of Vietnam operations" in fiscal 1965, $103 million. That figure seems low in view of the fact that U.S. troops in South Vietnam rose from 23,300 to 103,000 during that year. Presumably, a high proportion of the costs was financed from regular operations or by drawing down inventories of weapons and supplies previously purchased.

The significant impact of Vietnam on the Federal Budget and hence on the American economy began in the fiscal year 1966. The January 1966 Budget Document estimated that $14.0 billion of the requested appropriations and $4.4 billion of the estimated expenditures for the fiscal year then in progress—the year ending June 30, 1966—resulted from Vietnam. The actual amounts turned out somewhat higher, $14.9 billion in appropriations and $5.8 billion in expenditures. A review of the data in Table 1 confirms the fact that the fiscal year 1966 was the period of major expansion of American armed forces in Vietnam. Prior to July 1, 1965, U.S. armed strength stationed there had risen to 103,000. Between July 1965 and June 1966, there was an increase of over 200,000 American troops in Vietnam. To date, further increases have been somewhat in excess of 100,000.

As pointed out earlier, the basic detail in the defense budget is not broken down to show the Vietnam components of each item separately. Hence, it is necessary to infer the impact of this commitment from movements in the more aggregate figures. Thus, the escalation of the U.S. commitment in Vietnam, can, to some extent, be translated into economic impact by looking at the changing overall pace of military demand.

The data on total U.S. defense expenditures on a fiscal year basis show that the Nation's military spending was declining from $54.2 billion in fiscal 1964 to $50.2 billion in fiscal 1965 and did not turn up until fiscal 1966. A more precise pattern emerges when the annual data are divided into 3-month periods. It shows that the decline in military spending ended by January 1, 1965, the middle of the fiscal year, and that the last two quarters (January–June 1965) were higher than in the same period of the preceding fiscal year (see Table 3).

Moreover, the data on defense obligations—which include commitments currently being incurred for pay of the armed forces as well as defense contracts being awarded to private industry—show that the upturn began in January 1965. By the fourth quarter of 1965, defense obligations were running at about $9 billion higher than the last quarter of 1964, at seasonally adjusted annual rates. By June 1966, defense obligations were running $22 [billion] above the rate of the end of 1964. The January 1966 Budget Message stressed restraint in Federal fiscal policy, a theme that became even stronger in later public statements.

The January 1967 Federal Budget greatly clarified the pace of the military buildup resulting from Vietnam. It estimated that Vietnam spending would reach $19.4 billion in fiscal 1967 and $21.9 billion in 1968. By then the magnitude of the U. S. involvement in Vietnam, as well as its impact on the Budget and on the economy, was fairly clearly grasped by the public. The Pentagon estimated that it would spend $72.3 billion in the fiscal year 1968, for all military operations—a figure larger than any earlier period except the peak of World War II. Total military expenditures, excluding military assistance to foreign nations, is estimated to be two-thirds higher than at the Korean War peak and about twice the level reached during the post-Korean low. Nevertheless, the fiscal 1968 estimate represents a leveling of the rapid upsurge in military demand which has occurred since the Vietnam War escalated in the summer of 1965.

In retrospect, it appears that the latter part of 1965 and most of 1966 con-

TABLE 3   SELECTED MEASURES OF U.S. MILITARY SPENDING
[In billions of dollars at annual rates]

| Calendar year and quarter | Defense obligations | | Defense expenditures (budget basis) |
	Actual	Seasonally adjusted	
1964:			
1st quarter	$52.0	$55.2	$49.2
2d quarter	61.0	54.8	56.8
3d quarter	55.0	53.3	43.1
4th quarter	51.8	53.3	48.1
Total	55.0	54.2	49.3
1965:			
1st quarter	48.2	51.0	46.8
2d quarter	62.2	55.0	51.6
3d quarter	60.6	59.0	48.6
4th quarter	62.1	62.1	54.1
Total	58.3	56.8	50.3
1966:			
1st quarter	60.5	64.6	56.4
2d quarter	86.4	75.9	62.4
3d quarter	77.0	75.2	63.4
4th quarter	68.9	72.9	65.8
Total	73.2	72.0	62.0

SOURCE: Departments of Defense and Commerce.

stituted the period where the domestic consequences of this nation's commitment in Vietnam were not fully or generally understood. The year 1967 does not seem to be a period of equal uncertainty, although the possibility of another fundamental escalation in the level of the U.S. commitment persists. Hence, it seems both necessary and useful to review the earlier period in considerable detail, particularly in the hope of identifying some lessons for future economic policy.

B. The Economic Policy Response in 1966

The January 24, 1966 Budget message of the President estimated that Department of Defense expenditures would rise from $46.2 billion in fiscal year 1965 to $52.9 billion in 1966 and $57.2 billion in 1967. On both a cash and national income accounts basis, the Federal Budget was estimated to be in approximate balance in fiscal 1967; on the administrative budget basis, the deficit of $1.8 billion estimated for 1967 would be a reduction from the $6.4 billion deficit envisioned for fiscal 1966.

On this basis, the President stated in the January 1966 *Economic Report* that, "The fiscal program I recommended for 1966 aims at full employment without inflation."

The January 1966 Budget Message called for several steps that would increase Federal revenues, notably putting personal and corporate income taxes more nearly on a pay-as-you-go basis and temporarily reinstating the excises on passenger automobiles, and telephone service which had just been reduced.

On the expenditure side of the budget, despite statements on economy and efficiency, the customary items were found in the details of the document. For example, it was recommended that the Department of Agriculture start construction of 35 watershed projects and 1600 miles of forest roads, that the Bureau of Reclamation start work on three new projects with a total cost initially estimated at $1 billion, that the Corps of Engineers start building 25 new rivers and harbors projects and begin designing 23 more, that the General Services Administration finance construction of 33 government office buildings and design 10 more, and that the Government Printing Office acquire additional buildings.

The January 1966 Budget did not contemplate the firm policy of no new starts on public works projects that was maintained during the Korean War. It appeared, at least to many observers, that the Nation could afford simultaneously to wage a two-front war without raising taxes, the domestic war against poverty and the war in Vietnam. That theme was clearly stated in the Budget Message:

"We are a rich nation and can afford to make progress at home while meeting obligations abroad—in fact, we can afford no other course if we are to remain strong. For this reason, I have not halted progress in the new and vital Great Society programs in order to finance the costs of our efforts in Southeast Asia."

Secretary McNamara's testimony on the military budget in February 1966 clearly showed that the Administration was discounting any inflationary impact of the Vietnam buildup:

"As you can see, by itself, the defense program should not be a major factor contributing to inflationary pressures. I say this even though you are now considering a $12.3 billion supplemental to the fiscal year 1966 defense budget . . . defense expenditures will, in effect, be no more of an inflationary element in fiscal years 1966 and 1967 by virtue of their relative demand on the economy than they were in the period from 1960 to 1964, and therefore by themselves are not sufficient cause for predicting inflation."

In retrospect, things did not work out so well as anticipated. Although the unemployment rate declined below 4 percent, *the year 1966 witnessed the most rapid period of price inflation since the Korean War.* In striking contrast to the virtual stability during the period 1958–64, the wholesale index, which had been rising by about 1½ percent annually in recent years, mainly due to the rising cost of services, climbed more than 3 percent in 1966.

The second, related result of economic pressures in 1966 was the virtual collapse, at least temporarily, of the Council of Economic Advisers' wage-price guideposts. These were designed to reduce or avoid inflationary pressures in the economy by encouraging management and labor to hold wage increases to the trend increase in productivity in the economy as a whole. The CEA's guidepost of 3.2 percent was widely violated during the year, and prices rose even in the absence of cost pressures.

The basic explanation would apear to be that—despite the assurances in the Economic Report—*the increases in government civilian and military demand, coupled with the continued expansion in business expenditures for new plant and equipment, exceeded the capability of the economy to supply goods and services in 1966 at then current prices.*

Some perspective may be helpful prior to attempting to identify the specific factors which help to explain the 1966 circumstances. The United States has been engaged in a large-scale war; but it has not shifted to a war economy. Ours is truly a mixed economy: the Nation literally is concerned with social security as well as national security. The controls or runaway inflation often associated with war-time experiences are not present. Yet, the economy has been pressing very closely to the limits of available capacity and the nation is making choices somewhat analogous to guns versus butter, but not quite so. In a sense, as a country, we are choosing both more guns and more butter. However, we are also choosing less private housing and fewer automobiles while we are voting for more urban redevelopment and additional public transportation—thus simultaneously increasing both the military and civilian portions of the public sector in both relative and absolute senses (see Table 4).

TABLE 4   CHANGING PROPORTIONS OF GNP

	1964 4th quarter	1966 4th quarter
National Defense purchases	7.5	8.6
Consumer durables and residential housing construction	13.2	12.1
All other	79.3	79.3
Total	100.0	100.0

SOURCE: Department of Commerce.

An evaluation by the Federal Reserve Bank of New York of the role of military demand in the American economy was typical of that of many observers during the period: "The rapid growth of defense requirements was the largest single factor shaping the course of economic activity in 1966.

The Bank pointed out that although the share of GNP directly attributable to defense requirements was still only a relatively modest 8½ percent at the end of 1966, the significance of defense is suggested by the fact that enlarged *defense outlays for goods and services accounted for nearly 25 per-*

cent of the increase in GNP in 1966. This represented a striking shift from the earlier years of the current economic expansion when such spending contributed little or nothing to the overall growth of demand.

To cite again the words of the Federal Reserve Bank of New York, "The military buildup and the demand pressures associated with it affected virtually every sector of economic activity." The armed forces, in adding more than 500,000 men during the year, took over two-fifths of the total increase in the nation's available manpower, contributing directly to the tightening of civilian labor markets. A substantial share of the remaining expansion in the nation's work force was absorbed by the many firms with rising backlogs of defense orders.

The surge of military demands was obviously a sharp spur to activity in a number of industries, especially aircraft, ordnance and electronics, where employment during the year rose between 10 and 20 percent. This in turn led to intensified pressures on productive capacity. These industries reported some of the most rapid increases in expenditures for new plant and equipment. The result was further stimulus to the already high level of capital spending.

Also, the rapid rate of business inventory accumulation during 1966 was in good measure related to the expansion of defense demand. *About one-fourth of the increase in manufacturers' inventories during the year occurred in the aircraft, ordnance and electronics equipment, industries alone.*

C. The Underestimate in the Military Budget

One major factor helping to explain the emergence of inflationary factors in 1966 not anticipated in the January Budget and Economic Messages was the underestimate in military spending. The January 1966 Budget projected the cost of Vietnam at $10.2 billion in the fiscal year 1967. The current official estimate is almost double that—$19.4 billion (see Table 5).

TABLE 5   ESTIMATED APPROPRIATIONS AND EXPENDITURES
FOR SPECIAL SUPPORT OF VIETNAM OPERATIONS
[In billions of dollars]

Fiscal year	Appropriations		Expenditures	
	Estimated in 1967 budget	Estimated in 1968 budget	Estimated in 1967 budget	Estimated in 1968 budget
1965	$0.7	$0.7	$0.1	$0.1
1966	14.0	14.9	4.4	5.8
1967	8.7	22.0	10.2	19.4
1968	(1)	20.6	(1)	21.9

[1] Not available.
SOURCE: 1967 Budget, pp. 73-75; 1968 Budget, p. 77.

There are several facets to this substantial change in the direct expansion of Vietnam military demand. The January 1966 Budget Message contained what seemed at the time to be a very straightforward statement to the effect that "It provides the funds we now foresee as necessary to meet our commitments in Southeast Asia." The Message went on to state that if efforts to secure an honorable peace bore fruit ". . . these funds need not be spent." It appeared to the public observer that the U.S. role in Vietnam was fully funded. If there were any doubt about the matter, it seemed to be resolved by the statement, ". . . it would be folly to present a budget which inadequately provided for the military and economic costs of sustaining our forces in Vietnam."

In his testimony on the military budget, Secretary McNamara stressed that the budget was based on ". . . a somewhat arbitrary assumption regarding the duration of the conflict in Southeast Asia." This assumption—which was not mentioned anywhere in the January 1966 Budget—was that U.S. combat operations in Southeast Asia were to be budgeted only through June 30, 1967. "Should it later appear that combat operations will continue after that date at relatively high levels, it may be necessary to amend this budget request or supplement it later with additional funds," stated the Secretary of Defense.

The explanation for the need for a supplemental to the fiscal 1967 budget if the war were to extend beyond the fiscal year lies in the long lead-time of military procurement. In many cases, weapons required in the fiscal year 1968 would need to be ordered during 1967. This helps to explain also why the military appropriations requested for 1967 were lower than those for 1966 ($58.9 billion versus $61.8 billion).

Another factor revealed in the Congressional hearings was that, in order to avoid the buildup of surplus inventories that occurred during the Korean War, Secretary McNamara reduced the estimates of certain supply requirements below the consumption levels predicted by the services for the force levels then being planned for. He pointed out that if the services' initial estimates later proved to be correct, inventories could be drawn down to cover the difference or additional funds could be requested. The Secretary of Defense emphasized his concern that the Nation avoid the situation that occurred at the end of the Korean War when a vast quantity of surplus military stocks were on hand, far beyond any need at the time. The Department of Defense had unexpended balances of about $32 billion at the end of 1953. It took about five years to work the unexpended balances down to more reasonable levels.

It was estimated in the January 1966 Budget Document that the Department of Defense would end the fiscal year 1967 with unobligated funds totalling $10.4 billion and unexpended funds totaling $43.8 billion. Hence, it appeared that the Pentagon would be able to support a level of defense spending for Vietnam $10 billion above the original estimate for fiscal 1967.

During much of 1966, it was becoming clear that the military spending rate was exceeding that implied in the January budget. However, the Administration did not issue the traditional Midyear Review of the Federal

Budget in the Fall of 1966, which would have updated the estimates contained in the January budget. The reasons given were the uncertainties in Vietnam and the delay of Congressional action on budgetary legislation.

Nevertheless, *the lack of current estimates of military spending requirements made more difficult any intelligent public debate over appropriate economic policy.* Statements such as the following one by the Secretary of the Treasury in March 1966 indicated the difficulties faced by nongovernmental observers:

"At the same time let me emphasize that our current estimates of Vietnam expenditures remain, in the view of those most qualified to judge, an accurate evaluation of our needs so far as we can now foresee, and I would hope that, when the need for responsible restraint is so great, no one will base his economic decisions on the purely speculative assumption that our Vietnam needs will exceed current expectations."

A slowdown also occurred in the release of the most detailed public source of historical defense expenditure and obligation information, the Defense Department's *Monthly Report on the Status of Funds.* Through the Fall of 1966, when most business, financial, and other private observers were preparing and issuing economic forecasts for the calendar year 1967, the latest available issue of the *Monthly Report* was that for June 1966. The July and August issues never did appear; the September issue appeared too late in December to be useful for most of the forecasting work for 1967. More recently, the reports have been issued with only the customary lag.

The Budget for the fiscal year 1968, transmitted to the Congress in January 1967, did not contain any arbitrary assumption as to the termination of the fighting in Vietnam. The President's budget message, in discussing the Vietnam requirements, stated that the 1968 Budget ". . . provides for those requirements on a continuing basis, including the possibility of an extension of combat beyond the end of the fiscal year."

In the early February of 1967, the annual hearings before the Joint Economic Committee on the President's Economic Report were the occasion for some attempts at clarification of the earlier budgetary procedure. Senator William Proxmire, the Committee Chairman, opened the discussion of the underestimate of Vietnam expenditures with the following statement:

". . . in 1966 our Government made a serious economic policy blunder. Our fiscal policy was established early in 1966 . . . on the assumption that the Vietnam war would cost $10 billion . . . it is clear to me that we would have reduced spending and/or increased taxes—possibly both—if we had better and more accurate information."

The initial reply was given by Gardner Ackley, the chairman of the President's Council of Economic Advisers. He stated that one half of the difference between the original estimate of the cost of Vietnam during the fiscal year 1967 ($10.2 billion) and the revised estimate ($19.4 billion) reflected the assumption that the war would terminate by June 30, 1967. "The other half reflects the fact that there was a more rapid and efficient buildup of forces in Vietnam than had been initially considered possible, and second, increased requirements resulting from more intensive hostilities than had been initially assumed."

Mr. Ackley contended that the problem was "not a failure of communication," but due to the "uncertainty of the situation." The tenuous nature of the assumed June 30 termination was brought out during the subsequent dialogue between Senator Proxmire and Budget Director Charles J. Schultze:

"*Chairman Proxmire* . . . This assumption that the war would end on June 30, 1967, becomes more fantastic as I think about it, because, of course, the war could end on May 1 or June 1, and we still would have been $10 billion off, or very close to it. So we not only assumed that the war would end on June 30, but we assumed we would know about it well in advance, and we could have slowed down our procurement so we couldn't have procured anything to fight in the period subsequent to July 1, 1967, isn't that correct?"

"Mr. Schultze . . . I can't answer that yes or no."

D. The Underestimate of the Initial Economic Impact of Vietnam

The second factor explaining the growth of inflationary pressures in the American economy in 1966 relates to the point developed earlier in this study—the leads and lags in measuring the impact of government spending, and specifically in understanding how a military buildup affects the economy.

The key point is that, under our private enterprise system, the great bulk of military production is carried on in the private sector of the economy. As a result, when there is a large expansion in military orders, as occurred in fiscal 1966, the immediate impact is *not* felt in the government budget.

The initial impact—in terms of demand for labor, materials, and resources generally—is felt by the government contractors in the *private* sector. Hence, particularly during the early stage of a military buildup, we have to look at the private sector to see the expansionary effects. As pointed out earlier, this is hardly a new phenomenon. This timing relationship was the factor that contributed so greatly to the inflation that accompanied the first year of the Korean mobilization.

By just looking at the Government's budget during fiscal year 1951, it seemed that the public sector was following a policy of fiscal restraint. Policy officials generally overlooked the almost doubling in the volume of defense orders to private industry during that same period. Unfortunately, the same mistake was repeated during the first year of the Vietnam buildup. *The most rapid period of expansion in military contracts to private industry occurred in 1966; so did the most rapid rate of price inflation in recent years.* But that was the period when the Nation and particularly the Administration's economists were still congratulating themselves on the success of the 1964 tax cut and little need was felt, at least officially, for greater fiscal restraint.

Some detailed analysis of this point seems to be in order. As a benchmark, it may be recalled that in fiscal year ending June 30, 1965 total contracts placed, orders let, and other "obligations" incurred by the Department of Defense were about $54 billion. The concept of obligations is used here because it is a generic term, including both government payrolls and contracts with private firms. In the January 1966 budget, it was estimated that this rate of making new commitments would rise to well over $63 billion in fiscal year 1966. In retrospect, the January budget underestimated the rise in military demand during the fiscal year which was then in progress.

The actual amount of new obligations incurred during fiscal year 1966 was somewhat in excess of $67 billion, or almost one-fourth greater than in 1965. Actual expenditures increased at a much slower rate during the same period—17 percent. In other words, *obligations* are the more sensitive or leading indicator. Unfortunately from the viewpoint of analyzing business conditions, the supposedly most sophisticated measure of government finance, the so-called national income accounts budget, uses a concept that even lags behind actual government outlays—the delivery of completed military equipment. To compound the problem, the national income accounts budget picks up government revenues on an accrual basis, which precedes the actual receipt of cash by the government.

As was pointed out earlier, much of the impact on employment, production, an income of a military buildup occurs primarily at the points in time that budget recommendations are made, increased appropriations are enacted, and orders placed with military contractors. *However, the statement of Federal receipts and expenditures on national income account—the national income accounts budget—confines the measurement to the actual delivery of completed weapons and other military "hard goods."*

The policy implication of all this is that the official budget and economic reports were very slow to pick up the expansionary impact of the Vietnam buildup, but very quick to take account of the deflationary impact of the expansion in revenues. *The net result is that the Federal Government, though apparently following a non-inflationary economic policy in 1966, was actually a major source of inflationary pressure in the American economy during that time.*

Some statistical support for the foregoing is contained in Table 6. On the far left in Table 6 is the officially reported surplus or deficit in the so-called national income accounts budget. This, the Administration economists have contended, is the best measure of the economic impact of fiscal policy. On that basis, the Federal budget shifted from a position of ease in the second half of calendar 1965 (a deficit of $1.4 billion) to some restraint in the first half of 1966 (a surplus of $3.1 billion).

The next two columns in the table contain two alternative sets of rough adjustments for the fact that new contracts awarded may be a better indicator of the impact of a military buildup on the economy than delivery of completed weapons. The A series is essentially the excess of military obligations over expenditures during the period, seasonally adjusted and converted to an annual basis. One further change has been made. Over the years, about two to three billion dollars worth of obligations each year do not seem to result in actual expenditures. A number of technical factors are at work here, including some double counting of contracts awarded by one military agency in behalf of another military agency. Such a case might be Air Force procurement of aircraft for the Army, which may show up as an Army obligation to the Air Force, as well as an Air Force obligation to the airplane manufacturer. In computing both the A and B adjustment series, the annual obligation figures were reduced by $3 billion in each case to take account of the double counting and to assure that any error is on the conservative side.

It can be seen, referring to the A column on the right hand side of Table 6, that adjusting for defense obligations by this method results in

TABLE 6   FEDERAL SURPLUS OR DEFICIT: SOME VARIATIONS
ON THE NATIONAL INCOME ACCOUNTS BUDGET
[In billions of dollars at annual rates]

Calendar year	Federal surplus (+) or deficit (−) official basis	Adjustments for defense obligations		Federal surplus (+) or deficit (−) adjusted basis	
		A	B	A	B
1964:					
1st half	−4.3	−0.1	−0.1	−4.4	−4.4
2d half	−1.8	−4.4	−2.2	−6.2	−4.0
1965:					
1st half	+4.4	−2.0	−1.0	+2.4	+3.4
2d half	−1.4	−5.2	−2.6	−6.6	−4.0
1966 estimated:					
1st half	+3.1	−8.4	−4.2	−5.3	−1.1
2d half	−2.0	−5.2	−2.6	−7.2	−4.6

SOURCE: Data from Departments of Commerce and Defense. Adjustments are described in the text.

some significant changes in the usual measure of Federal fiscal impact. The second half of 1965 is now seen to be a period of much more substantial expansionary effect in the Federal budget than shown on the official basis. Of greater interest of course is the indication that the first half of 1966 was not a period of fiscal restraint but instead one with a substantial excess of outgo over income.

The B adjustment is a more conservative effort. It is a statistical compromise between the two approaches, the result of an arithmetic averaging of military obligations and expenditures for each period. The theoretical rationale that can be offered is that a more proper counterpart to the liability basis of the corporate revenue computations might be somewhere between the extremes of contract placement and governmental disbursement.

As would be expected, the B results are somewhat more moderate than the A series. The adjusted Federal deficit for the latter part of 1965 is rather large, but, on this basis, the first half of 1966 witnessed a deficit of somewhat reduced proportions. The adjusted deficit rises in the second six months of the year. Even the B series provides a very weak case for the widely made claim that fiscal restraint occurred during 1966.

E. Monetary and Fiscal Policy Complications

The mild fiscal policy restraints recommended in the January 1966 budget turned out to be inadequate to stem the inflationary pressures that were building up. Some private observers were more concerned over the inflationary impact of the January 1966 budget recommendation. A report prepared at Washington University in early February 1966, stated:

". . . the inflationary impact of the January 1966 Budget submission has been underestimated and that fiscal policy measures may need to be modified substantially . . . the current, immediate inflationary potential—during the fiscal year 1966—has been virtually ignored."

This report was picked up by a number of publications at that time, including the *Wall Street Journal* and *Business Week*. The latter referred to "skepticism of the degree of restraint that the Federal budget in fact provides for the economy."

To some extent, the inflationary pressures of the Vietnam buildup were accentuated by a rather liberal monetary policy in 1965, some of the results of which were continued to be felt in 1966. It has been pointed out that the rate of monetary expansion should have decelerated as early as 1965 as the economy regained reasonably full employment. Nevertheless, the rise in the money supply was allowed to pick up speed from an 8.0 percent annual rate in the first six months of 1965 to a 10.6 percent rate in the second half. Beginning in December 1965, the Federal Reserve Board undertook a series of steps to tighten the availability of credit. By April 1966, the steep rise in the money stock was halted and a slight decline occurred through the remainder of 1966.

The most dramatic, early action was the Fed's raising the discount rate from 4 to 4½ percent. Effective December 6, 1965, the interest rate charged member banks for borrowing from their district Federal Reserve Banks was increased in an effort to "maintain price stability." Simultaneously, the Federal Reserve Board increased the maximum rates that member banks were permitted to pay their depositors to 5½ percent on all time deposits and certificates of deposit having a maturity of 30 days or more. The latter action was to have serious repercussions on the savings institutions in 1966, a subject beyond the purview of this study.

A member of the Federal Reserve Board, J. Dewey Daane, explained shortly afterwards that the actions were taken because of "increasing evidence that aggregate demands were rising at an unexpectedly rapid pace and absorbing the remaining margin of unutilized capacity" of the national economy. He specifically noted that "over the summer, a step-up had been announced in the United States' participation in Vietnam, presaging an acceleration in defense outlays."

The Fed's action was sharply criticized at the time. Some Administration spokesmen contended that the Board should have waited until the January 1966 Presidential messages which would indicate both the expected future level of military spending and the degree of restraint in its fiscal policy. At least two members of the Board itself, Governors George W. Mitchell and Sherman J. Maisel, appeared to agree with the criticism in public testimony before the Joint Economic Committee in December 1965. Some Administration reaction was more general. Secretary of Labor W. Willard Wirtz stated, "There can be no tolerance for the suggestion that expansion of the economy must be slowed down, by increasing interest rates or in any other way, while there is still so much to be done."

At first, monetary policy was only mildly restraining. Member bank reserves continued rising, reaching a peak of $21.7 billion in April 1966, compared to $20.7 billion during the preceding Fall. Monetary policy tightened further in the Spring of 1966, with the total of member bank reserves remaining at the April figure through the middle of the year. The increased financial tightness also showed up in the money supply, which reached a peak of $171 billion in April and then declined, irregularly, to a low of $169 billion in November.

In the Summer and Fall of 1966, the Federal Reserve System took additional steps to slow bank lending. These included the unusual letter of September 1, requesting commercial banks to limit their loans to business. The letter indicated that the discount windows at the Federal Reserve Banks were open to banks conforming to these guidelines.

Other measures were taken to limit the ability of the commercial banks to compete for time deposits, including increasing reserve requirements against these deposits of over $5 million from 4 percent to 5 percent in July and to 6 percent in September 1966. By the end of September it appeared that the peak monetary stringency had passed. Most interest rates declined somewhat and bank reserves rose again. Late in December 1966, the monetary authorities rescinded their September 1 letter, once again encouraging banks to lend in their customary fashion.

In September 1966, the President proposed the suspension of the 7 percent investment tax credit and of accelerated depreciation on commercial and industrial buildings for a period of 16 months. The tax measure was passed, with some modifications, in late October 1966.

The January 1967 Budget Message recommended a general and temporary six percent increase in individual and corporate income tax rates, effective July 1, 1967. However, the recommendation was made conditional upon a later examination of economic developments. In March 1967, the President requested the Congress to restore the 7 percent investment tax credit which had been suspended in the Fall of 1966 as an anti-inflationary move. Apparently, the worst of the inflationary pressures resulting from the Vietnam buildup were over, barring another major escalation.

F. Resultant Economic Policy Problems for 1967

The previous criticisms notwithstanding, some positive impacts of governmental economic policy during this period also need to be acknowledged. A fundamental requirement on such policy was most successfully achieved— the large and rapid shift of resources from civilian uses or idleness to military programs.

In this vein, Budget Director Charles J. Schultze stated recently to the House Ways and Means Committee:

"Our military effort in Vietnam has not suffered in any way from a shortage of funds. We have provided every plane, every gun, and every cartridge needed to support operations in Vietnam."

At the same time, direct controls over prices, wages and materials generally were avoided (set-asides were in force for copper and a few other key materials). Moreover, economic growth and real improvement in the living standard of the average American continued despite the defense spending increases and the inflation.

In real terms—that is after making allowance for price rises—U.S. Gross National Product rose from $614 billion in 1965 to $648 billion in 1966 (in 1958 dollars), a growth rate almost equal to that of 1965. Increases also occurred in 1966 in real disposable income per capita and in personal consumption expenditures per capita.

In commenting on economic trends in the American economy in 1966, Gardner Ackley told the Joint Economic Committee the following:

"It is far from a perfect record. But I think if one looks at it in the large, in terms of the outcome for the year as a whole, it is a record of which we can be pretty proud.

Nevertheless, in retrospect, it can be argued that a major error occurred in domestic policy in the United States during 1966. In this era of sophisticated information systems, it still seems that a parallel can be drawn with the prehistoric brontosaurus whose internal communication system was so primitive that when another animal started chewing on the end of its tail, it lost its entire tail before the news reached the brain.

Somewhat analogously, *during much of 1966, especially the first half, the Nation and its economists were occupied with congratulating themselves on the success of the 1964 tax cut—when the problem suddenly had become combatting inflation rather than unemployment.*

A three-fold dilemma resulted from the various developments already covered in this study:

1. The Nation was not fully aware of the economic implications of the U.S. buildup in Vietnam.

2. Economists were not generally cognizant of the timing problems in evaluating the economic impact, and

3. Neither public officials nor private opinion were agreed as to either the need for or the nature of additional public policy measures to be taken.

Many, of course, were not convinced of the need for tighter fiscal policy, particularly in view of the Federal Reserve's tightening monetary policy. Others who would have preferred a tax increase to the extreme credit stringency did not believe that the Nation would accept so sharp a turn in fiscal policy—from tax reduction to tax increase—so quickly. Finally, even those who preferred the route of reducing government expenditures seemed to think that the Federal budget only contained two high-priority categories, defense programs and Great Society endeavors, overlooking the vast array of outmoded subsidies and special benefits.

It became clear also that, although the wage-price guideposts might be effective during a period characterized by mild cost-push inflationary pressures in an environment of some economic slack, they did not work as well during periods of demand-pull inflation such as characterized 1966.

Other negative results of the 1966 experience may be in terms of the legacy bestowed upon the future. To what extent will cost-push inflationary pressures dominate the American economy in 1967 after the aggregate demand-pull pressures may have subsided? Given the conditional tax increase recommended in the January 1967 Budget, to what extent does the Nation face the possibility of a tax increase coming after the major impact of the Vietnam buildup has occurred and the economy softened?

Perhaps more fundamentally, *the failure of the Nation either to under-stand how a military buildup affects the economy, much less to take prompt and effective action to curtail the excessive demand that results, does not augur well for a smooth economic adjustment to the hoped-for downturn in military spending after a successful termination of hostilities in Vietnam.* In such a case, the deflationary impact of defense contract cancellations and layoffs of defense workers might occur while defense expenditures and/or deliveries were still rising. If tax reduction or monetary ease or expansion in selected non-defense spending were to wait until sizeable declines in defense purchases showed up in the GNP, governmental economic policy once again would be too slow and too late.

·   ·   ·   ·   ·   ·   ·   ·   ·   ·   ·   ·   ·   ·

b] THE IMPACT ON THE DRAFT
[1] The Dubious Need for the Draft

MR. OI. I think the basic problem begins with the fact that the Nation presently allocates substantial quantities of its labor and material resources in maintaining a large Defense Establishment.

The Department of Defense has followed a practice of acquiring its material resources on the free market through a system of competitive defense contracts. Only in times of war has the Department of Defense seen fit to requisition strategic materials at below market prices.

·   ·   ·   ·   ·   ·   ·   ·   ·   ·   ·   ·   ·

MR. OI. It has only been in times of war that the Department of Defense has requisitioned material resources. However, when it comes to acquiring the necessary manpower resources, the Department of Defense has assumed an altogether different posture.

Conscription and coercion, which are the counterparts of requisition, have been the principal means of acquiring the necessary flows of labor.

I propose to argue that a draft and its compulsion are unnecessary in the light of the growing population pool, if we return to a strength of between 2.7 to 3 million men and if we raise pay substantially.

The four principal issues to which I have addressed myself in this paper are: No. 1, Who bears the burden of involuntary military service?

No. 2, What is the real cost of military service to those who are coerced to serve?

No. 3, What is the budgetary cost of meeting military manpower needs on a voluntary basis?

No. 4, and lastly, In the light of the current Vietnam situation, what steps can we take to formulate a rational military manpower procurement policy?

FROM Statement of Walter Y. Oi, Department of Economics, University of Washington, in *Economic Effect of Vietnam Spending*, Joint Economic Committee, U.S. Congress, 90th Cong., 1st Sess., I (1967), pp. 292–93 and 307–09. Used by permission.

First and foremost, the draft imposes a burden on American youths in four ways: Most obviously, some men are drafted.

Second, many youths reluctantly volunteer for enlisted ranks, officer commissions, and Reserve positions, in order to avoid being drafted. DOD surveys indicate that 38 percent of voluntary enlistments, 41 percent of officers, and 71 percent of enlistments to Reserve units can properly be regarded as reluctant participants who would not have volunteered in the absence of a draft.

The incidence of active military service has largely rested with the lower middle classes, men who do not have the wherewithal or the capabilities of continuing on to college, and, in this sense it has been a regressive incidence.

The two other burdens implicit in the draft, which I will mention and leave, are first, the uncertainty caused those youths who, rather than volunteer, would choose to wait and take their chances with the draft; and lastly, that because of the inordinately low pay levels associated with compulsory service, the true volunteers who want a military career are denied the higher pay they could have received under a voluntary system.

What is the real cost of service to those who are coerced or compelled to serve? Many of these costs cannot be put into dollars-and-cents terms. However, there is one undeniable fact.

The youth who is presently drafted earns a basic pay of somewhere in the neighborhood of $96 a month, including the value of his keep, his monthly income is in the neighborhood of $160, far below the minimum wage. If we went to a voluntary force, my estimate suggests that a pay of $325 a month would attract sufficient flows of volunteers.

The difference between that figure and $160 a month—or something over $1,900 a year—is a hidden tax borne by those men who are in our active duty forces, a tax burden some three times greater than the Federal income tax burden per average adult over 18 years of age, which is less than $650 per year. So we are taxing those who serve at a rate three times greater than the rate of taxation placed on all citizens, and this is a regressive redistribution of income.

Let me turn to the third question. What is the budgetary cost of meeting the manpower needs on a voluntary basis? If we move to a voluntary force, which will experience greater retention and consequently a lower personnel turnover than the present mixed force of conscripts and volunteers, we shall need fewer men to staff our forces.

DOD states that about 500,000 men per year are needed to sustain a force of 2.7 million men. With a lower personnel turnover of the voluntary force, I estimate that we will need only about 335,000 men per year in a steady state.

Under present circumstances, if by abolishing the draft we lose the draftees and the reluctant volunteers, there will be deficits between the supply of voluntary enlistments and the required accessions to maintain the force strength.

However, I estimate that we can attract enough men by increasing recruitment incentives, offering better housing, and most importantly, better pay. With the draft, we will need 27 percent of the male population to sustain a force of 2.7 million. Without a draft, and with lower personnel turnover, we will need only 19 percent of the population.

The necessary pay increase which I estimate is about 68 percent, which should give the private an early level pay of about $325 a month. The budgetary cost of this is about $4 billion.

My cost estimates can be criticized on a number of grounds, most of which are included in the full text; but I believe if anything these estimates err toward the high side. I have not taken account of potential savings in turnover. The one cost which I have omitted is the higher retirement benefits accruing to men reaching their 20th year.

However, from the data I have examined, I see no reason why we cannot meet our manpower needs on a voluntary basis.

Fourth, and finally, what steps do we now take? I am first proposing a 2-year extension of the draft, in the light of the Vietnam situation and the high replacement demand that will be confronting us within the next 2 years.

My second recommendation is that first-term pay be advanced sharply. It is inexcusable, I believe, to tax those who serve at a rate three times greater than that imposed on other citizens.

Third, I propose that under any system of induction we must be selective, given the growing manpower pools. Even with a draft, only 27 percent must serve in the active duty forces. Consequently, for every one who serves, there will be at least two qualified men who do not serve.

I am proposing, therefore, a lottery at age 21, rather than at age 19 as the Marshall committee stipulates, because according to my way of estimating, the Marshall Commission proposal to discharge the draft liability at age 19 would result in the loss of 112,000 voluntary enlistments.

The loss of each enlistment—who serves $3\frac{1}{2}$ to 4 years on the average— means that two men must be drafted. Consequently, moving the lottery to age 19 would create a greater need for the draft. More men would have to enter the service, run through the inefficient 2-year tour, and then be shoveled back into the civilian economy.

In suggesting a lottery at age 21, I estimate that without the pay increase, we would lose 40,000 enlistments. Given the proposed increase to eliminate the financial inequity of military service, I do not anticipate any loss of voluntary enlistments.

Lastly, I recommend that we thoroughly reexamine the role of the Reserves. During the entire Vietnam buildup, we have not activated the Reserves. If the Reserves are used to bolster the active duty strengths, the voluntary force can achieve the requisite flexibility that it needs. For these reasons I believe that the need for the draft has not been established, and I strongly endorse an intermediate program, advocating that we extend the draft for 2 years only, pending the course of events and with the ultimate objective of abolishing the draft.

Thank you, sir.

CHAIRMAN PROXMIRE. Thank you, Professor Oi.

.   .   .   .

[2] The Continuing Need for the Draft

MR. WOOL. Mr. Chairman, at the outset, I would like to differentiate my posture here from that of my two colleagues. As a civil service employee of the Department of Defense, I do not have quite the same scope in recommending policies as they may have as private citizens. The policy position of the Department of Defense, as well as of the administration, is on record in the recent Presidential message on the draft and in recent legislation recommendations.

As you know, in 1964, at the direction of President Johnson, the Department of Defense initiated a study which had as one of its principal objectives an assessment of the feasibility of meeting military manpower needs in the coming decade on a completely voluntary basis. The results of this study were submitted to the House Armed Services Committee by Secretary Morris last year, together with a large volume of supporting information. Its main conclusions, with respect to the all-voluntary-force alternative, may be summarized as follows:

First, it found that in the absence of a draft, military strengths would decline to a level of about 2 million or slightly higher in contrast to force levels of about 2.7 million required immediately prior to Vietnam, and to a current military strength of about 3.4 million.

Secondly, that the net budgetary cost of *attempting* to maintain military strengths at the pre-Vietnam level of 2.7 million on a completely voluntary basis would be very high, probably ranging from $4 billion to $17 billion, with $8 billion as the most probable estimate under a 4-percent unemployment rate level.

Third, that even these outlays would not assure an adequate supply of better educated manpower for the many professional and technical specialties needed by the Armed Forces, nor would it provide for adequate manning of our Reserve Forces.

Fourth, and perhaps most important, that there would be very limited flexibility under an all-voluntary system to increase military strengths even moderately within a short time period should the need arise.

It may be helpful to discuss briefly some of the basic research findings and assumptions which resulted in these conclusions. In particular, I would like to address myself to the question of the inherent reliability of the estimates and the reasons for expressing them in a rather broad range of possible costs.

The policy officials who initiated the study addressed some fairly simple questions, they thought, to the group of economists assigned to this particular task. First, would it be feasible to maintain military forces of the size required in recent years on a completely voluntary basis, in the coming decade?

Second, if so, how much will it cost?

It would have been tempting to submit simple, unqualified responses to

FROM Statement of Harold Wool, Director, Procurement Policy and General Research (Manpower), Department of Defense, in *Economic Effect of Vietnam Spending*, Joint Economic Committee, U.S. Congress, 90th Cong., 1st Sess., I (1967), pp. 313–17.

these questions. However, in spite of intensive research efforts, in which my copanelist, Dr. Oi, participated in the first year, this did not prove possible.

To do so, in my judgment, would have entailed a serious risk of grossly oversimplifying the many uncertainties and variable factors inherent in any projections of this type. The risks involved were the greater for the very reason that the problem we were dealing with was no theoretical exercise. It is directly related to our national security and to the ability of our Armed Forces to meet their commitments in future years.

It also clearly affects the lives of millions of young men in our country, and has significant implications for our civilian economy as well.

These uncertainties can be illustrated by examining two of the key steps in our estimating procedure, and there were many, Mr. Chairman.

These were: first, the projections of military recruitment capabilities in the absence of a draft.

Secondly, the estimates of the responsiveness of recruitment to increases in military compensation.

In the first area, I would like to emphasize particularly that our analysis of past recruitment trends in the Army, which always had the capability of accepting enlistments, showed a significant relationship between enlistment rates and the unemployment situation in normal years. We found that, for example, a given percentage change in unemployment rates would result in a closely corresponding percentage change in the Army enlistment rate.

Our initial estimates, which were developed in 1964, were based upon experience in a preceding period of years between 1956 and 1964, when the average unemployment rate was about 5½ percent. As we moved into the 1965 period, our experience, as you well know, was that unemployment declined significantly to a level which is now below 4 percent.

We subsequently, therefore, found it not only desirable but absolutely essential to present our estimates in some range of possible variation in unemployment rates. In addition to the 5½ percent assumption, we showed what recruitment would be under the lower 4 percent level of unemployment. These ranges were not designed to reflect either a desirable or possible variation in unemployment. They simply were designed to illustrate the implications for military recruitment of even limited variations in the level of civilian job opportunities.

The second and more difficult forecasting problem was to estimate the responsiveness of military recruitment under a voluntary system to increases in military pay.

I should note in this connection that increases in pay were only one of many management incentives explored in this study as a means of increasing volunteering, or eliminating reliance upon the draft. However, increases in pay are the conventional methods followed in the civilian economy, in attempting to attract additional labor supply, and particular interest has been expressed in the feasibility and cost of meeting our requirements voluntarily in this way.

In attempting to derive a supply curve for military recruits, our economists were in many ways moving into unexplored territory. It seemed almost self-evident that an increase in pay would produce some increase in enlistments. The precise relationship was much more difficult to forecast, particularly under conditions of a dynamic labor market.

The available research evidence drawn largely from studies by psychologists and sociologists indicates that many factors, in addition to pay, have influenced many young men in the choice of a job or career. An incomplete list of such factors, as listed by one leading psychologist, include: the person and his biological inheritance, parents, peers, relatives, teachers, social class, educational experience, geography, minority group status and location of opportunity.

Our own surveys of civilian youths have confirmed the fact that pay alone is a less potent factor in career choice than might be expected. We found that occupational values varied greatly with educational level.

Generally, the high school dropout or graduate who did not go on to college placed greatest emphasis on the training and job security aspects of jobs, whereas the college man placed much greater emphasis upon his inherent interest in the type of work and in various job status factors.

Pay, as such, was listed as the most important factor by less than 9 percent of those surveyed—pay, directly, as distinct from many of the indirect relationships which do exist.

With regard to military service, we found wide variations in basic likes or dislikes for military service, even among men with similar educational backgrounds.

Nevertheless, it was evident that, at the margin, substantial increases in military compensation would produce some increase in volunteering.

In order to measure this relationship, we compared Army enlistment rates in 1963 in each of the nine census geographic regions with two key economic variables: the median civilian income of young men, aged 16 to 21, and their unemployment rates in the regions.

We found a statistically significant correlation among these variables. As shown in the accompanying chart, the percent of qualified youth who enlisted in the Army—excluding those who reported they were influenced to enlist by the draft—was highest in the southern region where civilian income was lowest and unemployment rates relatively high. It was lowest in the Great Plains States where civilian earnings were slightly above the national average.

When geographic regions with similar unemployment rates were grouped together and compared, in all cases those with the lower civilian income had the higher enlistment rates.

This basic relationship, and a similar study for officers, based on ROTC voluntary enrollments, provided the limited empirical basis for the estimates of response of enlistments to pay used in our study.

I assure you that Dr. Oi and many of his colleagues strained very hard to find other meaningful data. This was the most meaningful relationship in this context which could be found and which did establish a certain statistical relationship between earnings and the propensity to volunteer.

However, I think it is very important to emphasize the limitations of these estimates, which were the best we could derive.

First, the relationship rests upon the inference that the differences in regional enlistment rates are in fact entirely due to differences in economic factors, such as income and unemployment, rather than to other influences such as regional differences in ethnic or racial background among these regions. We do not know, in other words, whether the young man from the Great Plains region would enlist at the same rate as the southern youth if his earnings and job opportunities were the same.

Secondly, the rates shown apply to one point in time. They refer to conditions as they existed geographically in the year 1963. In a dynamic society, with changing opportunities and values, we do not know whether these relationships would equally apply in future years.

Finally, it is particularly doubtful whether any assumed change in relative military pay, based on a cross sectional relationship, would produce a short-term increase in enlistments as great as that indicated by this supply relationship. We do know that attitudes towards occupational careers, including military service, are often formed early in adolescence, and that—as noted above—pay has not played a major role in shaping these attitudes.

For these reasons, it appeared essential that the resulting estimates be expressed in terms of a probability range, based upon the standard error of the regression coefficient derived from this analysis.

Although we cannot, therefore, place any great reliance upon any single cost estimate for an all-volunteer force, there are other relevant facts which—in my judgment—do clearly militate against this alternative as a viable method of maintaining our military force, at levels similar to those experienced in the recent past.

First, the proportion of volunteers who were motivated to enter service because of the draft was found in our surveys to be highest among men with the higher levels of educational achievement. Among enlistees with some college education, 58 percent stated that they would not have volunteered in the absence of a draft, as compared to 23 percent of high school dropouts. The greatest loss of volunteers, in the absence of a draft, would therefore occur among men who are best qualified for training in our many technical specialties.

Second, our Reserve enlistment programs would be particularly hard hit since 70 percent of those who were in these programs in 1964 stated that they had enlisted simply in preference to being drafted. In the event of any requirement for rapid augmentation of trained manpower, our Reserves would not be in very great shape to deliver.

Finally, military pay policy—or any similar combination of financial incentives—is a relatively inflexible recruitment method. Even if the Department of Defense were granted wide authority to adjust pay scales to changing market conditions and recruitment needs, it would be very difficult, if not impossible, to move pay rates up and down in response to these market factors. In effect, there would be a built-in tendency for a continued long-term escalation in relative military pay levels and related costs under such a policy.

The limitations of military pay policy as a recruitment method are perhaps best illustrated by recent experience in Australia. Australia has had a boom economy with the lowest unemployment rate of any of the countries

ARMY VOLUNTARY ENLISTMENT RATES AND CIVILIAN EARNINGS
AND EMPLOYMENT, MALES AGES 16 TO 21, BY REGION, 1963

Regions	Army enlistments without a draft[1]		Median civilian income, males 16 to 21[2]		Unemployment, males 16 to 21[2]	
	Rate (percent)	Index	Amount	Index	Rate (percent)	Index
New England	3.36	96.3	$3,567	98.5	11.3	99.1
Middle Atlantic	2.97	85.1	3,748	103.5	14.2	124.6
South Atlantic	4.65	133.2	2,849	78.7	9.4	82.5
South	4.93	141.3	2,441	67.4	13.9	121.9
Western South	4.25	121.8	3,148	86.9	9.2	80.7
Great Lakes	3.10	88.8	4,184	115.5	11.1	97.4
Great Plains	2.05	58.7	3,725	102.9	6.0	52.6
Mountain	3.25	93.1	3,640	100.5	9.8	86.0
Pacific	3.35	96.0	4,257	117.5	16.2	142.1
U.S. average	3.49	100.0	3,621	100.0	11.4	100.0

[1] Army enlistments in mental groups I-III, excluding those motivated by the draft, per 100 civilian out-of-school males, ages 16 to 21, who meet minimum enlistment standards.
[2] Derived from Department of Defense survey of civilian men, 16 to 34 years old. October 1964.

we surveyed in 1964—0.8 percent. It discontinued its draft in 1960. Entry pay for privates was increased to $163.50 per month by 1964, in American dollars, about twice the basic pay for privates at that time in the United States.

In spite of this high entry pay, Australia found it difficult to maintain a regular force of about 52,000, a strength corresponding to 1.9 percent of its 15-to-49 male population. This was less than one-third the relative size of the U.S. military force, and would correspond to a U.S. strength of only 860,000 men, based on our population in the same age groups.

Particular difficulty was experienced in recruitment of officers, technicians, and reservists. When a decision was made to increase Australian military strength by 14,000, or 25 percent, in 1964, it was therefore necessary to reinstitute a draft system, incidentally, with a lottery.

In conclusion, I would like to emphasize that the estimates discussed above relate to the feasibility of maintaining an all-volunteer force in the future at a level of about 2.7 million, corresponding to that period immediately before our military force buildup for Southeast Asia.

I have personally seen no responsible study which even suggests the feasibility of maintaining the current military force of about 3.4 million without reliance upon the draft, and would consider this to be grossly unfeasible.

For these reasons, much of the emphasis in recent studies has been directed to the immediate issues of assuring increased equity in selection for service, and of reducing the hardships and inconvenience of involuntary military service for those who must serve.

Further, the continuing objective of the Department of Defense has been, and will be, to minimize reliance upon involuntary induction through a wide range of career incentives and management efforts as described in recent official statements.

c] THE ABM DEBATE

[1] Defense Should Be Our First Priority

IMMEDIATELY after assuming office, I requested the Secretary of Defense to review the program initiated by the last administration to deploy the Sentinel ballistic missile defense system.

The Department of Defense presented a full statement of the alternatives at the last two meetings of the National Security Council.

These alternatives were reviewed there in the light of the security requirements of the United States and their probable impact on East-West relations, with particular reference to the prospects for strategic arms negotiations.

After carefully considering the alternatives, I have reached the following conclusions:

The concept on which the Sentinel program of the previous administration was based should be substantially modified.

The safety of our country requires that we should proceed now with the development and construction of the new system in a carefully phased program.

This program will be reviewed annually from the point of view of technical developments, the threat, the diplomatic context, including any talks on arms limitations.

The modified system has been designed so that its defensive intent is unmistakable. It will be implemented not according to some fixed, theoretical schedule, but in a manner clearly related to our periodic analysis of the threat.

The first deployment covers two missile sites: The first of these will not be completed before 1973. Any further delay would set this date back by at least two additional years. The program for fiscal year 1970 is the minimum necessary to maintain the security of our nation. This measured deployment is designed to fulfill three objectives:

Protection of our land-based retaliatory forces against a direct attack by the Soviet Union.

Defense of the American people against the kind of nuclear attack which Communist China is likely to be able to mount within the decade.

Protection against the possibility of accidental attacks from any source.

In the review leading up to this decision, we considered three possible options in addition to this program:

A deployment which would attempt to defend U.S. cities against an attack by the Soviet Union; a continuation of the Sentinel program approved by the previous administration; an indefinite postponement of deployment while continuing research and development.

I rejected these options for the following reasons:

President Nixon's Statement on Missile Defense Plan, March 14, 1969.

Although every instinct motivates me to provide the American people with complete protection against a major nuclear attack, it is not now within our power to do so. The heaviest defense system we considered, one designed to protect our major cities, still could not prevent a catastrophic level of U.S. fatalities from a deliberate all-out Soviet attack. And it might look to an opponent like the prelude to an offensive strategy threatening the Soviet deterrent.

The Sentinel system approved by the previous administration provided more capabilities for the defense of cities than the program I am recommending, but it did not provide protection against some threats to our retaliatory forces which have developed subsequently. Also, the Sentinel system had the disadvantage that it could be misinterpreted as the first step toward the construction of a heavy system.

Giving up all construction of missile defense poses too many risks.

Research and development does not supply the answer to many technical issues that only operational experience can provide. The Soviet Union has engaged in a buildup of its strategic forces larger than was envisaged in 1967 when the decision to deploy Sentinel was made. The following is illustrative of recent Soviet activity:

The Soviets have already deployed an ABM system which protects to some degree a wide area centered around Moscow. We will not have a comparable capability for over four years. We believe the Soviet Union is continuing their ABM development, directed either toward improving this initial system, or more likely, making substantially better second-generation ABM components.

The Soviet Union is continuing the deployment of very large missiles with warheads capable of destroying our hardened Minuteman forces.

The Soviet Union has also been substantially increasing the size of their submarine-launched ballistic missile force.

The Soviets appear to be developing a semi-orbital nuclear weapon system.

In addition to these developments, the Chinese threat against our population, as well as the danger of an accidental attack, cannot be ignored. By approving this system, it is possible to reduce fatalities to a minimal level in the event of a Chinese nuclear attack in the 1970's, or in an accidental attack from any source. No President with the responsibility for the lives and security for the American people could fail to provide this protection.

The gravest responsibility which I bear as President of the United States is for the security of the nation. Our nuclear forces defend not only ourselves but our allies as well. The imperative that our nuclear deterrent remain secure beyond any possible doubt requires that the United States must take steps now to insure that our strategic retaliatory forces will not become vulnerable to a Soviet attack.

Modern technology provides several choices in seeking to insure the survival of our retaliatory forces. First, we could increase the number of sea- and land-based missiles and bombers. I have ruled out this course because it provides only marginal improvement of our deterrent, while it could be misinterpreted by the Soviets as an attempt to threaten their deterrent. It would therefore stimulate an arms race.

A second option is to harden further our ballistic missile forces by putting them in more strongly reinforced underground silos. But our studies show that hardening by itself is not adequate protection against foreseeable advances in the accuracy of Soviet offensive forces.

The third option was to begin a measured construction on an active defense of our retaliatory forces.

I have chosen the third option.

The system will use components previously developed for the Sentinel system. However, the deployment will be changed to reflect the new concept. We will provide for local defense of selected Minuteman missile sites and an area defense designed to protect our bomber bases and our command and control authorities. In addition, this new system will provide a defense of the continental United States against an accidental attack and will provide substantial protection against the kind of attack which the Chinese Communists may be capable of launching throughout the 1970's. This deployment will not require us to place missile and radar sites close to our major cities.

The present estimate is that the total cost of installing this system will be $6-$7 billion. However, because of the deliberate pace of the deployment, budgetary requests for the coming year can be substantially less—by about one half—than those asked for by the previous administration for the Sentinel system.

In making this decision, I have been mindful of my pledge to make every effort to move from an era of confrontation to an era of negotiation. The program I am recommending is based on a careful assessment of the developing Soviet and Chinese threats. I have directed the President's Foreign Intelligence Advisory Board—a nonpartisan group of distinguished private citizens—to make a yearly assessment of the threat which will supplement our regular intelligence assessment. Each phase of the deployment will be reviewed to insure that we are doing as much as necessary but no more than that required by the threat existing at that time. Moreover, we will take maximum advantage of the information gathered from the initial deployment in designing the later phases of the program.

Since our deployment is to be closely related to the threat, it is subject to modification as the threat changes, either through lateral actions by the Soviet Union or Communist China.

The program is not provocative. The Soviet retaliatory capability is not affected by our decision. The capability for surprise attack against our strategic forces is reduced. In other words, our program provides an incentive for a responsible Soviet weapons policy and for the avoidance of spiraling U.S. and Soviet strategic arms budgets.

I have taken cognizance of the view that beginning construction of a U.S. ballistic missile defense would complicate an agreement on strategic arms with the Soviet Union.

I do not believe that the evidence of the recent past bears out this contention. The Soviet interest in strategic talks was not deterred by the decision of the previous administration to deploy the Sentinel ABM system—in fact, it was formally announced shortly afterwards. I believe that the modifications we have made in the previous program will give the Soviet Union even less reason to view our defense effort as an obstacle to talks.

Moreover, I wish to emphasize that in any arms limitation talks with the Soviet Union, the United States will be fully prepared to discuss limitations on defensive as well as offensive weapons systems.

The question of ABM involves a complex combination of many factors: Numerous, highly technical, often conflicting judgments.

The costs.

The relationship to prospects for reaching an agreement on limiting nuclear arms.

The moral implications the deployment of a ballistic missile defense system has for many Americans.

The impact of the decision on the security of the United States in this perilous age of nuclear arms.

I have weighed all these factors. I am deeply sympathetic to the concerns of private citizens and members of Congress that we do only that which is necessary for national security. This is why I am recommending a minimum program essential for our security. It is my duty as President to make certain that we do no less.

[2] Defense Spending Is Out of Control

BLANK CHECK FOR THE MILITARY

MR. PROXMIRE. Mr. President, I rise today to speak on a most serious matter. In my judgment the President and the Congress and, indeed, the country, have lost control over military spending.

No Adequate Critical Review

There is now no sufficiently critical review of what we spend or how we spend it. There is no adequate machinery, either in the executive or legislative branch to control the total amount spent or the way in which military funds are disbursed. This is especially the case with respect to contracting for major weapons systems. The results are vast inefficiencies in procurement, waste in supply, and less security for the country than we could get by spending smaller amounts more efficiently.

When former President Eisenhower left office, he warned against the danger of "unwarranted influences, whether sought or unsought, by the military-industrial complex."

Danger Is Here

I speak today not to warn against some future danger of this influence. I assert that, whether sought or unsought, there is today unwarranted influence by the military-industrial complex resulting in excessive costs, burgeoning military budgets, and scandalous performances. The danger has long since materialized with a ravaging effect on our Nation's spending priorities.

FROM speech of Senator William Proxmire to the U.S. Senate on March 10, 1969, *Congressional Record* (March 10, 1969), pp. S2518–21.

In the first place, we are paying far too much for the military hardware we buy.

But, in addition, and perhaps even more shocking, we often do not get the weapons and products we pay the excessive prices for.

Major components of our weapons systems, for example, routinely do not meet the contract standards and specifications established for them when they are bought.

All of this puts the country in a most ironic position. On the one hand, we have a supply of missiles and weapons which could literally destroy the world. There is little doubt about that.

On the other hand, we find ourselves unable to defend ourselves even against military incidents where relatively minor amounts of force are involved. The *Pueblo* incident is a case in point.

While it is not my purpose to argue what action we should or should not have taken during that incident, I do say that it was shocking that apparently we were unable to take appropriate action at all, even if we had determined to do so.

Supposedly, forces to protect the *Pueblo* were on alert and ready to defend the ship if necessary. They were allegedly "on call." But in the case of the *Pueblo,* as the testimony at the inquiry clearly showed, the forces supposed to be on call were not on call. For a period of about 24 hours after the initial attack took place, we were unable to bring to bear, even if we had desired to do so, the relatively small force from the vast military might of this country needed to protect that ship.

Thus, while we have sufficient military might to create an atomic holocaust and blow up the world, we are at times incapable of countering even a relatively small military force. There are times when we are like the giant Gulliver who was tied down and made immobile by the Lilliputian dwarfs.

This example from this military side is symptomatic of the general situation we face with respect to procurement and contracting. It epitomizes our dilemma.

Situation Out of Control

The problem of defense spending is out of control. The system is top heavy. The military-industrial complex now writes its own budgetary ticket.

This situation is, in part, a result of the highly ambivalent attitudes the country has taken toward our defense over the years. Looking at the long view, we seem to have a roller coaster policy. During the 1930's when the threat from Germany, Italy, and Japan was obvious for all to see if only they would look, we starved our military services and placed the security of our country in deadly peril.

Then, after World War II, we overreacted with respect to contracts for weapons systems. Nothing was too good for the military. We have followed a policy of "gold plating." It might even be called "All This and Heaven Too." Americans, in general, have even felt slightly guilty about raising the question of excessive defense spending and whether we were getting our money's worth. The military has had a blank check. It could be said that we have had over two decades of "carte blanche for defense."

Surfeited With Excesses

The result is a system not unlike the medieval knight who was so encased in armor that he was unable to move. We are now so surfeited with excesses that we are almost unable to fight.

This uncritical policy should end. It should end because it is wasteful and costs too much money. It should end because it reduces the real security of the United States.

The military should lighten its pack. It should get into fighting trim.

We Pay Too Much for What We Buy

But whatever mistakes we have made in the past and whatever warnings we may make about the future, at the present time we face a condition and not a theory.

That condition, first of all, is that we pay too much for what we buy.

The evidence that this is true is overwhelming. This is particularly the case on contracts for large weapons systems. Let me cite some of the evidence.

Mr. Robert S. Benson, formerly in the office of the Assistant Secretary of Defense, Comptroller, has just written in the March issue of the Washington Monthly that—

> Few Americans are aware that about 90 percent of the major weapons systems that the Defense Department procures end up costing at least twice as much as was originally estimated.

The services from time to time admit this as well. In the official Air Force Guidebook for May of 1966, the Air Force stated, in arguing for a new concept of total package procurement, that—

> Thus, the history of defense procurement was replete with cost overruns, less than promised performance which were at least in part the result of intentional buy-in-bidding, and this has been the case even in the situation where there has been no substantial increase in the then state of the art.

This was not only true in 1966, but it continues, believe me, to be true today. We have just held a series of hearings on this matter under the auspices of the Subcommittee on Economy in Government of the Joint Economic Committee, of which I am chairman. The C–5 airplane is the major example of a weapon system or plane secured under the concept of "total package procurement." This was a method introduced, it was said, to overcome the terrible inefficiencies.

But our hearings established that the C–5A will probably cost the American taxpayer $2 billion more than the original contract ceiling of $3 billion. The Air Force itself admits that the cost overrun will amount to at least $1.2 billion. And they would admit, I am sure, it would cost $2 billion if they included the cost of spares, which are essential, which would be in the neighborhood of $800 million more.

Delayed Delivery

And, as we have seen in the past few days, delivery is to be delayed now from June until next December. So we face the same old problems of cost overruns and late delivery that the total package concept was supposed to cure.

Profits Up

Let me cite more evidence. When Admiral Rickover testified before our committee, he stated that the Pentagon's "weighted guideline" system of profit determination had resulted in an increase of about 25 percent in profits on defense contracts without regard to the contractor's performance.

He stated that the suppliers of propulsion turbines are now insisting on a 20 to 25 percent profit as a percent of cost as compared with 10 percent a few years ago.

He testified that profits on shipbuilding contracts based on cost had doubled in the last 2 years.

Cost Reimbursement Contracts

Assistant Secretary of the Air Force Robert Charles, in his testimony before the Economy in Government Subcommittee in January, quoted with approval a study by C. H. Danhof for the Brookings Institution on "Government Contracting and Technological Change," which said:

> During the 1950's, virtually all large military contracts reflected an acceptance by the military agencies of contractor estimates which proved highly optimistic. Such contracts ultimately involved costs in excess of original contractual estimates of from 300 to 700 percent.

Secretary Charles further stated that—

> A substantial amount, however, was due to the fact that most contracts for major systems were of a cost reimbursement type which provided little, if any, motivation for economy, and were not awarded on a price competitive basis.

From the evidence we have from a wide variety of sources, there is no question whatsoever that we have routinely paid more than double the original price for the procurement of major weapons systems.

There is no convincing evidence that the use of "total contract packaging" or other devices has changed this at all. In fact, the specific evidence on the C–5A, where that method was used, shows an overrun of some $2 billion. The testimony of Admiral Rickover is equally convincing. This situation continues and, in my judgment, has been intensified during the last 2 years because of the buildup of procurement for the Vietnam war.

Funds Could Be Cut

Mr. Benson, a former official of the Office of the Assistant Secretary of Defense, comptroller, whom I quoted earlier, believes that $9 billion can be cut from the Pentagon budget; and I quote this Defense Department expert: "without reducing our national security or touching those funds earmarked for the war in Vietnam."

He says even under those circumstances spending can be cut $9 billion.

Admiral Rickover testified that by establishing uniform standards of accounting for recording costs and profits—which, of course, would be entirely separate from the Benson concept—we could save "at least 5 percent" of the defense procurement budget. That is $2 billion for that item of waste alone.

The editors of Congressional Quarterly recently interviewed highly placed sources in the Pentagon and in industry about the 1969 defense budget. Those sources agreed that the 1969 budget was loaded with "fat" and said that $10.8 billion could have been cut from the fiscal 1969 budget without in the slightest way impairing our level of national defense.

There are other items as well. We spend a disproportionate amount of our resources on marginal items such as post exchanges, commissaries, and ship's stores. Vast funds are spent for military public relations.

The Congressional Quarterly recently pointed out how topheavy we were in the field. It pointed out that we had 20 officers in Vietnam for every command post.

Excess Supplies

I will cite just one further example. On June 30, 1968, the value of the excess and long supply in our military supply pipeline was $12.7 billion. This was 28 percent of the $45.8 billion value of the supply system stocks on hand. This is the excess.

While the proportion of excess and surplus items has dropped considerably since 1961, it is still correct to ask, "What kind of a supply system do we have when 28 percent of the value of the supply system stocks are in excess of requirements? What kind of supply system is it that generates such vast surpluses and excesses?"

Contracts Fail to Meet Standards

Not only are we paying too much for what we buy, but often we do not get what we pay for.

This, it seems to me, should shock all of those who are concerned about our defense, whether they support enthusiastically the amount we are spending, and feel we should have more in national defense, or whether they are critical of it. We do not get what we pay for.

A most shocking example of this is to be found in a paper by a Budget Bureau specialist, a very distinguished and able man, Mr. Richard Stubbings, entitled "Improving the Acquisition Process for High Risk Electronics Systems."

Mr. Stubbings shows that in the procurement of some two dozen major weapons systems costing tens of billions of dollars during the 1950's and 1960's, the performance standards of the electronic systems of these weapons seldom met the specifications established for them.

How far they fell below their specifications is a real shock.

Of 11 major weapons systems begun during the 1960's, only two of the 11 electronic components of them performed up to standard. One performed at a 75-percent level and two at a 50-percent level. But six—a majority of them—of the 11 performed at a level 25 percent or less than the standards and specifications set for them.

But that is not all.

Excessive Costs—Late Delivery—High Profits

These systems typically cost 200 to 300 percent more than the Pentagon estimated.

They were and are delivered 2 years later than expected.

The after-tax profits of the aerospace industry, of which these contractors were the major companies, were 12.5 percent higher than for American industry as a whole.

Those firms with the worst records appeared to receive the highest profits. One firm, with failures on five of seven systems, earned 40 percent more than the rest of the aerospace industry, and 50 percent more than industry as a whole.

One other company, none of whose seven weapons systems measured up to the performance specifications, had earnings in excess of the industry average.

Think of that, Mr. President (Mr. HUGHES in the chair). A company not one of whose weapons systems measured up to performance specifications still had earnings in excess of the industry average.

This is a shocking situation. We are talking about the computers, radar, and gyroscopes—the key to performance—in our major weapons systems.

No Bang for a Buck?

In the past, the system managers and efficiency experts have talked about "More bang for a buck." But the analysis of Mr. Stubbings raises the question, "Are we not approaching the time when there will be 'No bang for a buck'?"

These revelations raise the most serious questions.

We have high profits without performance.

Rewards are in inverse relationship to the time taken and the funds spent.

Failures are rewarded and minimum standards seldom met. Prices soar. Profits rise. Contracts continue.

This is what I mean when I say that military spending is out of control. This is what I mean when I refer to the "unwarranted influence by the military-industrial complex." This is what I mean when I assert that we face a condition of excessive costs, burgeoning military budgets, and scandalous performance.

This is why we could get more security for the country by spending smaller amounts, but spending them more effectively.

Same Dangers Ahead

The conditions I have cited above are not only a condition of the 1950's and 1960's. The same dangers lie ahead. There are numerous additional huge weapons systems for the future. Some of them are already authorized.

Some have begun to be funded. We may wake up some morning soon and find that we are committed to billions upon billions of future expenditures where costs will burgeon and performance will be substandard. The fact is that things may soon become a great deal worse.

One of the ablest men we have had on the financial side of the Government in recent years is Charles Schultze, who was Budget Director under President Johnson for a number of years. Mr. Schultze recently wrote an excellent article in the Brookings Agenda papers, which lists some of the programs now contemplated, authorized, or funded. Among them are:

Minuteman II, which is being improved, and Minuteman III, which is in the offing. Estimated cost: $4.6 billion.

Thirty-one Polaris submarines to be converted to carry 496 Poseidon missiles. Estimated cost: $80 million per submarine, or almost $2.5 billion.

Two hundred and fifty-three new FB–111 bombers. Mr. Schultze does not give the cost estimate.

The thin Sentinel system—the ABM system. Estimated cost was $5 billion. I am now told on excellent authority that it is $10 billion and that this figure does not include funds for the Sprint missiles. If the thin system becomes a "thick" system, the total estimated cost is said to be in the neighborhood of $50 billion. And in a very fascinating analysis the other day by one of the real authorities in Congress on defense, the former Secretary of the Air Force, the Senator from Missouri (Mr. SYMINGTON), he estimated that the cost could go as high as $400 billion.

Incidentally, this is a system that even its supporters agree would protect the country for only a limited period of time, perhaps a decade. So that would mean spending $40 billion a year, or half of the total military budget as of now.

Four nuclear-powered carriers. These cost $540 million each, or $2.16 billion.

A new destroyer program. Mr. Schultze does not give the original estimated cost.

Five nuclear-powered escort ships. The cost is estimated at $625 million.

An advanced nuclear attack submarine. Again no cost estimate.

A new Navy fighter—VFX–1—to replace the F–111.

Mr. Schultze, and he should know—as I say, he was Budget Director for a number of years, and an outstanding, and brilliant young man—concludes that:

> One fairly predictable feature of most of these weapons systems is that their ultimate cost will be substantially higher than their currently estimated cost.

Mr. President, that is the understatement of the year. We have seen a doubling in the estimated cost of the Sentinel system alone in a period of 1 year. And we all know that what the military has hoped to do is to convert it into a "thick" system as a defense against a Soviet as well as a Chinese attack.

. . . .

Uncritical Approach

What is so discouraging about both the past and the future is the cavalier way in which increases and overruns are shrugged off by the military.

Two billion dollars is a very great amount of money. That is the estimated overrun for only one plane—the C–5A.

Five billion dollars is a tremendous amount of money. But that is the increase in the estimated cost of the thin Sentinel system in less than a year.

It is virtually impossible to get such funds for housing, jobs, or poverty programs. But the examples I have given are merely the increases and overruns for only two of the many defense weapons systems.

An article published not too long ago in the Washington Post indicated the dimensions involved in the matter. It was pointed out that $5 billion, the overrun on the military system, is more than we spend in a year in the entire foreign aid program plus everything we put into housing and urban development. The Pentagon handles it as if it were small change.

What appalls us is the uncritical way in which these increases are accepted by the military. To be consistently wrong on these estimates of cost, as the military has been consistently wrong, should bring the entire system of contracting under the most detailed scrutiny. But there is not the slightest indication that this is being done by the military. In fact, when such questions are raised, we find the services far more defensive than they are eager to improve the system.

But let me give this solemn warning. The time has come when many of those willing to provide this country with the defense it needs are unwilling to vote funds or authorize new weapons systems or accept the military justifications for them except after the most critical review.

The time of the blank check is over.

.   .   .   .

[3] Nixon Wins Senate ABM Battle by One-Vote Margins

A FTER AN epic legislative battle which became one of the longest, closest and hardest-fought in recent Congressional history, the Senate Aug. 6 narrowly supported President Nixon's controversial Safeguard antiballistic missile (ABM) system.

On suspenseful 50-51 and 49-51 roll-call votes a coalition of mostly Republicans and Southern Democrats rebuffed vigorous attempts to delay or block the Safeguard proposal.

The showdown took place as the Senate closed out a month of debate over a $759.1-million authorization for research and the beginning stages of deployment on the Safeguard system. This amount was contained in a bill (S 2546) requesting $20 billion for the military services and the Defense Department's research and procurement operations for fiscal 1970.

FROM *Congressional Quarterly*, August 8, 1969, pp. 1432–35. Copyright 1969 Congressional Quarterly, Inc.

DEBATE OVER

Although the ABM debate was seen as momentarily ended, it was expected to resume later in the session when the plan comes up in other bills. In addition, numerous challenges to other programs in the bill were also expected, ensuring that S 2546 would keep the Senate occupied into September.

The ABM votes came on an amendment by Sen. Margaret Chase Smith (R Maine) to prohibit anything but research on other antimissile defense and an amendment by John Sherman Cooper (R Ky.) and Philip A. Hart (D Mich.) to allow only research on the Safeguard network.

The Senate by an 11-89 vote earlier had rejected another amendment by Sen. Smith to forbid any work on the Safeguard ABM. A last-ditch attempt to curtail work on the program also failed by a 27-70 vote Aug. 7. That bid, termed a compromise by its sponsor, Thomas J. McIntyre (D N.H.), would have allowed research and installation for the initial stages of the system but prevented any acquisition of operational missiles.

The decisions climaxed 29 days of debate on the proposal on which President Nixon had banked the prestige and the political muscle of his 6-month-old Administration. President Nixon and his supporters argued that the ABM was necessary to protect U.S. retaliatory strength in the face of a mounting Soviet arsenal. Opponents argued that the system was probably unworkable or unnecessary, could wreck prospective arms negotiations by scaling up the arms race and would drain needed funds from vital domestic projects. This protracted discussion of the issue made the debate one of the longest since World War II.

TWO-YEAR FIGHT

The crucial votes also capped a two-year struggle against ABM plans supported by the Johnson and Nixon Administrations. Also involved was a growing sentiment of suspicion and doubt which had dogged defense expenditures in 1969.

The debate had been accompanied by the most intense publicity and lobbying as Members of Congress, Administration officials, scientists, news media and citizens and pressure groups sought to sway votes before the anticipated close outcome.

Entering the final week of the debate, only four Senators still had not announced how they planned to vote. They were Clinton P. Anderson (D N.M.), Warren G. Magnuson (D Wash.), Mike Gravel (D Alaska) and John J. Williams (R Del.). During that last week both Magnuson and Gravel declared their opposition to the ABM plan. Projected forecasts indicated that their announcement had tipped the vote to 50 against, 48 for the plan and two undecided.

But in the final day of debate most of the drama was provoked by Sen. Smith, the Senate's only woman Member. The ranking Republican member of the Senate Armed Services Committee and an avowed opponent of the

Johnson and Nixon Administration ABM plans, Mrs. Smith had been counted on to support the Amendment offered by Hart and Cooper, which was seen by some as being a compromise between outright rejection and delay of the ABM.

FIRST SMITH AMENDMENT

Mrs. Smith introduced her first amendment, a substitute for the Cooper-Hart measure, on Aug. 5, the day before the crucial ABM vote. The Smith amendment would have prevented funds in the bill from being used on any aspect of the Safeguard system.

She said, "The Hart-Cooper amendment is a partial approval of the Safeguard ABM system in that it proposes a compromise authorization for research, development, testing, evaluation and normal procurement incident thereto for the Safeguard ABM system. I do not approve of such a compromise and such authorization for the Safeguard ABM system. It would be a 'foot-in-the-door' authorization for a system in which I have no confidence. . . . Why vote to develop a system when you are opposed to deployment of such a system?"

In her soft voice, she told the silent Senate chamber, "Let me make it crystal clear that while I do not believe in the ABM, I do believe in America. I do believe in our form of government—but I do not believe in the ABM. I do believe in our Republic—but I do not believe in the ABM. I do believe in free enterprise—but I do not believe in the ABM. I am for the American way of life—but I do not believe in the ABM. The ABM is not an acid test of patriotism."

Albert Gore (D Tenn.), a leading ABM opponent, offered modifying language to the Smith measure which spelled out that funds for radar and computer components for other weapons systems would not be affected. Mrs. Smith agreed to Gore's language, but Barry Goldwater (R Ariz.) blocked its addition to the pending amendment, a move which required unanimous consent.

Just before the vote, the Senate suspended proceedings for a few minutes to greet Horace Maybray King, Speaker of the British House of Commons. During that break, Mrs. Smith met off the floor in a conference with Hart, Cooper, Gore, Stuart Symington (D Mo.) and Jacob K. Javits (R N.Y.) to work out strategy for the second Smith substitute.

When the session resumed, 11 Senators backed the first Smith amendment and 89 opposed it. George McGovern (D S.D.) originally voted against it, but switched his vote to support it.

SECOND SMITH AMENDMENT

When the time for debate on the Cooper-Hart amendment expired, Mrs. Smith offered another substitute for it. The second amendment stated that no funds could be used for research, development, testing, evaluation or procurement of "the antiballistic missile system known as the Safeguard" or any part or component of it. But the funds would not affect work on any other advanced ABM system or other weapons system, it stated.

Cooper said that he and Hart supported the new substitute. "Her amendment, in a different way, but as precisely and perhaps more clearly, accomplishes the purpose of our amendment," the Kentucky Republican said.

Javits said that the second Smith provision made "a very substantive difference in opening up" development of other weapons systems. "This does not mean that if Safeguard has a transistor that we cannot deal with that transistor in another system, or a weapon, or a Sprint, or a PAR (perimeter acquisition radar), or anything else that happens to be in the Safeguard system." What it did do, he added, was "to reject Safeguard as the system upon which the research and development will be focused."

Richard B. Russell (D Ga.), President Pro Tempore of the Senate, said that backers of the Cooper-Hart amendment had been arguing for additional research and development instead of deployment.

The Smith language, he said, "will kill all the research and all the development of the so-called Safeguard system after Senators have stood here on the floor day after day and stated they were in favor of research and development, but not deployment. This strangles it in the crib."

Another ABM supporter, Howard H. Baker Jr. (R Tenn.), said that the Smith amendment would prevent "evolutionary development" to improve the Safeguard system. "I do not believe we intend to scrap what we have done so far and require our scientists to start over from scratch with some other system," he added, but that was "the inevitable effect" of Mrs. Smith's proposal.

Stennis called the new amendment "a legislative monstrosity, when there is not time to analyze, to find the meaning of words, to check and double-check. . . . It is legislating in the dark where we do not know what these words mean."

When the voting ended, Mrs. Smith had joined the backers of the Cooper-Hart amendment but the two Senators whose positions were not known, Anderson and Williams of Delaware, lined up with the Administration.

Under Senate rules an amendment needs a clear majority to carry, and although Vice President Agnew cast a "nay" vote to break the tie, this was not necessary to defeat it. The final vote on the second Smith amendment was 50-51, with 36 Democrats and 14 Republicans in support of it, and 21 Democrats and 29 Republicans plus Agnew against it. Of the 21 Democrats who opposed the amendment, all but five were Southerners. All but seven Northern Democrats supported it.

COOPER-HART AMENDMENT

Voting on the Cooper-Hart amendment followed immediately after the defeat of the Smith provision. There was a rush of murmurs when Mrs. Smith changed her previous position to vote against the anti-ABM measure. Hers was the only switch, setting the tally at 49-51.

MCINTYRE AMENDMENT

The next day, McIntyre tried to rally the anti-ABM forces to support his limited deployment compromise. The amendment would allow installation of radars, computers and electronic equipment at two Air Force bases in North Dakota and Montana, but would prevent deployment of operational missiles or acquisition of other sites.

He called the Aug. 6 votes "a hollow victory indeed" for the Nixon Administration. Since "the Senate is in great disagreement among itself" over the Safeguard, he said, the bill should spell out what Defense officials could do rather than give them latitude to act.

Stennis objected to the McIntyre amendment. "Just a few hours ago 51 Senators put their stamp of approval on phase one (of the Safeguard system)." The McIntyre amendment "cuts some pieces out of phase one," he said.

Fulbright said he did not understand how McIntyre's amendment would limit the Pentagon. The amendment "affirmatively authorizes two bases . . . which are intended to be operative bases," he said. He said he would support it "if I could be convinced it is truly restrictive in a meaningful way."

The vote, the last on the Safeguard ABM during consideration of S 2546, was 27-70. Five Republicans and two Southern Democrats voted for it.

Following the votes, President Nixon was reported by White House spokesman Ronald L. Ziegler as "pleased . . . and gratified by the results and the bipartisan voting that was apparent in the outcome."

In another reaction the vote was interpreted by the Soviet newspaper Izvestia as a victory for the antimilitary forces in the United States.

FUTURE CONTROVERSY

However, continued attempts to block the ABM system were certain later in the session in the Senate where the opposition is centered. Some opponents vowed an attack when the annual defense appropriations bill with funds for the plan is considered later in the session.

In addition, many who opposed the ABM also plan to attack other programs authorized in the bill. The ABM funds authorized in the bill amounted to $759.1 million out of a total of $20 billion contained in S 2546. The remaining funds were designated for numerous research and procurement programs by all military services and the Defense Department. Many of these programs had become centers of controversy and criticism during the growing debate over defense spending and contracting and national priorities.

About 20 amendments were either already offered or were being considered on the bill assuring that debate would continue for several weeks. Senate Majority Leader Mike Mansfield (D Mont.) Aug. 6 indicated that debate on the measure would probably continue past the three-week Congressional recess beginning Aug. 13.

The controversial development of chemical-biological warfare weapons was the subject of seven amendments to curtail, oversee or cut back such operations.

William Proxmire (D Wis.), an ardent critic of defense spending, introduced several amendments to oversee job changes of executives between defense contractors and the Pentagon and of contracts and profits.

Proxmire also offered an amendment to tighten spending on the Air Force's controversial C-5A transport plane, for which costs had increased significantly during its construction.

Other amendments were offered to curtail or end spending on the Army main battle tank program, defense research programs, the defense contingency fund and to limit troops strengths. Still others would require reports from the Pentagon on contract progress and release of studies by Defense "think tanks."

PART V

The Legacy of the Cold War: The Military-Industrial Complex

INTRODUCTION

❪ The phrase "military-industrial complex" was made popular by President Eisenhower in his "farewell speech" three days before he left office in January, 1961. Eisenhower believed that international crises would continue to occur and that in meeting these crises, the military and the industrialists, who stand to gain thereby, would pose costly defense programs as simple solutions. Eisenhower believed that such programs would be dangerous to our economic and political well-being unless a balance was maintained between the private and the public, the foreign and the domestic, and the present and the future. "We must guard against the acquisition of unwarranted influence . . . by the military-industrial complex," Eisenhower declared, "in order to balance, and to integrate these and other forces, new, and old, within the principles of our democratic system." Otherwise, if political and financial considerations, rather than strict military needs, are allowed to prevail, said Eisenhower in another speech on March 11, 1959, "we are finally going to a garrison state." Eisenhower believed, moreover, that the military services were rarely satisfied with the amounts allocated to them, and that unjustified military spending was a distorted use of the nation's resources. Because Eisenhower feared that his successor would not fully understand how the military-industrial complex operated, and hence would be vulnerable to its pressures, he decided to warn the country. This warning is printed in full below.

"Could the United States become a garrison state in which most of its energies are devoted to arms?" This is the question that Jack Raymond, writing for the *Harvard Business Review,* attempts to answer. After amassing evidence that such a complex does in fact exist—and suggesting certain countervailing safeguards that mitigate excessive power, by that complex—he concludes that we are not yet a garrison state. But Raymond warns us to be alert and knowledgeable, lest the industrialists' desire for profits and the politicians' fear for our safety lead to that eventuality.

As Gar Alperovitz has pointed out, the Cold War really began with the advent of nuclear weapons. The bomb also brought scientists into the field of military planning and gave rise to a whole new discipline—deterrent strategy. Although to propagandize the public for the military is not the main function of these deterrent theorists, many of whom are associated with the RAND Corporation, still their numerous and sophisticated writings do tend to "legitimize" Pentagon thought. By rationalizing the pronouncements of the leaders of the military-industrial complex and supplying a theoretical substructure to assumptions of the inevitability of conflict, these writers have supplied a raison d'être for the military-industrial complex beyond the mere need to keep our economy healthy.

No deterrent theorist is better known than Herman Kahn. He believes that the Soviet Union is our mortal enemy, and that in order for us to survive, the problem of nuclear security must be examined as objectively and as completely as possible. Kahn's book *On Thermonuclear War* met with wide approval when it was first published in 1960. His basic thesis there is that it is unrealistic to believe that nuclear wars will never be fought because the ensuing destruction would be too horrible. They will be fought, but they will not mean the end of humanity. Therefore we should prepare for them. This, according to Kahn, requires two major efforts: (1) that we take seriously the "fact" that the Soviet Union is our mortal enemy; and (2) that we be willing to allocate all the national resources necessary to defend ourselves against this enemy. Selections from Kahn's book are reprinted below.

Philip Green, an unusually perceptive writer, is very critical of deterrent theorists in general and Herman Kahn in particular. In his book *Deadly Logic* (1966) he maintains that deterrent thinking was largely responsible for the decision to overcome the so-called missile gap by building a first-strike force. The Russians then responded "in accordance with the best principles of deterrence logic" by developing an antiballistic missile (ABM) system. We, in turn, responded to their ABM system with plans to build a "thin" ABM system of our own. Thus, the arms race continues to spiral.

Green believes that deterrent theory is intellectually bankrupt, but he is pessimistic that this underlying ideological buttress will soon disappear. Excerpts from Green's book serve as a conclusion to this book. They are not simply a criticism of the military-industrial complex but a searching examination into the intellectual condition of our whole society.

The questions raised in the final chapter are of course of great significance to our society and the world community. Are our national interests really threatened? If not, has our preoccupation with foreign wars been used as an excuse to postpone domestic goals, thereby undermining the values of liberal democracy? Has the power of the military-industrial-scientific complex reached such proportions that it now can determine its own needs and dictate to the American people the sacrifices that are expected of them in order to sustain this complex in power? In other words, is our system of nuclear defense a greater threat to the survival of freedom today than the Communist movement, aggressive or not? If so, are demonstrations—including violence—an effective way to oppose its power? If not, is it realistic to think that a reversal of policy can emerge via normal political channels? Moreover, does the public have the ability or the time to understand such technical issues even if given all the facts? Even when all of the facts cannot be released for reasons of security, could not more data be released than at present—especially to congressional committees? Finally, in light of Clark's data in the introduction—suggesting that past wars have retarded human progress but that current wars may actually further human progress—is it possible to make a dispassionate judgment while we are in the midst of the Cold War? On the other hand, by the time such a judgment *is* possible, will it really matter? That is, will we have lost the opportunity to make significant changes in our policy, or worse, will the dogs of war already have been unleashed?

THE READINGS

1] The Military-Industrial Complex Concept

M Y FELLOW Americans, three days from now, after half a century in the service of our country, I shall lay down the responsibilities of office as, in traditional and solemn ceremony, the authority of the Presidency is vested in my successor.

This evening I come to you with a message of leavetaking and farewell, and to share a few final thoughts with you, my countrymen.

Like every other citizen, I wish the new President, and all who will labor with him, Godspeed. I pray that the coming years will be blessed with peace and prosperity for all.

Our people expect their President and the Congress to find essential agreement on issues of great moment, the wise resolution of which will better shape the future of the Nation.

My own relations with the Congress, which began on a remote and tenuous basis when, long ago, a Member of the Senate appointed me to West Point, have since ranged to the intimate during the war and immediate postwar period, and, finally, to the mutually interdependent during these past 8 years.

In this final relationship, the Congress and the administration have, on most vital issues, cooperated well, to serve the national good rather than mere partisanship, and so have assured that the business of the Nation should go forward. So, my official relationship with the Congress ends in a feeling, on my part, of gratitude that we have been able to do so much together.

We now stand 10 years past the midpoint of a century that has witnessed four major wars among great nations. Three of these involved our own country. Despite these holocausts America is today the strongest, the most influential and most productive nation in the world. Understandably proud of this preeminence, we yet realize that America's leadership and prestige depend, not merely upon our unmatched material progress, riches, and military strength, but on how we use our power in the interests of world peace and human betterment.

Throughout America's adventure in free government our basic purposes have been to keep the peace; to foster progress in human achievement, and to enhance liberty, dignity, and integrity among people and among na-

President Eisenhower's Farewell Address to the Nation, January 18, 1961.

tions. To strive for less would be unworthy of a free and religious people. Any failure traceable to arrogance, or our lack of comprehensive or readiness to sacrifice would inflict upon us grievous hurt both at home and abroad.

Progress toward these noble goals is persistently threatened by the conflict now engulfing the world. It commands our whole attention, absorbs our very beings. We face a hostile ideology—global in scope, atheistitc in character, ruthless in purpose, and insidious in method. Unhappily, the danger it poses promises to be of indefinite duration. To meet it successfully, there is called for, not so much the emotional and transitory sacrifices of crisis, but rather those which enable us to carry forward steadily, surely, and without complaint the burdens of a prolonged and complex struggle—with liberty the stake. Only thus shall we remain, despite every provocation, on our charted course toward permanent peace and human betterment.

Crises there will continue to be. In meeting them, whether foreign or domestic, great or small, there is a recurring temptation to feel costly action could become the miraculous solution to all current difficulties. A huge increase in newer elements of our defense; development of unrealistic programs to cure every ill in agriculture; a dramatic expansion in basic and applied research—these many other possibilities, each possibly promising in itself, may be suggested as the only way to the road we wish to travel.

But each proposal must be weighed in the light of a broader consideration: The need to maintain balance in and among national programs—balance between the private and the public economy, balance between cost and hoped-for advantage—balance between the clearly necessary and the comfortably desirable; balance between our essential requirements as a nation and the duties imposed by the Nation upon the individual; balance between actions of the moment and the national welfare of the future. Good judgment seeks balance and progress; lack of it eventually finds imbalance and frustration.

The record of many decades stands as proof that our people and their Government have, in the main, understood these truths and have responded to them well, in the face of stress and threat. But threats, new in kind or degree, constantly arise. I mention two only.

A vital element in keeping the peace is our military establishment. Our arms must be mighty, ready for instant action, so that no potential aggressor may be tempted to risk his own destruction.

Our military organization today bears little relation to that known by any of my predecessors in peacetime, or indeed by the fighting men of World War II or Korea.

Until the latest of our world conflicts, the United States had no armaments industry. American makers of plowshares could, with time and as required, make swords as well. But now we can no longer risk emergency improvision of national defense; we have been compelled to create a permanent armaments industry of vast proportions.

Added to this, 3½ million men and women are directly engaged in the defense establishment. We annually spend on military security more than the net income of all U.S. corporations.

This conjunction of an immense military establishment and a large arms industry is new in the American experience. The total influence—economic, political, even spiritual—is felt in every city, every statehouse, every office of the Federal Government.

We recognize the imperative need for this development. Yet we must not fail to comprehend its grave implications. Our toil, resources, and livelihood are all involved; so is the very structure of our society.

In the councils of government, we must guard against the acquisition of unwarranted influence, whether sought or unsought, by the military-industrial complex. The potential for the disastrous rise of misplaced power exists and will persist.

We must never let the weight of this combination endanger our liberties or democratic processes. We should take nothing for granted. Only an alert and knowledgeable citizenry can compel the proper meshing of the huge industrial and military machinery of defense without peaceful methods and goals, so that security and liberty may prosper together.

Akin to, and largely responsible for the sweeping changes in our industrial-military posture, has been the technological revolution during recent decades.

In this revolution, research has become central; it also becomes more formalized, complex, and costly. A steadily increasing share is conducted for, by, or at the direction of, the Federal Government.

Today, the solitary inventor, tinkering in his shop, has been overshadowed by task forces of scientists in laboratories and testing fields. In the same fashion, the free university, historically the fountainhead of free ideas and scientific discovery, has experienced a revolution in the conduct of research.

Partly because of the huge costs involved, a Government contract becomes virtually a substitute for intellectual curiosity. For every old blackboard there are now hundreds of new electronic computers.

The prospect of domination of the Nation's scholars by Federal employment, project allocations, and the power of money is ever present—and is gravely to be regarded.

Yet, in holding scientific research and discovery in respect, as we should, we must also be alert to the equal and opposite danger that public policy could itself become the captive of a scientific-technological elite.

It is the task of statesmanship to mold, to balance, and to integrate these and other forces, new, and old, within the principles of our democratic system—ever aiming toward the supreme goals of our free society.

Another factor in maintaining balance involves the element of time. As we peer into society's future, we--you and I, and our Government—must avoid the impulse to live only for today, plundering, for our own ease and convenience, the previous resources of tomorrow.

We cannot mortgage the material assets of our grandchildren without risking the loss also of their political and spiritual heritage. We want democracy to survive for all generations to come, not to become the insolvent phantom of tomorrow.

Down the long lane of the history yet to be written America knows that this world of ours, ever growing smaller, must avoid becoming a community of dreadful fear and hate, and be, instead, a proud consideration of mutual trust and respect.

Such a confederation must be one of equals. The weakest must come to the conference table with the same confidence as do we, protected as we are by our moral, economic, and military strength. That table, though scarred by many past frustrations, cannot be abandoned for the certain agony of the battlefield.

Disarmament with mutual honor and confidence, is a continuing imperative. Together we must learn how to compose differences, not with arms, but with intellect and decent purpose. Because this need is so sharp and apparent I confess that I lay down my official responsibilities in this field with a definite sense of disappointment.

As one who has witnessed the horror and lingering sadness of war—as one who knows that another war could utterly destroy this civilization which has been so slowly and painfully built over thousands of years—I wish I could say tonight that a lasting peace is in sight.

Happily, I can say that war has been avoided. Steady progress toward our ultimate goal his been made. But, so much remains to be done. As a private citizen, I shall never cease to do what little I can to help the world advance along that road.

So—in this my last good night to you as your President—I thank you for the many opportunities you have given me for public service in war and peace. I trust that in that service you find some things worthy; as for the rest of it, I know you will find ways to improve performance in the future.

You and I—my fellow citizens—need to be strong in our faith that all nations, under God, will reach the goal of peace with justice. May we be ever unswerving in devotion to principle, confident but humble with power, diligent in pursuit of the Nation's great goals.

To all the peoples of the world, I once more give expression to America's prayerful and continuing aspiration:

We pray that peoples of all faiths, all races, all nations, may have their great human needs satisfied; that those now denied opportunity shall come to enjoy it to the full; that all who yearn for freedom may experience its spiritual blessings; that those who have freedom will understand, also, its heavy responsibilities; that all who are insensitive to the needs of others will learn charity; that the scourges of poverty, disease, and ignorance will be made to disappear from the earth, and that, in the goodness of time, all peoples will come to live together in a peace guaranteed by the binding force of mutual respect and love.

2] The Growth of the Military-Industrial Complex

COMPLEX ANATOMY

. . . .

TO UNDERSTAND and assess the military-industrial complex, we must identify it and consider its magnitude, its composition, and the interaction of its component parts.

The military-industrial complex includes all those elements of American society—economic, political, and professional—that have a material or philosophic stake in a large defense establishment. It includes not only the Armed Services and the companies that produce for them, but politicians in and out of government, workers and union leaders, ordinary citizens and local officials, teachers in schools, and academicians—in short, all who for reasons of "pork or patriotism" support the Armed Forces' requirements.

It may be simplistic to bundle diverse elements of the military-industrial complex into a single "it," but "it" is very real, as former Secretary of Defense Robert McNamara attested after seven years in his post. Characteristically, McNamara asserted he rarely lost to "it." He told an interviewer, "I'd say in this area we haven't lost more than 2% of the cases to the so-called military-industrial complex—and in those instances we failed to present our case properly." But what about the magnitude of the cases lost? Even a straight-across-the-board 2% of Pentagon expenditures in the nine budgets McNamara worked on in seven years, including estimates for fiscal year 1969, totals $10.3 billion—twice the estimated cost of the anti-China ABM defense system, which is considered by many to be the "complex"'s latest prize.

Our Beneficent Budget

The Pentagon's spending program supports not merely the tactics and strategy of the fighting fronts; it reaches into the lives of all of us on the domestic front. Allocations for military research spin off into jobs and products that can and do become important to the civilian economy. The decision to open a base or close one can affect grocery store owners and church fathers as well as night club operators and liquor dealers. The confluence of interests in the military budget thus results in unusual alliances as varying segments of society, motivated by monetary or social objectives, seek each other's support for shares of Pentagon expenditures.

The defense budget that President Johnson presented to Congress in 1968 totaled $79.8 billion, an increase of about $3 billion over the current year's

FROM Jack Raymond, "The Growing Threat of Our Military-Industrial Complex," *Harvard Business Review*, vol. XLI (May–June, 1968), pp. 56–64. © 1968 by the President and Fellows of Harvard College; all rights reserved.

budget (for the fiscal year ending June 1968). Although a new budgeting system appeared to reduce the proportion allocated for defense in the total federal budget of $186.1 billion, supplementals inevitably will add $10 billion or so and restore the defense proportion to at least half of the total. While much of the increase in the January budget was due to heightened military operations because of the war in Vietnam, and some $3 billion in savings was planned through consumption of inventories, the budget nonetheless called for $25.8 billion for the procurement of military equipment ranging from shoelaces to nuclear weapons.

The detailed budget is fascinating in the multiplicity and variety of "things" that are needed to equip and maintain the Armed Forces. It provides, for example, $6,000 for flowers for American battle monuments. Flower growers, too, can be part of the military-industrial complex.

Most of the total defense procurement is accounted for in several large programs. About half the increase in planned procurement is earmarked for three nuclear weapons systems—(1) the controversial ABM system that Senators Joseph Clark and Wayne Morse condemned as fuel for the military-industrial complex; (2) the Minuteman land-based ICBM network; and (3) the Poseidon submarine-launched ballistic missiles which are to replace the Polaris missiles. The new budget calls for $600 million in hardware purchases in addition to the $500 million to be spent in continued research and development on the ABM system, about $200 million in "super-hardening" the concrete silos in the Minuteman-ICBM network, and an undisclosed amount for the purchase of long lead-time items for the Poseidon missiles. Specific items help to make clear the industrial stakes involved:

The 1968 budget message disclosed plans to start constructing 25 ships of various kinds and sizes and to modify or convert 43 ships, bringing total expenditures on ships to $1.6 billion; procurement of 2,943 new aircraft, mostly helicopters, for an expenditure of $8.9 billion; production of 163 F-111A and F-111D swing-wing airplanes (the controversial TFX's) for a total of $1.1 billion; and outlays of another $350 million for 30 F-111B's for the Navy, despite indications that the Navy might decide not to use the plane. The F-111's are a product of the General Dynamics Corporation.

The 1968 budget also calls for $500 million worth of C-5A cargo transports built by the Lockheed Aircraft Corporation, $670 million worth of A5 attack aircraft built by Ling-Temco-Vought, $576 million worth of F-4 supersonic fighters built by the McDonnell-Douglas Corporation, $169 million worth of A6 attack aircraft built by Grumman Aircraft Engineering Corporation, and $630 million for development work on the Air Force's manned orbiting laboratory (MOL)—a space laboratory the Pentagon hopes to launch in 1971.

Although the United States has meticulously sought to differentiate between its civilian space programs and the military space requirements, the budget of the National Aeronautics and Space Administration is as noteworthy as the Pentagon's insofar as military-industrial links are concerned. Thus, while the budget request for the space agency was reduced considerably from the figures for previous years, it still totaled $4.3 billion.

Numerous Beneficiaries

There are various ways of looking at Pentagon spending. To begin in quantitative terms, consider the spread of contracts:

Some 22,000 prime contractors and 100,000 subcontractors enjoy the defense business that is generated in different military programs.

A total of 76 industries, from aircraft to X-ray apparatus, are classed as defense-oriented.

Plane makers and shipbuilders derive more than half their income from defense contracts.

About 5,300 U.S. cities and towns boast at least one defense plant or company doing business with the Armed Forces.

The Armed Forces have swelled to more than 3,490,000, a jump of about 800,000 in two years. The number of persons employed directly or indirectly because of military spending has risen to 4,100,000 men and women—about 1,000,000 more than last year. The number of Americans in the uniformed services and in defense-generated employment of all kinds is said to account for nearly 10% of the entire U.S. labor force of 78,000,000.

Then there are the Pentagon's direct economic holdings. The Pentagon is landlord over some 27.6 million acres of land in the United States; this land is value officially at $38.4 billion—and some of the values have been calculated in terms of prices of more than a century ago! The Military Services and Defense Agencies, after a calculated effort to rid themselves of costly installations, still maintain some 470 major bases, camps, and installations and about 5,000 lesser ones around the nation. The Department of Defense budget for nine arsenals in the current fiscal year totals $3.9 billion, up $2.6 billion from last year. These arsenals employ 57,000 workers and are operating at full capacity because of the war in Vietnam.

Big Contractors

Another way of looking at the defense contracting business is to examine the military prime contract awards of $10,000 or more which the Pentagon regularly lists by state, region, and commodity categories. In fiscal year 1967, the most recent period for which figures have been made available, 100 companies accounted for 65.5% of the military prime contracts.

The top military contractor for that year was the McDonnell-Douglas Corporation, which represented the merger of two companies that had been among the country's leaders. This company received over $2.1 billion in defense contracts, accounting for 5.4% of the total awarded. McDonnell-

Douglas produces the F-4 Phantom series of fighters and reconaissance aircraft. The General Dynamics Corporation, with over $1.8 billion in defense contracts, accounting for 4.7% of the total, was second on the list. General Dynamics, whose contracts include the F-111 (TFX) aircraft, as previously mentioned, also produces missiles and ships. Lockheed Aircraft Corporation was the third largest contractor in fiscal 1967, with $1.8 billion; General Electric Company was fourth, with more than $1.2 billion; and United Aircraft Corporation was fifth, with nearly $1.1 billion. The top ten included the American Telephone and Telegraph Company, in eighth place with $673 million in defense contracts.

Some states are well favored by the largest contractors and therefore possess stronger interests than others in the perpetuation of the system. California was at the top of the list, with over $6.6 billion, which comprised 17.9% of the total. The identity of the second state on the list led one reporter to write:

> President Johnson's home state of Texas, which only a few years ago ranked seventh among the states getting prime defense contracts, now has nosed out New York for No. 2 spot, Pentagon figures showed today.

Although there are many changes from year to year in the list of prime contractors, the cluster at the top is a "hard core." Eight of the top ten prime contractors in fiscal 1967 were in the top ten in the period 1958–1960; seven, in the period 1951–1953; and six, in the period 1940–1944. Four companies—Douglas (now part of McDonnell-Douglas), Lockheed Aircraft, General Electric, and United Aircraft—have been in the top ten for the past 23 years.

Marietta on the Make

The benefactions of defense contracting appear more dramatic still when specific examples are considered. One good illustration is the city of Marietta, Georgia. Lockheed-Georgia Company, a division of Lockheed Aircraft Corporation, is located in Marietta and is the largest single industrial organization in the Southeast. About 90% of Lockheed-Georgia's business stems from defense contracts, the most important of which now are for the development and building of the C-5A military transport (worth about $1.4 billion) and for production of the C-141 Starlifter (worth another $600 million or more).

Lockheed-Georgia pays about $200 million a year in wages to 26,000 workers drawn from about 55 of Georgia's 159 counties—about one third of the state. Marietta's mayor, Howard Atherton, has said the impact of Lockheed-Georgia on his city's economy is "almost immeasurable." Robert Cox, a Machinists Union leader in Marietta, said defense spending "would almost have to be considered a major ingredient in the continuing low rate of unemployment in the metropolitan Atlanta area." Lockheed buys everything from soft drinks to metal parts from Georgia suppliers. Last year, the company spent $113 million with about 1,720 suppliers, many of them small businesses.

Lockheed-Georgia offers so good an example of spreading prosperity in a defense-oriented economy that the Pentagon cited it proudly in its *Defense Industry Bulletin,* as follows:

> Major subcontractors and subsystems contracts on the Starlifter are shared by 33 companies over the United States. Whatever the total of the employees of the subcontractors and vendors who draw their paychecks from funds derived from the C-141, it can be multiplied by five to give a truer estimate of the number whose livelihood is affected by this defense program. This is because in the communities involved there are grocers, clothiers, furniture dealers, appliance dealers, etc., who feed, clothe, house and, generally, care for the needs of those who are working specifically on a defense contract.
>
> After receiving the prime contract on the airframe of the C-141 from the Air Force Systems Command's Aeronautical Systems Division, Lockheed's plant in Georgia sublet the wing to Avco Corporation in Nashville, Tenn., in competitive bidding. The wing includes a fuel pump. The Tennessee subcontractor in Avco obtained the fuel pump from Pesco in Bedford, Ohio. To build the fuel pump, Pesco needed, among other things, a switch and a cannon plug. The Ohio firm bought the switch from the Micro Devices Company of Dayton, Ohio and the cannon plug from a concern in Los Angeles, California.
>
> At this point, the defense dollar really begins to flow into communities over the United States. Micro of Ohio gathers components for the switch from the following areas: wire, from Westbury, N.Y.; glass, Shanton, Conn.; electrical material, Chicago and New York; disc, Cincinnati, Ohio; springs, Cincinnati; ceramics, Paramoit, Calif., and Sun Prairie, Wis.; epoxy, Canton Mass.; and silver from New York City. The Los Angeles firm providing the cannon plug for Pesco's fuel pump follows a similar pattern in obtaining components from companies spread out over the nation. . . .
>
> A tracing of the path of the defense dollar through the subcontracting and vending program involving other parts of the Starlifter would find it in virtually every state going from prime contractor to major subcontractors into the third and fourth levels, to vendors and suppliers ad infinitum. For example, Rohr Corporation of Chula Vista, Calif., largest C-141 subcontractor, sublets 49% of its contract on engine nacelles. Companies receiving this 49% from Rohr, in turn sublet 40% of their part to other firms. Rohr's subcontractors at the time the study was made totaled $85.9 million; since then additional millions are being negotiated for follow-on C-141's.

Arms for Sale

No review of U.S. defense business would be complete without inclusion of the government's own mercantile interest in it, for the United States engages in the sale of arms as a source of revenue for the Treasury. In fact, the United States is the world's principal arms supplier. This is not surprising, or novel. The United States was the arsenal of democracy in two world wars.

And in the period immediately after World War II, it maintained its role as arms supplier in order to bolster Western Europe against threatened Communist aggression.

From 1949 to 1962 the U.S. Government alone (not counting private arms sales) sold $16.1 billion worth of military arms to other countries and gave away about $30.2 billion. Since 1962, when the current arms sales program began, Pentagon officials have been as aggressive as private arms merchants, with the result that the United States has sold over $11.1 billion worth of arms. In a speech in Los Angeles in the spring of 1966, the Pentagon official in charge of the sales program proudly estimated that it had yielded $1 billion in profits for American industry and 1.2 million man-years of employment for companies throughout the country.

So aggressive has been the Pentagon in selling abroad that for several years it managed to use the Export-Import Bank to provide easy credit for poorer, underdeveloped nations, much like the easy-credit terms that flourish between retailers and ghetto inhabitants.

Congress, angered by disclosures of so-called "Country X" accounts, ended the practice in 1967 and put ceilings on the grants and sales of arms to Latin America and Africa. However, the sale of arms abroad continues to be a big—very big—business.

PRESSURE ON THE PENTAGON

An easy way to dramatize the potential for what Eisenhower labeled as "unwarranted influence, whether sought or unsought," is to personalize it. Shortly after Clark Clifford was designated Secretary of Defense, early in 1968, columnists Drew Pearson and Jack Anderson pointed out that his law clients had ranged "from the far-flung duPont de Nemours to the Radio Corporation of America, from General Electric to El Paso Natural Gas and Phillips Petroleum." Although the insinuation may have been a nonsequitur, since many of Clifford's predecessors also had come from the ranks of big business, including defense business, the story had an ominous ring.

Equally ominous to some has been the practice of defense contractors who hire military men for big jobs. Shortly before Eisenhower's farewell speech, a House subcommittee disclosed that more than 1,400 retired officers of the rank of major or above, including 261 of general or flag rank, were employed by the leading 100 defense contractors. General Dynamics, headed by former Secretary of the Army Frank Pace, led with 187, including 27 retired generals and admirals.

There have been no recent similar estimates, but there is ample evidence that defense contractors continue to recruit avidly among retired high-ranking officers. To mention just a few instances:

General Curtis E. LeMay, retired Air Force Chief of Staff, is President and Board Chairman of the Networks Electronic Corporation, Chatsworth, California.

General Lauris Norstad, former Supreme Allied Commander in Europe, is President of Owens-Corning Fiberglas Corporation.

General Mark E. Bradley, former chief of the Air Force Logistics Command, is Assistant to the President of Garrett Corporation, in Los Angeles.

Vice Admiral William Raborn, developer of the Polaris submarine missiles and former Director of the Central Intelligence Agency, is a Vice President of Aerojet-General Corporation, Azusa, California.

General Paul L. Freeman, the former Commanding General of the Continental Army Command, is a Vice President of the Mellonics Systems Development Division of Litton Industries.

Several years ago, as a reporter on a television panel show, I asked the then Secretary of the Air Force, Dudley C. Sharp, whether he thought high-ranking officers should be barred from taking top defense-industry jobs. His reply was:

I would hate to see this happen. I think that the officers that take jobs in private industry contribute a great deal to the defense of this country because of the knowledge that they can offer industry.

When I followed up with a question about whether there might not be some danger, precisely because they had special knowledge, that they would provide their new bosses with an unfair advantage, Sharp replied that he did not believe the Pentagon was "subjected to that kind of pressure."

I often remember that statement in recalling the classic Congressional testimony of the late Admiral William M. Fechteler, who, after he retired as Chief of Naval Operations, took a job as consultant to the Atomic Products Division of General Electric. Admiral Fechteler explained to a House subcommittee that he had arranged some appointments for one of the vice presidents to his company:

"I took him to see Mr. Gates.[1] I took him in to see Admiral Burke.[2] He had not met Admiral Burke before. And then I made appointments for him with the Chief of the Bureau of Ships. But I did not accompany him there, because those are material bureaus which make contracts, and I *studiously* avoid even being in the room when anybody talks about contracts."

Aggressive Lobbyists

The military-industrial complex includes certain pressure groups. The most obvious of these are the organizations of the Army, Navy, and Air Force supporters, led by men with strong emotional and careerist ties to the services and virtually financed by the defense contractors.

The Association of the U.S. Army, the Air Force Association, and the Navy League—each with chapters throughout the country—are composed of active, reserve, and retired members of the Armed Forces, and of defense contractors, community leaders, and other supporters. These organizations are financed by membership fees, payments for contractors' exhibits at an-

---

[1] Thomas L. Gates, then Secretary of the Navy, later Secretary of Defense.
[2] Arleigh Burke, then Chief of Naval Operations.

nual conventions, subscriptions to dinner meetings and rallies, and advertisements in official publications. They are regarded as the civilian "arm" or "spokesmen" of their respective services, and their officers maintain close contact with the active civilian and military leaders of the services. They unabashedly campaign in behalf of policies advocated by the active Army, Navy, and Air Force leaders. Occasionally they even choose sides between the military and the civilians in government, usually in favor of expanded military forces and bigger and better weapons, and in opposition to policies that suggest reduced "preparedness."

In its annual meeting of 1967 the Association of the U.S. Army welcomed the decision to produce and deploy the ABM system which the Army had so long advocated (more on this presently); in its annual meeting the Air Force Association urged "contract definition" of an advanced manned strategic bomber, procurement and deployment of an improved manned interceptor, the F-12, and production of the SST supersonic transport; and in its annual meeting the Navy League called for additional ships—especially nuclear-powered carriers and submarines.

The Military Services, of course, carry on their own direct lobbying and public relations campaigns. They maintain legislative liaison staffs with officers stationed in the Capitol and concern themselves with legislation on the budget, broad military policies, pay, promotion, retirement, housing, medical care, and—not least—the military construction programs that provide most of the "pork barrel" projects. The Military Services thus keep members of Congress informed and solicit their interest in particular programs. In this way they have consistently created Congressional support for certain expanded arms programs, even when the White House has opposed them.

Of course, many members of Congress are active reservists, come from areas dependent on weapons manufacturing, or are dependent on other forms of military largess—a military base, for example. It is by now an old saw that if Georgia, the home state of the chairman of the Senate Armed Services Committee, received another military installation, it would sink.

Wooing of the TFX

The TFX story is probably the most outstanding example of the pressures that can be identified in the military-industrial complex—pressures that are still reverberating, in this case, more than five years after the initial Pentagon announcement of the award of a potential $7 billion contract to the General Dynamics Corporation.

The TFX (Tactical Fighter, Experimental), later named the F-111, a jet fighter-bomber, was the biggest contracting plum since World War II. The competition for the contract developed between Boeing, with headquarters in Seattle, and General Dynamics, with corporate headquarters in New York. Boeing planned to place the work in its Wichita, Kansas plant; General Dynamics planned to develop and build the plane in its Convair division at Fort Worth, Texas.

Inevitably, the politics of geography drew public notice. The then Vice President, Lyndon B. Johnson, was from Texas; the first Secretary of the

Navy in the Kennedy Administration, John B. Connally, was Governor of Texas and a close friend and associate of Johnson; and the then Secretary of the Navy, Fred Korth, was one of the most prominent citizens of Texas. A Congressional committee brought out the fact that the bank of which Korth had been president held the General Dynamics checking account in Fort Worth.

Meanwhile, a number of members of Congress were also interested in the TFX award:

Several of them were in touch with Secretary of the Air Force Eugene Zuckert during the contract negotiations. One of them, Senator Mike Monroney of Oklahoma, said later he had visited Zuckert's office "to remind him of the vast government-owned plant in Tulsa, Oklahoma, which the Douglas Aircraft Company operates, and its large unused machinery and manpower capabilities."

Senator Stuart Symington of Missouri, a former Secretary of the Air Force, visited Zuckert to discuss the possibility of Missouri companies obtaining subcontracts from whichever manufacturer got the prime contract.

Senator Warren Magnuson of Washington inquired about the status of the competition. His fellow Washingtonian, Senator Henry M. Jackson, frequent butt of the jape that he is the "Senator from Boeing," openly said he had insisted on an investigation when Boeing did not win the contract.

Senators Frank Carlson and James B. Pearson, and Representative Garner E. Shriver, all of Kansas, where Boeing had an idle plant at Wichita, visited Zuckert as a group and told the Air Force Secretary that Boeing could do the job better than its competitor.

Representative Jim Wright of Fort Worth, Texas, made no bones about his interest and the reason for it:

"In the absence of a substantial contract of this type, the General Dynamics team at Fort Worth was faced with dismemberment. It meant the difference between employment or unemployment for thousands of my constituents. Let me be completely frank. I talked about this subject with everybody I could get to listen, both military and civilian officials. That does not in my judgment amount to undesirable political influence. The same sort of thing was being attempted by the other side."

Unnecessary Contracts

In the case of the TFX there was at least general agreement on the desirability of such an airplane. However, some large weapons programs have been pushed hard by the military-industrial complex when there were contentions that they were not needed at all. The United States has spent almost $19 billion since World War II on missile systems that either were never finished or were out of service when finished because of obsolescence. And the story might have been worse. The B-70 is an example of a major weapons system that Air Force leaders—and security-minded supporters, including contractors—persistently advocated; it was rejected successively by the Eisenhower, Kennedy, and Johnson administrations on the ground that it was (or soon would be) outmoded. Score that one *against* the power of the military-industrial complex.

Controversial ABM: Only the future will tell us how to score the $5 billion ABM system which is being designed to protect the United States against a possible ballistic missile attack by Communist China in the 1970's.

The Army has been pushing an antimissile defense for more than ten years and has patiently suffered the scorn of those who first said that it was impossible and now argue that it is too expensive.

As long ago as 1957, General Maxwell D. Taylor, when he was Chief of Staff of the Army, appealed for a $3 billion start on such a system, and he found means of getting his top-secret proposal into the press after he ran up against opposition in the Eisenhower Administration. In 1961, with Taylor back in favor at the White House under Kennedy, the Army renewed its campaign. *Army,* the magazine published by the Association of the U.S. Army, featured articles by generals praising the Nike-Zeus ABM system and advertisements by Western Electric and eight subcontractors for the project. The issue contained a map showing 37 states that were already sharing in the research and development work and were likely to get more if production were approved. Next the House and Senate rang with speeches calling for Nike-Zeus production to start immediately. And in 1963 Senator Strom Thurmond, a reserve general in the Army, forced the first secret session of the Senate since World War II in an effort to win an appropriation for a production start on an American antimissile defense. He lost. The Kennedy Administration successfully resisted that pressure.

But now, ten years after the start of the campaign, the Johnson Administration has relented in part. A full ABM defense network against a possible missile attack from the U.S.S.R. is still considered pointless to undertake —it would cost more than $30 billion under existing conditions—because the Soviets' ballistic missile force is so powerful that the ABM defense admittedly could not cope with it. But for a decade, at least, a so-called "thin" defense against China is said to be worthwhile. Why? Near the end of his term as Secretary of Defense, McNamara tied himself in knots explaining why, the heart of his justification being that a ten-year insurance policy against a relatively small Chinese Communist nuclear missile force was worth $5 billion. Arguments that this might start a new arms race were rejected.

Votes for ABM: Long before McNamara made his announcement, Frederic W. Collins, Washington correspondent for the Ridder newspapers, drew attention in an article in *The New Republic* to some of the ingredients that finally may have broken resistance to the ABM. He noted the favorite ploy of the industrial side of the complex, this time an advertisement in *The New York Times* financial section by the investment firm of Arthur Wiesenberger & Co., which offered a special report on nine companies involved in the research and development of Nike-X (forerunner name of the ABM).

The advertisement listed the 28 potential corporate beneficiaries of a Nike-X development program. Collins estimated that the 28 companies had about 300 plants in 42 states plus Puerto Rico and Washington, D.C., and offered a "conservative guess" that they provided jobs for 1,000,000 employees. The writer then noted that the plants were in the domain of 84 Senators and 172 Representatives.

AWARDS TO ACADEME

The list of the 100 largest prime contractors for the military in 1967 includes Massachusetts Institute of Technology, in sixty-second place with $94.9 million of contracts, and Johns Hopkins University, in seventy-third place with $71.1 million. The ranking of these universities among the leading defense contractors is hardly surprising. We have long been accustomed to the vital participation of the academic community in national defense, from the first nuclear chain reaction at the University of Chicago in World War II to the recent arrangements between many universities and the Central Intelligence Agency. And the Eisenhower farewell speech brought out, as no high government official before or since has done with equal candor, the "prospect of domination of the nation's scholars by Federal employment, project allocations and the power of money."

The Pentagon awards some $700 million a year in contracts to universities, colleges, and other nonprofit institutions. Without this kind of money, as noted in a report of the Carnegie Foundation for the Advancement of Teaching, "the whole character of many universities' research programs (and in consequence their instructional programs) would change. Faculties in many instances would shrink. Many research efforts would have to be abandoned completely. Others would be sharply curtailed." Thus, as Eisenhower warned, many universities have indeed become dependent on the government, not only for research activities, but also for faculties and instructional programs. Perhaps his own experience as President of Columbia University and his brother's as President of Johns Hopkins made Eisenhower specially conscious of this problem.

Recent incidents on campuses across the country have called attention to a general uneasiness, if not rebellion, against government research contracting on purely political grounds. At the University of Pennsylvania, two $1,000,000 research contracts for measuring the effectiveness of chemical-biological warfare were canceled after some professors threatened to wear gas masks at commencement. At Cornell University the faculty voted to cut ties with the Cornell Aeronautical Laboratory because the laboratory had received a $1,500,000 contract to plan counter-insurgency projects in Thailand.

Even such a relatively independent and well-enduring institution as Harvard University has encountered serious government pressure on "how things are to be done in laboratories and who may or may not appear in them," Dr. Nathan M. Pusey, President of Harvard, once complained. He referred specifically to the arrangement with the Atomic Energy Commission for maintenance of the $12 million electron accelerator on the university grounds. The government paid the cost of construction; Harvard and M.I.T. shared a $5 million-a-year contract to operate it. It was intended for "free and unfettered academic research of an unclassified nature," but the government insisted on federal security regulations that seemed more appropriate to a military site than a university campus. Harvard resisted and won many concessions, but finally signed the contract.

CONCLUSION

Having identified, described, and examined certain aspects of the military-industrial complex, we must consider its implications for us. Could the United States become a garrison state in which most of its energies are devoted to arms? Could the pressures of war and the frustrations of international affairs pave the way to a military coup such as that depicted in the novel *Seven Days in May?* Are the appeals for peace and disarmament being selfishly balked by the vested interests of the military-industrial complex? These are ancient forebodings in U.S. history, and the fact that they linger reveals a national awareness of our vulnerability. For it cannot be denied that the military-industrial complex flourishes in war and during the threat of war.

Checks and Balances

Yet this awareness of our vulnerability itself constitutes considerable protection for us. For example, we are often troubled by the intervention of the military in "civilian" affairs. But we can take encouragement from the very openness of that intervention. When General Earle G. Wheeler, the Chairman of the Joint Chiefs of Staff, boldly and publicly disagrees with the Secretary of Defense on policies for the war in Vietnam or on the desirability of constructing a full-scale antiballistic missile defense system; and when General Wallace M. Greene, the commandant of the Marine Corps, publicly demands a greater national devotion to the war in Vietnam than to the social revolution in the streets of America—these expressions by the military serve to identify them publicly with recognizable political attitudes. By joining the public debate in a manner that is authorized under our system, they also set themselves up as targets in that debate.

Moreover, as we have learned from experience, the military are not always unanimous in their professional view of the world and in their demands on the budget. Their rivalries for funds have sometimes exploded in fierce public lobbying and internecine bureaucratic warfare. This, too, mitigates against concerted action by the military to influence public policy. In addition, far from challenging civilian control, the military leaders in recent years have complained of civilians dominating the military in their professional competence. The complaint does honor to the principle of our democratic system.

Insofar as the economic threat of the military-industrial complex is concerned, it appears to reflect largely the familiar dangers of huge concentrations of economic power. And there is recurring evidence of the government's capacity to cope with the industrial giants. During the Kennedy Administration we saw the Secretary of Defense lead the charge against a sudden increase in the price of steel. In the Johnson Administration, in November 1965, the Defense Secretary also led in thwarting aluminum and copper price increases by threats to use the national stockpiles.

Another safety factor is that not all states and communities share equally in the defense business despite the fervent Administration efforts to spread the dollars. This inequality of benefits tends to create challenges to the activities of the military-industrial complex, even within its own constituencies. The result is high-pitched competition involving defense contractors and their political, military, legislative, and other allies. A single defense appropriations bill usually occupies several dozen members of Congress and several committee staffs for the better part of six months, and not all of these Congressmen have the same concerns and motives.

The competing demands of special interest groups that focus on major decisions often cancel each other out. A Congressman, for example, might be an Army reservist with a strong tendency toward its doctrine of national strategy which calls for certain types of military preparedness and weaponry; but he would vote for an Air Force appropriation if it meant a factory for his home city, a Navy appropriation if he were rallied by his political leaders on Capitol Hill, and an across-the-board economy cut if he needed to trade a vote with Wilbur Mills, Chairman of the House Ways and Means Committee.

Taking Nothing for Granted

The problem that confronts us is whether we can continue to depend on these countervailing pressures; or whether at some point in our future—nearer than we like to imagine, perhaps—the disparate impulses that go into the military-industrial complex, ranging from a crass desire for profits to honest fear for the safety of the country, may coalesce in such a powerful advocacy of more and better weapons and in such potent opposition to arms control that the entire country will be drawn to support this position.

I am not suggesting that the threat of our industrial-military complex is based in any way on a military-industrial conspiracy. There is no more of a conspiracy here than in numerous other matters where legitimate lobbies influence public policy makers, or where conflicts of interest affect decisions of the legislative and executive arms of government. The free enterprise system is frequently compromised, and political judgments influence every aspect of our national security—but not because of conspiracies. Rather, I am urging that we keep in mind the Eisenhower admonition: "We should take nothing for granted. . . . Only an alert and knowledgeable citizenry can compel the proper meshing of the huge industrial machinery of defense with our peaceful methods and goals, so that security and liberty may prosper together."

3] The Raison d'Etre of the Military-Industrial Complex

a] THINKING ABOUT THE UNTHINKABLE

. . . There are at least three kinds of insurance which a survival-conscious person might wish to add, the first being *Insurance for Reliability*. We will label the view that *worries about the details* of obtaining a "punishing" retaliation, but does not want any more strategic capability than this, the *Finite Deterrence* strategy. In many ways, and with some inconsistencies, this is the official U.S. view. The believers in Finite Deterrence do not quite accept the idea that reliable deterrence can be obtained simply by stocking thermonuclear bombs and having a weapon system which could deliver these bombs in peacetime. They notice that when the problem of retaliation is studied, rather than asserted, it is difficult to retaliate effectively, since the enemy can do many things to prevent, hinder, or negate retaliation. Evaluation of the effectiveness of retaliation must bear in mind that the Russians can strike *at a time and with tactics of their choosing*. We will strike back, no doubt, but with *a damaged and not fully coordinated force* which must conduct its operations in the *postattack environment*. The Soviets may use *blackmail threats to intimidate our postattack tactics*. Under these conditions, the Russian defense system is likely to be *alerted*. Indeed, if the strike has been preceded by a tense period, their active defense forces would long since have been *augmented,* and their cities may be at least partially *evacuated*.

Any of the considerations referred to by italicized words can change the effectiveness of a retaliatory strike by an order of magnitude. Yet almost all of them are ignored in most discussions of the effectiveness of our deterrent force. Sometimes they are even relegated to the position of unimportant "technical details." They are far more than this. The possibilities indicated by the italicized words will be discussed at some length in Lecture II. I only want to mention here that the believer in Finite Deterrence is somewhat aware of these problems; he wants to have ready more than the bare minimum force that *might* be able to retaliate effectively (the Minimum Deterrence position). The advocate of Finite Deterrence wants enough forces to cover *all* contingencies. He may even want mixed forces, considering that it may be possible for a clever enemy to discover an unexpected countermeasure against a single kind of force no matter how large. Thus he may well want different types of missiles, bombers, strategic submarines, aircraft carriers, and so forth. In addition, sober advocates of Finite Deterrence wish to have the various weapons systems so deployed and operated that they will have a guaranteed capability, even in a crisis in which the enemy has taken

---

FROM *On Thermonuclear War*, by Herman Kahn (Copyright © 1960 by Princeton University Press), published for the Center of International Studies, Princeton University. Reprinted by permission of Princeton University Press. [Footnotes omitted—J. L. C.]

extraordinary measures to negate the capability. They want these forces dispersed, protected, and alert; the arrangements for command, control, and communications must be able to withstand degradation by both peacetime and wartime tactics of the enemy. These sober believers in Finite Deterrence tend to insist on an objective capability as opposed to one that is only "psychological." And even those believers in Finite Deterrence who would be satisfied with a façade yearn for an impressive-looking façade. One might characterize the Finite Deterrence position as an expert version of the Minimum Deterrence position, held by an expert who wants to look good to other experts.

The notion of Finite Deterrence is therefore not as dramatic as the notion of Minimum Deterrence. The believer in Finite Deterrence is willing to concede that it takes some effort to guarantee Mutual Homicide, that it is not automatic. However, the notion of Finite Deterrence is still dramatic, since most followers of this doctrine believe that *the advent of thermonuclear bombs has changed the character of an all-out war in such a way that if both opponents are prepared the old-fashioned distinctions between victory, stalemate, and defeat no longer have much meaning*. It was once believed that if one country had forces twice as large as those of another country, the first country was the stronger. Those who believe in Finite Deterrence challenge this view. Sometimes they rest their case on this idea: the only purpose of strategic forces is to deter rather than to fight; once one has the ability to damage seriously, say, 10 or 20 enemy cities, this is enough force to deter, and therefore enough force. More often, backers of Finite Deterrence take a more extreme position. They argue that you can do no more than kill somebody once, to overkill by a factor of ten is no more desirable than overkilling by a factor of two—it is simply a waste of effort. They also usually argue that with some thought it should be easy to design strategic systems that can overkill, even in retaliation. Once we procure the limited (i.e., finite) forces required to do this job we have enough strategic forces and do not need any more—no matter what the enemy does.

In the year 1960 I believe that even adherents to an extreme Minimum Deterrence position tended to agree, under pressure, that the nation should buy whatever insurance is needed to make retaliation at least "look" potentially reliable and effective. In this sense, the orthodox Minimum Deterrence School is no longer as respectable as might once have been inferred from the remarks of the most enthusiastic proponents of a defense built solely around small Minuteman and Polaris systems. Most of the more sober analysts have come to talk about *Finite* Deterrence, by which they mean having a generous adequacy for deterrence, but that is all they want for the general war. Specifically, they often tend to be against any counterforce capability, (The word "counterforce" includes not only an active counterforce that can destroy or damage the enemy's force on the ground, but also other methods of countering the opponent's force, such as Active and Passive Defense).

Some believers in Finite Deterrence are against counterforce as a useless diversion of forces; others would not even be interested in having any counterforce even if it were free, because they consider it destabilizing. They notice at least one circumstance in which an enemy is likely to attack even if he is worried about the retaliatory destruction that he will suffer. This

circumstance occurs when he believes his attack is pre-emptive, that by striking first he is only forestalling an attack being launched on him. Most
believers in Finite Deterrence are so convinced of the efficacy of their deterrence that they believe such an idea could only arise as a result of miscalculation, since no rational man could order an attack against an enemy
who has made at least moderate preparations to ward it off. However, they
recognize that if both forces are in a condition of super alert it may be easy
to have such a misunderstanding. Or equally likely, there is the problem
that Thomas Schelling of Harvard (and RAND) has called "the reciprocal
fear of surprise attack," where each side imputes to the other aggressive intentions and misreads purely defensive preparations as being offensive.
There are unfortunately many postures possible in which a disastrous train
of self-confirming actions and counteractions could be set into motion. In
order to prevent this from occurring, some believers in Finite Deterrence
think it is important for us to disabuse ourselves of the idea that there can
be any circumstance in which it makes sense to attack the Soviet Union, and
they want us to adopt a posture which makes it clear to the Soviets that we
are so disabused. As part of this posture we should make as few preparations
as possible to alleviate the effects of the war or protect ourselves from Soviet
retaliatory strike. This will convince the Soviets that we do not intend to
attack them except in retaliation; they will then be able to relax and not
be trigger-happy. As one (partial) adherent to Finite Deterrence, Oskar Mor-
genstern, explained: "In order to preserve a nuclear stalemate under conditions of nuclear plenty it is necessary for *both* sides to possess invulnerable
retaliatory forces. . . . it is in the interest of the United States for Russia to
have an invulnerable retaliatory force and vice versa [i.e., one may wish to
strengthen the enemy's retaliatory capability and weaken one's 'Counterforce as Insurance']."

Many who accept the Finite Deterrence view have another reason for not
defending or protecting anything but the retaliatory capability; they see
no need for programs to protect people and property, because they think it
is not feasible to protect either people or property. These people often argue
that it does not matter whether one dies immediately from blast, heat, or
radiation, or dies later from the effects of radioactivity, disease, or starvation
—as long as one is going to die. And they go on to assert that modern war is
so horrible that everyone or almost everyone will be killed immediately—or
will eventually be destroyed by one of the aftereffects.

A surprisingly large number of official military experts and planners seem
to hold views, at least unconsciously, which are really a variation of the
Finite Deterrence view that the only purpose of the strategic forces is to
deter. This is illustrated by the following apocryphal quotation:

TABLE 2   ONE PROFESSIONAL'S VIEW OF HIS PROFESSION

"If these buttons are ever pressed, they have *completely failed* in their purpose! The equipment is useful only if it is not used."

                                                              — General Aphorism

Even though the above statement may be intended to be rhetoric rather than policy, it is far from innocuous. If one were to deduce the beliefs of some policy makers from the decisions they make, he would find that in a rather high percentage of cases the planners seem to care less about what happens after the buttons are pressed than they do about looking "presentable" before the event. They show slight interest in maintaining an appreciable operational capability on the second day of the war; if deterrence should fail, they, as well as many scientists, could not be less interested in the details of what happens—so long as the retaliatory strike is launched.

It is my contention that failure to launch an effective retaliatory attack is only the first of many possible failures. Even if one retaliates successfully, there can ensue significant and meaningful failures. These will occur one after another if the attitude exemplified in the above quotation becomes too universal in either the making or execution of policy. And even Deterrence Only advocates should realize that there are subtle but important differences between a posture which is to be a façade to impress the enemy and one which is supposed to have an objective capability.

Insurance Against Unreliablity. Some of the proponents of Finite Deterrence do not have an antipathy toward all forms of counterforce. They are willing to insure against unreliability. That is, even though deterrence has been made as reliable as they think it can be made, they realize that it may still fail; for example, from accident, human irrationality, miscalculation, or unauthorized behavior. Given this nonzero probability of a war, they find it difficult not to go through the motions of doing "something" to mitigate its effects. Even totally convinced "mutual annihilation" decision makers may be unwilling to admit openly that there are no preparations to alleviate the consequences of a war. It is difficult for any government to look at its people and say in effect, "We can no longer protect you in a war. We have no answer to blackmail except a counter-blackmail threat, and we have no preparations to deal with accidental war except trying to make it so dreadful that everybody will be careful in advance."

A façade of being able to alleviate may also be useful in international relations. It reassures one's allies about one's resolve and induces uncertainty and (hopefully) fear in the enemy. Even if it were true that both sides in the cold war conflict were unwilling to risk a thermonuclear war over any issue that could arise between them, it would weaken their diplomatic strength to admit this openly since the admitting power would be conceding that the other power could always get its way by staking a little more.

Some decision makers who accept the Finite Deterrence view are willing to pay for insurance against unreliability for more than political or psychological reasons. Even those who hold that war means mutual annihilation are sometimes willing for us to act beyond their beliefs—or fears. While this is inconsistent, it is not neccessarily irrational. They understand that paper calculations can be wrong and are willing to hedge against this possibility. Sometimes these decision makers are making a distinction that (rather surprisingly) is not usually made. They may distinguish, for example, between 100 million dead and 50 million dead, and argue that the latter state is better than the former. They may distinguish between war damage which sets the economy of a country back fifty years or only ten years. *Actually, when one examines the possible effects of thermonuclear war carefully, one notices that there are indeed many postwar states that should be distinguished.* If most people do not or cannot distinguish among these states it is because the gradations occur as a result of a totally bizarre circumstance—a thermonuclear war. The mind recoils from thinking hard about that; one prefers to believe it will never happen. If asked, "How does a country look on the day of the war?" the only answer a reasonable person can give is "awful." It takes an act of iron will or an unpleasant degree of detachment or callousness to go about the task of distinguishing among the possible degrees of awfulness.

But surely one can ask a more specific question. For example, *"How does a country look five or ten years after the close of war, as a function of three variables: (1) the preparations made before the war, (2) the way the war started, and (3) the course of military events?"* Both very sensitive and very callous individuals should be able to distinguish (and choose, perhaps) between a country which survives a war with, say, 150 million people and a gross national product (GNP) of $300 billion a year, and a nation which emerges with only 50 million people and a GNP of $10 billion. The former would be richest and the fourth largest nation in the world, and one which would be able to restore a reasonable facsimile of the prewar society; the latter would be a pitiful remnant that would contain few traces of the prewar way of life. When one asks this kind of question and examines the circumstances and possible outcomes of a future war in some detail, it appears that it is useful and necessary to make distinctions among the results of thermonuclear war. The figures in Table 3 illustrate some simple distinctions which one may wish to make at the outset of his deliberations in this field.

TABLE 3   TRAGIC BUT DISTINGUISHABLE POSTWAR STATES

Dead	Economic recuperation
2,000,000	1 year
5,000,000	2 years
10,000,000	5 years
20,000,000	10 years
40,000,000	20 years
80,000,000	50 years
160,000,000	100 years

Will the survivors envy the dead?

Here I have tried to make the point that if we have a posture which might result in 40 million dead in a general war, and as a result of poor planning, apathy, or other causes, our posture deteriorates and a war occurs with 80 million dead, we have suffered an additional disaster, an *unnecessary* additional disaster that is almost as bad as the original disaster. If on the contrary, by spending a few billion dollars, or by being more competent or lucky, we can cut the number of dead from 40 to 20 million, we have done something vastly worth doing! The survivors will not dance in the streets or congratulate each other if there have been 20 million men, women, and children killed; yet it would have been a worthwhile achievement to limit casualties to this number. It is very difficult to get this point across to laymen or experts with enough intensity to move them to action. The average citizen has a dour attitude toward planners who say that if we do thus and so it will not be 40 million dead—it will be 20 million dead. Somehow the impression is left that the planner said that there will be *only* 20 million dead. To him is often attributed the idea that this will be a tolerable or even, astonishingly enough, a desirable state!

The rate of economic recuperation, like the number of lives saved, is also of extreme importance. Very few Americans can get interested in spending money or energy on preparations which, even if they worked, would result in preindustrial living standards for the survivors of a war. As will be explained later, our analysis indicates that if a country is moderately well prepared to use the assets which survive there is unlikely to be a critical level of damage to production. A properly prepared country is not "killed" by the destruction of even a major fraction of its wealth; it is more likely to be set back a given number of years in its economic growth. While recuperation times may range all the way from one to a hundred years, even the latter is far different from the "end of history."

Perhaps the most important item on the table of distinguishable states is not the numbers of dead or the number of years it takes for economic recuperation; rather, it is the question at the bottom: "Will the survivors envy the dead?" It is in some sense true that one may never recuperate from a thermonuclear war. The world may be permanently (i.e., for perhaps 10,000 years) more hostile to human life as a result of such a war. Therefore, if the question, "Can we restore the prewar conditions of life?" is asked, the answer must be "No!" But there are other relevant questions to be asked. For example: "How much more hostile will the environment be? Will it be so hostile that we or our descendants would prefer being dead than alive?" Perhaps even more pertinent is this question, "How happy or normal a life can the survivors and their descendants hope to have?" *Despite a widespread belief to the contrary, objective studies indicate that even though the amount of human tragedy would be greatly increased in the postwar world, the increase would not preclude normal and happy lives for the majority of survivors and their descendants.*

My colleagues and I came to this conclusion reluctantly; not because we did not *want* to believe it, but because it is so *hard* to believe. Thermonuclear bombs are so destructive, and destructive in so many ways, that it is difficult to imagine that there would be anything left after their large-scale use. One of my tasks with The RAND Corporation was to serve as project leader for a study of the possibilities for alleviating the consequences of a thermonuclear war. That study was made as quantitatively and objectively as we could make it with the resources, information, and intellectual tools available to us. *We concluded that for at least the next decade or so, any picture of total world annihilation appears to be wrong, irrespective of the military course of events.* Equally important, the picture of total disaster is likely to be wrong even for the two antagonists. Barring an extraordinary course for the war, or that most of the technical uncertainties turn out to lie at the disastrous end of the spectrum, one and maybe both of the antagonists should be able to restore a reasonable semblance of prewar conditions quite rapidly. Typical estimates run between one and ten years for a reasonably successful and well-prepared attacker and somewhat longer for the defender, depending mainly on the tactics of the attacker and the preparations of the defender. In the RAND study we tried to avoid using optimistic assumptions. With the exceptions to be noted, we used what were in our judgment the best values available, or we used slightly pessimistic ones. We believe that the situation is likely to be better than we indicate, rather than worse, though the latter possibility cannot be ruled out.

Exactly what is it that one must believe if he is to be convinced that it is worth while to buy Counterforce as Insurance? Listed below are eight phases of a thermonuclear war. If our decision makers are to justify the expense (and possible risk of strategic destabilization) that would be incurred in trying to acquire a capability for alleviating the consequences of a war, they must believe they can successfully negotiate each and every one of these phases, or that there is a reasonable chance that they can negotiate each of these phases.

TABLE 4   A COMPLETE DESCRIPTION OF A THERMONUCLEAR WAR
Includes the Analysis of:

1. Various time-phased programs for deterrence and defense and their possible impact on us, our allies, and others.
2. Wartime performance with different preattack and attack conditions.
3. Acute fallout problems.
4. Survival and patch-up.
5. Maintenance of economic momentum.
6. Long-term recuperation.
7. Postwar medical problems.
8. Genetic problems.

I repeat: To survive a war it is necessary to negotiate *all eight* stages. If there is a catastrophic failure in any one of them, there will be little value in being able to cope with the other seven. Differences among exponents of the different strategic views can often be traced to the different estimates they make on the difficulty of negotiating one or more of these eight stages. While all of them present difficulties, most civilian military experts seem to consider the *last six* the critical ones. Nevertheless, most discussions among "classical" military experts concentrate on the *first two*. To get a sober and balanced view of the problem, one must examine all *eight*.

As an example of the necessity to be concerned about the last six phases, it might be appropriate to quote from testimony before the 1959 Johnson subcommittee on military preparedness during the hearings on the Berlin crisis (italics mine).

> MR. WEISL: General White, I hate to keep you here so long, but there are some matters that *we feel ought to be in the record to make it complete.*
> On March 9 of this year Dr. Libby, a Commissioner of the United States Atomic Energy Commission, in a public speech stated as follows:
>
> > "Now the fallout we fear in the case of a nuclear attack on this country, or in any other country for that matter, is the local fallout, and this arises solely from bombs which hit the surface."
>
> Then I go on to what I consider the important quote:
>
> > "But in any case, the area covered can amount to several thousand square miles at such an intensity that it would be hazardous to life to stay out in the open for more than an hour, and the density would be high enough *so that farmland in this area would be ruined for something like 40 years* for anything except the culture of feed for beef cattle, or possibly swine, because of the strontium-90 that would be taken into any other kind of farm product."
>
> I don't know whether it is fair to ask you whether you agree with that or not, but at least that is the statement of a responsible member of the Atomic Energy Commission.
> GENERAL WHITE: I think there are other responsible scientists, though, who do not agree. I think Dr. Edward Teller is one such. While I agree that fallout is a terrific hazard and one that we don't know as much about as I hope we are going to know, and it is certainly a consideration in atomic war, I don't think that every horror story should be accepted 100 per cent.
> MR. WEISL: I do agree that every horror story should not be accepted, but coming from a responsible member of the AEC, whose duty is to look into these problems, one must take account of it and not look upon it, at least I wouldn't look upon it, as solely a horror story.
> SENATOR SYMINGTON: If the counsel will yield, Dr. Teller has opposed those who believe that strontium-90 and cesium-137 will be too damaging from the standpoint of current testing. If there is anything he has said from the standpoint of strontium-90 in answer to Dr. Libby, on the premise of an all out war, with nuclear surface blasts, I wish you would put it in the record at this point.
> GENERAL WHITE: I think the only thing I can say is I am sure there is disagreement among scientists as to the exact effects. I can't go beyond that.

It is clear that if "farmland in this area would be ruined for something like 40 years," recuperation will be difficult. In that case we had better abandon Counterforce as Insurance and retreat to the Finite Deterrence position. However, we are going to consider the strontium-90 problem quantitatively below and will come up with some different results. The only point to be made now is that those waging a modern war are going to be as much concerned with bone cancer, leukemia, and genetic malformations as they are with the range of a B-52 or the accuracy of an Atlas missile. Senior military advisors in particular will increasingly be forced to deal with what would once have been called "nonmilitary" problems. They will need to be armed with documented studies rather than opinions.

Once one accepts the idea that deterrence is not absolutely reliable and that it would be possible to survive a war, then he may be willing to buy insurance—to spend money on preparations to decrease the number of fatalities and injuries, limit damage, facilitate recuperation, and to get the best military result possible—at least "to prevail" in some meaningful sense if you cannot win.

Insurance Against a Change in Policy. One of the things which I will try to make clear in Lectures II and III is that *the military problem really is complicated and that it is impossible for fallible human beings to predict ahead of time exactly what capabilities they will wish or need.* This does not mean, of course, that one has to buy everything. Resources may not be as limited as some of the more budget-minded people think, but they are still quite limited. However, it does mean that whenever it is *cheap* to do so (and sometimes when it is moderately expensive), we should be willing to hedge against changes in our desires. The fact that it is expensive to buy and maintain a complete spectrum of military capabilities in being does not mean that we should not have what might be called "mobilization bases" for a complete spectrum of adequate military capabilities. The government, relying on current doctrine, current military capabilities, its estimates of the capabilities and intentions of potential enemies, or some aspects of the political situation, might be satisfied with current allocations for national defense. But it should still be willing to hedge against the possibility that circumstances may so change that the reluctance to spend money will also change, either increasing or decreasing. This hedging can be accomplished by spending a relatively small amount on advance planning and physical preparations. We will then be in a position where we can make the most rapid and effective use of larger funds if they become available, or we will be able to get the most value out of a smaller military budget if it seems desirable to cut back on expenditures.

There are many different kinds of programs that come under the heading "Hedging Against a Change in Policy." It is obvious that there is need for very broad research and development programs. While research is not cheap, it is far from true that research is so expensive that it can be afforded only on clearly needful items. The opposite is true. The penalty for not having researched on an item that turns out to be useful is so great that we must have an extremely broad program to be certain that all the things that could conceivably be useful will in fact be investigated. Development is somewhat more expensive than research. As a result, we cannot afford to have quite as broad a menu. But even here we should *develop* many more items than we actually *procure.* We may also procure some systems in part, even if we do not feel they are absolutely needful. Requirements can change.

For example, many people today feel that in the ballistic missile age *air defense* is obsolete. As I will try to explain later, this is by no means true. But even if it were true that air defense should be termed obsolete because it might be unable to give protection against Soviet missiles, we might still be willing to have a "base" for air defense because we may be able to discover an answer to the missile threat, or we may later decide we want air defense against countries like China—or ultimately even smaller countries. We may find it easy to protect against small bomber forces, which could be very lethal if they had a free ride—very much more lethal, indeed, than any small missile forces these same countries might procure. (Of course, such an air defense system might look quite different from our current one.)

Similarly, while it might be our policy at a given moment to fight limited wars with atomic weapons, we may still be glad to have a large reserve force armed with conventional high-explosive equipment. After all, it is relatively cheap to keep up such reserves, and we recognize that we might change our minds—as we did in Korea. The existence of such a force could enable us to fight a war which otherwise we would have to lose by default, simply because we were unwilling to use nuclear weapons when the occasion actually arose.

There is a special type of mobilization base which I will call a "Preattack Mobilization Base." This can be extremely important. It is a capability for being able to improve rapidly our ability to fight or to threaten to fight either a limited or a general war. It includes preparations for putting in *adequate civil defense programs*. It also includes the procurement of very long *lead time* items for our strategic air defense and air offense, so that by just spending money rapidly we could bring all of these capabilities up to an adequate level. There is a very broad spectrum of preparations possible here. One kind of preparation would be useful only if a situation occurred in which substantial tactical warning (hours) was available; another set of preparations would be most useful in situations in which we had strategic warning—days, weeks, or even months. And still another set of preparations could be made to improve our ability to compensate for a possible deterioration in the international situation or an increase in our standards for an acceptable level of defense. I will defer to Lecture II discussion of the role that a Preattack Mobilization Base might play in deterring and correcting provocations or providing extra insurance against a failure of deterrence. I will only make here the obvious point that what might be called the Finite Deterrence function of the strategic force is too important to depend on warning. There should always be an adequate capability *in-being* to deter a surprise attack.

There are large resources available for defense if it becomes necessary to use them. Many economists have estimated that the United States could allocate between 40 and 50 per cent of its gross national product to military purposes for some years without subjecting individual citizens to any appreciable physical hardships. (Postattack living standards would be adequate by almost any reasonable standard. The situation would be much like World War II where we spent, at peak, about 43 per cent of our GNP on military products, and we could still buy phonograph records even if we could not buy phonographs.) In fact, if we make allowances for current unutilized resources, the country should be somewhat better off than in World War II. Such spending would undoubtedly leave a very unpleasant post-crisis legacy of debt, economic dislocation, some inflation, and so on. But if it ever came to a serious question of choosing between such spending and a high risk of national defeat, I think there is no question that the United States would choose to spend between $200 and $300 billion annually on national security —rather than face the alternative. We are actually spending today about one-fifth of this potential. Clearly there is an enormous amount of fat which could be converted into muscle if we felt that circumstances warranted this step. The problem is, Could we move fast enough? Whether we could would depend not only on how critical the military situation was, but also on our stop-gap military preparations, on our ability to recognize that circumstances have changed, on our resolve, and on the preparations already made for such an expansion. It would be most important that the actual physical plant and equipment of the Department of Defense (including installations) be such that it could be used as an existing base for a higher capability.

b] THINKING ABOUT DETERRENT THEORISTS

THE IMPORTANCE of *On Thermonuclear War* cannot be overestimated. Since the appearance of this book, proponents of both armament and disarmament strategies have had to cope with Kahn's unassailable demonstration that policy-planners cannot simply choose between end-of-the-world nuclear annihilation and total nuclear "peace," but must be prepared to deal somehow with the possibility of a whole series of in-between states of nuclear war. All sides to the arms debate have benefited from this demonstration. Professional and academic military planners have been pushed to new levels of sophistication in their development of strategic alternatives, as have the opponents of nuclear armaments in their counterarguments. The advocates of a nuclear strategy have been given material to show how difficult must be the achievement of a stable state of nuclear disarmament; their opponents, on the other hand, have been given material to show how equally difficult must be the achievement of a stable state of nuclear armaments. All students of this complex subject, clearly, must be grateful to Kahn for grappling so well with this difficult new material.

At the same time, however, *On Thermonuclear War* is significant as much more than a "compleat strategysts" guide to the arms race. For the most noteworthy of the creative efforts at strategic thinking contained in that work has been Kahn's attempt to infuse deterrence doctrine with the stuff of science: an attempt that has apparently impressed many authoritative members of the executive branch of the United States government as being successful. Since we are investigating the connection between the uses of social science and the development of deterrence theory, I shall concentrate on this aspect of Kahn's work, though it bears remarking here—and repeating later—that Kahn's prescriptive concepts, as distinct from his purely analytical ones (a distinction hard to make in any event), are tightly bound up with his claims to scientific rigor.

What is the nature of these claims? In the course of his two major works on nuclear war, Kahn makes repeated reference to computered studies at the RAND Corporation, which use the tools of mathematics to give answers to the question of survival, and illustrate the benefits of "Systems Analysis" and "Operations Research" for the study of military affairs. These references to systems analysis and operations research are supported by tables, graphs, and other simplified models for illustration, the whole often taking on the appearance of the report of a laboratory experiment.

The question that immediately comes to mind is whether Kahn has used these methods properly, given the nature of his subject. Has he made out a case, first, that they are truly tools for scientific work, and, second, that they are helpful in the policy discussions that are so markedly a feature of both *On Thermonuclear War* and *Thinking about the Unthinkable?*

In attempting to answer this question, one must offer a necessary caveat. What is called systems analysis obviously offers some important benefits in the formulation of military strategy. A recent collection of essays written under the auspices of RAND, *Analysis for Military Decisions,* makes these benefits clear. For example, summarized there is one of the earliest examples of systems analyses: out of the systematic study by a RAND team of factors in the selection of overseas bases for the Strategic Air Command emerged the first clear definition, in a concrete setting, of the operational demands of a *second*-strike strategy, and of the way in which these demands differ from those implied by a *first*-strike strategy. Other real and paper examples of both the monetary savings and the strategic (and tactical) clarity and control that can be generated by the use of rigorous analytical methods are adverted to throughout these essays, as well as in Hitch and McKean's *Economics in the Nuclear Age.*

However, there is a common ground between all the various examples of systems analysis referred to in these essays that does not exist between any of them and Herman Kahn's (or RAND's) civil-defense study. To put the case most broadly: the value of a given method of work is determined by asking the opinion of those who have hired it done. Several ways of accomplishing a stated objective are proposed. If the employer is satisfied that the best option has been conclusively demonstrated (or if only obvious bias or stupidity is keeping him from being satisfied), and if over time his satisfaction is justified, then the method of study that indicated the selection of that option is justified (except perhaps to philosophers).

In the case of all the various studies of comparative cost effectiveness of competing weapons systems that are referred to by systems analysts—even in the case of the bases study—the relevant employer is the Department of Defense or some branch of the armed services. But when certain kinds of broad policy questions are being asked, the employer who asks them is not

the Department of Defense but the public; and the answers being sought
are not technical estimates of cost-effectiveness but complex and indissolubly
political judgments . . .[1] It is important to keep in mind that we are making a distinction not merely between two types of subject matter—"strategic"
vs. "tactical," or "broad" vs. "narrow" questions—but also and more fundamentally between two different clients for the product of a given study. The
DOD, the Air Force, etc., commission research in order to help them fulfil
their missions. But what is good for the Air Force is not necessarily good
for the country. As to the latter, in democratic theory "the people," or their
representatives, are the final judges, and political recommendations must be
designed to help them make their ultimate choice among competing policies.
What we want to know, therefore, is how helpful for this purpose are rigorous scientific procedures for arriving at technical answers to technical
questions? We shall see that a close look at Kahn's work, keeping this distinction always in mind, suggests a decisive conclusion.

II. THE METHOD OF SYSTEMS ANALYSIS

It must be said at first that no matter how much one reads on the subject
one simply cannot find out what "systems analysis" is. The various attempts
at definition one encounters are not very instructive:

> [S]ystems analysis might be defined as inquiry to aid a decision maker
> choose [*sic*] a course of action by systematically investigating his proper
> objectives, comparing quantitatively where possible the costs, effective-
> ness, and risks associated with the alternative policies or strategies for
> achieving them, *and formulating additional alternatives if those exam-
> ined are found wanting.* Systems analysis represents an approach to, or
> way of looking at, complex problems of choice under uncertainty, such
> as those associated with national security. . . . It offers a means of dis-
> covering how to design or to make effective use over time of a techno-
> logically complex structure in which the different components may have
> apparently conflicting objectives; that is, an approach to choosing a
> strategy that yields the best balance among risks, effectiveness, the costs.
> Its purpose is to place each element in its proper context so that in the
> end the system as a whole may achieve its aims with a minimal expendi-
> ture of resources.

> The systems analyst must take a systems approach; that is, he must
> attempt to look at the problems as a whole.

> [I]n complex problems of military force composition or development,
> we are dealing with a field so broad that no one can be called expert. A
> typical systems analysis depends critically on numerous technological
> factors in several fields. . . . No one is an expert in more than one or
> two of the subfields; no one is an expert in the field as a whole and the

---

[1] Although we may not be absolutely clear about the precise line of demarcation between the technical and the political. "It is common, indeed usual, to be uncertain of a
boundary but quite certain of what lies well to the east or west of it."

interrelations. So, no one's unsupported intuitions in such a field can be trusted.

Systems analyses should be looked upon not as the antithesis of judgment but as a framework which permits the judgment of experts in numerous subfields to be utilized—to yield results which transcend any individual judgment.

At its best, operations research or systems studies in national defense should be conceived as the quantitative method of science applied to the refractory problems described.

Insofar as possible, a systems analyst should try to use the methods of science and to establish the same traditions. He should be objective and quantitative; all his calculations, assumptions, data, and judgments should be made explicit and subject to duplication, checking, criticism, and disagreement.

What I mean by conflict systems design and analysis . . . is the *explicit* outline and study of alternative systems of interdependent parts where the comparative performance of a system is affected not only by the machines and the men who are elements in the system but also by the opposing behavior of men and machines outside the system. In particular, I mean the design of systems on the basis of an explicit analysis of the effects of opposing strategies.

Systems analysis is the comparison of . . . enlarged systems of interrelated elements. . . .

Evidently systems analysis has something to do with looking at a problem as a whole, looking at it over time, being quantitative where possible, being realistic about potential conflict, and drawing on a wide range of technical expertise. The guiding principle seems to be to start with a simple model for a "system" of goals and capabilities and then to make it progressively more realistic by adding, step by step, such constraining factors as cost, competing objectives and their costs, an opponent's capabilities, degradation or otherwise of all these elements over time, chance, etc.[2] In other words, as far as I can gather, one analyzes a system by trying to see the real-world context of its operations, rather than by simply imagining its ideal performance without further sophistication of analysis.

The use of this method, it should be added, is supposedly necessitated by the fact that the old-fashioned way of analyzing the workings of military systems is no longer feasible because of the progressive technological revolutions of the nuclear era. As Klaus Knorr remarks in the "Foreword" to *On Thermonuclear War,* "The problems of defense have become inordinately complex, and their solution is not susceptible to the rules of thumb, often called principles, which the military derived from past experience." That is, the study of experience, which no one really has, is to be replaced by the study of hypothetical but relevant models of systems, using all the techniques here mentioned.

Unfortunately, all this seems very much like saying that "systems analysis"

2 Any techniques that will help explicate the implications of the model are used for this purpose; *viz.,* "scenarios," war-gaming, formal game theory, computer programs, etc.

is "thorough analysis" or "good analysis." Apparently there are no generalizable principles of the science of systems analysis that can help us understand what is particularly thorough or good about it, why it is being used, what it adds to some other method of study, etc. Thus if we want to test its adequacy for the study of what I have called broad policy questions, we can only do this by looking at systems analysis in action: to be specific, by studying Kahn's description and use of his *RAND Report R-322-RC, A Report on a Study of Non-Military Defense,* which has been incorporated (with some flamboyance) into *On Thermonuclear War.* When we do this we are also studying the workings of Kahn's strategic logic qua logic, for the two elements of his thought are so intertwined that to analyze one is really to analyze the other. Kahn's grand strategy of what he calls "multistable deterrence," based on the possession by the United States of both a second-strike and a "credible first strike" nuclear force, is necessarily dependent on his proposal for the development of a credible civil-defense posture. This is so because, as he frequently asserts, one cannot plausibly threaten to start a nuclear war unless one is prepared to "ride out" the likely retaliation. Thus all of Kahn's complex strategic theorizing hinges on the answer to the pivotal question: would the kind of civil-defense system he proposes have enough of a chance to work to make the proposed strategy seem acceptable? Kahn's answer to this question is conveyed in his report of the civil-defense study. As we shall see, to call the logic of the latter into question is thus to call into question not only the relevance of systems analysis but also the substantive logic upon which the most important school of deterrence theory has created its view of the arms race.

III. THE CIVIL-DEFENSE STUDY: DATA AND ASSUMPTIONS

For understanding what has actually been accomplished by Kahn's civil-defense analysis, we should be interested in answers to, among others, the following questions:

1. What kinds of "hard" data are available for studying the outlines of possible nuclear and deterrence crises?

2. Where do the assumptions upon which the analysis is based come from? How compelling are they? If alternative assumptions are neglected, why are they neglected?

3. Is the analysis which produces whatever conclusions are reached compellingly rigorous or merely personal? If the latter, what reasons are there for preferring it to other ways of looking at the same subject-matter?

4. How has the problem for study been formulated? Are there alternative, equally good, or better ways of formulating it?

In discussing Kahn's development of data in his analysis, to begin with, we need not repeat the various figures and other evidences of "fact" that he adduces. Where necessary, these will be brought out in the discussion of the interior logic of the civil-defense study. Here I rather wish primarily to distinguish the types of materials that Kahn presents as data from those that he presents as assumptions.

When one does this, one finds that Kahn's empirical material—his handle, so to speak, on the real world—consists of the following: (1) A numerical statement of "permissible peacetime standards" for exposure to radioactivity, and calculations, based on those figures, of expected genetic damage under assumed conditions of radioactivity resulting from nuclear war. (2) Statements about the expected effects of nuclear attack: that is, the fallout to be expected from different levels of attack, in the short and long run. (3) An estimate of the life-expectancy shortening effects of radioactivity. (4) The expected incidence of bone cancer due to the fallout of Strontium-90, and the possibility of the human organism's tolerating that incidence. (5) Charts and tables quantitatively descriptive of certain aspects of the American economy during the 1950's.

With the exception of the last-named item (which I shall consider later), all of Kahn's descriptive data fall in the general area of facts about the effects of radioactive fallout. It would seem on first thought that this is a rather limited amount of empirical information on which to base such a study. Of course it is quite possible for systematic scientific work to suggest important conclusions on the basis of very little accurate data. This result can come about if the hypothetical assumptions with which the researcher manipulates his data are powerful assumptions: that is, are either derived from a prior body of "verified" theory or simply turn out to have been reasonable on an intuitive basis. Since Kahn refers to no body of theory, we must be interested in the apparent reasonableness of his assumptions. No doubt, as John Polanyi remarks, those who find Kahn's conclusions convincing will tend to feel the same about his assumptions; but in any case it is worth knowing what those assumptions are, and measuring them against whatever other knowledge or theory may be available in the area of his interest.

Essentially the assumptions are of two kinds. The first kind is strategic: statements of the level of attack that we ought reasonably to expect (or the worst we ought reasonably to expect). Thus Kahn, in *On Thermonuclear War*, postulates two possible attacks, an early (light) and a late (heavy) attack. In the early attack 500 bombs are dropped on 150 targets (including 50 cities); in the late attack 2000 bombs are dropped on 400 targets. (Although Kahn varies his assumptions so frequently that one can never be sure quite what they are at a given moment, it appears that the most fearful test he envisages for his civil-defense system—the total destruction of America's 53 largest metropolitan areas—is meant to be, roughly speaking, a possible result of the late attack.) Implicit in these suggested figures is also an unstated assumption about the size of nuclear arsenals up to about 1970 (the projected period for the late attack), the strength of bomb (or missile) warheads, and the amount of megatonnage that we can expect to be delivered per target point.

In addition, throughout Kahn's discussion of civil defense there is a general though unstated, assumption: that of rationality in decision-making. This notion is perhaps at the core of all his strategic thinking, even though he often explicitly disowns it (in common with many other deterrence theorists, as we shall see). The idea that opponents in a cold (and hot) war may hopefully be expected to act "rationally" is central to all the strategic concepts—limited nuclear reprisals, limited strategic war, controlled counterforce war, limited general war, and postattack blackmail—which Kahn and his colleagues have developed to illustrate the idea that a nuclear war can be *fought* with some chance of "success," rather than merely being deterred on the one hand or being the occasion for a spasm of destruction on the other. (In sum, these are all the strategies which together make up Kahn's proposal for developing a credible first-strike capability, a capability itself dependent on the successful development of the civil-defense capability that is at the heart of his discussion.)

This is not to say that Kahn asserts warring opponents will always or even usually be rational. Rather he assumes that there is enough of a chance of their being rational to make strategic planning for such a contingency a more realistic option than planning based on a different assumption. The crucial point is that whenever he is confronted with the necessity of making predictions based on either expected rationality or expected irrationality (whatever that might be), he invariably prefers the former. He assumes on behalf of any and all participants in a nuclear war that that strategy which minimizes damage to one's self will be preferred; that one's enemies will be expected to have the same preference; and that the result of these dual analyses of preferences will be that each side will actually choose the mutually preferred strategy.

There is one apparent exception to Kahn's assumption of rationality. Presumably, the 50- and 150-city attacks are what he thinks of as irrational city-busting attacks—outside chances that might come about if we adopt one of his first-strike strategies, and which must therefore be investigated to discover if we can survive even the worst. But there are two points about this "exception" that diminish its importance. First, the assumption that these are the worst attacks at all likely to befall us is itself based on an assumption of rationality, since worse could befall us if our enemies were so moved. . . . Second, whenever Kahn talks about probabilities rather than mere possibilities, the assumption of rationality colors his judgment. This is true with regard to such questions as whether a given assumption is "optimistic" or "pessimistic"; or whether a given likelihood is worth worrying about or not (e.g., what will be happening during the period immediately following a nuclear war that must be spent in fallout shelters, about which Kahn says, ". . . a war is likely to continue for a few days after the first strike and then terminate . . . probably by negotiation. . . . "). More important, it is true of all his discussions of casualties, as we shall see when considering those. It is only the assumption of rationality that enables Kahn to suggest, for example, that "counterforce plus avoidance" and "straight counterforce," the two types of nuclear attack most directly designed to keep casualties down, are the attacks most likely to occur. It is only this assumption that explains his apparent preference for the 2–20 million range when he is estimating casualties, among all the other possibilities he develops. . . . Most important of all, an assumption of rationality is implicit in the idea that the kind of massive civil-defense program Kahn ultimately proposes is a feasible one. All he says in this regard is that the economy can "afford" it—a statement that as he himself points out is quite meaningless, since the economy can "afford" anything the people want badly enough. The real question is, on what grounds do the people (or their representatives) decide what they "want," and this question is never discussed. Thus the effect of his treatment of this issue is to deny the relevance of politically determined fiscal restraints, as well as all other kinds of psychological and cultural restraint, against the adoption of any course of behavior that a "rational" analyst has proved will "pay off."

The second kind of assumption that Kahn makes concerns the ability of American society to recuperate from the effects of nuclear war, economically and socially. These are assumptions, in other words, which have to do with (1) the effect of devastating crisis on human personality and social organization; and (2) the effect of massive destruction on an organized economy. In this context, Kahn rarely makes his assumptions sufficiently explicit; the only way in which one can clearly see what he has in mind is to cull from his presentation the relevant passages and put them together to form some kind of whole.

On the first problem, Kahn has little to say; the following passages appear to indicate his views:

> The fifth optimistic element in our calculation was the assumption that people would be willing to work at reconstructing the country and would have a productivity at this task about equal to that of their prewar work. To many this seems like a rather bold assumption. . . . Nations have taken equivalent shocks even without special preparations and have survived with their prewar virtues intact. In past years these shocks were spread over many years; the one we are considering would take place in only a few days. But . . . from the viewpoint of character stability it is better to take this kind of shock in a short time rather than in a long one.
>
> It is my belief that if the government has made at least moderate prewar preparations, so that most people whose lives have been saved will give some credit to the government's foresight, then people will probably rally round. . . . It would not surprise me if the overwhelming majority of the survivors devoted themselves with a somewhat fanatic intensity to the task of rebuilding what was destroyed. . . .
>
> One of our most important assumptions was that it would be possible to adopt "workable" postwar health and safety standards—workable in many senses: that people would be willing to accept them from both the political and individual point of view; that they would not be so high as to result in any large economic costs or so low that the medical

problems get inordinate. . . . Doing this may be very difficult because
it may make the people setting up the standards look somewhat
callous. . . .

Earlier, Kahn has also appended a more or less parenthetical—and well-
known—passage that seems to imply a great deal about his view of the relationship between human nature, social organization, and catastrophe, not to
mention his sensibility as a social commentator in general:

> Now just imagine yourself in the postwar situation. Everybody will have
> been subjected to extremes of anxiety, unfamiliar environment, strange
> foods, minimum toilet facilities, inadequate shelters [sic], and the like.
> Under these conditions some high percentage of the population is go-
> ing to become nauseated, and nausea is very catching. If one man
> vomits, everybody vomits. Almost everyone is likely to think he has
> received too much radiation. Morale may be so affected that many sur-
> vivors may refuse to participate in constructive activities, but would
> content themselves with sitting down and waiting to die—some may
> even become violent and destructive.
>
> However, the situation would be quite different if radiation meters
> were distributed. Assume now that a man gets sick from a cause other
> than radiation. Not believing this, his morale begins to drop. You look
> at his meter and say, "You have received only ten roentgens, why are
> you vomiting? Pull yourself together and get to work."

Concerning economic organization, Kahn is somewhat more explicit. He
begins by positing a distinction between the urban part of the nation that
will be largely destroyed in the late attack, and the relatively undamaged
non-urban remainder of the nation; these he calls respectively the A country
and the B country. His argument then consists almost entirely of the assertion that, despite the contrary beliefs of "many laymen, professional economists, and war planners," the B country could prosper—re-create or rather
maintain an undestroyed, livable economy—even though the A country had
been destroyed, together with its "one-third of the population," "half the
wealth," and "slightly more than half of (the) manufacturing capacity" of
the United States. The key steps in his argument, which may be taken to
denote his theory of economic activity, are as follows: (1) The United States
can "about double its GNP every fifteen or twenty years," so the level of
destruction being considered would merely set us back "a decade or two"
and destroy many "luxuries" rather than being a "total economic catastrophe." (2) The calculation sounds "naïve" if we think of highly integrated
modern economies as organisms, but the "organism analogy" is false, at least
for purposes of "long-term recuperation": actually the economy is more
"flexible than a salamander," and "no matter how much destruction is
done," the survivors, if there are any, "will put *something* together." Thus
even if a critical part of the economy is destroyed, one can use the remaining
parts, as one could not with an organism, in the reconstruction effort. (3)
Specifically the A and B countries are in the relationship of "a mother coun-

try and a vigorous, wealthy, and diversified colony." Thus the B country can "survive without the A country and even rebuild the A country" in about 10 years; in fact its problems will be easier than those faced by the U.S.S.R. "in constructing the Soviet Union of 1955 from its 1945 base." Here, with the remark that "We tend to exaggerate . . . the impact of losing valuable people, equipment or resources," Kahn's theory of economic development comes to an end. No sources of any kind are cited in support of the two key points in the last paragraph (or any other, for that matter).

Kahn then proceeds, as he might put it, to quantify the problem. First, he lists the total "tangible wealth" of the United States in a table (17) and estimates that "at current rates of investment" this represents a generation's worth of economic activity: indeed we would be in even better shape than that statement indicates because "we are likely to work harder and consume less" and (again) "much of the destroyed wealth will be a luxury." He follows this remark with an example: "[If] half of our residential space is destroyed, then, even if everyone survives, these survivors will be better housed than the average (very productive) Soviet citizen." The only part of our assets both "in danger of being destroyed" and "critically needed in the immediate postwar period," is "producers' durables and manufacturing structures," and "business inventories." These remarks appear to sum up Kahn's thinking about the sociology of economic organization.

Next, in Table 18, we are shown that the B country contains "more than one-fourth of our capacity in almost all industries," which during reconstruction would undoubtedly operate "at more than their theoretical capacity." The table doesn't take into account possible bottlenecks, but these might be avoided by "advance preparations" such as stockpiling; and anyhow, "entrepreneurs and engineers are very capable at 'making do' when necessary." In Table 19, finally, Kahn gives the value of "capital goods used in industry" and estimates "the minimum that should survive." He adds that our problem is to have in the short-run postwar period "a manufacturing industry that at current prices would be worth something like 100 billion dollars," and concludes that "if we can do this, protect a few items, and use the things that will automatically survive, such as people, land, transportation facilities, rural areas with their power stations, utilities, non-manufacturing industries, and so on, *there is every expectation that we will have an economy able to restore most of the prewar gross national product relatively rapidly. . . .* "

Kahn next notes "seven optimistic elements" contained in his analysis, although he believes that on balance "the calculations are more likely to be pessimistic than optimistic." These elements are, first, "that we will be permitted to reconstruct"; second, that society will, concurrent with the war's "end," start to function again at the level of basic necessities such as clearing up debris, restoring "minimum communications," reestablishing credits and markets, providing basic transportation and utilities, etc.; third, that economic activities particularly will "be started rapidly, even though society can live for a time on inventory and stocks"; fourth, "that there be no specific crippling bottleneck problems"; fifth and sixth, that peacetime work habits survive at the same time that people are willing to accept "workable"

postwar health and safety standards . . . ; and finally, that there be no
"catastrophic" side-effects of the war, such as unexpected "effects of lingering
radioactivity," "unsuspected ecological consequences," disastrous fire storms,
etc.

. . . .

VI. DATA, ASSUMPTION, AND ANALYSIS: SUMMARY

If we attempt, then, a summary answer to the questions I asked earlier,
the results are not promising. To begin with, Kahn's data are not only
unsatisfactorily accounted for, but they appear to be inevitably so given the
kind of study he has undertaken—an analysis of the hypothetical strategic
future. Because of this, and because the study is in any event so completely
speculative, it is often difficult to tell, as we have seen, whether there is any
truly logical connection between Kahn's data and premises, and the extrapo-
lations he makes from them. The premises themselves are at best ex-
ceedingly questionable, as the assumption of (partial) rationality or the
idiosyncratic view of the economy; at worst they are grounded either in
arbitrariness or sheer fantasy, as the various "factors" of decontamination.
And no reasons are given in *any* of the reports of the civil-defense study for
choosing the assumptions that were chosen.

Of course science always proceeds by the making of assumptions: but not
by the making of tendentious assumptions; not by the making of argumenta-
tive assumptions for which no justification is offered, and which have not
been fully debated in the relevant scientific community; and not by the
assuming away of the most important and dynamic questions in the field of
inquiry being investigated. Worst of all, we have seen that when merely
one or two of these many arbitrary assumptions are varied somewhat, the
whole tissue of the conclusions begins to fall apart, and it becomes possible
for Kahn, forgetting what assumptions he has made in the past, to write a
few years later that in an all-out nuclear war the Russians, "unless their
strike had been extraordinarily successful . . . would be likely simply to disappear as a nation—or at least to be set back 25 to 100 years in industrial
and material wealth." Flexibility is a virtue in policy studies, but it ought
to have its limits.

This last comment raises another point: namely, that the systems "analysis" really contains very little true analysis at all. For most of Kahn's
"calculations" are not really calculations but merely assigned values. Thus,
for example, in the study of economic recuperation, the figures concerning
the B country's resources and their putative postwar value do not in fact
support the assumption about the B country's "survivability," but merely
illustrate it; similarly Table 3 illustrates rather than supports the argument
that there is a relationship between number of dead and time required for
recuperation. To rest the proof of a proposition on an illustration of how it
could be true is circular, and thus almost all Kahn's work on recuperation
is a circular development of his own assumptions. And although he does

make calculations based on his genetic data, the calculations and the data are both useless except in the context of Kahn's assumptions about the shape and size of a future nuclear war.

How much value, after all, can an empirical study have when it is almost all utterly deductive? The result in this case can only be a neat illustration of one possible result of a nuclear war—probability unspecified. As a representation of what would be *likely* to happen, however, the study does not compel belief, for no true investigation of the world has gone into it: and nothing will come out of nothing.

.   .   .   .

VIII. SYSTEMS ANALYSIS AND NATIONAL POLICY: CONCLUSION

The above discussion, of course, should not be taken as asserting the general uselessness of systems analysis. Such an assertion would be egregious: any method is useful if it produces answers we feel we can use.

What is at stake here, rather, is the claim that our expectations ought to be higher when we are dealing with a systems analysis than with other forms of study: that is, the claim to be doing work that is peculiarly scientific. We have noted Kahn's reiterated references to having performed "scientific" studies. Those references are incorrect. Science is not merely a "method," as it is continually being referred to in the systems analysis text, *Analysis for Military Decisions*. It is rather the mating of a method and a subject that are relevant to each other. The method described by various systems analysts may indeed be relevant to the subject of, say, whether to build jet interceptors or jet bombers, or how to compare active air defense with other methods of defense or deterrence. But as Charles J. Hitch, himself an economist who has engaged in the economic analysis of military operations, and who is presently Comptroller of the Department of Defense, has remarked, "the proportion of the relevant reality which we can represent by any such model or models in studying, say, a major foreign-policy decision, appears to be almost trivial."

Thus we must reject the argument of Wohlstetter, the most sophisticated polemicist on behalf of systems analysis, that those who employ "the method of science" in "the analysis of political-military-strategic alternatives" are *ipso facto* more important as spokesmen on matters of strategy than those who do not:

> In the letter that Bertrand Russell sent in 1955 to heads of state enclosing a call for what later became the Pugwash Conferences, he began: "I enclose a statement, signed by some of the most eminent scientific authorities on nuclear warfare." The signers were indeed without exception eminent scientists, but among the ten physicists, chemists and a mathematical logician who were included, not one to my knowledge had done any empirical study of military operations likely in a nuclear war.

Indeed Russell's statement is hyperbole, but no more so than is the counterclaim of Wohlstetter and Kahn. The "method of science" has not been shown to be relevant to the study of our nuclear future, nor is there anything "empirical" about available studies of "nuclear war."

As for the chief *substantive* contribution of the application of systems analysis to matters of national policy, our conclusion must surely be implicit in what has been said so far. It is extremely difficult to justify the particular exotic nuclear strategies that have sprung out of Kahn's fertile mind and are now generally accepted as realistic options in the community of deterrence theorists. If we were not fairly sure that civil defense would work well, would we dare to think of invoking nuclear weapon strategies such as limited strategic nuclear war, controlled counterforce war, etc., to which the likeliest responses are either surrender or escalation to a higher level of nuclear destruction? Kahn himself, in his latest work, reveals that he doubts the efficacy of these strategies more than most deterrence theorists. But he is always able to find a good word for "limited" nuclear strategies, and that good word is always dependent on the assumption of a workable civil-defense program.

What Kahn has produced is not scientific analysis but prophetic science fiction; unless it strikes our literary imagination it has neither more nor less merit than any other of its kind. How unsystematic does a systems analysis have to be before we balk at taking such uncalculated risks with our fate on the basis of such a "rigorous" method?

CONCLUSION

THE COLD WAR has created a world-wide industry based largely upon fears generated by conflicting ideologies that now uses up economic resources well in excess of $125 billion each year. Three-fourths of this total is accounted for by the two superpowers, the United States and the Soviet Union. In the United States, 10 percent of our personal income and 20 percent of our manufacturing output are derived from this war industry. Indirectly, the livelihood of twelve to fourteen million Americans, including two-thirds to three-fourths of our scientists, now depends on this industry. The defense sector has had the fastest rate of growth of any area in the economy, and it accounts for more than half the research done in this country since the Cold War began.

This military-industrial establishment is a new social fact in American history and is rapidly changing the basic structure of our economy. Large corporations are emerging—about a third of them defense-oriented—that no longer operate according to the laws of supply and demand. Supply and demand is now largely planned by these corporations and the federal government. In the defense sector the buyer (government) decides what to buy and usually finances it; the price is largely determined by reimbursement of actual costs to the corporation plus a fee agreed upon in advance. Consequently, the old division between "public" and "private" is breaking down. What is now needed is recognition of the quasipublic nature of industries in the defense establishment and the institution of effective controls of these industries in the public interest.

The rise of the military-industrial complex has unquestionably spurred the economy to new heights, but the benefits have passed most people by. The rich have been getting richer because the bulk of the defense work is done by the well-educated in high income areas, whereas the poor have received only "crumbs from the table of Mars." What is true of industry is also true of universities—those already financially well-endowed and bulging with prestigious faculty receive the bulk of research grants while the others are left wanting. Over the years, vested interests in politics, industry, and the universities have developed to keep defense expenditures high, while more numerous but less powerful and often less-informed citizens continue to foot the bill.

This whole system has been built upon the philosophy that Communism is expansionistic and that power equals security. Seldom have we studied the national interests of our enemies that motivate their actions, and rarely have we seriously considered non-military solutions. Only recently have we become aware of the fact that our resources are limited, and that monies spent on defense necessarily reduce our options in solving pressing domestic needs. But this knowledge has not yet reversed the trend toward ever higher defense budgets, more arms, and increased commitments abroad.

It may well be, however, that the Cold War is now reaching a turning point. The war in Vietnam has shown clearly that the United States cannot have guns and butter too, nor can we have a war without wartime controls and still avoid inflation. Criticism, beginning most dramatically with Senator Eugene McCarthy, is now focusing on the ABM system, the draft, "overkill," ROTC, and the war itself—this despite the fact that the rate of domestic spending from 1958 to 1969 climbed almost three times faster than the rate of military spending. Can the civilian sector of the economy continue to support a growing number of military adventures? The continued diversion of limited human and natural resources for military purposes and the rising need for controls that might permanently affect social relations are issues well worth everyone's consideration. The debate will undoubtedly continue, and it should be as informed as possible. It is for that purpose that these materials were assembled.

Suggested Readings

(Books and articles from which selections have been reprinted in this volume are not listed below.)

ABSHIRE, DAVID M., and RICHARD V. ALLEN, eds., *National Security: Political, Military, and Economic Strategies in the Decade Ahead,* part V, "Meeting Strategy Requirements in the Free Economy." New York, 1963.

BENOIT, EMILE, "The Monetary and Real Costs of National Defense," *American Economic Review,* vol. 58 (May, 1968), 398–416.

BENOIT, EMILE, and KENNETH E. BOULDING, eds., *Disarmament and the Economy.* New York, 1963.

BOLTON, ROGER E., *Defense Purchases and Regional Growth.* Washington, D.C., 1966.

BOWEN, WILLIAM, "The Vietnam War: A Cost Accounting," *Fortune,* vol. 73 (April, 1966), 119.

CENTER FOR STRATEGIC STUDIES, GEORGETOWN UNIVERSITY, WASHINGTON, D.C., *Economic Impact of the Vietnam War.* New York, 1967.

CHAMBER OF COMMERCE OF THE UNITED STATES, *After Vietnam: A Report of the Ad Hoc Committee on the Economic Impact of Peace After Vietnam.* Washington, D.C., March, 1968.

Defense Industry Bulletin (a monthly publication of the Assistant Secretary of Defense, Public Affairs), 1965 to date.

DRAPER, THEODORE, "The American Crisis: Vietnam, Cuba and the Dominican Republic," *Commentary,* vol. 45 (January, 1967), 27.

DUSCHA, JULIUS, *Arms, Money, and Politics.* New York, 1965.

ENKE, STEPHEN, ed., *Defense Management.* Englewood Cliffs, N.J., 1967.

GILPATRIC, ROSWELL, "Our Defense Needs: The Long View," *Foreign Affairs,* vol. 42 (April, 1964), 366.

HITCH, CHARLES J., and ROLAND N. McKEAN, *The Economics of Defense in the Nuclear Age.* Cambridge, Mass., 1960.

KAUFMANN, WILLIAM W., *The McNamara Strategy.* New York, 1964.

LAPP, RALPH E., *The Weapons Culture.* New York, 1968.

LEONTIEF, WASSILY W. and MARVIN HOFFENBERG, "The Economic Effects of Disarmament," *Scientific American,* vol. 204 (April, 1961), 47.

McGOVERN, GEORGE, "New Perspectives on American Security," Speech in the U.S. Senate, August 2, 1963, *Congressional Record,* vol. 109, part 10, p. 13986.

McKEAN, ROLAND N., ed., *Issues in Defense Economics.* New York, 1967.

MELMAN, SEYMOUR, ed., *Disarmament, Its Politics and Economics.* Boston, 1962.

MILLIS, WALTER, *Arms and the State: Civil-Military Elements in National Policy.* New York, 1958.

National Planning Association, *Community Adjustment to Reduced Defense Spending: Case Studies of Potential Impact on Seattle-Tacoma, Baltimore and New London-Groton-Norwich.* Washington, D.C., 1966.

National Science Foundation, "Federal Support to Universities and Colleges, Fiscal Years 1963–66," NSF 67–14.

Nef, John U., *War and Human Progress.* Boston, 1950.

Nelson, Richard R., "The Impact of Arms Reduction on Research and Development," *American Economic Review,* vol. 53 (May, 1963), 435.

Phillips, James G., *et al.,* "The Military-Industrial Complex," *Congressional Quarterly Weekly Review,* vol. 26 (May 24, 1968), 1155.

Schelling, T. C., *Arms and Influence.* New Haven, Conn., 1966.

Schwarz, Urs, *American Strategy: A New Perspective.* Garden City, N.Y., 1966.

Smith, Bruce L. R., *The RAND Corporation.* Cambridge, Mass., 1966.

Steiner, George A., *National Defense and Southern California, 1961–1970.* Los Angeles, 1961.

Stillman, Edmund, and William Pfaff, *Power and Impotence.* New York, 1966.

Swomley, John M., *The Military Establishment.* Boston, Mass., 1964.

"The Changing Cold War," *The Annals* (of The American Academy of Political and Social Science), vol. 351 (January, 1964).

U.S. Bureau of the Census, *Defense Indicators.* Washington, D.C. (Published monthly.)

U.S. Bureau of the Census, "1963 Census of Manufactures; Shipments of the Defense-Oriented Industries," Washington, D.C., 1966.

U.S. Bureau of the Census, "Shipments of Defense-Oriented Industries, 1966," Washington, D.C., 1968.

U.S. Congress, Joint Economic Committee, *Background Material on Economic Aspects of Military Procurement and Supply: 1964.* Washington, D.C., 1964.

U.S. Congress, Joint Economic Committee, *Economics of Military Procurement.* Washington, D.C., 1968. See Hearings and Report.

U.S. Congress, Joint Economic Committee, *Impact of Military and Related Civilian Supply and Service Activities on the Economy.* Washington, D.C., 1964 and 1966.

U.S. Congress, Joint Economic Committee, *National Security and the American Economy in the 1960's,* Washington, D.C., 1960.

U.S. Department of Commerce, *Statistical Abstract of the United States, 1968.* See sections entitled "National Defense and Veterans Affairs" and "Science."

U.S. Department of Defense, "Five Year Trends in Defense Procurement, Fiscal Years 1958–1962." Washington, D.C., 1963.

U.S. Department of Defense, "Military Prime Contract Awards by Region and State, Fiscal Years 1962–1967." Washington, D.C., 1968.

U.S. Department of Defense, "Prime Contract Awards by State." Washington, D.C. (Published quarterly.)

U.S. Senate, *Defense Department Sponsored Foreign Affairs Research,* Hearing before the Committee on Foreign Relations. Washington, D.C., 1968.

U.S. SENATE, Committee on Labor and Public Welfare, *Convertibility of Space and Defense Resources to Civilian Needs: A Search for New Employment Potentials, Selected Readings in Employment and Manpower,* vol. 2. Washington, D.C., 1964.

U.S. SENATE, Committee on Labor and Public Welfare, Subcommittee on Employment, Manpower, and Poverty, *The Impact of Federal Research and Development Policies upon Scientific and Technical Manpower.* Washington, D.C., 1966.

WARBURG, JAMES P., *Disarmament: The Challenge of the Nineteen Sixties.* New York, 1961.

WRIGHT, QUINCY, *A Study of War.* 1942.

	0
B	1
C	2
D	3
E	4
F	5
G	6
H	7
I	8
J	9